DIETRICH BONHOEFFER—
THE LAST EIGHT DAYS

DIETRICH BONHOEFFER— THE LAST EIGHT DAYS

THE UNTOLD STORY OF THE JOURNEY TO FLOSSENBÜRG

JOHN McCABE

BAYLOR UNIVERSITY PRESS

Cover and book design by Elyxandra Encarnación. See the cover art legend in the front matter for details on the cover art.

Library of Congress Cataloging-in-Publication Data
Names: McCabe, John, Rev., author.
Title: Dietrich Bonhoeffer—the last eight days : the untold story of the journey to Flossenbürg / John McCabe.
Description: Waco, Texas : Baylor University Press, [2024] | Includes bibliographical references and index. | Summary: "A new telling of the story of Bonhoeffer's last eight days, focusing on the others who travelled with him as he made the journey to Flossenbürg concentration camp" — Provided by publisher.
Identifiers: LCCN 2024004689 (print) | LCCN 2024004690 (ebook) | ISBN 9781481321679 (hardback) | ISBN 9781481321709 (adobe pdf) | ISBN 9781481321693 (epub)
Subjects: LCSH: Bonhoeffer, Dietrich, 1906-1945—Imprisonment. | World War, 1939-1945—Prisoners and prisons, German. | Prisoners of war—Germany—Biography. | Theologians—Germany—Biography.
Classification: LCC BX4827.B57 M39 2024 (print) | LCC BX4827.B57 (ebook) | DDC 940.53/18092 [B]—dc23/eng/20240605
LC record available at https://lccn.loc.gov/2024004689
LC ebook record available at https://lccn.loc.gov/2024004690

For Gela and Kieran

CONTENTS

PREFACE

In 1946, after the defeat of the German armies, personnel of the Canadian Intelligence Corps (CIC) remained in Germany to assist in the liquidation of the German Intelligence Services, the disbandment of the Nazi Party in all its manifestations, and the denazification of German institutions. Similar activity took place in Holland, where large German forces whose escape to Germany had been cut off by the Canadians were screened. Some two thousand Canadians remained until the spring; the Canadian headquarters in the Netherlands was disbanded on May 31, 1946. As this process was underway, James Hudson, then a twenty-four-year-old serving officer of the CIC, was tossed a copy of *Mein Kampf*. The numerous copies in the office being cleared out were quite naturally valueless and superfluous. The 1943 copy, which documents for the record that the total print run of this violent outpouring then stood at 10,190,000 copies, is in my possession today. James Hudson became my stepfather in 2003, and later gave me the book. In conjunction with this volume, I also inherited a hollowed-out Bible with a padded space for a handgun,[1] presumably from that same office clear-out process.

The *Mein Kampf* edition contains a blank loose-leaf sheet of Gestapo headed stationery. It bears the Wilhelmshaven address Am Rathausplatz 4, presumably the location of the stash of stored—and distributed—volumes. This building was destroyed entirely in an air raid on October 15, 1944, and the Gestapo had to move. Today signs of that era are few. Yet by a curious coincidence of timing it was on April 1, 1939, exactly six years before the start of the period covered by this book, that Hitler visited Wilhelmshaven to launch Germany's battleship the *Tirpitz* in front of eighty thousand spectators. It was then to be known for the benefit of future generations as "Hitler day." Hitler was on genial form that day and sufficiently charmed by Hermann Göring's wife, Emmy, to kiss her hand.

The volume's frontispiece, which I show below, is revealing:

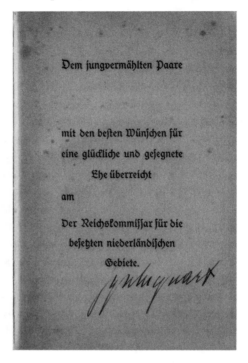

Dem jungvermählten Paare

mit den besten Wünschen für
eine glückliche und gesegnete
Ehe überreicht

am

Der Reichskommissar für die
besetzten niederländischen
Gebiete.

Fig. 0-1. Frontispiece of copy of *Mein Kampf*
Author's collection. Photo: John Hogg.

Translated, the text states, "To the newly wedded couple, with best wishes for a happy and blessed marriage . . . presented on [date left blank] . . . Reichkommissar for the Occupied Dutch Territories [signature of Seyss-Inquart]."[2]

By 1943, for a good number of years already in Germany, wedding couples had been provided with this rambling screed. This edition bears frightening testimony to the expansion of this custom to the "Occupied Dutch Territories." Quite how the convoluted contents of *Mein Kampf* could be contributory in any conceivable way towards the blessing of any marriage continues to be a puzzling question. But this inscription and frontispiece serves at the very least as a poignant and powerful reminder of the outworkings of the process of *Gleichschaltung*. In it the "whole of life" was to be subsumed under the banner of adherence to the Nazi movement. In the course of that territorial encroachment, much of what was good in Luther's "orders" for the governance of life—marriage and family, political and civil life, and the order of priestly office—was corrupted on a scale of no small magnitude and recast by some into ill-fitting Nazi clothing.

On the subject of the edition's signatory, following a brief period in 1945 as Hitler's successor, Seyss-Inquart, a virulent anti-Semite, was executed at Nuremberg in October 1946. The combined impact of his signature, plus the headed notepaper with its innocuous-looking and helpfully provided telephone number, together with the feel of the 1943 *Mein Kampf* edition, is chilling. One wonders: How many transportation orders were expedited from the Wilhelmshaven office? How many killings ordered? How many homes and lives utterly devastated by a call from that telephone number?

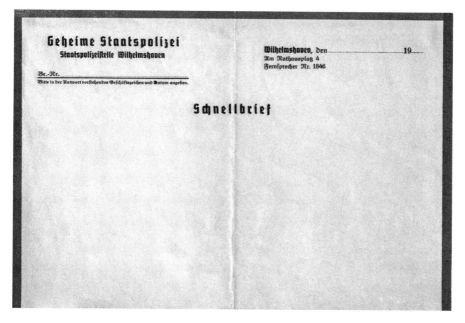

Fig. 0-2. Gestapo letterhead from copy of *Mein Kampf*
Author's collection. Photo: John Hogg.

Holding these volumes in my hand has in part inspired me to address in more earnest the study of Bonhoeffer's final week. Where possible, I have acquired copies of the editions he was reading at the time—more precisely, the period between Sunday, April 1, and Monday, April 9.

The story of those momentous days still calls out for further study and investigation.

ACKNOWLEDGEMENTS

Since I embarked on this project at the midpoint of a 2017 sabbatical, the list of people to thank has continued to grow; it is today a long one. My primary thanks go to my wife, Pippa Ross-McCabe, for her wonderful support. Our children—Jeremy, married to Bani, and Jessica, married to Marco—have made significant contributions. As an author dealing with a pandemic that frustrated travel plans and closed libraries, I have been particularly grateful for the kindness extended to me by those I have met as a result of undertaking the work. My boundless gratitude goes to Dr Tilman Pünder, son of Dr Hermann Pünder, for his invaluable collaboration, encouragement, and support. Sadly Tilman died before *The Last Eight Days* was completed. His family, especially Professor Hermann Pünder and Katinka and Matt Cousins, have continued to reach out to me with great generosity. Of equal worth have been the contributions of Maria Sarda Villargarda, whose infectious warmth, kindness, and Herculean labours in leading the project of scanning and transcribing (and, in some cases, translating) the Spanish, German, and English handwritten diaries and notes of Erich and Maria Heberlein have been second to none. From the Heberlein family, Sofia Ceballos Garcia-Escudero has been endlessly encouraging and patient, and her willingness to make the short sections of these valuable family documents that appear here available for the public record has been heartwarming. A full rendition entitled *The Heberlein Diaries: Hitler's Non-compliant Ambassador* is due out in the near future.

Thanks to the family of Horst Hoepner, especially Giesela and Sophie Potente. Thanks, too, to Evelyn Smith, the daughter of Hugh Falconer, who successfully brought to publication her father's wartime account in 2018, and who has been an inspiring companion throughout, bringing sparkle to the (sometimes painful) process of offering enhancements and corrections to my own understanding of the text. Thanks to the Petersdorff and Einsiedel families: Friedrich Petersdorff, Winand von Petersdorff-Campen, and Sebastian Graf von Einsiedel (and other members of the family) have provided practical assistance, long-term encouragement, as well as appreciated suggestions and rephrasings!

My warm thanks go to Victoria Barnett, a Dietrich Bonhoeffer scholar and series editor of the English edition of the Dietrich Bonhoeffer Works, whose input and wisdom over a sustained period have been exceptional. She has provided the project with seminal help and direction, not least in suggesting I approach Barry Harvey of Baylor University for funding from the International Bonhoeffer Society (IBS). In this respect I am most thankful to the IBS for the funding award that has enabled this book to be written. Stephen Plant's constant availability at crucial moments of the project's gestation, as well as his encouragement to apply for a research associate position at the Von Hügel Institute in Cambridge, have proven a truly remarkable blessing. I am especially grateful to Wojciech Szczerba for the introduction to Fiammetta Curcio, whose story about her father's prison friendship with Bonhoeffer is new information. My enduring thanks go to Lidia Ripamonti, to the team and fellow associates at the institute, and to directors Philip McCosker and Vittorio Montemaggi in particular.

My thanks go to Professor Tom Greggs for his support in this application. Separately, I am also grateful to Jane Williams for introducing me to Dietrich Bonhoeffer's life story some twenty-five years ago.

In Schönberg itself, Bernd Bachhuber is a local historian and author of note. Together with his wife, Elfriede, he welcomed me from the outset into their home. To them both, for invaluable help and support, my sincere thanks. Bernd also kindly introduced me to Martin Pichler, Schönberg's mayor, and the (most helpful) Very Reverend Michael Bauer of the Katholisches Pfarramt St. Margareta, and accompanied me along Bonhoeffer's route from Schönberg to Flossenbürg. He has subsequently, with seemingly endless patience, provided answers to countless questions of detail, including (recently) transcribing an extended essay from the diary of Erich Heberlein, and has been generous enough to take and send many photographs and images, including one of Neustadt. I am also greatly indebted to him for his help in establishing warm contacts with a number of other German historians. Included among these is Johannes Molitor, who provided the name of the bridge Bonhoeffer crossed in Deggendorf. Further afield, Bernd provided me with a warm introduction to the archivists Peter Seiwald and Walter Boaretto, of the Pragser Wildsee / Lago di Braies Hotel, the inspiring destination in the Italian Dolomites that will always remain associated with the "rescue" of the 139 hostages who, unlike Bonhoeffer, survived the war. An already memorable and brilliantly hosted research trip there in late April 2019 was made even more special by the generous hospitality of Caroline Heiss, niece of Emma Hellenstainer, and the (timely) arrival overnight of a twelve-inch snowfall. Following my trip there, I contacted Robert Riebling, who readily made available to me in soft copy a full English translation of Hans-Günter Richardi's *SS-Geiseln in der Alpenfestung* (SS hostages in the Alpine Fortress), for which I am most grateful.

My particular thanks are due to Bernhard Schünemann, who introduced me to Dietrich Bethge, Bonhoeffer's godson, at the vicarage in Dulwich. I count it a moment of great privilege that Dietrich readily consented to my reading him the words Bonhoeffer composed for him at the time of his baptism, and an even greater honour that he claimed, perhaps with exceptional generosity, to be unaware of them! Dietrich not only played the part of what he is fond of describing as "Exhibit A" in such circumstances; he also later obligingly fact-checked a point of record that I had raised with him. I am also grateful to Mathias Bonhoeffer for answering my persistent questions on behalf of the wider Bonhoeffer family. A five-star vote of thanks goes to Wilfried Schulz, secretary of the German section of the IBS, whose advocacy, patience, and practical support have been exceptional. To Wilfried I owe thanks, among a veritable host of other things, for a spectacular introduction to the Herrnhuter archivist Olaf Nippe. Wilfried also spent two hours travelling halfway across Berlin on the metro during lockdown on my behalf sourcing the last remaining copy in any Berlin library of the fourth edition of Anneliese Goerdeler's *Verschleppt*, only to find the library closed. The situation was retrieved by the librarian hand delivering the text to his home in an act of exceptional generosity on behalf of both parties!

I am very much indebted to Karina Gandur in St Petersburg for her sourcing, transcription, and translation in 2018 of a considerable body of Russian-language texts pertaining to Vasily Kokorin, immediately before Ian Sayer "broke" Kokorin's story. My thanks too to the Russian author Vyacheslav Zvyagintsev for his warm help. Given my own limitations with regard to the Greek language and script, I also owe particular thanks to Nadia Valavani for her tenacity and warm support concerning the Papagos text, which was written in the (old) polytonic system, outdated since the 1970s, which proved correspondingly challenging to transcribe. In this respect I express sincere thanks to Dionysia Lagou of Newport Shipping, who (in her lunch breaks!) located and applied a particular software "fix" enabling the original 1945 text to be captured and edited in soft copy. Hat tip to Samantha Fisk for the introduction!

All non-fiction authors are indebted to librarians and archivists, whose kindness often goes more than the proverbial second mile. I owe my deep appreciation for answers to multiple questions to Dr Ralf Breslau of the Handschriftenabteilung in Berlin's Staatsbibliothek. Also there, in this case from the hidden depths of the Kartenabteilung, Holger Scheerschmidt has provided first-rate support over a sustained period, which has been unstintingly good-humoured and generous. My thanks are also due to Axel Braisz from the ITS Arolsen Archives. At London's Wiener Holocaust Library, the team were obliging and helpful throughout, particularly Elise Bath, who also kindly read and commented on early drafts of this work as the project took shape. Thanks too to *Gedenkstätte* Flossenbürg's Timo Saalmann, Jörg Skribeleit, and Johannes Ibel, the latter also for his unsolicited hospitality; and to Tanja Fichtner, whose conversation with an elderly neighbour provided pertinent weather information for April 8, 1945. My thanks are due to the Imperial War Museum's Bryn Hammond; to the custodian of Baylor University's Texas Collection, Paul Fisher; to the Bundesarchiv's Lutz Möser in Berlin; and to the director of Eulenburg's Universitäts- und Stadtmuseum in Rinteln, Stefan Meyer. My thanks go also to Manuela Bonfissuto of Battenberg-Geitel Verlag for the introduction to Peter Schmoll, who provided accurate information on wartime Regensburg. To Michael Löffelsender in Buchenwald's *Gedenkstätte*, many thanks. I also recruited non-writer family members and friends to read and amend chapter drafts. Thank you, Charles and Rachael Holland, John and Linda Marjot, and Jennifer Hogg. Many thanks also to John Hogg for his photographs. Heartfelt thanks go out to Schönberg's Edith Doeringer for such generosity, diligence, and persistence in sourcing and obtaining photographs together with the needed permissions.

As a brand-new author, I have much leaned on fellow authors for guidance and support. My heartfelt thanks go to Ian Sayer, who was not only quick to offer me a full soft copy of his publication *Hitler's Last Plot*, but has also been a ready provider of ongoing coaching, proofreading, and direction. I must thank him for showing me the Bonhoeffer inscription in his copy of *Nachfolge* and hence enabling me to make a connection that has not, to my knowledge, previously appeared in print. My thanks go out warmly to Christiane Tietz for providing the text of Bonhoeffer's ordination service in that respect. I have much appreciated the kindness and wisdom of Gela Van Horen in Australia and Teresa Edlmann in South Africa from the project's infancy and throughout. I am most thankful to German author Heiko Suhr, who has written a biography of Admiral Wilhelm Canaris, and provided English-language draft corrections and project structure guidance at the highest level. Hans-Joachim Ramm, German author of *Mich trägt mein*

Glaube, on General Rabenau, who has also provided exceptional support, kindly effected that welcome introduction. I am much indebted to Steve Tyas, co-author of *Himmler's Diary, 1945,* who provided research advice and actual research, at times setting the bar very high. He also assisted in many generous telephone consultations and on numerous occasions went out of his way to help with fact checking. Nick Rankin has offered appreciated coaching and encouragement. Mikael Nilsson kindly engaged with my questions about Hitler. Sylvie Young has kindly provided proofreading support, as did Professor Andrew Parker. Thomas Harder kindly helped out with textual amendments. Stephen Kippax's SOE network of authors has been an exceptionally rich resource of wisdom, perspective, information, and humour. To Steve I owe my lasting thanks for inviting me to belong to a network where I am readily welcomed, despite clearly being an impostor. From this network, in addition to those already mentioned, I am grateful in particular to David Tremain, Martin Briscoe, Peter Dixon, Nigel Jones, Rod Bailey, Clare Mulley, Richard Sisk, David O'Keefe, Nick Fox, Gary Henderson, Francis Suttill, Alan Judge, David Hendy, and Gabrielle Rothwell. Xavier Riaud kindly assisted with my questions on Flossenbürg's dental processes. Erik Arjan/Callaerts notably and generously undertook research on my behalf during lockdown.

Given that this book grew out of and alongside full-time parish ministry, I owe a special debt of thankfulness to the parishioners of St Mary's Byfleet. My thanks are due to Anne Haring, for her Spanish-language help with the Heberlein diaries; to Claire Calder, for transcribing a lengthy interview with Evelyn Smith; and to Penny Weiss, for an extensive project in the deciphering and transcribing of page upon page of transcripts from the BBC archives. My thanks go to Phil Way for his proofreading support. To Rob Knee, Bernice Rust, Dave Whymark, Kerry Tucker, and Dominic Mitchell, whose preaching duties enabled my regular rhythm of writing weeks, I extend my lasting appreciation. To Bruce Bovill's map creation and research collaboration skills I owe more than one flash of insight about the actual route travelled by Bonhoeffer, in contrast to that described in previous publications. Without him I would have been wholly unable to investigate, "think together," and understand the events of the week at the required level of detail. To Bruce I express my most profound admiration and gratitude.

Finally, and perhaps most importantly, I express my special thanks to R. David Nelson and the reviewer team at Baylor University Press. Without the constancy of your support, over a sustained period, and your corrections and reshaping, this book would most likely never have found its way into print. All errors and mistakes are my own.

ABBREVIATIONS

I have left the names of German source texts untranslated unless the text has appeared in English or the title in German alone would be unhelpful. Place names are as the places were known in the Germany of the time, and if it has subsequently changed, the current name is mentioned. In the case of German surnames prefaced by *von*, the *v* is not capitalised. For military operation code names and cyphers, the capitalisation of source texts has been preserved.

All citations from Bonhoeffer are from the German editions (DBW) unless otherwise indicated (DBWE).

AEL	*Arbeitserziehungslager* (camp for "re-education into work")
ATS	Auxiliary Territorial Service
BA/MA	Bundesarchiv/Militärarchiv (Federal Archives/Military Archives, Freiburg, Germany)
BAB	Bundesarchiv, Abt. Berlin
BK	Bekennende Kirche (Confessing Church)
BRT	*Bruttoregistertonne* (also gross registered tons)
ECG	Electrocardiograph
GRO	General Register Office
HASAG	Hugo Schneider Aktiengesellschaft
IfZ	Institute für Zeitgeschichte (Institute for Contemporary History, Munich, Germany)
IMT	International Military Tribunal (Nuremberg, 1945)
ITS	International Tracing Service (for Holocaust victims)
JU52	Junkers aircraft used for heavy loads
KL	*Kriegslager* (concentration camp)
KZ	*Konzentrationslager* (concentration camp)
NKVD	People's Commissariat for Internal Affairs (interior police of Soviet Interior Ministry)
NSDAP	Nationalsozialistische Deutsche Arbeiterpartei (Nazi Party)
OKH	*Oberkommando des Heeres* (Army General Staff)

OKW	*Oberkommando der Wehrmacht* (Armed Forces General Staff)
POW	Prisoner of war
RAF	Royal Air Force
RFSS	Reichsführer-SS (Head of SS)
RSHA	Reichssicherheitshauptamt (Head Office for Reich Security)
SA	Sturmabteilung (a paramilitary organisation associated with the Nazi Party)
SD	Sicherheitsdienst (Security Service—the Nazi Party intelligence service)
SIS	Special Intelligence Services (covert Allied counter-intelligence service)
TNA	The National Archives of the UK, London
USAAF	United States Army Air Force
USSR	Union of Soviet Socialist Republics

FIGURES AND MAPS

COVER ART LEGEND

DIETRICH BONHOEFFER
THE LAST EIGHT DAYS

THE UNTOLD STORY OF
THE JOURNEY TO
FLOSSENBÜRG

① Vasily Kokorin   **⑦** Dietrich Bonhoeffer

② Heidel Nowakowski   **⑧** Hugh Falconer

③ Friedrich von Rabenau   **⑨** Erich Heberlein

④ Horst von Petersdorff   **⑩** Payne Best

⑤ Alexander von Falkenhausen   **⑪** Horst Hoepner

⑥ Hermann Pünder   **⑫** Margot Heberlein

Fig. 0-3. Cover Art Legend
1 Courtesy of Vyacheslav Zvayagintsev / **2** Courtesy of Ian Sayer / **3** Bundesarchiv, Bild 183-C05190 / Dometh / CC-BY-SA 3.0 / **4** Private collection of Heinrich von Einsiedel / **5** Bundesarchiv, Bild 146-2008-0155 / Kropf / CC-BY-SA 3.0 / **6** Courtesy of Prof Dr Hermann Pünder / **7** Private, by permission of the German Resistance Memorial Centre / **8** Courtesy of Evelyn Smith / **9** Courtesy of Sofia Ceballos Garcia-Escudero / **10** Western Morning News/mirrorpix / **11** Courtesy of the Potente family / **12** Courtesy of Sofia Ceballos Garcia-Escudero. Not pictured: Sigmund Rascher.

Introduction

On July 20, 1944, a bomb that had been smuggled into Hitler's presence, with the intention of killing him, exploded. That objective was not achieved. The consequences for all involved in any way with this attempt were of course severe. Almost all of them, even those only distantly connected, were soon engulfed in a tidal wave of arrests, torture, and executions. For example, "having access to treasonable information and failing to report it" was an offence that carried the death penalty. One such contributor was Dietrich Bonhoeffer. Although he had already been incarcerated for over fifteen months at the time, his ties to the inner circle of conspirators readily classified him in the eyes of the Gestapo as a prime potential suspect.

Meanwhile the chaos unleashed by the events of World War II, already extreme, intensified still further. Within Germany, dissolving support for the regime, which propaganda struggled vainly to combat, meant inexorably a greater recourse to terroristic repression. Across Europe, especially for civilians and the incarcerated, the early months of 1945 were among the most precarious. The population was increasingly forced into line in the total war drive. Any incautious remarks or signs of what might be deemed defeatism were ruthlessly punished.[1] For combatants, the knowledge that the end of hostilities was imminent did not necessarily mean that the intensity of the fighting would slacken. For the fortunate few, the final ten months of the war involved a winding down and mopping-up operation: for the majority, the bitter and costly conflict continued. By April 1945 millions of people were on the move. At the time, German SS concentration camp guards chose to obey orders not to allow inmates to be "captured" (in reality, liberated) by advancing Allied troops. Those charged with responsibility harried totally ill-equipped and undernourished prisoners in their thousands out onto death marches—at an appalling human cost.

This tsunami of suffering, of which events in Germany were only a part, would abate only with Hitler's suicide on April 30. Against this backdrop the untimely nature of Bonhoeffer's death on April 9 has been, to borrow a phrase, greatly exaggerated. Not least, the sound from the oft-cited "rumble of US gunfire" apparently audible in the distance on that date would have to have travelled a distance of one hundred kilometres.[2] More substantially, the reality is that the Flossenbürg executions (of April 9) were a consistent expression of the values and modus operandi of those continuing in power, which, apart from the actual arrival of US troops two weeks later, nothing short of a wholesale regime change could have altered. It was not only that the collapsing system continued to elicit passionate loyalty, sacrifice, and murderous acts. The existing processes developed by the "machinery" of wrongdoing had their own gathered momentum. For example, the offence of forging a bread coupon, perhaps by a forcibly deported and half-starving French slave labourer, was elevated by the prevailing justice system to the status of a political crime of the highest possible calibre. The guillotining of hapless victims continued not just intermittently but on an industrial scale, right throughout the latter part of April. It was also the case that those who had been far-sighted (or courageous) enough to resist were not well regarded. As a result, the spree of "settling scores" with regime opponents still had weeks left to run, and those with weapons and power often chose unflinchingly not to exercise mercy. It was genuinely the case that many reasoned that if they were not to taste victory, those who had opposed Nazism should not live to see the fruits of Allied victory either. Late on April 22, as Berlin fell to the Russians, a small Gestapo team led a group of sixteen prisoners, including Bonhoeffer's brother Klaus, a small distance outside the prison where they were being held and shot them.[3]

All this was not just out of pure vindictiveness. At the time, the flames of twisted ideologies generating a conflagration of hatreds and abuses that had long predated Nazism were not simple to extinguish. One instance of this occurred as late as May 13, 1945. German soldiers under Canadian control convened a makeshift court and executed two Germans for desertion. When challenged about why they wanted to kill people on a beautiful day after the end of the war, one of those involved commented that "if they were allowed to go home and have children, the minds of the children would be dirty, too."[4] A further such instance took place at Kaufbeuren hospital, one of the facilities that under Nazism had become dedicated to the efficient ending of "unworthy life." This institute had developed a speciality in killing children, usually by sheer starvation. This was deemed efficient as costs were kept to a minimum and numbers were high. On May 29, 1945, thirty-three days after US troops had occupied the local area, and twenty-one days after Germany's unconditional surrender, the hospital's medical director, Dr Valentin Falthauser, oversaw the "medical" killing of Richard Jenne. The child was four years old. The Americans had not occupied the building because they had been warned that it might contain typhus patients. Falthauser and his staff had simply "got on with their work."[5]

Hence, for a host of reasons, including such as these, following Germany's capitulation, a very substantial amount of time would need to elapse before the nation would begin to come to terms with what had transpired. A further generation and a half would be required for resisters to be exonerated. For example, the Law for the Revocation of Unjust Sentences Passed by Law under National Socialism (exonerating, among others, Bonhoeffer) was passed in 1998, and revised in 2002 and 2009. For such as these to be widely appreciated and honoured would take longer. Bringing things more up to date, it was only in 2021, for example, that a key legal textbook/commentary originating under Nazism, effectively a "Bible" for law students—*Maunz*—was finally renamed.[6] The process of self-understanding and the bringing of compassionate perspective for all involved in issues of such depth and magnitude is hence still an ongoing one. This book aims to contribute a small part to that wider process.

Almost eighty years have passed since the death of Dietrich Bonhoeffer, and the time is apt for a fresh look at the final days of his life. A number of new documents have become available. It could be argued that with the passing of time, our minds have cleared somewhat in relation to his life, his times, and aspects of his legacy. The friend who became his biographer later wrote about Bonhoeffer,

> At the age of thirty he was barred from his academic post; when he was thirty-four, the pulpit was closed to him; at thirty-five, written publication was forbidden; and with his imprisonment at thirty-seven, even conversation with his friends was denied him . . . but as the outer circle of his activities and communication increasingly narrowed . . . his acting and thinking gained power . . . and when he was silenced for good at thirty-nine, he began to speak more loudly than ever before.[7]

This book will illustrate from a wide-ranging selection of sources the experience of both civilians and combatants caught up in the raging currents of those April days so that the circumstances of Bonhoeffer's death, unencumbered by oft-repeated inaccuracies, may be better free to speak for themselves. Bonhoeffer's death on April 9 did not take place on the final day of World War II. Unhelpful invented stories in this area, such as the account of Bonhoeffer kneeling to pray before his hanging, have proven misleading for decades, and have, in some instances, provided source material for sincere (but misguided) writings. On this subject, Hitler's valet Heinz Linge wrote upon his return after ten years in Soviet captivity that he was "surprised" to discover that "the only architect there had ever been in the Third Reich was Albert Speer" and went on to name a further eighteen, together with the details of their projects.[8] Linge's publication was first released in English in 2009. The point is clear: newly released publications and material enable us to correct oversimplified understandings and to understand and appreciate in a more rounded sense the poignancy of Bonhoeffer's final days. In the opening section of *Europe: A History*, Norman Davies observes that

> current affairs cannot become "History" until half a century has elapsed, runs one opinion, "until documents have become available and hindsight has cleared our minds." . . . Four hundred years ago, Sir Walter Raleigh, writing under sentence of death, understood the dangers perfectly. "Whosoever in writing a modern history shall follow the Truth too near the heels," he wrote, "it may happily strike out his teeth."[9]

As Germany disintegrated, Reichsführer-SS Heinrich Himmler, primary architect of the camps and the Nazis' other genocidal schemes and the most powerful man in Germany after Adolf Hitler, was collecting and gathering hostages from all realms of his empire of death who might be of personal benefit to himself. Previously, he had held hostages as an inducement to dissuade resistance movements from acts of sabotage.[10] Now he was assembling together some who might rather in some way prove valuable in helping him and Germany from going down in flames with Hitler. One select group, a mixed bag of political and "clan custody prisoners"[11] were being transported by the Gestapo under armed guard in generally a southerly direction towards the so-called "Southern Redoubt," the theoretical bulwark area of last defence that never quite materialised.

This book traces the story of the characters in a subset of that much larger hostage group, namely those who were "thrown together" with Dietrich Bonhoeffer during his final week.[12] Those executed on the same day, from whom he was kept in strict isolation, are not included. By dint of revisiting original, newly published, and unpublished sources in six languages, much translation work, and establishing contact with numerous families of contemporaries, a detailed study of the week's events has been undertaken.[13] It is now possible to list with confidence the thirteen members of the subgroup who were present on the morning of April 8 for Bonhoeffer's final service in Schönberg.[14] It was a truly eclectic group. In order of their Buchenwald cell numbers, they are General Friedrich von Rabenau, Pastor Dietrich Bonhoeffer, Dr Hermann Pünder, Erich and Margot Heberlein, Vasily Kokorin, General Alexander von Falkenhausen, Squadron Leader Hugh Mallory Falconer, Colonel Horst von Petersdorff, Heidel Nowakowski, Dr Sigmund Rascher, Captain Sigismund Payne Best, and Dr Horst Hoepner.[15]

A brief background to the inclusion of each of these people in the transport is outlined below. A fuller introduction to each of the members of the travelling party, insofar as it is known, is included by stages in different chapters over different days of the week.

Those who know something of Bonhoeffer will find, perhaps to their surprise, that so much of this volume is devoted to a selection of wider historical events of the relevant days in question. The aim of this choice is to correct the imbalance caused by the omission of the war context that has been known to characterise other works. This pattern has had the unfortunate result of making historical events appear almost as though they were secondary to whatever biographical narrative is being related, whereas the reverse is of course true. In this volume, by contrast, the biographical intentionally takes second or even third place to the surrounding and all-engulfing events of the time.[16] The reader's "companions" for this book are hence not merely Bonhoeffer and those travelling with him but also a rich catalogue of testimony from the days in question. In harmony with the diverse nature of the group of Bonhoeffer's hostage companions, the accompanying events are also drawn from an eclectic range of sources. To set the scene in its wider context, daily events from the Far East theatre and political developments at a world leader level are included. Insofar as possible, a detailed study of the German leadership's contributions, representative of the regime that Bonhoeffer resisted, stands centre stage. These include, for example, Josef Goebbels' diary entries at the time. Along the same lines, the book traces coverage of the "Werewolf" project, which played more than a walk-on part in the terrible closing stages of the war. This phase represented Germany's encouragement to its own citizens in the closing days of the war to become, on home soil, actors of a truly chilling sort: the very partisans and *francs-tireurs* they had so abundantly massacred throughout Europe. As a further example of the consequences of the Hitler dictatorship, the plight of more than one city faced with impossible demands to fight to the last, such as Königsberg, is detailed. In recognition of the fact that in his final week, unbeknown to Bonhoeffer, he experienced an undercover sabotage operation, courtesy of a member of the Special Operations Executive (SOE), one that arguably almost saved his life, a selection of SOE operations are mentioned. The harrowing tale of the death marches, a subject suitably documented only relatively recently, is portrayed, even as it unfolds, on successive days. As new towns and cities fall into Allied hands on a daily basis, the wide variety of situations experienced is documented. Equally varied, but sadly widespread, is the nation's transient captivity to a fear-based mentality that finds expression in the murder of helpless victims, for example those escaping from Allied air attacks on trains carrying concentration camp inmates. Its graphic scenes are set forth here. For the purpose of contrast and balance, intentionally mundane accounts of contextual events that are referenced in this project also include diary notes from other actors who managed to survive the war. The two resisters of differing hues followed in this respect are Marie "Missie" Vassiltchikov,[17] a regime opponent, and Victor Klemperer,[18] a Jewish professor. As a further example of the suffering unleashed through Nazism, the inclusion of details from Sarah Helm's exceptional work on Ravensbrück, Hitler's concentration camp for women, enables another (painful) consistent thread to be followed throughout the book. So too does the background story of Allen Dulles' *The Secret Surrender*, the high-stakes undercover negotiations between the Allies and the Axis powers. Testimony from a variety of individual German and Allied soldiers is referenced throughout, including that of Guy Sajer's *Forgotten Soldier*. The BBC daily news reports of the period from across Europe and beyond provide detail and add colour to the backdrop.

This approach has a purpose. As the weight of misery continuing to be unleashed by Nazism is recounted and documented on every page, so too stands in relief the courage of those known to have been resolute in their opposition to it.

Sunday, April 8, 1945

Flossenbürg, Germany: Destination Schönberg

Just after dawn on a beautiful spring morning, the week after Easter, a black Mercedes emerged into the chilly morning air from the SS garage immediately outside the camp. The Flossenbürg camp itself was a death factory of colossal proportions, and had for some months now been responsible for a daily execution quota of up to ninety people. Today would be no exception, and there had already been comings and goings since 4:00 a.m. that day. The plain-clothed driver and passenger, both members of the SS, had clear orders: to collect and return a prisoner from within a larger group. It involved, for them, a decidedly perilous daylight round trip of some 320 kilometres. A dusting of snow covered the camp and its environs, but the roads were still passable. A crucial bridge en route was still intact. The vehicle wound down the hill, took the road to Neukirchen, and forged south, towards Catholic Lower Bavaria, heading towards Schönberg and a schoolroom temporarily repurposed for hostage accommodation. For that prisoner, Dietrich Bonhoeffer, they would be the messengers of death.

(Nearby) Erbendorf, Germany

Close by, vestiges of normal and agreeable German life, in this case in connection with the seasonal rhythms of the church, somehow managed to continue, despite the momentous circumstances. In Erbendorf, only forty kilometres to the north of the camp, the eight-year-old Magdalena Helm was already preparing for a memorable event. In the church calendar, the first Sunday after Easter is White Sunday, when new confirmands receive Holy Communion for the first time: a special festive day when all the new communicants dress in white.

Zur Erinnerung

an meine
erste hl. Kommunion
empfangen am
Weissen Sonntag
(8. April 1945)

in der
Mariä Himmelfahrt-Pfarrkirche
zu Erbendorf.

———

Magdalena Helm

Fig. I-1. From a 1954 re-creation "marking" White Sunday
It reads, "In celebration / of my / first Holy Communion / received on / the second Sunday of Easter / (April 8, 1945) / at the Mariä Himmelfahrt Church / in Erbendorf / Magdalena Helm." Records accessed by Roswitha Heining, Erbendorf Parish Office, January 8, 2021. Author's collection. Recreated by Bruce Bovill.

Magdalena woke early as the family needed to be at the Mariä Him-melfahrt Church in good time for the Mass. They decided to walk, spend-ing much of the day watching in some alarm and wonderment as many bombers flew overhead, targeting destinations further south and locations unknown to them. After the service, along with the sixty-one others also partaking in their first Holy Communion, they enjoyed cakes in celebra-tion. Magdalena felt thankful that the day of her special event did not fall a week later, when sustained attacks from low-level flyers were experienced, and they could not have ventured outside. She still recalls the particu-larly beautiful weather of that day.[19] The brightness of the April sunshine formed a stark contrast with the darkness of events taking place close at hand as the day progressed.

Fig. I-2. View from Schönberg schoolroom window (unchanged)
Author's collection.

Schönberg, Bavaria, Germany

Much further south, the weather was also fair. In Schönberg that Sunday morning, thirteen people—prisoners—awoke in the schoolroom, undisturbed by any camp or guard routine. As they stirred, the feeling of normal life was tantalisingly close. For the second morning in a row, they could hear the church clock striking, and also from outside, the encouraging sounds of a subdued civilian life were audible. Since arriving here on Friday, they had had no guard presence in the room and, in contravention of their respective incarceration orders up to this point, had been able to converse freely with one another. The weather had been kind: there was a fabulous view from the window.

Adding to their sense of pleasurable disbelief, the room was even heated. There was no food, but they had beds with sheets—a dramatic improvement. Not only had they been accustomed to the rudimentary SS cells just outside Buchenwald concentration camp, but they had also spent three uncomfortable nights on the road that week: two in a claustrophobic police van, and one on the floor of an overstretched local prison.

In one week—so much had happened. As April progressed, and as the distance from Berlin increased, so too in proportion did the sense flourish for all members of the group of having a better chance of escaping from the persecutions and settling of old scores being meted out by the collapsing regime. The dread feeling of death being visited upon them at any moment, at the hands of brutal captors, or by an arbitrary decision of the authorities, had even begun to thaw, just a little. After all, they were now in Bavaria, around 560 kilometres south of Berlin. One member of the group, Hermann Pünder, a devout Catholic, even had with him a *Schott*, a Catholic lectionary with Bible readings, and from the adjacent bed allocation asked Bonhoeffer that morning to lead a Sunday service. He demurred, citing respect for the Russian, whose company he was so clearly enjoying but whose country was officially atheist. However, Kokorin insisted, and the time was fixed for 10:00.[20] Holding this service was a landmark, not just for the small group in the schoolroom, but also for Bonhoeffer. He allowed himself to be encouraged, albeit informally, to reinhabit his role as ordained pastor. The fact that Bonhoeffer acceded to this request among this group after eight and a half months of awaiting a certain death sentence speaks volumes. The unfreezing effect of the extending journey, the companionship of the others, and no doubt the beauty of the surroundings in Schönberg made a contribution to his decision. Perhaps he might after all survive the war. On that sunny Sunday morning, Bonhoeffer was wholly unaware of the approach of the SS guards already underway since earlier in the day on their long drive with orders to arrest him. Thoughts of a future with his young and beautiful fiancée, for so long an implausible dream, may have crossed his mind. It was not to be so.

The "companions in adversity" during this period were:

General Friedrich von Rabenau

Rabenau was a senior Wehrmacht officer with a strong Christian faith. He had initially welcomed Hitler but as a person of faith soon began to work with the resistance to oust him. Rabenau was arrested on July 27, 1944. He was a military historian of some note and in early retirement had studied theology. By all accounts the fellowship he and Bonhoeffer shared in Buchenwald, playing chess every afternoon on a set lent by Payne Best, was highly agreeable. By April, despite being on SS (double) rations, Rabenau's weight had fallen by one-third, from fifteen stone to ten.

Dietrich Bonhoeffer

Bonhoeffer was ordained as a Lutheran clergyman in 1931. He was on track for a brilliant academic career, but a "turn" in the trajectory of his faith meant, among other things, that he came to throw his energy into opposing the National Socialist regime. From his London base in 1934, he encouraged English-based German congregations not to support the German "Reich" Church until being tasked with leading a seminary for illegal ordinands back in Germany. Despite its closure by the Gestapo in 1937, Bonhoeffer persisted as a trainer and mentor of illegal ordinands until war broke out. He travelled back from a fresh job opening and possibility in New York in August 1939 to "share Germany's destiny," and in 1940 accepted an unsalaried undercover post in Germany's military intelligence organisation, the Abwehr, which plunged him into a hazardous shadow existence: his new line manager would disclose sensitive military information to nations about to be invaded. Bonhoeffer was arrested in April 1943 and remained in custody from then on. The nature of his covert identity as an overseas contact link for the German resistance was unknown to the group.

Hermann Pünder

Hermann Pünder was Germany's state secretary from 1926 to 1932. Rather than continue to serve under the dubious arrangements of Franz von Papen's cabinet, he resigned when the latter took office. Pünder was then ousted from his subsequent role as president of the administrative

district of Münster and forced into early retirement on grounds of political unsuitability. He took to farming a smallholding. A decorated World
War I veteran, he enlisted in the army reserve in 1939, being promoted to
the rank of major, before being arrested in the post–July 20, 1944, roundup.
Along with many others, he was apparently deemed by the regime to be
of questionable political loyalty. He appeared before the so-called People's
Court (Volksgerichtshof) that December and, unusually, was cleared of all
charges on the basis of insufficient evidence. In a pattern that was also customary for the Gestapo in such circumstances, he was instantly rearrested
and returned to prison. This continued without any further charges being
brought or any information being provided about any further hearings or
possible release.

Erich and Margot Heberlein

Erich and Margot Heberlein were a diplomatic couple and well known in
Madrid's high society. At home, the main language spoken in their household was English, in addition to German and Spanish. Erich was deputy
German ambassador to Spain and, as war progressed, was summoned,
together with his direct superior, Ambassador von Stohrer, back to Berlin
in March 1943. Their arrival in the German capital brought them face
to face with the horrors of Nazism and the reality of Germany's imminent defeat in the war. Heberlein immediately requested leave in order to
resolve personal matters, and persisted in asking, until leave to return to
Spain was grudgingly granted in August. From there, on June 17, 1944,
both he and Margot were kidnapped, separated, and dragged from one
prison to another across France before finally reaching Berlin on July 12.
There Erich was interned in isolation in the Gestapo general headquarters prison on Prinz-Albrecht-Straße. Margot was held under the same
conditions in Potsdam. On December 12, 1944, the lobbying of friends
and family finally paid off, and Erich and Margot were both transferred to
Sachsenhausen concentration camp under better conditions. They were
even allowed to hear news from their son. Ten weeks later, part of the
camp was evacuated and they were taken to Buchenwald, where they were
housed in the section reserved for VIP prisoners.

Vasily Kokorin

In Buchenwald's camp records, Vasily Vasilyevich Kokorin declared he
was born in 1921 in the village of Bronivka, Volochysk, in Proscurov
Province. It was a part of the fabrication "sold" to his captors about his

being the nephew of Vyacheslav Molotov, a former Soviet prime minister and second in command in the leadership to Joseph Stalin. In fact, Kokorin was born in 1923 in the village of Moloki, a village situated in the Kumensky District, which itself lies within the Kirov Region of the Soviet Union. Kokorin was captured in Demyansk-Leningrad on April 11, 1942. He was not Molotov's nephew—any more than many of the captured British POWs called Churchill were, as they claimed to be, relatives of the British prime minister—but rather an inventive survivor who also became a Gestapo informer. By agreement, he also provided his warders with information on other Soviet POWs in Sachsenhausen. From the Allied perspective, he was in truth a collaborator.

The reason for his inclusion as a VIP hostage in the prisoner transport covered by this book is testimony to his convincing ability to sustain his false identity before the Gestapo—and also among at least his sympathetic fellow prisoners. His invented tale remained virtually unchallenged for almost seventy-five years outside the Russian-speaking world.

General Alexander von Falkenhausen

Tenaciously wearing not only his uniform but also his Pour le Mérite medal, Germany's highest honour, awarded in 1918, was sixty-seven-year-old General Alexander von Falkenhausen. He had been until relatively recently Germany's military governor general of occupied Belgium. When originally coerced back onto German soil from a brilliantly successful retirement posting in China, he made no effort to hide his sentiments and was never to receive a front command. His contacts with the opposition began, unsurprisingly, in early 1939. The group had no idea of his links to the July 20 plotters, and he did not make them known. As a serving soldier, he was inexorably drawn into serving the ruthlessness of the regime and while in post in occupied Belgium was a party to war crimes. It was his nonconformity that led to his dismissal and his multiple contacts with the German resistance to Hitler that placed him under suspicion. Falconer's words about him are a pertinent although incomplete summary: "Von Falkenhausen was by anybody's standards a complete gentleman."

Squadron Leader Hugh Falconer

A fluent French speaker, Falconer began his war service with the RAF, but on July 5, 1941, was released in order to volunteer for the SOE.[21] As an undercover radio operative, he played a key role in Torch, the Anglo-American invasion of Vichy French North Africa, in November 1942.

When the US armed forces went into combat, for a period of three days it was only Falconer's low-level radio post housed in a cave in the Rock of Gibraltar (an improvised radio network, created by dint of persuasion and cunning out of rudimentary materials) that kept the Allied commander Eisenhower in touch with his ground forces. Later captured in Tunis, he was tortured. He eventually adopted the identity of a downed pilot, and by dint of acting the part of a very important captive, Falconer was selected for transport by rail via Florence directly to the Gestapo's Prinz-Albrecht-Straße headquarters in Berlin. After an interval of some duration, he was moved to Sachsenhausen concentration camp, and from there, eventually, to Buchenwald.

Colonel Horst von Petersdorff

Horst von Petersdorff was born on March 9th, 1893. His military connections were established from a young age. He served with exceptional distinction and bravery throughout World War I, despite losing an arm. After the war he was involved in the Freikorps, and was an early joiner of the Nazi Party. He did not like all that he found and left the party in 1932. He was associated with the SA[22] under the leadership of Röhm, and only narrowly escaped with his life in the Night of the Long Knives in June 1934. Petersdorff was reactivated to military duties in 1939. He took part in the Polish campaign, and for service in France was awarded the Knight's Cross of the Iron Cross. Despite the fact that he continued to take part in the war, being wounded a further four times, Petersdorff came to loathe Hitler and abhor the Nazis. Following the July 20 plot, he was expelled from the General Staff of the SA on October 18, 1944. Petersdorff was tried by the Volksgerichtshof but, unusually, found innocent—and yet was reimprisoned. The reasons for his inclusion in the hostage group are unknown.

Heidel Nowakowski

In her book *Reise durch den letzten Akt* (A journey as the curtain falls), Isa Vermehren makes disparaging mention of Nowakowski. In his account Best puts her age as being in her early twenties, whereas she is in fact in her early thirties, with Best noting that "she might, but for her short stature, have posed for a model for a youthful Germania. . . . According to her own account she had worked for some Allied Intelligence Service, and while imprisoned at Ravensbrück, had been tortured by having two teeth extracted in slow fashion. Here, befriended by an SS officer, she had been freed and moved to lodgings (but not work) in the camp brothel. . . . Blonde, she firmly believed she was very beautiful and that she was desired by all men; being a good-natured girl she felt it her duty to bring joy to them, and her readiness was so great that restraint was both necessary and difficult."[23] Currently her flirtations were being extended in the direction of a much-disliked and gregarious member of the group, SS doctor and mass murderer Sigmund Rascher. Given her status as a single woman in her early thirties, her improvised bed in Schönberg had been firmly positioned next to the beds of a married couple, the Heberleins, to discourage any untoward night-time activity.[24] For over fifty years she remained, disconcertingly, without even a surname in the prolific retelling of this part of Bonhoeffer's story, until Richardi revealed her surname in 2010. In 2019 Sayer provided the photograph used on the front cover. It is possible she became a VIP hostage through smart manoeuvring, as did others. While in captivity, Heidel gave Payne Best two addresses where she could be contacted—both in the Essen area—along with a telephone number. She told Hugh Falconer she was from Düsseldorf, which is close to Essen. Within the prisoner group itself, most commentators presume her to have been an informer who also used sex work, but no evidence of informing has been found.

Sigmund Rascher

In the current (eighth) revised edition of Bethge's thousand-page biography of Dietrich Bonhoeffer, Rascher is simply listed as a "fellow prisoner."[25] It is a telling omission. A regular Gestapo informer, Rascher is known to have murdered at least two hundred people in his "medical" experiments.

The reasons for Rascher's inclusion in the party of VIP hostages are unclear. Rascher and his wife, Nini, fell out of favour with their patron Heinrich Himmler following the revelation that between them they had falsely claimed Nini had given birth to four children, who were in fact adopted. A Gestapo investigation into the saga, while concluding that Rascher was "duped," did not overly add credibility to Rascher's status as a qualified doctor. They were placed in separate camps. In Buchenwald Rascher was admitted as a priority "English" prisoner and befriended by British former spy Payne Best. Here he came to be a member of the group of hostages who are the subject of this book.

Captain Payne Best

Payne Best, a fluent German speaker, was a British intelligence officer who had served with great distinction in World War I. His interwar years had been spent moving in the highest social circles amid a network of con-tacts well suited to exploitation for spying purposes. During the course of the 1930s, one of those he met and charmed was Heinrich Himmler. When war was declared, Best was responsible for espionage conducted via the British SIS (Secret Intelligence Service) in Holland. Against his better judgement and counsel he was drawn, with another, less experi-enced British agent (Richard Stevens), into discussions in 1939 with a so-called group of resisters, in reality agents of Himmler's Gestapo, who were purportedly unhappy with Hitler's regime and aiming to negotiate (despite the fact that war had been declared) with the British prime minister. In a daring and violent abduction, and to the excruciating and lasting embarrassment of the British government, Best and Ste-vens were kidnapped from the Café Backus on the outskirts of Venlo in November 1939. After initial harsh treatment and his disclosure to the Germans of copious amounts of intelligence information, much of questionable value, Best was awarded prisoner conditions of (relative) luxury for the duration of the war in Sachsenhausen. He was visited in person there by Himmler, presumably in relation to his prior acquain-tance, in 1942, after which his VIP prisoner status increased still fur-ther. He was generally well liked and regarded by SOE operative Fal-coner as a collaborator.

Dr Horst Hoepner

Horst Hoepner was the son of Dr Kurt Hoepner and his wife, Elizabeth, née Kienast. He was born on June 19, 1889, in Torgau: the third boy, a younger brother to Erich and Kurt from a long clergy family line.[26] After completing his doctorate in science and business,[27] and before military service, Horst was employed in business. He spoke fluent English, no doubt a business asset in the 1920s and 1930s. After the July 20, 1944, bomb plot, Horst's well-known older brother General Erich Hoepner, who became a defiant resister of Hitler's commands, was seized and shortly thereafter executed, on August 8. Horst himself was also arrested in Paris, where he was serving with the army, on July 24. He was kept in Fresnes prison, mainly in solitary confinement, until August 1, 1944, when he was transferred to Buchenwald. Horst received extreme inhumane treatment at the hands of the Gestapo, enduring physical and psychological torture. In Payne Best's 1950 account, Hoepner's (by now) broken mental health is the subject of scorn by the author. The reasons for his inclusion in the hostage group are unknown.

For much of the period from Tuesday, April 3, to Friday, April 6, Bonhoeffer and the others travelled in a wood-burning Grüne Minna (Green
Minna), a police van developed in the 1930s to run on alternative fuel.
It was designed to transport four to six people. This group initially comprised sixteen people, and possessed, with the notable exception of Payne
Best, only scant small items of luggage. The small window panels of the
vehicle in question had additional bars to deter thoughts of escape.[28] The
twin aspects of wood storage and wood smoke had been somewhat overlooked at the design stage of the vehicle, with the result that despite being
ahead of its time (and green), in other respects it provided a difficult experience for those unfortunate enough to be obliged to travel in it. Indeed,
its very name was believed by some to be derived from a story about a
child's uncomfortable experience of travelling in one (Minna), who was
reputed to have turned green at the time. A museum picture of this vehicle
is included here (fig. I-3).

Fig. I-3. Die Grüne Minna
www.polizei.autos.de, M. Weber

As mentioned above, one member of the party, Sigmund Rascher, had
taken the lead in murdering dozens of prisoners in Dachau, in experiments
of great cruelty. His participation in the various schemes was notable for
its extent and alacrity. Compared with the others in the vehicle, he was
privy to a lot more inside knowledge about the innovative methods that
Hitler's Germany had employed to murder people. As the journey began,

he was sufficiently alarmed by the vehicle's wood fumes to cry out, "It's a gas van—we're being gassed!" For most of the hostages, being squashed alongside Rascher was both unpleasant and excruciating. Pünder writes,

> Rascher chatted as if on friendly terms and openly and he [without being asked] shared intimate details of the "medical work" of the SS. As a young medical officer, he'd been ordered to be part of the freezing experiments in the last year. Here prisoners had been experimented upon concerning how low temperatures could be lowered, and for how long, before death ensued. When the naïve SS doctor noticed with what disgust [Abscheu] we turned away from him, he changed course and confidentially advised us that as a result of pursuing these investigations he had "got into trouble" with his superiors, and for that was now a KZ [concentration camp] internee.[29]

But the Rascher story as relayed in this passage is another entirely fabricated tale. The more complex and disturbing story of the initiative behind the experiments, as well as the real reasons for the arrest of Rascher and his wife, is recounted in full in chapter 13. Hence even this brief exchange illustrates at the very outset (1) how limited was most of what the people on the transport knew about each other at the time, and even as they later wrote memoirs; and (2) how little was in fact true.

Such was the diversity of these so-called enemies of the Third Reich. Their rich part in Bonhoeffer's story has at best remained a footnote, and at worst repeatedly been superficially or wrongly reiterated, or simply dismissed. The purpose of this book is to help that part to be more fully told.

1
Dietrich Bonhoeffer

So what had led this mild-mannered German pastor to be incarcerated in the Schönberg schoolroom? Growing up, the thought of becoming a resister would hardly have entered his mind. Bonhoeffer and his twin sister, Sabine, were born on February 4, 1906.[1] Dietrich and Sabine were the sixth and seventh of what would soon become eight children in a household that included a cook, a nanny, and a housekeeper, and—as the children grew and developed—an abundant repertoire of tutors across a dazzling variety of subjects and interests.[2] When Bonhoeffer was only five months old, his Silesian hometown of Breslau, a place today within Poland and now called Wrocław, received a visit from Winston Churchill.[3] The young Churchill was there at the invitation of no less than the Kaiser himself, Wilhelm II, to attend and observe German army manoeuvres. It was a sure sign that current relations between the two nations were indeed cordial. Few, if any, could have seen the stark and dire reversals in what so soon lay ahead. By comparison with Churchill, who was always delighted to dress up in full regalia, the Bonhoeffer family would have had scant interest in the show-manship of the Prussian military, and it is fair to state that the international significance of this visit will have most likely eluded them. Perhaps a more auspicious accolade for the city of Bonhoeffer's birth than that of receiving the future British prime minister was that, like many similar places of that era, Breslau/Wrocław also saw a healthy fourfold increase in the ratio of mixed Jewish-Christian marriages in the period 1870–1915. Indeed, the subsequent marriage of Bonhoeffer's twin sister, Sabine, to Gerhard Leibholz would subsequently become one such mixed marriage. It proved a good match, and a source of genuine blessing to Dietrich as well. Of course, Bon-hoeffer's childhood was not immune from the anti-Semitism prevalent in Germany at that time, but there is an illustrative story on the subject. Once, after Bonhoeffer had thumped another, presumably Jewish, boy of his own age, the child's mother accused him, and his household, of anti-Semitism.

His mother's comment that he "could not have heard of such a thing in her house" has the ring of truth. When war came, it would bring tragedy: the family were absolutely devastated by the death of Dietrich's older brother Walter in 1918. His loss left scars that would never heal. Otherwise inconsolable, his mother took what comfort she could from retaining the Luther Bible she had given him at the time of his confirmation.

Work, rest, and play, in good measure, were all important in the Bonhoeffer family, in the wider context of a total commitment to profession and related activities. Play was important in this household, but one had to know its place.[4] What *really* counted was "what you do." The career of Bonhoeffer *père* was a distinguished one: a Berlin S-Bahn station was later named after the Berlin University Neurological Clinic, where he was director, and still bears that name today.[5] Bonhoeffer forged a relationship of lasting respect with his father and grew up homeschooled by his diligent mother (and, as alluded to, multiple helpers) in a house where the man's role was self-evidently to work with an unstinting commitment to work itself. It was not just theory: something of the level of the Bonhoeffer family's work ethic can be discerned in the letter written by Bonhoeffer's mother, Paula, to her son at a much later date and in dark days: on November 11, 1943, eight months after her son's arrest earlier that April, she wrote, "Your father will not disengage himself from his work despite his being 75 years old."[6] Stephen Plant notes, "Bonhoeffer's brothers prepared for careers in science and law; his sisters married similarly solid professionals."[7] Musical ability and similar or related accomplishments, despite being taken very seriously, along with the relatively effortless acquisition of additional languages, were all things that were nice to have, especially if they happened to be professionally useful, but fitted more into the background "wallpaper" of what it meant to be a well-rounded young German in that walk of life.

Dietrich would be different. When Bonhoeffer was fourteen, German hyperinflation was about to devastate the nation, and yet somehow the family were able to emerge unscathed. Later, in 1932, looking back at himself as he had been at that age and time, Bonhoeffer would write about a "classroom moment": considering seriously the study of theology and then lying awake all night as a result. This is readily understandable, considering that his family hardly attended regular church services. The Bonhoeffer clan were not "religious" and had a tradition of reading aloud the Scriptures at Christmas. They also had a pattern of celebrating the transition into the new year by reading Psalm 90. So in relational terms, despite the number of theologians in the wider family and the encouragements of his uncle and godfather,

Hans von Hase, the stakes were high when vocational choices—not least in the context of economic disaster—were under discussion, and especially Bonhoeffer's particular choice: to study theology. It did not readily offer the prospect of financial self-sufficiency and hardly promised glamour—but it was his alone. He would later write, "From the time I was twelve, it was clear to me that I would study theology."[8]

Encouragements towards this particular pathway would not be slow in arriving. One came when he was only fifteen, through his language teacher Richard Czeppan. He wrote to Bonhoeffer on the occasion of his confirmation in March 1921,[9] calling him a "budding theologian." Many more were to follow. His mother chose the occasion to present him with Walter's Luther Bible, a volume that Dietrich would treasure and keep in his possession from then on right up until the final moment of his life.

In summary, Bonhoeffer's family and his formative years were for him a backdrop of significant goodness: a liberating environment, as opposed to a controlling one. Later, Bonhoeffer would have more than adequate resources for outgrowing any unhelpful "captivity of the clan." He would readily be able to forge his own path. Meanwhile he completed his doctoral thesis at the age of twenty-one. It, and a sequel, were both soon published—with all the positive signals towards a career in academic theology that such accolades would bring.

From these beginnings Bonhoeffer embarked upon a series of formative and often international experiences. These would prove vital in shaping him for the matter-of-fact self-confidence with which he was later able, by 1933, to confront the adherents of Nazism when they came to power in Germany. He spent a pre-ordination training year in a German parish in Barcelona, which proved formative. He won a scholarship to the United States to spend a year at Union Theological Seminary, which proved significant in his faith journey.[10] Bonhoeffer was ordained in 1931.

Soon he would change, as things also changed rapidly around him. There was a "turn" in Bonhoeffer's life at some point during the year 1932, which took place before the winter semester of that year began. In 1936, looking back, he would write about that phase, "I came to the Bible for the first time."[11] As part of his international ecumenical work, he wrote that year,

> The job of responsible theological work, supported by the ecumenical world, is to strengthen and support that proportion of Germans and Christians in Germany who are fighting against Hitler.[12]

Just at the very moment Hitler came to power, Bonhoeffer gave a radio broadcast in January 1933 about leadership principles. It was cut off at the end—not because of any Orwellian controlling editorial decision, but because the schedule had run over. It was a prescient moment. Inspired by his time in America to engage with the project of making faith more accessible to a wider audience, that year he delivered a series of lectures on Genesis chapter 3 entitled "Creation and Fall." These proved so popular at Berlin University that there was "standing room only," with class members hanging on his every word.

At the same time, he became deeply involved in the early days of the German "Church Struggle" under Nazism. For Bonhoeffer, an early run-in with the authorities—in this case, the Gestapo—would ensue. Unusually within Europe, Germany had, and still has today, an almost equal proportion of Catholic believers to those connected with Protestant denominations. On coming to power, the new regime had soon effectively neutralized resistance to Nazism from the otherwise socially active Catholic Church by the skilful negotiating and signing of a "Concordat" with Rome. The regime was also seeking at the same time to infiltrate and dominate the voice of Protestant churches by various means. These would, sooner or later, include

- removing non-Aryan clergy from their posts by legislation,
- having Synod motions passed by packing out meetings with Brownshirt bullies,
- promoting pro-Nazi clergy who were happy to adorn their churches and communion tables with swastika flags,
- obtaining control of clergy stipend payment mechanisms,
- forbidding duplication and distribution of newsletters and the like, and
- restructuring authority and allegiance channels so as to manipulate the election via church structures of a Hitler-nominated newly to-be-appointed Reich bishop.

Already Bonhoeffer's hackles were up, and he was busy printing and distributing leaflets encouraging voters not to cooperate. But these leaflets were being banned and confiscated by the Gestapo. In order to level the playing field, Bonhoeffer sought out an audience with the current head of the Gestapo, Rudolf Diels. He appeared in Diels' office in the subsequently infamous Prinz-Albrecht-Straße building with a suitably dressed clergy colleague, who was wearing the Iron Cross won in the 1914–1918 war.

What was said is not recorded, but the two did secure a truce. Bonhoeffer did subsequently reveal that being despatched to a concentration camp as punishment for such disruptive behaviour as he had just demonstrated was "mentioned."[13] The seeds of a determination to resist were being sown.

But by this time Bonhoeffer had found that the cost and frustration levels of these activities had become very high. One the one hand, there was the deep exasperation with the tortuous process of rounding up and energising clergy to go on strike or resist, or even break away. For example, one such area where Bonhoeffer called upon clergy to go on strike, and where he was roundly and soundly ignored, was in the making available to the authorities of data contained only in church records to establish Aryan or non-Aryan ancestry.[14] On the other hand, there were the overall difficulties involved in the process of finding his own clergy work. Together things had become sufficiently galling to move him to offer himself for much-needed employment in another overseas German parish, this time in Sydenham, London. From here, greatly to the irritation of the new *official* German church authority structures, he operated as a dynamo of energy in undermining the aspirations of the by-then Reich Church to be regarded exclusively as the official church of Germany. In Bonhoeffer's short stay in the UK, working full time as an incumbent, his parishioners and his parents proved fulsomely supportive of his endeavours. On one memorable occasion, a key senior London parishioner, wholly in agreement with Bonhoeffer's views on developments within Germany, threw the visiting German ambassador, Ribbentrop, out of his office. At another level, Bonhoeffer's ministerial stipend proved completely inadequate to financing the telephone bill costs arising from his anti-Nazi activism. On this occasion Bonhoeffer benefitted greatly from the unprecedented generosity of the Post Office in writing off most of a bill deemed simply too high to pay. The balance, as was the case with his frequent travel, was covered by his parents.

Bonhoeffer's time in England was punctuated by enough trips back to Germany to earn him frequent-flyer status at London's Croydon Airport. But it was foreshortened by a call back to Germany from the newly outlawed Confessing Church. He was asked to direct an illegal seminary for courageous and unfunded ordinands at the remote places of first, Zingst, and subsequently, Finkelwalde. Given that Bonhoeffer had been there right at the start of the movement (for an alternative church to the now-corrupted Reich Church to come into existence), the making to him of this particular offer, which he did accept, was a moment of brilliance on the part of the much-under-duress Confessing Church. Throughout his time in London, Bonhoeffer had been sending his weekly sermons to a girl he was in love with in an unspoken way, called Elizabeth Zinn.[15] Bonhoeffer's choice to perceive the new opening to direct a seminary in the end as a "call"—one he felt was not a role for someone with the responsibility of a spouse—was also a constituent part of his calling time on his not-quite-acknowledged relationship with Elizabeth Zinn.

Once he was back in Germany, events moved fast. Bonhoeffer flourished in the role of Finkenwalde's seminary director, and in addition took on seemingly endless cases of support for beleaguered regime opponents. He was soon banned from lecturing, which for him meant in turn that, from now on, there was no way back to be found in any academic work. Yet despite the fact that all the training for the illegal ordinands was done on a shoestring, somehow things worked together well enough for a total of seventy ordinands to be trained up over the course of the next two years. Ordaining them into a context of complete uncertainty was just something to be accepted. Given the levels of persecution and harassment that active Christians were experiencing at the time, with every term bringing with it news of a new wave of arrests, it is remarkable that Finkenwalde was able to remain open all that time, and the fact that it was may largely be due to the Olympics being staged in Germany in 1936. Without them Bonhoeffer's seminary might well have been closed down a full year earlier. As a part of putting on a show for the favourable consumption of the world's media, arrests were curtailed, and among these appeasement measures, thousands were released from concentration camps. Bonhoeffer came across a sign in a Berlin bookshop at the time that was very revealing:

Nach der Olympiade	After the end of the Olympics
hau'n wir die BK	We'll beat the CC [Confessing
zu Marmelade	Church] to a pulp
dann schmeissen wir die Juden raus	Then we'll kick out the Jew
dann ist die BK aus!	Then the CC's finished too!

The entirely predictable did indeed occur. From an international public relations viewpoint, the Olympics proved a resounding success for Hitler's Germany, but when they came to a close, it was soon "back to business as usual" for the authorities. In 1937 a group of Christian leaders wrote a letter to Hitler asking some difficult questions: it produced nothing except for two imprisonments and the martyrdom of one other individual, bludgeoned to death in Buchenwald. Amid all this, and another bruising encounter with the Gestapo over the arrest of pastor Martin Niemöller, Bonhoeffer also wrote up his lectures to students and his thinking on the Sermon on the Mount into still another book, *Nachfolge* (Discipleship), which was published in Advent 1937, only months after the Gestapo had physically bolted shut the main door and closed down the seminary at Finkelwalde. Bonhoeffer was forced to teach seminarians on, if possible, an even more ad hoc basis. With the seminary closed, Bonhoeffer now had no base to keep any of his possessions. His books were his work and he loved them—mainly theological ones, as well as novels—but he also owned a motorcycle, some paintings and an icon, a piano, and a car. He would resort to keeping things stored at interim locations, including his parents' home in Berlin. Over the next phase of harassment, the motorcycle would come in very handy. It was agreed between Bonhoeffer and what was left of the Confessing Church that although he was now banned from lecturing and running any training institution, and would soon have to start reporting in to a local police office to help the Gestapo keep tabs on him, he could still meet with illegal ordinands and continue their formation in bursts, in different venues and groupings.

In a circular letter from Gross-Schlönwitz around the turn of the year 1937, at a time when twenty-seven seminarians who had studied under him had been arrested, Bonhoeffer wrote about transience in a meaningful way:

> For some time now we have grown accustomed to the fact that we cannot count on having long periods of time. We neither could nor should do so. Learning obedience each new day is enough for us.[16]

When the book was published, he somehow managed to finance the distribution of copies of the book to most of the ordinands. In one, presented to Otto Lerche,[17] he signed the inside and included the verse from John 15:16:

> You did not choose me, but I chose you and appointed you so that you might go and bear fruit—fruit that will last—and so that whatever you ask in my name the Father will give you.

The passage he chose follows on from the ordination promises he himself had made in Berlin six years earlier, and in that sense represents the faithful "handing on" of a charge. At that service the presiding bishop had asked all the candidates, once they had listened to a selection of Scripture passages, whether they were willing and ready to undertake the office of preaching with which they were being entrusted. Once they had replied individually that they were, he prayed, "May God bless you, that you might bear much fruit, and may that fruit endure eternally."[18] Neither Bonhoeffer nor Lerche would survive the war—and perhaps in their lifetime neither was granted an answer to some of their deepest prayers—but in a time of disintegration and fragmentation, they both trusted in God's promise that lasting fruitfulness from their lives might ensue.[19]

The pressure on active Christians became more intense as bans on meetings and duplicated communications came into force. In Bonhoeffer's case he was also subject to travel restrictions. With parental help he was able to overturn a ban on his visiting Berlin. "Underground" teaching, with its accompanying nomadic existence, became the new order of the day. There was also a final parting of the ways with the Confessing Church after its capitulation on the issue of a loyalty oath to Hitler in July 1938. No doubt in connection with this, an early contact with military resisters was established. Key pages were duly torn out of the Bonhoeffer diary. His ability to pull a few strings, plus the fact that his local reporting station was by this time in (relatively sleepy) Pomerania, proved very useful when it came to military call-up papers. When these arrived, the available options were clear-cut: "conscientious objection," punishable by death,[20] or reporting for duty. Bonhoeffer gave serious consideration to the military chaplaincy option.

Meanwhile, he was able to write another book: *Life Together*. Then, as 1939 progressed, he obtained a military leave of absence while he explored various work openings in the USA. After less than three weeks there in June, he chose to return to Germany to share in his country's destiny, fully aware of the likely cost.

A curious confluence of circumstances led to the appointment of Bonhoeffer's brother-in-law Hans von Dohnanyi to the staff of Admiral Canaris, an appointment that had Hitler's personal sanction. It was needed because the brilliant young lawyer had taken a particular stance pleasing to Canaris but in the process made enemies, who in turn swiftly pointed out his Jewish lineage. It was through this family link that Bonhoeffer was invited to meet with the Abwehr's fiercely anti-Nazi Colonel Hans Oster on March 24, 1940. In some ways the head office of the Abwehr, with its impressive location in Berlin, was well placed to be at the centre of a conspiracy. It was an organisation known to work successfully with unusual strategies. Any suspicions or even complaints about staff engaged on operations could easily be brushed aside as a counter-intelligence ruse. As a consequence, with breathtaking rapidity Bonhoeffer became one of only around seven Germans[21] who were privy to the knowledge at the time that Oster was revealing invasion dates to the Western powers. Bonhoeffer agreed with Dohnanyi that in so doing, Oster was acting in the best interests of Germany. The result was that between March 1940 and April 1943, the date of his eventual arrest, no other Confessing Church pastor led quite such an unusual life as did Dietrich Bonhoeffer. For example, as of mid-1940 his accommodation and travel costs were covered under Abwehr expenses. Bonhoeffer was assigned to Abwehrstelle Munich. He was able to undertake the (pastoral) work he wanted to do in Prussia, on the basis that he submit a report to his brother-in-law Dohnanyi, who would redraft it so as to make it appear as a military intelligence-gathering exercise in preparation for the coming eastward attack. His double life was balanced on a knife-edge. Bonhoeffer's Munich line manager in the service of the Abwehr, Josef Müller, suggested that he take up residence at Ettal Monastery, where Bonhoeffer was able to benefit greatly from the seclusion and write. For him it was not a hardship posting. At Christmas 1940, when Bonhoeffer had already spent the autumn in Ettal Monastery, he was joined there by the Dohnanyis.[22] Through these unusual connections, Dietrich enjoyed sustained periods of quiet—writing in remote locations and working on yet another book, which later became *Ethics*—interspersed with a hectic national and international travel schedule—covering thirty thousand miles of travel on assignment in the period between 1940 and March 1943. These activities, which of course at the time would have been deemed conspiratorial by the Nazi regime, and would form a backdrop to Bonhoeffer's eventual arrest and execution, are recounted in more detail elsewhere.[23] Amid all that was going on, Bonhoeffer also met and entirely fell for a beautiful and much younger woman, Maria von Wedemeyer—this time proposing to her, and being accepted. No sooner, it seemed, had they declared their love than Bonhoeffer was imprisoned. The date was April 5, 1943.[24]

Bonhoeffer in Prison

Bonhoeffer's time in prison started with poor treatment. However, things changed when his kinship with Berlin's military governor, von Hase, became known and special privileges began to be made available, something that did not endear Bonhoeffer to a number of other prisoners.

Meanwhile, on the outside, the war situation intensified. Bonhoeffer remained incarcerated in Berlin's Tegel prison. He wrote many letters, a number of which his friend Bethge would gather over time and publish after his death. But Bonhoeffer's circle of resisters would never recover from the investigations linked to the "*Depositenkasse* affair," the original cause of their arrest.[25] Bonhoeffer was interrogated on both minor charges, ones that he had been able, with considerable ingenuity, to deflect, and major charges, for which there was insufficient evidence. But after the failure of the July 20, 1944, attempt on Hitler's life, Bonhoeffer knew he was too closely linked with numerous conspirators to escape for long. Hundreds were arrested, and there was a dramatic ramping up of the pursuit of the wider group who had made (or in any way been associated with) plans for a coup. On September 21, 1944, a large dossier documenting widespread resistance plans reaching as far back as 1938, Dohnanyi's "Chronicle of Shame," was gifted to the Gestapo investigators.[26] As a dreadful sign of intent, seventeen days later, Bonhoeffer, together with other key resisters, was rehoused away from the relative luxury of Berlin's Tegel prison. The shocking information reached his family and fiancée that same day: "They've moved Dietrich to Prinz-Albrecht-Straße! Where Fabian [von Schlabrendorff] is!" The news fell like a hammer blow in the family circle. Dietrich's fiancée, Maria, by now a familiar face in the Bonhoeffer home, was visibly upset. The place being named with such dismay was the head office of the RSHA (Reichssicherheitshauptamt, the state security and police apparatus), base of the notorious Gestapo interrogators. The SS men in black uniforms were infamous for the cruelty and brutality of their methods—and this was the very nerve centre of all their operations in Berlin. Its impressive exterior, in period architecture, spoke reassuringly of Imperial German respectability and world standing. But the high ceilings and long corridors inside bore silent witness to the unimaginable brutality and inhumanity taking place behind closed doors there, particularly in the dungeons. It was a name that spelt disaster for any who were incarcerated there, and news of a transfer to that destination was almost certainly a death sentence.[27]

As a priest—particularly a priest of the despised church—Bonhoeffer was not shown mercy in the ensuing Gestapo interrogations. He was initially allowed a small ration of visits from his fiancée, Maria, but after he was moved again in February 1945 to become a part of Himmler's collection of hostages, she was not allowed to be informed of his whereabouts. Bonhoeffer's interim destination at the time was Buchenwald. He would remain there until April 3.

Sunday, April 1, 1945

Map 1 of Bonhoeffer's Germany: Chapters 2–6

Philippsburg	On Easter Sunday the First French Army under General de Lattre de Tassigny crosses the Rhine here.
Lake Comacchio	A British Commando unit breaks out of the (static) Allied battle-line in Italy, and on April 1 surprises the German 162nd Division, taking many prisoners.
Aschaffenburg	Intense fighting between the 45th US Infantry division, March 25–April 3, 1945. On the German side are troops from Kampfkommando Aschaffenburg.
Balf	On April 1, Red Army forces enter Balf, Hungary. Some Jewish survivors of an SS massacre crawl out of a mass grave.
Creuzburg	Resistance in Creuzburg finally ceases late on April 1.
Erfurt	Erfurt is attacked, but resists until April 6.
Eisenach	On April 1 US Army troops cross the border into Thüringia at Eisenach.
Hersfeld	On April 1, American troops break out from Hersfeld towards the Werra.
Upper Silesia	Upper Silesia has been captured by Konev, Chuikov's forces are controlling Küstrin, Zhukov's are across the Oder river, and the 2nd and 3rd Ukrainian fronts are nearing the gates of Vienna.
Vienna	Missie Vassiltchikov attends a "surreal" Mass in the Stefansdom.
Falkenstein	Viktor and Eva Klemperer continue their circuitous journey.
Hela Peninsula	An extensive German sea evacuation project, which includes Guy Sajer, is underway.
Zellingen	Karl Weiglein is cut down on Easter Day after being hanged by a Flying Court Martial on Good Friday.
Ravensbrück	Swedish Red Cross "Rescue" bus drivers are instructed to wait.
Buchenwald	Bonhoeffer and the larger group of prisoners hear news of their imminent departure.

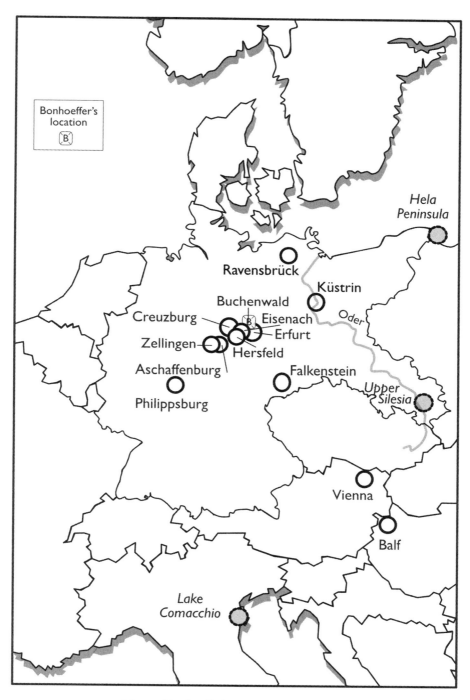

Map 1 of Bonhoeffer's Germany: Chapters 2–6
Staatsbibliothek zu Berlin-Kartenabteilung/Bruce Bovill

2
One Week Earlier

The Global Conflict: Okinawa

While the hostages might be hopeful that hostilities across all theatres of war would soon cease, this latest week would prove to be still another disappointment. In the global conflict, Easter Sunday began with the launch of the greatest land battle of the Pacific War: Operation Iceberg, the invasion of Okinawa. That morning fifty thousand American troops landed on Okinawa along an eight-mile beachhead. Twice that number of Japanese were entrenched on the island. The initial landing, for some reason, was unopposed, leading the US troops to change their slogan from "Golden Gate in 48" to "Home Alive in 45."[1]

Moscow

In Russia, on the evening of March 31, American and British ambassadors and top military advisors had arrived at "the Little Corner," Stalin's informal residence, for a meeting of the Allies. US ambassador Harriman handed Stalin a Russian translation of a communiqué from President Roosevelt, explaining that his top priority was the encirclement and destruction of German forces in the Ruhr region.

As he listened, knowing that Upper Silesia had been captured by Konev, that Chuikov's forces were controlling Küstrin, that Zhukov's were across the Oder river, and that the 2nd and 3rd Ukrainian Fronts were already nearing the gates of Vienna, the normally suspicious dictator seemed to open up. He praised the plan, saying it would accomplish the goal of cutting Germany in half. The next morning, April 1, he received Marshals Zhukov and Konev in his large study in the Kremlin, with its long conference table and the portraits of Suvorov and Kutuzov on the wall. Immediately thereafter he wrote formally approving the proposal of his trusting ally, noting agreeably that "Berlin has lost its former strategic importance: the Soviet command will send only second-rate forces against it," adding,

"However, this plan may undergo certain alterations, depending upon circumstances."[2] Historian Antony Beevor describes this note as "the greatest
April fool in modern history."[3]

World Leaders: Tensions

Another hope prevalent among Germans, particularly those offering resistance to the Allies, was that some form of rift would take place
between the Allied nations and provide a "way out" for Nazi Germany.
Certainly, by April 1, 1945, among the Allies prosecuting the war, the
deep tensions between the leaders of the "Big Three," which had been
simmering away for some considerable time, were abundantly ready to
boil over. Stalin, bearing by far the overwhelming burden of both military
and civilian casualties, had by now little need for Allied recognition of his
by now dominant world leader status, paid for in blood. As the days of
British imperial greatness passed into history, Churchill was in the painful process of being sidelined by the new realities of global conflict. His
rapidly diminishing influence on events could be partly offset by his eye
for publicity, as in his dangerous meander with news media present on
the far side of the Rhine the previous week, but it could not be concealed.
Roosevelt had only twelve days left to live, and was growing deeply, and
understandably, weary of Stalin's insatiable appetite for the expression and
exploitation of distrust and recrimination.[4]

London, England

In London the government was at pains to encourage Germany towards
the cessation of hostilities and at home to mark the beginning of a transition from over five years of war towards the longed-for peace. Public
morale needed careful stewarding. The first BBC news for April 1 was read
by Stuart Hibberd:[5]

> With Field Marshal Montgomery's front now more than seventy
> miles beyond the Rhine, R.A.F. pilots have caught and bombed big
> German traffic movements out of Northern Holland. At least four of
> the American armoured columns ranging through central Germany
> are less than two hundred miles from Berlin. The Russians have
> thrust deep into Austria: they're only a dozen miles south of Wiener
> Neustadt and less than forty from Vienna; to the east, they're sixty
> miles from the Austrian capital and within twenty-five of Bratislava,
> the Slovak capital. At home, the new rationing period brings news of
> a halving of the points needed for raisins.[6]

The British government could afford some loosening of austerity. On that Easter Sunday, the French 1st Army under General de Lattre de Tassigny crossed the Rhine at Philippsburg.[7]

Berlin, Germany

Across much of Germany and Austria, Easter Day was a beautiful day. Yet such a small mercy was of scant consolation to the population at large. Germany had been a country so much at the heart of the worldwide Christian faith, for so many hundreds of years. But after over a decade of intense persecution of the church at the hands of the authorities, 1945 was for once a year when the joyful message of Easter, where and if there was still any way of proclaiming it, was understandably muted. In Berlin Josef Goebbels, not known for his Christian connections, noted it in his diary as the most miserable Easter of his life.[8] As for Adolf Hitler, the idea of attending an Easter service would not have featured high on his priority list that morning. He had no time whatsoever for people of faith. The high point of the Führer's faith masquerade was now twelve long years behind him. At the time of his accession to power, in a crafted appeal over the radio on the evening of February 1, 1933, he had asked the German people to give him four years, ending with a solemn benediction, which no bishop could have made more imposing: "May Almighty God take our work to His grace, give true form to our will, bless our insight, and endow us with the confidence of our Volk."[9] But that was in 1933. By 1945 Hitler's true sentiments about the clergy were well known: "The parsons will be made to dig their own graves. They will betray their God to us. They will betray anything for the sake of their miserable little jobs and incomes."[10] By 1945 it no longer suited Hitler to maintain the illusion of having any connection with faith, still less a faith community, and that particular deception had long since been dispensed with. In Hitler's view traditional values like compassion and respect for the law were nothing but man-made shields behind which the weak could cower and protect themselves from the fate he saw as naturally theirs. It was no accident that the two professions Hitler hated above all others were lawyers and priests.[11] For Hitler the subject of faith was also intrinsically linked with the vexacious awareness that in particular some people of faith had proven consistently troublesome in bending to his vision and will. On April 1 Hitler moved his headquarters from the Chancellery building to a bunker system behind the Chancellery, and deep below it.[12] It was part of a consistent trajectory. For many weeks now, he had been in the pattern of rising very late, somewhat depending upon the medications his advisor[13] had procured him, holding a midday briefing, and reaching the most important military decisions together with key staff between 2:00 and 3:00 in the morning, the only sure time when there would be a tranquil interlude from the onslaught of Allied bombing.

3

Heinrich Himmler

Germany's Reichsführer-SS, Heinrich Himmler, was the controlling energy behind the hostage convoy. It is important to understand his actions throughout Bonhoeffer's final week largely because he was excluded from the role he wished to play. In truth, Himmler had been shielding the Abwehr's Admiral Canaris (and hence Bonhoeffer) for many years.[1] This book will trace the story of his being "blindsided," which in turn enabled the executions of the entire group of resisters with which Bonhoeffer was associated.

Somewhat like Hitler and Goebbels, Himmler had little interest in the Christian message of Easter Sunday. He saw the faith as "the destroyer of every nation."[2] His own answers to the challenges facing Germany were drawn from other sources. A central component in his repertoire for enforcing discipline among troops and civilians had long been the punishment of the utmost severity for non-compliance—and the more the overall situation deteriorated, the more stringent and severe Himmler became.[3] In this way he could appease Hitler, the source of all his power, but with whom his star was no longer in the ascendant.[4] Nonetheless, Himmler was still inextricably joined to the implementation of Hitler's will. One instance of this, a major reflection of the enhanced emphasis on repression and terror, came within the decree issued on Hitler's orders on February 15. In this the Reich justice minister, Otto Thierack, introduced the establishment of summary courts martial (*Standgerichte*) in areas threatened by the enemy. Each court was to be chaired by a judge and to comprise in addition a political leader of the NSDAP (Nazi Party) or one of its affiliates and an officer of the Wehrmacht, the Waffen-SS, or the police. The members of the court were to be nominated by the Gauleiter, as Reich defence commissar for the region. The court was to deal with all offences that could endanger fighting morale and could issue only three verdicts: death penalty, exoneration, or transfer to a regular court. On

Hitler's behalf, party secretary Bormann issued guidelines that gave clear enough indication that the new courts had little to do with conventional justice. They were, in fact, no more than a facade for increasingly arbitrary and wild terror—"instruments of destruction in legal drapery." Death sentences were scarcely more than a formality, since the judges themselves were under pressure to show their loyalty.[5]

This summary justice became if possible even more arbitrary and unconstrained after March 9, when their reach was extended by Hitler's decree creating the "flying court martial" (*fliegendes Standgericht*). These courts travelled around Germany dealing with those accused of undermining the war effort in whatever way and wasted no time before reaching their verdict, normally sentence of death, meted out by the senior officer presiding over the court, and without any appeal. Disobedience to Hitler's "verbrannte Erde" (scorched earth) orders for German soil carried the death penalty. It fell to commanders who reported to Himmler to carry these out. Such was the wholesale corruption of the German legal and justice system and its transformation into an arbitrary intrument of terror that prevailed by April, when Dietrich Bonhoeffer would be subject to its worst machinations. One example of this had taken place on Good Friday.

Zellingen, near Würzburg, Germany

In Zellingen, on the previous Good Friday, fifty-nine-year-old farmer Karl Weiglein was hanged by the flying court martial of Major Erwin Helm. Weiglein's crime was associated with his call-up to the Volkssturm, the local defence force.[6] He was assigned to a company led by a local teacher, Alfons Schmiedel, a fanatical Nazi who also led the local Hitler Youth. On March 25 the battalion had lined up for a roll-call in the village square and listened to a short speech from the battalion commander, Dr Mühl-Kühner, who said that with the war coming closer, regulations would be tighter and anyone who did not obey orders would be shot. A group in the first battalion including Karl Weiglein replied, "Oh-oho!" Around the same time, some anti-tank obstacles were removed from a nearby road, and a false rumour went around that Weiglein had something to do with it. On Tuesday, March 27, the Nazis blew up a bridge connnecting Zellingen with the neighbouring village of Retzbach in order to prevent the advance of American troops. Weiglein, whose house was near the bridge, said to one of his neighbours, "Those idiots who have done this, Schmiedel and Mühl-Kühner, ought to be hanged!" Schmiedel overheard the remark and reported it to Mühl-Kühner. The flying court martial convened at midnight to condemn Weiglein to death as an example to others. Two local farmers brought in as "assessors" to validate proceedings were peremptorily dismissed for refusing to cooperate and were later threatened with a court martial themselves. At 1:30 a.m. Weiglein was taken out to the pear tree Major Helm had selected for his hanging. He was made to wear a sign around his neck that read, "Sentenced to death because of sabotage and destruction of fighting strength." The pear tree was only five metres from Weiglein's home, and he called out to his wife of more than forty years, "Oh Dora, Dora, they are hanging me!" She opened the kitchen window and shouted at Helm and the others, "Leave my husband alone! He hasn't done anything to you!" Helm's Lance Corporal Michalsky shouted back, "Shut up and close the window!" Her husband was hanged in front of her by Helm with Michalsky's assistance. His body was left hanging at the tree for three days, guarded by two soldiers. He was allowed to be cut down on Easter Sunday.[7]

Himmler's Easter Concessions

At precisely the same time as he was administering unmitigated terror, it was becoming more important for Himmler to appear as the voice of reason within Germany's command structure towards the Allies. He adopted various measures in this respect. Among them was the ultra-secret condoning of peace talks.

Peace Negotiations via Switzerland

Since the end of February 1945—unknown to the outside world—emissaries and messages had been passing secretly between German forces and the USA's OSS (Office of Strategic Services) mission in Switzerland, headed by Allen Dulles. These channels were seeking the means to end the fighting on the front in Italy, in the (legitimate) hope that a Nazi surrender there would bring in its wake a general surrender in Europe. Of the many and varied similar attempts to hold behind-the-scenes peace talks, only this one, code-named "Operation Sunrise,"[8] was to prove both genuine and fruitful. Dulles' German counterpart was Himmler's former chief of staff, and now the highest-ranking SS commander, Karl Wolff.[9] Wolff, unlike Himmler and Kaltenbrunner, who were both senior to him, had the relational confidence with Hitler, when summoned to give an account of his actions, to emerge unscathed. Through him, behind-the-scenes discussions with the Allies were close to taking place. Wolff, springing a surprise on his counterparts, had actually shaken hands on March 19 with Allied generals Airey and Lemnitzer.[10]

Himmler's list of activities were designed to present himself as a man with whom the Allies could work. Also featuring high up on it was his gradual agreement to allowing the release of small groups held in concentration camps. He opened a line of communication that, by April, had taken the shape of regular meetings with Count Bernadotte of the Swiss Red Cross. On that Easter Day, Count Bernadotte met Himmler an hour north of Berlin at Hohenlychen for a second time. As an example of his keeping his options open, earlier that day, in Hamburg, maintaining his outward show of loyalty to Hitler, Himmler had assured the beleaguered city council that disagreements among the Allies, as well as the imminent use of German jet aircraft in large numbers, would give Germany decisive breathing space.[11]

But Himmler was serious about "playing both sides." On the afternoon of the same day—Sunday, April 1—Count Bernadotte was given Himmler's permission via the Red Cross to fetch a number of Norwegian and Danish women from the concentration camp at Ravensbrück. The resulting concessions needed swift enacting. One of the prisoners in the concentration camps system was Frenchwoman Marie-Claude Vaillant-Couturier. In her Ravensbrück diary entry for April 1, 1945, she noted, "The sick were sent to the gas chambers yesterday and today we get their share of Ovaltine as an Easter treat!" In another French block, prisoners spent the day chatting around the stove, warming their Easter drinks, as truckloads of bodies continued to trundle past.[12] Soon a line of white buses, each painted with a huge red cross, appeared outside the gates of the camp. Given that for six years the International Committee of the Red Cross had refused to take a stand on the concentration camps, the arrival of their rescue buses outside Ravensbrück was, as the prisoners themselves would say, "a miracle." Now, learning that their rival neutrals, the Swedes, were finally acting, the Swiss did not want to be outdone. However, the bus drivers—themselves Canadian prisoners of war freed by the Germans as part of the deal—were made to wait. The reason given was that the women had not been selected and properly prepared. The reason not given was that there was still some gassing and burning to be done. So the drivers of the Swiss Red Cross buses parked a little way back in the trees, and waited for three more days.

The net result of such delays meant that the rate of killings continued unabated while Himmler continued to do everything in his power to present himself to the Allied leadership as the voice of reason within Nazi Germany. Such was the channel of "compromise" in which Heinrich Himmler, the "protector" of last resort for Bonhoeffer and the Canaris group, was involved.

4
The Speed of Events

Hela Peninsula, Germany

The hostages were firmly under SS guard. But elsewhere, German military forces were collapsing in droves. April 1 also marked the start of a sea evacuation project from the Hela Peninsula in northern Germany, on the shoreline of the Baltic Sea. Over the coming fortnight, ships would transport westwards 96,000 wounded, 81,000 civilians, and 66,000 soldiers.[1] Among them was a soldier from the proud Grossdeutschland Division, a unit that had fought longer than most. Guy Sajer writes,

> We finally learned that it was Sunday . . . in the throng of anxious refugees camping out on the narrow Hela Peninsula. . . . The last victim I was to see was a dirty white horse. . . . A Russian plane had been hit, and was disintegrating above us. We all watched as the forward part of the plane, whose racing engine gave a long howl, plunged towards the ground. The noise terrified the animal, which slipped its collar and galloped, whinnying, towards the spot where the roaring mass of metal would land. It must have taken about 3 steps before it was hit. Its flesh was scattered for over 15 yards in all directions.[2]

But soldiers being evacuated by ship, despite the dangers involved, were among the more fortunate: countless thousands who were on the move found themselves harried, with scant or no sustenance, onto forced marches of extreme duration. One such was Charles Waite. Captured in Abbeville, in May 1940, he was subsequently held for the entire duration of hostilities as a POW. Between January and April 1945, with the Soviets approaching, he was forced to walk from Marienburg in East Prussia to Schwerin on the Baltic coast, southwards to Halle, and onwards via a circuitous route to Berlin, covering a total of 1,600 kilometres. He reported that he only survived thanks to the judicious gift (from his mother) of a new pair of boots. On Sunday, April 1, he reached his lowest ebb: "Much worse now. Three have died. . . . Rations very poor. We are working. Very, very little chance of Red Cross. War. News is good. We are all hoping it will finish. God help us."[3]

Mauthausen, Austria

The chaos and intensity of these days led to and reinforced extreme inhuman behaviours. One instance was that of Josef Eger, a forty-four-year-old Volkssturm member. He later wrote, "I had to shoot a Jew near the village of Strettweg because he had opened his arteries. . . . I tried to shoot him in the neck. I think I missed him. . . . On the way toward Pöls . . . I shot another Jew . . . because he tried to escape." This was a reality that was repeated endlessly. Two or three Volkssturm men were ordered to accompany a group of Jewish prisoners for a short time as they plodded slowly through their village and on to the next one on their way to Mauthausen. Over that short distance, some of the Volkssturm guards turned into murderers. At the beginning of April, Stefan Knaus, a forty-two-year-old Volkssturm man, and several of his comrades received orders to accompany a group of Jews coming from the direction of Graz. When the prisoners passed the village of Frohnleiten, one of them went over to Knaus and pleaded for a chunk of bread in return for his boots. The commander of the column, Franz Iskar, who was riding his bicycle alongside the column, warned Knaus not to dare to agree. Farther on, several prisoners tried to tear lumps of flesh off carcasses of horses lying at the roadside. Then too Iskar threatened to shoot anyone who did this. Some time later, prisoners began to collapse, unable to continue walking. One of the guards, Rupert Schmer, shot them. About nineteen prisoners were shot by the guards along the nine-mile (fourteen-kilometre) stretch of road. A more wide-scale massacre occurred near the village of Frensdorf. Twelve Jewish prisoners were taken, on orders from Kreisleiter Johann Brandber, to the cellar of a building in the village and shot there. In the town of Gratwein as well, several Jews unable to continue the march were murdered. They were led to a bomb crater and shot by one of the guards. This murder was committed before the eyes of local residents, "who heard the Jews pleading for their lives before being shot."[4]

The Speed of Events

Sometimes the sheer speed at which events were moving contributed to the disaster when groups of people were suddenly faced with making choices. According to Soviet field regulations, a mechanised column was supposed to move 150 kilometres in a day, but the 200th Rifle Division of the 49th Army managed to cover 358 kilometres in just twenty-five hours.[5] One war correspondent travelling with front-line units wrote about the improvisations made by troops seeking to make rapid progress in their advance. In some cases, where they had no vehicles at the outset, they simply seized anything they could get hold of from the Germans: bakers' and butchers' vans, post office trucks. They did not even bother to repaint them. He even saw one man in a steamroller. Anything to get forwards. In such a context, things did not look good for anyone at the mercy of the concentration camp authorities: at least a million prisoners were thought to be alive in April 1945 in Himmler's concentration camps. As the speed of advance increased, so too in proportion did the likelihood of the camps being overrun (and liberated) increase. It was generally assumed that it was a dereliction of duty to allow prisoners to be taken alive by the enemy. Repeatedly a grim consensus among guards emerged that it was safer to kill everyone, just to be sure that a court martial for "disobedience to orders" (even when there were none) could be avoided. Hence almost all those being held in custody were at risk of massacre in these last days.

Sopron, Hungary

So it was in Hungary, in Balf camp, south of the Hungarian border town of Sopron. On April 1, 1945, at about 9:00 a.m., Red Army forces entered Balf. About 1,500 Hungarian Jews had worked on the site, which had been evacuated on March 28. Prisoners who were too sick to endure the evacuation had remained behind. The previous day, March 31, 176 of them had been murdered by an SS unit, whose identity was never fully clarified after the war. The Jewish victims were led to anti-tank trenches that had been dug some time beforehand by the prisoners themselves and ordered to stand alongside them. Two SS men armed with automatic weapons apparently began to shoot these feeble human beings, who fell into the trenches. The massacre lasted half an hour, and then one of the killers turned to his colleague and asked: "Have they all been finished off?" ("Sind sie alle kaputt?"). Then the murderers left. Several prisoners survived the slaughter, because the killers were careless in checking that all of them were dead. Once they were sure that the Germans had gone, they crawled out of the mass grave.[6]

Vienna, Aschaffenburg, and Saxony, Germany

Elsewhere across Europe the war also advanced rapidly and in bleak earnest. In Vienna, facing the imminent reality of the city's capture by

Soviet forces, Marie Vassiltchikov, who had been working for much of the
war as a PA to July 20 resister Adam von Trott (executed by the Nazis
on August 26, 1944), took a break from her nursing work and chose to
attend a surreal High Mass at the Stefansdom that day. She caught herself wondering if she would ever see the building again. Further west, in
Aschaffenburg (see map), a devastating battle between unevenly matched
forces was in its fourth day of destruction and devastation. These concluding days epitomised the dilemma faced by countless German citizens.
Aschaffenburg's leader, World War I veteran Major Emil von Lamberth,
had issued a proclamation in the days beforehand: "Soldiers, men of the
Wehrmacht, comrades—the fortress of Aschaffenburg will be defended
to the last man. . . . As of today everyone is to give to his last. I order that
no-one shall rest more than 3 hours out of 20. I forbid any sitting around
or loafing. Our belief is that it is our mission to give the cursed enemy
the greatest resistance and to send as many of them as possible to the
devil." To give substance to these words, and following Napoleon's dictum
"Morale is to the physical as three is to one"—to ensure loyalty and obedience in the ranks—Lamberth even had a man hanged in public.[7]

5

Surviving Hitler's Demands

In step with these proceedings, on that Easter Sunday the Deutschlander radio, in a national broadcast, proclaimed, "Hate is our prayer" and "Revenge is our battle cry."[1] For Germany, the land of Goethe and Brahms and Tillich, it was truly a low point.

The low-lying cloud cleared on day four of the battle for Aschaffenburg, Easter Sunday 1945, and on the liberating side an increasingly frustrated General Frederick was able to call in air support. He had the P-47 fighter-bomber squadron use .50-calibre ammunition, because of fears that bombing might kill Americans below in the burning and shattered city. It proved ineffective, so the air crews were ordered to bomb specific targets such as Gestapo headquarters. One thousand Germans kept on fighting. For the first time in Europe in World War II, it was decided to use napalm in a civilian area.[2] The air strikes seemed to make no difference; nor did the napalm. Still the defenders held out. Four times that Easter Sunday, Germans who had been dislodged from their hiding places in ruins still managed to creep back through sewers and remains of buildings to rejoin the hand-to-hand fighting in the town centre and inflict casualties.

When US troop commander Felix Sparks finally reached the town centre of Aschaffenburg, he found two (more) German soldiers hanged from a gallows, executed on Commander Lamberth's orders. The sign attached to them stated, "This is the reward for cowards." In all this Lamberth was not acting out of step with orders from above, but rather enacting entirely the scenario demanded on pain of death by the Nazi leadership. It was not an inviting prospect for even the most loyal of soldiers. Corporal Helmut Fromm, facing the Russians in Saxony, aged sixteen, wrote in his diary that Easter, "May God have mercy on his people. This has been a long crusade, strewn with corpses and tears. Please grant us an Easter followed by redemption."[3]

German Soldiers and Führer Orders

But a thought such as redemption was far from being on Hitler's mind. Emulating Stalin, from March 1945 Hitler expressly omitted from state support the families of those who had been captured without being critically wounded. The intent was plain: further to harden the resolve of every combatant never to give any ground, and at the same time to brand surrender, even against impossible odds, as shameful. Yet as a strategy, these measures did nothing to improve military morale. Hitler's leadership instincts were failing him. The tide of those surrendering to the Western Allies rose from half a million men in the first quarter of 1945 to 4,600,000 a month later. These men (rightly) calculated that they had less to fear in British or American captivity than from the random violence being meted out by their own side.[4] That same Easter Sunday, Hitler's deputy, Martin Bormann, despatched a message in Hitler's name to members of the party. It ran,

> After the collapse of 1918 we devoted ourselves life and limb to the struggle for the right of existence of our people. Now . . . Gauleiter and Kreisleiter, other political leaders and heads of affiliates are to fight in their Gau and district, to conquer or to fall. Any scumbag who leaves his Gau when under attack without express order of the Führer, anyone not fighting to the last breath will be proscribed and treated as a deserter. Raise your hearts and overcome your weaknesses! Now there is only one slogan: conquer or fall! Long live Germany! Long live Adolf Hitler![5]

For ordinary people, Bormann's message was clear, but also terrifying in its consequences. Equally severe, but rather more confusing, was the message that also came that day from Goebbels in the launch broadcast of the new Radio Werewolf. Germans of all ages were urged, following any defeat by Allied troops, and ensuing local ceasefire, to form partisan movements and to rise up and kill any Germans collaborating with the occupiers, as well as occupying forces. "There is no end to revolution," Germans were exhorted; "a revolution is only doomed to failure if those who make it cease to be revolutionaries."

In a transparent attempt to reverse the despair felt at the incessant bombing, the radio station's message actually welcomed the bombs that fell nightly, continuing, "Together with the monuments of culture there crumble also the last obstacles to the fulfilment of our revolutionary task. Now that everything is in ruins, we are forced to rebuild Europe. In the past, private possessions tied us to a bourgeois restraint. Now the bombs, instead of killing all Europeans, have only smashed the prison walls which held them captive. . . . In trying to destroy Europe's future, the enemy has succeeded its past, and with that, everything old and outworn has gone."[6] While Goebbels congratulated himself on the seriousness with which (rightly) the Allies responded to the news of the launch of the Werewolf movement, and Hitler's obvious delight at the concept, Goebbels' support only made things, if possible, still more chaotic; most Germans simply reached for the "off" switch.

Some Survivors; Life Goes On: Falkenstein, Germany

One such (elderly) couple were Victor Klemperer and his wife, Eva.[7] After years of persecution in Dresden, they had been fleeing since the city there was destroyed on February 13. They had simply removed the "J" stars they were required by law to wear, in order to make good their escape. On April 1 Klemperer notes in his diary,

> While we were eating potato salad at Meyer's, there was a pompous report on the "Werewolves," men and girls taking up the fight against the enemy in the territory occupied in the West. They have a transmitter, Greater German broadcasting will pass on their news. With that, this franc-tireur, partisan group . . . is not only glorified, but also officially recognised. It was immediately followed by a corresponding appeal by the Party to all men and women. "The supreme test," fight to the bitter end. What will the Anglo-American answer be? Destruction of every house from which a shot has been fired, even more intense air attacks. And no-one in Germany puts an end to this murderous government.[8]

6

Buchenwald, Bonhoeffer, and the Hostage Convoy

Meanwhile, as hostilities raged across Europe and beyond, in the vicinity of Weimar, Bonhoeffer and the other political and clan custody hostages who form the subject of this book were by now around three hundred kilometres south-west of Berlin. They were being held in converted SS barracks around a kilometre outside the lethal electric fence of the Buchenwald concentration camp. Its gate bore the chilling sign "Jedem das Seine" (Each to their own).

Buchenwald was one of the Reich's oldest concentration camps, founded in the early years of the Nazi regime. It had been designed as part concentration camp, part SS training centre, and part playground for the Nazi elite—equipped with stables, hunting and falconry facilities, and even a zoo, in addition to the vast SS barracks. The main camp itself, in which the mass of prisoners lived, was enclosed by a high-current electrified fence and watchtowers; outside was the SS complex and an armaments factory and quarry in which the inmates laboured, all enclosed by a ring of sentries.[1] The layout plan of Buchenwald in April 1945 may be seen from a mid-1944 sketch (see p. 51). It shows in different colours the prisoner area, the work area, and the SS sport and relaxation areas. It was in this latter area that one of the most important VIP prisoners also being held in the Buchenwald complex that Easter morning was lodged. Léon Blum, the former prime minister of France, together with his wife, Jeannot, did not live with the other special category prisoners, or *Prominenten*, but had special private quarters, and even the services of an SS orderly, in the SS falconry complex.[2] Blum would soon write a vivid account of these days entitled *Le dernier mois* when he embarked on the same journey as Bonhoeffer.

At the centre of the SS compound was a large set of barracks named "Special Camp Fichtenhain" (Spruce Grove), where, according to camp records, on April 1, sixty-seven prisoners were housed, and where the group very soon to become Bonhoeffer's travel companions, the *Sippen-häftlinge*, or *Prominenten*, were interned.[3] Bonhoeffer himself was part of a separate group of (at this stage) seventeen political prisoners, plus an SS camp doctor, accommodated in "Bau 16": the converted cellar of what had previously been a detention centre for Waffen-SS guards deemed guilty of infringing camp regulations.[4]

The Shared Prisoner Experience

On Easter Sunday, for the political prisoners in Bau 16, things were look-ing up. Falconer wrote in his diary, "On Easter Sunday we hear gunfire to the West—the Americans are attacking Erfurt."[5] But hopes needed to be tempered. News had been delivered that day to just two of the prisoners, Payne Best and Léon Blum, that they were shortly to be embarking upon a journey with an unknown destination. As the news permeated to the hostage group, it was received with apprehension. Every prisoner had a different set of circumstances and hopes. Of course, they would not shed a tear to leave Buchenwald behind. Here the cells, according to Hermann Pünder, were ice-cold[6]: yet while the accommodation had no refinements or hot water, and there were petty harshnesses inflicted by the guards, plus a ban on both writing and receiving letters, as well as leaving the building for any exercise, there were upsides. One was that VIP prisoners came under the personal stewardship of the camp commandant, Piester. In Buchenwald this group had by definition been exempted from forced labour. For these hostages there was even access to limited medical treat-ment. Furthermore the rations card demonstrates that all political pris-oners received full SS food allowances, the standard of which was better in February than in April. Although their accommodation was not luxu-rious, it had certain advantages. Writing in the 1970s (published in 2018), Falconer comments that the work done to convert this basement into cells "had obviously been done in a great hurry, possibly by prison labour, for the work had been done carelessly and with very little skill. . . . The walls separating the cells were made of thin concrete blocks, unpointed and unplastered, and the whole effect was of a temporary structure intended for demolition at no very distant date."[7] But there were windows in each of the cells, some double, some single, with the width clearly having been dictated by the spacing of the original cellar windows, allowing one win-dow per cell. These were high up in the cell walls so that their bottom edges were about six inches above the level of the ground outside, and did not open, but as they were of clear glass, "one merely had to stand on

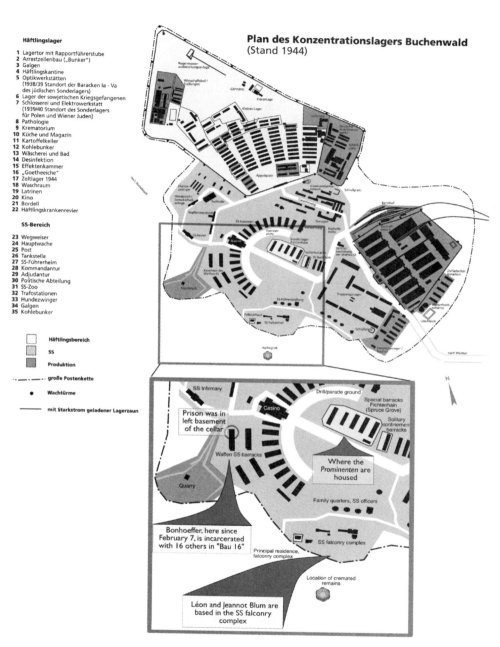

Häftlingslager

1 Lagertor mit Rapportführerstube
2 Arrestzellenbau („Bunker")
3 Galgen
4 Häftlingskantine
5 Optikwerkstätten
 (1938/39 Standort der Baracken Ia - Va
 des jüdischen Sonderlagers)
6 Lager der sowjetischen Kriegsgefangenen
7 Schlosserei und Elektrowerkstatt
 (1939/40 Standort des Sonderlagers
 für Polen und Wiener Juden)
8 Pathologie
9 Krematorium
10 Küche und Magazin
11 Kartoffelkeller
12 Kohlebunker
13 Wäscherei und Bad
14 Desinfektion
15 Effektenkammer
16 „Goetheeiche"
17 Zeltlager 1944
18 Waschraum
19 Latrinen
20 Kino
21 Bordell
22 Häftlingskrankenrevier

SS-Bereich

23 Wegweiser
24 Hauptwache
25 Post
26 Tankstelle
27 SS-Führerheim
28 Kommandantur
29 Adjudantur
30 Politische Abteilung
31 SS-Zoo
32 Trafostationen
33 Hundezwinger
34 Galgen
35 Kohlebunker

Häftlingsbereich
SS
Produktion
große Postenkette
Wachtürme
mit Starkstrom geladener Lagerzaun

Plan des Konzentrationslagers Buchenwald
(Stand 1944)

SS Infirmary
Drill/parade ground
Casino
Special barracks
Fichtenhain
(Spruce Grove)
Prison was in left basement of the cellar
Solitary confinement barracks
Waffen SS barracks
Where the *Prominenten* are housed
Quarry
Family quarters, SS officers
SS falconry complex
Bonhoeffer, here since February 7, is incarcerated with 16 others in "Bau 16"
Principal residence, falconry complex
Location of cremated remains
Léon and Jeannot Blum are based in the SS falconry complex

Fig. 6-1. Buchenwald plan
Provided by Bruce Bovill. Original adapted with permission of *Gedenkstätte*
Buchenwald and Mittelbau-Dora Memorial.

the chair to have an excellent view of all that went on outside, obstructed only by the window bars."[8] Having that ability just to look outside was of some, but perhaps modest, comfort: on one side of the building there was another SS barrack, and on the other, the "Steinbruch"—literally, stone-breaking—a forced labour quarry area for prisoners immeasurably less well treated than this group. Fortunately there were washbasins and showers, and especially when allowed access to these for their daily ablutions, the prisoners made every effort to ascertain who the others all were, and what were their respective chances of survival.

See fig. 6-2; the allocation of cells was originally made on the night of February 7–8 and then redone on February 24, as shown in Best's diagram, with modifications.[9]

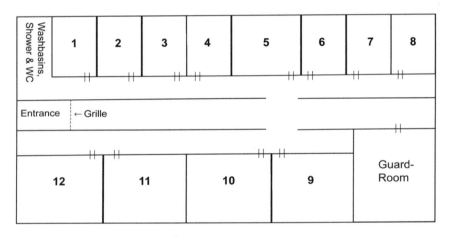

Fig. 6-2. Buchenwald cells, possible layout
Cell 1: General von Rabenau and Pastor Bonhoeffer; cell 2: Dr Pünder and Commander Franz Liedig; cell 3: Erich and Margot Heberlein; cell 4: Vasily Kokorin; cell 5: General von Falkenhausen and Dr Gerhard Schiedlausky or Dr Hoven; cell 6: Squadron Leader Falconer; cell 7: Dr Josef Müller and Captain Ludwig Gehre; cell 8: Count Werner von Alvensleben and Colonel von Petersdorff; cell 9: Heidel Nowakowski; cell 10: Dr Rascher; cell 11: Captain Best; cell 12: Dr Hoepner. Diagram compiled by the author.

In Best's account a select few of the rooms were double-sized. However, one unpublished account disputes this.[10] Bonhoeffer clearly enjoyed sharing cell 1 with General von Rabenau. If the distance from the guard room is anything to judge by, the authorities did not anticipate much trouble from Bonhoeffer and Rabenau. Next door to them, in cell 2, were Franz

Liedig[11] and Pünder. Sharing cell 5 with the esteemed General von Falken-hausen was an SS doctor,[12] whose identity—while both Falconer and Müller testify to the presence of this character—remains uncertain. In a transparent attempt to ingratiate himself with resisters who might sur-vive, the individual, who may have been there anyway for his own reasons, provided a tip-off: he imparted to Müller (in cell 7) the unwelcome, but not wholly unsurprising, news that Müller's cellmate and fellow resister, Ludwig Gehre,[13] had (disastrously) come to a deal with the SS and had agreed to spy on him. The background to this is explained by Müller. He recounts how, while imprisoned in Buchenwald, he became frustrated at the constant loud arguing that he could not help overhearing between the occupants of the cell next door, cell 8: Count Werner von Alvensleben[14] and Petersdorff. When he requested to be moved, he was surprised to be told it was on the basis of "orders from above" that he was to share his cell with Gehre. Puzzled, he was indeed soon to discover the basis for those orders. Müller writes, "At one point an SS doctor whispered to me, 'Be careful, your cell companion is writing reports for the SD [Sicherheits-dienst]." Müller continues, "I went straight to him and asked him, 'You are always writing. Are you also writing about me?'" Gehre was, Müller reports, an inwardly shattered person. He broke down. "Yes." Now con-fronted in Buchenwald's Bau 16 by Müller, Gehre confessed that he had been tasked by the SD to use "conversations that seemed as innocent as possible" to extract more information: in this case, out of Müller. In exchange, the Gestapo had made their usual meaningless promise of a reprieve.[15] The result of this confession rendered Gehre's treacherous deal innocuous: "You keep on writing," Müller asserted, "but from now on you will show me all reports in advance and agree them with me. And you will explain everything you have written about me already. I bear you no ill will; I know you are no blackguard; I know what you've been through."[16]

Next door, the two arguing occupants of cell 8, Alvensleben and Peters-dorff, were another well-matched pair, who were even distantly related by marriage.[17] Falconer reports that Alvensleben was excluded from the list of political and other hostages and was separated from the group the next day, April 2.[18] His spirit unbroken, he would survive the war. Alvensleben's cell companion in argumentation, Petersdorff, some seventeen years his junior in age, was an equally strong character, and was introduced earlier; he had, as mentioned, taken an entirely different path towards incurring the regime's disfavour.

Closest to the guard-room (cell 9) was the only single female, Heidel Nowakowski. From the Buchenwald sketch, it can be seen that the allocation of cells put Nowakowski and Rascher as next-door neighbours. Best also mentions that Heidel was romantically successful in capturing the interest of Vasily Kokorin, in cell 4. Around this time of cell juxtaposition, Nowakowski transferred her romantic attentions away from Kokorin (cell 4) towards Rascher (cell 10).

In Buchenwald's converted barrack cellar, it was forbidden for prisoners to communicate with each other. Ingenuity and determination were required. The daily routine was simple. Every morning in turn, starting at 6:00, prisoners would go to the washroom and after that remain in their cells. The washroom arrangements consisted of a row of washbasins, a row of WCs, and two or three primitive showers. During these crossover moments, there were ample opportunities, if prisoners were circumspect, to get to know more about other prisoners and obtain war status updates. By April 1 the guards, who had always been nervous, were even more so. Quite understandably, the closer the Allied troops came, the more their anxiety grew and their commitment to serving under the structures of the Third Reich began to evaporate. Isa Vermehren writes about two of the guards, both female:

> Miss Knocke has in her heart of hearts already cast aside her uniform and now assiduously courts the sympathies of the prisoners entrusted to her. She adopts an intellectual veneer and frequently uses, and misapplies, many words borrowed from other languages. In the eight days of our stay here, she undergoes a visible transformation: initially put on for show, her rather patronising posture of superiority retreats more and more into an overwhelming anxiety . . . an out-of-control condition seeking release in precipitous flight from the camp . . . [including] hysterical flattery. Another, a Miss Raffoth, although . . . a robust and ordinary person . . . yet at night throws her 75-kilo frame onto a creaking chair and repeats loudly and raucously over and over again the refrain "Night time zone: can't be alone."[19]

The male guards, too, were starting to make plans. As a part of wishing to appear amenable towards the prisoners, the guards invited General von Falkenhausen in cell 5 to join them in the guardroom to listen to the news bulletins. The general had managed to retain in his possession a high-quality military map, against which the progress of the advancing

Americans could be traced, and when updates were shared, this contribution was much appreciated by the group.

During a bombing raid, Falconer from cell 6 at one point played the senior officer card, which was no small feat given the group he found himself among. No doubt the approach of Allied troops played a role. Summoning the Oberscharführer, he demanded in no uncertain terms that during raids, cells were to be unlocked, so that prisoners were able to move to the relative safety of the corridor. In this way, on one occasion the group enjoyed five hours of mingling. In some cases they were renewing acquaintances, and in others, getting to know fellow hostages for the first time.[20] Falconer reports that this concession, too, was designed to curry favour with him, and that what the guard wanted in return was a certificate of some kind, attesting to humane treatment of them all.

Conditions in the Bau 16 cellar were harsher for the prisoners than in the *Prominenten* (see fig. 6-1) accommodation only a few metres away: Stauffenberg, accommodated there, was able to sing not only the "Te Deum" with others in the corridor on Easter morning at 8:00, but also "Lobet den Herrn" (Praise the Lord) and "Fest soll mein Taufbund stehen" (The promise of my baptismal bond shall stand firm).[21] The Bau 16 political prisoners were also not allowed to send or receive letters, so Hermann Pünder adopted the practice of writing letters to his family and *imagining* that they had received his earlier ones, which he retained. This Sunday was his fifty-seventh birthday. Given that it was Easter Sunday, for the very first time since his birth in 1888, Pünder's birthday and Easter Sunday coincided! Buchenwald is certainly not where Hermann Pünder had imagined spending that anniversary. He had decidedly set his hopes on already being released by then, and, in some disquiet had continued counting the number of days since then, in part as a record of the further injustice being meted out to him at the hands of the regime. On Easter Day the number reached 101. His cellmate, Liedig, donated him some crispbread with Greek raisins on top. Although it was a meagre offering, it was an appreciated one. But news of one event that took place elsewhere that day would have brought him real comfort, had it reached him, which it did not: the taking possession by US troops of the estate of his close relatives, who lived in Everswinkel, near Münster, a moment that included the safe liberation of his own wife and both children. By contrast, in a visit from Gestapo headquarters on the day beforehand, the senior official Obersturmführer Valentin had stated that Hermann Pünder was not in the category of VIP prisoner (*Ehrenhäftling*) but that of an ordinary prisoner. The Gestapo official stated that Pünder's exoneration before the Volksgerichtshof on December 21 had "changed nothing." Faced with this, Pünder had to console himself on Easter Day with a thank-you note from fellow hostage General von Falkenhausen (see fig. 6-3):

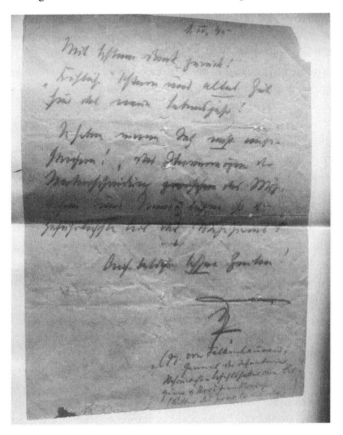

Fig. 6-3. Von Falkenhausen note

The note is warm, with a suitable birthday and "Happy" Easter greet-ing. It is dated April 1, 1945, nestled inside the jacket of the book, and is still in the family's possession today. In it Falkenhausen thanks Pünder for the loan of a book called *Julian der Abtrünnige* (Julian the Apostate), which he had lent first of all to Bonhoeffer and then to Falkenhausen during their time in Buchenwald.[22] It includes a memorable citation from the book and reads,

Mit bestem Dank zurück! (Returned with warm thanks!)

"Fröhliche" Ostern und alles Gute für das neue Lebensjahr! ("Happy" Easter and all best wishes for the year ahead!)

Das Unvermögen der Unterscheidung zwischen dem Möglichen und dem Unmöglichem ist die gefährlichste Art des Wahnsinns. (The inability to differentiate between the possible and the impossible is the most dangerous form of madness.)

Auf baldige bessere Zeiten! (Here's to better days soon!)

> **General von Falkenhausen**
> **General der Infanterie**
> **(Ritter . . . Pour le Mérite)**

Given that at least two hostages, including Bonhoeffer, were reading this book during this period, it is worthwhile alluding to its content.

Julian the Apostate

The character of Julian, Roman emperor from 361 to 363, has continued to fascinate people down the ages. This laudatory biography portrays him as an heroic figure, the tragic victim of an early and untimely death. His conduct towards Christians as, with considerable dexterity, they are ousted, is portrayed as honourable. Here his (in one sense) apostate and profound spirituality appears in a disarmingly Christian light: Julian instructs his new class of (heathen) priest, "We must serve the gods in the conviction that they are always present, that they see us, and that their gaze is more penetrating than any beam of light and reaches into the most secret corner of our hearts."[23] For Julian, "Misdeeds and mistaken thoughts are of a kind [*zweierlei*]: above all, you must set a guard over your thoughts, for your thoughts will seduce your tongue to participate in its mistakes and sins."[24] Julian believes it is how people act towards others, notably the weak, that determines character. As emperor-to-be, Julian is grounded and wise: in an early phase of his public life, it is said of Julian that "the joy and enthusiasm of the crowds being directed towards him did not obscure his solid understanding of human nature, nor wrap it in any fog."[25]

The book touches profoundly on the theme of call. Here the reader is introduced to a reluctant emperor, for whom to step up and accept his calling is an act of courage. When being offered the original opportunity to be crowned—initially as Caesar—by the preceding emperor, Julian reportedly does some serious soul-searching:

> And you [yourself], who number yourself not among ordinary people, but among the wise and the just—are you walking away from the will of the gods, and not allowing them to do with you as they please? Where is your courage? When have you concealed it? Is your conduct not laughable? Do you really want to creep and flatter out of fear for your life?[26]

With this higher call, and challenge to disavow cowardice, comes the imminent possibility of death. Indeed, Julian's reign is such that he is very soon mortally wounded, and his deathbed words contribute to his standing as an enigma. As he lies dying, fatally wounded at an unknown hand, he understands the sun (the object of his worship) to be a soulless body, created to give light, but indifferent to, and silent in the face of, suffering. Before he gives over his soul to the devil, he takes a couple of drops of blood from his wound into his hand, holds them up towards heaven, and says, "Galilean, you have the victory."[27] To the Christian reader familiar with Romans 10:13—"Whoever calls on the name of the Lord shall be saved"—these words do not have the hallmark of an apostate unbeliever. Julian dies a man of faith, courage, and integrity.

In Buchenwald Bonhoeffer had precious little choice in reading matter, but would have resonated with this thoughtful account. There was much more to Julian than, as some have characterised him, one "chasing after a world forever gone."[28] Bonhoeffer had, for example, previously much appreciated the writing of Georges Bernanos. Bernanos writes incisively about the reality of human sinfulness and explores in some depth the subject of pride and spiritual pride within Christians, especially those who claim to have some kind of calling. For his own part—as mentioned in the introduction—Bonhoeffer had since very early in life been clear about his own purposes, and in 1939 he also felt a further call to return from America to Germany to share in the country's destiny, whatever might be the cost. He had also engaged frequently and openly with the subject of death, talking about it at a very early age with his twin sister, later revealing he had a clear sense he might die at age forty. But at this stage of the war, in love with his fiancée, and (as alluded to in the introduction) with Berlin feeling some distance away, Bonhoeffer's hopes for survival may well have been slowly rekindling.

It was only gradually dawning on some of those incarcerated in Buchenwald's Bau 16 that they might be used as currency. The very idea of his being a hostage was a proposal Bonhoeffer very much resisted, when presented with it, in conversations with Falconer, claiming he could not possibly be of any value in any negotiations. In this Bonhoeffer, rather than being modest, was completely correct, more than Falconer could know: the British government saw no value in any Germans who had resisted Hitler at this point in the war. After the failure of the July 20 plot, the British government had adopted a posture akin to mockery, even publishing names of resisters for the Gestapo to execute. But Falconer had worked things out correctly, checking out his suspicions with one guard after another: most of this group were by April 1 indeed in the process of being gathered together from different locations to comprise a remarkable convoy—of hostages.

7
General von Rabenau

The remarkable convoy of hostages being assembled together included Bonhoeffer's chess-playing friend and cell companion General Friedrich von Rabenau, who certainly counts among the hitherto most underrated characters of the anti-Hitler resistance. Rabenau was born in Berlin on October 10, 1884, into an old Meissen family of nobles originally from Rabenau-on-Dresden, the third child and second son to his parents, Friedrich and Wally (née Noebel) von Rabenau. As with Bonhoeffer, his father was from a medical background: Friedrich *père* was a gynaecologist. When young Friedrich was only six months old, his father died from a research-related infection: his mother moved the family to her parents' home in Eberswalde. Here Friedrich learned, among many other things, to play the piano fluently by ear without having lessons, an ability that he also shared with Bonhoeffer, and went on, also like Bonhoeffer, via philosophy, to the further study of Hebrew as a major. He originally wanted to become a priest, but financial constraints meant that he was accepted as a career officer into the 72nd Field Artillery Regiment in 1903. In 1909 he married Eva Kautz, with whom he had two daughters, Eva-Dorothee and Edelgard. Rabenau served with great distinction throughout World War I and was promoted with rapidity. A list of the medals he was awarded over the duration of his military career includes the Iron Cross, 1st and 2nd class; the Knight's Cross of the Royal House Order of Hohenzollern with Swords; the Fredericks Cross; and the Military Merit Cross, 3rd class with War Decoration (Austria-Hungary).

Always a committed Christian soldier, Rabenau soon embarked on a concurrent writing career, and in 1925 published a book entitled *Die alte Armee und die junge Generation* (Army tradition and the young generation). In it he pronounces against the idea of the excessive figure of a "Führer" embodying both military and political leadership. He writes, with uncanny prescience,

A very great leader will always be of a demonic nature, someone possessed, driven by a lust for tearing down and building up according
to their own sense of right and wrong, accountable to no one but
themselves.[1]

Rabenau goes on to make the case for the army always to be "above party
politics," reasoning that "to be involved [in politics] is a bridge too far and
an impossible step for active soldiers." They were words that, seen with the
benefit of hindsight, carried a prophetic ring, and even at the time proved
to be the subject of a heated discussion at a meeting on May 26, 1925, in
the Reichstag.[2]

By 1930 Rabenau, while still an increasingly senior ranking officer,[3]
had become more a "dual-career" soldier/academic and theologian. He
specialised initially in military biographies, and forged a connection
with the war history faculties of Breslau and Münster Universities. His
academic work was of sufficient merit for the Faculty of Philosophy in
Breslau to award him an honorary doctorate in 1934, with Münster University awarding him the title of Honorary Citizen in 1935.

With the upheavals of the 1930s came also a revisiting of old loyalties.
As a result of army chaplaincy over time, Rabenau was friendly with Ludwig Müller, but when the latter threw in his lot with the pro-Hitler Deutsche Christen (German Christians), Rabenau broke off contact with him
and had his first grandchild baptised by his own cousin Eitel-Friedrich
von Rabenau, a founding member of the Pastors' Emergency League (an
organisation set up in an attempt to resist the unwelcome interferences of
Nazism in church life). But while he had no time for the Deutsche Christen, Rabenau would not "sign up" with the (opposing) Confessing Church,
which grew out of the Pastors' Emergency League. In this respect Rabenau
was, again like Bonhoeffer, a lifelong committed ecumenist. Both these
men also forged profound friendships with Catholic believers during the
course of the war. Rabenau's understanding of interconfessional church life
led him from early on to see the claims of the Confessing Church as "too
absolute" and "one-sided." In his front-line service, he "lived" ecumeni-
cally and beyond confessing boundaries in pastoral conversations, in military services, or in battlefield situations. His sense was that soldiers were
invariably interconfessional, with the corollary that what was shared was
more important than what divided. But, at the same time, he was entirely
capable of taking a stand: as the tensions between the army and the SA
peaked in June 1934, in Breslau, Rabenau chose (successfully) to confront

the local and much-hated SA leader Heines, a particularly brutal, violent, and untrustworthy individual, with military force. Following the demise of Heines the next day in the events of June 30, 1934, presumably quite without Rabenau's awareness, the anonymous death threats to Rabenau's family ceased. His promotion to major general came that October.

It has been observed that Rabenau cared little for his external image. This may account for some slowing down of his military advancement, but what is certainly true is that by the time of his transfer to Münster later that year, he was growing ever more engaged with the study of theology. A copy of the Bible was an ever-present feature on his desk. It was a small sign of hope amid gathering storm clouds.

In 1936 Rabenau was already director of Germany's Military Archive. He was ideally suited to the work in both experience and temperament. As a researcher, soldier, scholar, and author, Rabenau applied energy and rigour to the project of capturing records accurately for posterity. At that time Rabenau was charged with a full-time assignment by the Reich war minister, Werner von Blomberg. It was to write and publish a biography on a well-known and much respected figure in recent German military history, General Hans von Seeckt, who died in 1936. But seeing things clearly and speaking the truth as he saw it would become a troublesome attribute in the Third Reich. That same year, after a speech given in Cologne about "the Führer principle in the army" during the course of his regular work, which was attended by General Kluge, Rabenau was branded an "arch-conservative." In the ensuing complaints process, Düsseldorf's Gauleiter, Friedrich Florian, called for him to be banned from speaking in public. Florian's campaign against Rabenau persisted for the next five years. One accusation that the Gauleiter would level against Rabenau in 1939 was that "Rabenau ist geistig falsch fundiert,"[4] which, when translated, means "Rabenau is [in error to the point of being] mentally ill, or deranged [and hence unfit for office]." But the truth, in the context of National Socialism, was more the reverse: Rabenau was seeing clearly what others were at pains to deny.

In 1938 Rabenau duly published volume 1 of General von Seeckt's significant biography. In subsequent collaboration with Frau Seeckt, the wife of the deceased general, in preparation for the release of volume 2, Rabenau found that she had greatly amended the text in order to make her husband appear as a National Socialist, which he had not been. Rabenau became exposed to a vast "interference" and editing process, one that included the army, the party, and the Auswärtiges Amt (Foreign Office) because Hitler's name was mentioned. He found that conformity with the LTI—the *Lingua Tertii Imperii*[5]—(the language of the Third Reich) was required of him. Accordingly, *Zweigleisigkeit* (double entendre) became his style. Juxtaposing sentences with mild contradictions were offered as a "clue" to the discerning reader. In the earlier phases of his writing, Rabenau refrained from openly criticising National Socialism. His criticism of Hitler was nuanced, using irony and camouflage, just as, in a different way, Bonhoeffer's writings also were in the same period. In one instance of this, Rabenau describes the Nazi Wilhelm Busch as "the greatest philosopher since Kant." This he quite clearly was not. In the same way, in Rabenau's publications, the phrase "genial Führer" appears at times; it is an intended irony, indeed, a veiled critique of Hitlers' self-styling as the "Greatest Military Commander of all time." In the unusual world of Nazism, it would be sufficient camouflage to dupe the *Bonzen*[6] assigned to proofreading and textual amendment duties.

But actual acts in defiance became necessary. In May 1939 Rabenau stood up for a colleague, Wilhelm Groener, who, although previously chief of the German General Staff in 1919 and a holder of the prestigious Pour le Mérite medal, had by the time of his death been declared persona non grata. An edict had been issued that all officers from the army were banned from attending the funeral. While Rabenau did not join the only officer to defy the ruling, Kurt von Hammerstein-Equord, at the funeral, he did travel to Groener's home and, taking over his personal papers and writing legacy, prevented their seizure by the Gestapo.

That defiance spilled over into his relationships and his published works. Rabenau is thought to have played an early role in linking General Beck, the leader of the resistance to Hitler from within the German military, with his civilian counterpart, Carl Goerdeler. Writing in 1940, at the height of Hitler's accomplishments in the West, in *Geist und Seele des Soldaten* (The soldier's heart and mind), Rabenau warns against

> making comparisons between current military triumphs and victories of the past, especially the victories of Attilla the Hun over the heathen Goths of the East. The purpose of a war cannot be the "destruction of the enemy as a nation. . . . A decisive conflict is not the same thing as destruction."[7]

In these words Rabenau is alluding unfavourably to the persecution of the Jews, as well as to the impending clash between Stalin (in the East) and Hitler (in the West).

Even more forthright is Rabenau's comment in another 1940 publication, *Soldatentum* (Being a soldier today):

> A war can be justified only if the organically grown problems of international human relations can be solved by no other means.[8]

Rabenau also further developed the thinking he had formulated about the soldier's need for purpose and meaning. In 1940 he had written,

> How is a young man to go calmly to his death without any concept of the transcendent? Without any concept of the transcendent, a hero's death is just a jump into the abyss.[9]

In the unpublished manuscript *Ernste Laiengedanken* (Serious lay thoughtfulness), which he drafted in 1940/1941, Rabenau extends this line of thought by highlighting the unhelpful nature of the *gottgläubig* concept prevalent at the time. He points out that "a simple *Gottglaube* [deism] without responsibility towards the Almighty is in any case meaningless (*ein Nichts*)."[10] One can hear the army chaplain in him witnessing as Rabenau writes, "In Jesus Christ I can find the support I need when I come before God's throne when I die."[11] Still more firm in antithetical stance towards the policy and conduct of the authorities is the line "Of course being a Christian does not depend upon racial origins."[12]

Instances of courageous Rabenau protest would increase. From 1941 onwards the Gestapo monitored his telephone conversations and written correspondence. That same year, the regime chose the moment of its greatest triumphs to embark (while the favourable news coverage allowed) on a long-cherished policy of the "requisitioning"/expropriation of vast numbers of church properties and related assets. Rabenau was approached, possibly at the initiative of Münster's outspoken bishop Count von Galen, via a Catholic contact, Monsignor Alfred Büttner, and asked to intervene on behalf of the Maria Laach Benedictine abbey. Rabenau did not have to think for very long before deciding to go in his general's uniform and meet Himmler in person. The result of his visit surprised everyone: Himmler agreed that the policy was mistaken, the abbeys must be preserved, and Himmler wanted to learn more about Gregorian chant. In the context of wider protests, Hitler even outlawed further such "requisitioning" in July 1941.[13]

For a while, Rabenau sought for confirmation that Hitler had no part in the evil acts being committed, the clear evidence of which was reaching him first hand in his capacity as director of the Military Archives. But within a year of the outbreak of war, it had become clear to him that Hitler was indeed the source of the evil. In 1940 Joachim von Stülpnagel reported to trusted associates that Rabenau "detested Hitler with all his might."[14] This sentiment was reciprocated on the Führer's behalf by Gauleiter Florian, who, upon reading Rabenau's above-cited publication *Geist und Seele des Soldaten*, protested furiously to Hitler's deputy, Rudolf Hess, about the Eher Verlag print run of 300,000 copies and demanded that Rabenau be banned from publishing. The reason given was that Rabenau's statements were "church-friendly" and "influenced by the Christian faith."[15]

But it was not only the hubris and the crimes being committed that, for Rabenau, proved decisive. His engagement with theology became more serious as a result of his role as an active and serving soldier and (by now) general. He studied, insofar as service demands allowed, in order to put his Christian theological arguments onto a more researched footing. He also changed his writing style to include criticisms, the use of National Socialist vocabulary, mentions of Hitler and other top Nazis, and citations from *Mein Kampf* and National Socialist poets. Rabenau's insight was that the regime was adopting its own world-view in the place rightly occupied by the domain of faith—in other words, that it was putting the finite in the place of the Eternal. Here Rabenau's theology aligned with Bonhoeffer's. For both men it was self-evident that resistance against any dictatorship—in this instance, the Nazi one—invariably had an existential dimension. It's possible that Rabenau called his family together and said he was obliged to resist this system and thus endanger them. Both his daughters had married soldiers. Eva-Dorothee's husband, Karl Linnebach, twenty-one years older than her, and five years her father's senior in age, had served as an officer in World War I. Rabenau's other son-in-law, Wilhelm von Kornatzki, married to his daughter Edelgard since 1934, was, like him, a currently serving soldier. By 1942, Kornatzki was already on the front line in Stalingrad. In 1943 he would perish in Soviet captivity. If Rabenau did make this choice it would not have been an easy conversation. His wife, Eva, stood resolutely at his side, as she would throughout the dark days ahead.

From then on, Rabenau's tracks led him more into conflict with the regime and closer to the centre of the military and civilian resistance. Using his military travel as cover, he met with numerous senior military and civilian figures, apparently in attempts to sound them out about an end to the atrocities and standing up to Hitler. Rabenau himself was opposed to Hitler's assassination. On behalf of Carl Goerdeler, the leader of the civilian resistance, and Ulrich von Hassell, a diplomat working in covert opposition to the regime, he sounded out the chief of staff of the army,

Field Marshal Brauchitsch. Bethge reports that "after a meeting Hassell, Oster and Dohnanyi had with General von Falkenhausen, von Falkenhausen and General von Rabenau went again to Brauchitsch but were unable to persuade him to make any move at all against Hitler."[16] In another visit Rabenau spent time winning over another troubled soldier, General Guderian, who apparently—following a subsequent meeting with Hitler's paladin, General von Manstein—changed his mind. But in one respect the contact with Hassell did have a consequence. Hassell and Rabenau were both members of the prestigious Protestant Order of St John.[17] This Order was clear about the regime's anti-Christian stance. In Christian confidence and courage, Rabenau elected to write with an offer of help to all the Gauleiters of Germany. In an open letter he stated,

> Dear Gauleiter, in the matter of relations with the Churches, the Party is making one mistake after another. If you could obtain for me the necessary authorisations from the Führer, I guarantee that I will succeed within a few months in arranging peace with the Churches once and for all.[18]

The response was swift. Party secretary Martin Bormann's reaction to the idea that the party was making one mistake after another was to issue a writing ban on Rabenau. Army chief of staff General Halder noted in his diary on November 26, 1941, "Von Rabenau's writings are now banned. He is withdrawing all his publications from circulation."[19] Within a few days, on November 30, 1941, Rabenau met not just with Hassell but also with Hans von Dohnanyi and Colonel Hans Oster, both of whom were at the heart of the military resistance.[20]

From then on, events took a familiar trajectory. In 1942, in an act of breathtaking sycophancy, an individual named Scherff prepared a so-called historical document entitled "Lived Genius" about Hitler, which he presented for the *Führergeburtstag* moment of April 20, 1942. The ploy, although transparent, was a success: Scherff was appointed "Director of Army Archives," responsible for the (re)writing of military history, on June 6, 1942.[21] On July 1 Rabenau was transferred to the *Führerreserve*, the list of the Führer's retired officers, at his own request. Only one voice was raised in protest at the sidelining of General von Rabenau, that of General Halder.

Once prematurely retired, Rabenau pressed ahead with his theological study and writing. In words that could equally have been written by Bonhoeffer, in an unpublished script, believed to date from 1942, he urges,

It needs to be made clear to people afresh that we are responsible
to God, and that God asks something of us. . . . The Christian faith
is not something fixed, or static, but rather, essentially dynamic. It
is not something just "there" but instead, it's about becoming and
acting. . . . Along this path towards God we find ourselves unavoid-
ably confronted by the teachings of Jesus.[22]

In this Christian boldness, Rabenau's affinity with the Catholic Christian
faith deepened still further. His friendship with the Catholic Monsignor
Büttner, whom he had so visibly helped, flourished, the latter becoming a
frequent house guest. Clearly the rigours of war had the unusual benefit of
bringing the "open Lutheran" Rabenau and his wife into contact with Catholics in new and meaningful fellowship, just as it did for Bonhoeffer. No
doubt in connection with Büttner and other Catholics, Rabenau prepared
a shared Lutheran/Catholic intercessory prayer for use interconfessionally
in 1943. Because it was to be published, Goebbels became involved, and the
Völkischer Beobachter, the main party propaganda and news organ, relegated
it to the second inside page. Learning of this loss of impact, Rabenau let the
authorities know in no uncertain terms of his displeasure. The telephone
call he made in this respect is thought to have had ramifications for him
after July 20, 1944. At that time those charged with investigating the assassination attempt decided that Rabenau's contacts with high-placed Catholic
clergy could be a sufficient basis for suspicion as they sought to establish a
connection between the Catholic bishops and the July 20 attempt.[23] Certainly Rabenau succeeded, either in connection with this or another matter,
in making an enemy of Goebbels, who saw in him a prime example of the
generals' lack of trust in Hitler. Goebbels wrote in his diary,

Rabenau, who has now been replaced as Director of the Military
Archive, now proposes to study theology, in order to foster opposition to the Führer. These people have no shame in collecting a State
pension but still wish to attack both State and regime.[24]

Following Goebbels' comment, the commander-in-chief of the army,
Field Marshal Wilhelm Keitel, swiftly banned Rabenau from speaking in
public and from further writing.[25] He was also banned from accessing the
very military library he had himself so diligently created. From August 31,
1943, at his own choice, he no longer wore the uniform of a general on
any occasion, wanting "nothing more to do with these people." He continued with his theological studies at the Evangelische Konsistorium of

Mark Brandenburg, obtaining a lay preacher's licence on March 9, 1944. But with the war situation deteriorating rapidly, he was moved to offer his services again, albeit as a military chaplain. He applied for a chaplaincy post and was rejected. When he telephoned the adjutant of the chaplain general of the army to make good his offer of service whenever a vacancy arose, he was told, "Vacancies are not being filled." He responded, "So now you are officially lying." "Aber Herr General . . . [But, General . . .]," came the response. "That's enough," Rabenau interjected, before closing off the call: "Please just report this conversation to the chaplain general."[26]

Rabenau was not involved with the July 20 bomb plot but—perhaps unsurprisingly given all of the foregoing—was visited by the Gestapo almost immediately afterwards, on July 25, 1944. He was asked if he knew of the whereabouts of Carl Goerdeler. When he replied that he did not, he was arrested anyway. As he left, he said to his wife, "I'm not coming back." It was to prove so.

His time in prison was shattering. Following September 9, 1944, Rabenau was placed for three months in solitary confinement in Berlin's Moabit prison. His wristwatch was removed, so that he would lose track of time, and he was subjected to artificial lighting being shone on a continuous 24-7 basis. Bedcovers were not allowed to be drawn over the face of the prisoner, and he was totally cut off from the outside world. His cell had dimensions of six square metres. Rabenau established that by completing over 1,500 mini-laps, he would be able to walk twenty kilometres on a daily basis. This he did, covering a distance of 1,200 kilometres by December 1944. He was diabetic and no allowances were made for his health. Food allowances for prisoners were intentionally insufficient so as to weaken a prisoner's resolve and ability to withstand interrogations. He rapidly lost twenty kilograms in weight. On October 10, the day of his sixtieth birthday, allowed to wear shoes again for the first time since August 8, he received an apple from one of the guards, which he described as one of the most meaningful birthday presents he had received in his life. It helped restore his faith in human nature. He wrote, "A couple of absolute devils one is thence more readily able to overlook."[27] In the case against him, no link was made between Rabenau and Goerdeler or Rabenau and Hassell in the Kaltenbrunner reports, although Goerdeler in his own sufferings opted for the fullest disclosures. On rare occasions Rabenau's wife, Eva, was permitted to visit him.

In early February 1945, in a curiously hospitable decision, Buchenwald's camp commandant, Piester, elected to room Bonhoeffer together with Rabenau. Others soon noticed how amenable was their fellowship. As can be readily understood from this chapter, summarised in the table below, they soon found they were more than "brothers in adversity" but people of shared faith with a remarkable commonality and solidarity in their respective experiences at the hands of the authorities.

A Shared Story of Anti-Christian Harassment, Maltreatment, and "Liquidation": Bonhoeffer and Rabenau (Both Lutheran)

	Bonhoeffer		Rabenau
1924	PhD awarded (theology)	1934	PhD awarded (hon. philosophy)
1937	Banned from lecturing or running any public institution (Gestapo close Finkenwalde)	1936	Following speech in Cologne, Gauleiter Florian calls for him to be banned from public speaking
1940	Forbidden to speak in public (required to report location regularly to police)	1940	Publicly attacked by Gauleiter Florian for being "church-friendly." Study of theology intensifies
1941	Banned from printing or publishing	1941	In-person meeting with RFSS Himmler: intervention/protest over *Klostersturm*, the regime's confiscation of Catholic property. Banned from writing or publishing
1943	April: arrested/imprisoned/interrogated. Charges unclear. Begins smuggled correspondence in which deep, questioning faith shines through	1943	Ridiculed by Goebbels; banned by Keitel from public speaking and writing/accessing library
1944	Permitted minimal contact with fiancée, Maria von Wedemeyer	1944	Banned from chaplaincy work. Awarded lay preacher's licence. Arrested July 25 / imprisoned. No charges brought. Permitted minimal contact with wife. Begins smuggled correspondence in which strong faith shines through
1945	February: shares cell and hostage experience with Rabenau	1945	Shares cell and hostage experience with Bonhoeffer
1945	April 9: executed after sham trial following orders issued in Berlin (not known if authorised by Himmler)	1945	April 14/15: executed by order issued in Berlin (not known if authorised by Himmler)

Bonhoeffer and Rabenau were to be each other's warm companions in faith, doubt, and adversity for the short remaining duration of their lives.

Monday, April 2, 1945

8
Double Summer Time: Russian Resolve

Yet the warmth of companionship that Bonhoeffer and Rabenau shared, welcome as it was, could not of course hide the seriousness of the situation that engulfed the hostages and Germany as a whole. Failing a fulsome capitulation, which Hitler would never countenance, the serious business of war had to continue, until the bitter end. That end was nearing, but its coming was still elusive.

As the hostages struggled to sleep in Buchenwald, across Europe, April 2 began with a silent act. It was one that was not collaborative, but which was shared across many countries: at 2:00 a.m. that Monday, the clocks in the UK went forwards by one hour, as they did in Germany.[1] The BBC news that morning was read by Frederick Allen, and while including a local warning about ground frost, also noted that this was the first such warning it had been possible to give since the war began; so low was the likelihood of UK weather information being of any possible relevance or advantage to the retreating German armies. It was a poignant snub for Hitler: after November 5, 1940, he had created a special group (*Meldewesen*) for weather forecasting, because of his distrust for the army. The group was headed by a top meteorologist selected, pointedly, from the Luftwaffe. This harassed individual had to report almost daily to the Führer, who would not be satisfied with any forecast without being told the origin of its principal data. If it was derived from army sources, he was inclined to downgrade it or even voice the thought that it had probably been tampered with.[2] Now the BBC was prepared for Hitler to have first-hand access to any weather data he cared to tune in to.

The bulletin continued, "Today the American First Army have thrown back all attempts by the vast German Army Group 'B,' estimated at a hundred thousand men, to break out from the Ruhr, where they were surrounded yesterday by the link-up between the American 'Ninth and First' at Lippstadt.... The work of destroying [this army group] is not holding up our advance deeper into Germany. Further south, Third Army spearheads are now only ninety miles from Czechoslovakia. . . . The main news from the Eastern Front is of the converging Red Army drives on Vienna—one of them now within twenty-five miles of the Austrian capital."[3] Indeed, the Germans were surrendering "with fanatical persistence" to the Americans, in Russian journalist Ilya Ehrenburg's contemptuous phrase, while conducting a desperate last-ditch stand against the Russians.[4]

World Leaders

The unique task for the Allies was to cooperate with such a great power as Russia, one in whom they had no trust whatsoever. Clearly, whoever was first to seize Berlin would be in a commanding position. Indeed, it was necessary to recognise that from wherever the Soviets got to first it would hardly be feasible, at any subsequent point, to dislodge them.[5]

It had become very apparent to Churchill that Stalin could not be trusted, and that while he was a necessary ally in the defeat of Nazism, the (related) battle was now on for post-war dominance. In this respect, Russian military might was, by this stage, overwhelming. By December 1943 the victories at Stalingrad and Kursk had turned the Soviet Union into a major world power. After a row with the British, Allied supreme commander Dwight D. Eisenhower had left open the capture of Berlin as a "distinct possibility." In orders issued to Lieutenant General Simpson, the 9th Army was told to "exploit any opportunities for seizing a bridgehead over the Elbe and be prepared to continue on to Berlin or to the north-east."[6] But the Allies were being outmanoeuvred. For his part, Stalin observed wryly, "Now the fate of Europe is settled, we shall do as we like, with the Allies' consent."[7]

In Russia itself, at a time when the future shape of the world hung in the balance, Clementine Churchill and her companions arrived at Moscow airport on April 2. Here from the moment of their arrival they were "overwhelmed" with gifts and received with the utmost goodwill. The BBC news reported,

> Mrs Churchill arrived at Moscow airport this morning after a non-stop night flight from Cairo. Mrs Molotov was there to meet her with Mr and Mrs Maisky, the British and American Ambassadors and Soviet Red Cross and Foreign Office officials. Mrs Churchill was wearing her British Red Cross uniform. "We have all (she said) followed with admiration and respect, awe and wonder and affection the great exploits of your wonderful Army and of your men and women. I have looked forward with great pleasure to my visit here." Then she thanked

the Royal Air Force pilot and crew who'd brought her safely to the beginning of her tour.[8]

Clementine Churchill's visit remains a fine example of an un-lauded, but well-conducted, behind-the-scenes diplomatic initiative. But off the world stage, relations were fraught with tension. Despite the public posturing, many saw this, including Hitler. On April 2, in a postscript to the "Table Talk" memoranda given to Bormann and recorded by him, Hitler delivered the last of his Table Talk monologues, in effect a political testament to the German nation. He states,

> I have been Europe's last hope. . . . If Germany was to suffer defeat after all, it would be utter and complete . . . and a tragedy for Europe as well as for the German people. . . . With the defeat of the Reich and pending the emergence of the Asiatic, the African and perhaps the South American nationalisms, there will remain in the world only two great powers capable of confronting each other—The United States and Soviet Russia.[9]

For his part, Churchill could also see the future very clearly. In a reply to General Eisenhower, which rather crossed in the post with Eisenhower's note politely suggesting he be allowed to conduct the war as he saw fit, Churchill continued, as the by now weakest voice among the Allies, to emphasise the need for the Anglo-Americans to "shake hands with the Russians as far east as possible." That was in public. Privately, with Soviet troops in Europe enjoying a four-to-one numerical superiority over those of the other Allies, supported by advantages in tank deployment, there were real fears that further hostilities might break out following the German surrender. As a result, Churchill ordered contingency plans to be drawn up that were based on a hypothesis that Hitler's defeat simply marked the end of a chapter, rather than an end point in itself. The name given to these plans concealed the reason why they had been prepared in the first place: Operation Unthinkable was eminently thinkable in the minds of British planners.[10]

Hegyeshalom, Hungary

Russian resolve did not waver. On Monday, April 2, Soviet forces on the Danube front reached the Austrian border at Hegyeshalom, less than seventy miles from Vienna, and Bulgarian troops captured Nagykanizsa, the centre of the Hungarian oilfields. With this defeat Germany's last hope of any even partly adequate fuel supply was lost, ironically and decisively in this instance, because there was insufficient fuel for the tanks leading the German counter-attack under General Student.[11] The German counteroffensive was postponed until April 4, when it was (unsurprisingly to all save Hitler) cancelled outright. Without fuel the inevitable wholesale German collapse was now only a question of time. Hitler had been obsessing about fuel supplies for months. The pain of the day's news was compounded for Hitler closer to home when his physician, Dr Karl Brandt, warned him personally that one-fifth of all needed medicines no longer existed and that stocks of two-fifths would run out completely in two months.[12] But Hitler refused to accept even the possibility of surrender and, in a message sent on April 2 to Kesselring, ordered the replacement of every commander in Italy who failed to stand firm.[13] Hitler's "no withdrawal" stance was by now entirely predictable.

9

Germany's Leadership: Out of Touch

Equally predictable was Hitler's racist understanding of world events. One historian noted that "in his last days Hitler kept execrating the Jews in racial terms." On April 2 he again stressed that "after the war, in the [white] world, only peoples showing themselves capable of eradicating the deadly Jewish poison from their system . . . would have the strength to face an emergent Asia, Africa and South America."[1] It was part of a continuing pattern of vitriol. One historian observed,

> The discussions of Germany's military situation in the early months of 1945 are rambling, confused, and futile. The leadership was not only morally, but also intellectually, bankrupt. Hours were wasted in discussion of questions of detail and local operations, interrupted by reminiscences and recriminations. Hitler no longer shows any grasp of the situation. His orders became wilder and more contradictory, his demands more impossible, his decisions more arbitrary. . . . Without bothering to investigate the facts he ordered the dismissal, degradation and even execution of officers who, after fighting against overwhelming forces, were forced to give ground. . . . His one answer to every proposal was: no withdrawal.[2]

But denial could not stem the flow of events. Even Josef Goebbels, confiding in his voluminous diary, noted in his entry for that day that the German situation was completely desolate, with reports he found distressing streaming in from every conceivable quarter. He comforted himself with insightful observations on the now-public lack of harmony in Anglo-American and Soviet relations and by (rightly) noting that the impact of the publication of the Morgenthau Plan[3] would be to stiffen German resolve to fight on. But Goebbels was a deluded man. His remarks about the Werewolf[4] radio transmissions are self-congratulatory, as is the account of his own stinging attack on a Lieutenant Colonel Balzer

for demonstrating a "defeatist" attitude: an accusation readily capable of
attracting for its object the death penalty. Perhaps more importantly, for
someone who was at the heart of things, his information on the speed
of the Allied advance on the Western Front is either "redacted" or out of
date, simply because territory was being lost at a rate he could not grasp.
He notes the presence of US troops in Vacha, Thuringia, whereas by the
next day they were already much further east, and, accordingly, far closer
to the centre of the Reich.[5]

Berlin, Germany

With the German leadership increasingly out of touch with reality, a
small miracle of communication occurred in the German capital. Newly
released, to her immense relief, from the horrors of Ravensbrück, Norwegian Gerda Schröder somehow managed to make contact on Easter
Monday by telephone with a humanitarian cell of Norwegian exiles at
Gross-Kreuz, near Potsdam. She arranged to meet Wanda Hjort in Berlin,
and miraculously, in the turmoil, they managed to find each other. Wanda
brought with her Norwegian professor Arup Seip. They met in a small café
near the central station, where trains were still arriving, though the front
was so close now that they could see the wounded soldiers being brought
in on the S-Bahn. All over the city, the streets were plastered with notices
saying, "Berlin will never surrender."[6]

10

Himmler's Hostage Plans

Close to Berlin, in the fast-shrinking remnant of what remained of Nazi-controlled Germany, Himmler remained active on many counts. His thorny problems with SS-General Ernst Kaltenbrunner's desire to run the show, and place himself in the frame to connect with the Allies, continued to increase. In a blatant attempt to make the regime look better to a post-war world, on April 2, 1945, Kaltenbrunner wrote to the chief of the International Committee of the Red Cross, Carl Burckhardt, saying Himmler had agreed to release Karolina Lanckoronska—on condition the countess stay silent and conduct herself loyally in respect of the Reich.[1] It was a fraught example of Kaltenbrunner, in a relationship that was fast breaking down, on this occasion working at Himmler's behest. It would be only three days before Kaltenbrunner would take a direct order from Hitler and implement it in the full knowledge that Himmler would most likely have objected.

But if Kaltenbrunner's mutiny was simmering, at least there were some loyal soldiers Himmler could still count on. One of these was Adolf Eichmann, whom he had recalled from Hungary to Berlin in January 1945. There, every day, Eichmann's boss and former mentor, Kaltenbrunner, would lunch with all his departmental heads—except Eichmann. Covering their tracks to avoid post-war retribution, they never invited Eichmann to sit and eat with them—most of them avoided this pariah, who in his diligence towards the implementation of their "Final Solution" plans had executed their own wishes. In early April Himmler ordered Eichmann to Theresienstadt, due for liquidation as the Allied armies approached. The instructions Eichmann received were to select one to two hundred prominent Jews and bring them to a safe place in the Austrian Tyrol as "pawns" in possible negotiations with the Allied Supreme Command. A wide-ranging "insurance policy" was in the process of being constructed. Hostages were being selected. Among these so-called "pawns" were former

French prime minister Léon Blum and Gemma La Guardia Glück, sister of New York's popular mayor Fiorello H. La Guardia, currently imprisoned in Ravensbrück. Though Eichmann himself looked upon Himmler as the most prominent rat deserting the sinking ship, and had even at one point harangued Red Cross guests against Himmler's "humane line," he was not one to disobey an order unless he could exceed it. Heading into Austria, he began to search for a mountain sanctuary for his hostages. In the Tyrolean town of Brixlegg, he survived a heavy bombardment. In Innsbruck the Gauleiter Franz Hofer was too busy to see his Berlin visitor, but one of his department heads found a couple of villages in the Brenner Pass between Austria and Italy that had empty hotels, and these were put at Himmler's disposal.[2] It would be to one of these that the hostage group as a whole would, eventually, be directed—but by then, without Bonhoeffer.

11

Germany: Reaping the Whirlwind

For Germany it was a time of reaping what had been sown. One soldier, writing in April 1945 from the front, said he had heard in the last days several times from older soldiers who had experienced the first two years of the Russian campaign that "all guilt is avenged on earth." They saw reports, he thought partly exaggerated, of Bolshevik[1] atrocities in the occupied eastern parts of Germany as proof of this. "Many think consciously of the things they themselves saw or had to carry out and which had to be set against what is allegedly taking place now. . . . We are guilty ourselves, we've earned it—that is the bitter recognition that many struggle through to."[2] The problem of the day of judgement arriving in the form of Allied troops was a pressing one. Before Auschwitz was evacuated in January 1945, the SS had gone around shooting any kapos who might have had evidence of what had happened. All of the *Sonderkommandos*—the special work forces who had worked in the gas chambers or crematoria—were to be executed. Just before their execution, the Auschwitz *Sonderkommando* had revolted, and several had escaped.

Ravensbrück, Germany

Presumably to forestall any similar rebellion in Ravensbrück, Himmler's concentration camp for women, the eleven men who had worked in the crematorium and gas chamber were taken to the camp bunker and locked up. Also in early April, Vera Salvequart, the camp nurse, learned she was to be shot.[3] Elsewhere in the Ravensbrück camp, on Easter Monday the French women lined up to be part of the constant selection and deselection rituals accompanying the camp's final weeks. In these cruel scenes, the women would be told they had been selected for departure, and lined up accordingly for hours, only for the process to lead nowhere, and begin again on the same or another day. By the end of the Easter weekend, all the prisoners bundled onto lorries had been gassed—as many as 2,500—and the air was thick with burning smoke.[4]

The Black Forest, Baden-Württemberg, Germany

Across Germany even devoted followers of the Führer found their faith in "final victory" shaken. "In the last few days we have been shaken by events," an army officer on the staff of an SS corps in the Black Forest wrote in his diary on April 2. "Düsseldorf lost, Cologne lost, the disastrous bridgehead at Remagen. . . . In the south east the Bolsheviks have reached Wiener Neustadt. Blow upon blow, we are coming to the end. . . . Do our leaders see perhaps a possibility? Does the death of our soldiers, the destruction of our cities and villages make any sense now?" Yet he still felt they should fight on until told to surrender.[5]

Aschaffenburg and Thuringia, Germany

Across Germany Allied progress was mixed. In Aschaffenburg, as described in chapter 5, the battle raged on. As the last of the SS hold-outs fell, some three thousand remaining civilians tried to surrender. US soldier Harry Eisener caught sight of a crowd of around a hundred civilians moving towards him. Then he heard rifle shots and saw civilians fall dead, fired upon by their own countrymen. Others kept on walking and running, undeterred. He picked up and carried to safety a severely wounded girl with a faded blue dress and a pigtail, holding in the contents of her insides with her bare hands, and handed her gently on to the care of a US medic. He felt his heart pounding as he saw the medic tend to her.[6]

Much closer to Bonhoeffer's location in Buchenwald, the town of Creuzburg, situated approximately ninety kilometres to the west of Buchenwald, was the first Thuringian town to experience the onslaught of US forces. After heavy fighting throughout Easter Day, resistance in Creuzburg had ceased late in the evening of April 1, leaving the demolished town a smouldering pile of rubble and destroyed buildings. The medieval bridge, intact since 1225 and a sought-after crossing point of the Werra river, had been detonated at the approach of US tanks from General Patton's 3rd Army. In the small hours of the night of April 2, the first Americans crossed the river in inflatable rafts. The construction of a pontoon bridge began immediately. The town, like so many, paid a heavy price for its compliance with Gauleiter Fritz Sauckel's orders to fight to the death.

Schloss Holte-Stukenbrock, Germany

Meanwhile in central Northern Germany, near the town of Schloss Holte-Stukenbrock, the rapidly advancing US 2nd Armoured Division freed the POW camp Stammlager Vik (Stalag 326), thus liberating 7,890 malnourished prisoners of many nationalities. Here conditions were utterly appalling: sixty men had been forced to live in a room measuring twenty square feet. Report writer Major Wayne Culp, of the 3rd Battalion, 117th Infantry, was so amazed to find that among the starving men there were Russians who had been forced-marched there from as far away as Moscow, a distance of 2,184 kilometres, that in his shock and disbelief, when compiling his official report about the liberated prisoners' place of capture, he wrote the word "MOSCOW" in capital letters. It was a telling exposure of the brutalities of war and of the policies of the regime. In this instance it was the case that such was the treatment meted out to racially inferior groupings. In itself that was, in the regime's eyes, defensible. But how the world's media would react to learning the truth about the German treatment of regime opponents kept in concentration camps was as yet unknown. Accordingly, the policy of not surrendering captives, but instead sending them on forced marches as enemy troops approached, would gain ascendancy.[7]

Breslau, Germany

Further south-east in Pomerania, in Breslau, non-stop bombing raids obliterated practically the entire town centre. The city was paying a terrible price for Gauleiter Hanke's decision in January to obey orders and defend "Fortress Breslau" to the last. Within a week, though, to his complete delight, Hanke was for this conduct awarded the Golden Cross of the German Order. Yet this "hero" had no intention of going down with the city he had condemned to near total destruction. Hours before Breslau's capitulation on May 5, Hanke would make his escape in a Fieseler Storch, perhaps the only plane ever to leave the improvised airstrip within the city, for which houses had been bulldozed on his own orders, inflicting further misery upon the inhabitants.[8]

Map 2 of Bonhoeffer's Germany: Chapters 12–16

Lippstadt	On April 2 the American First Army throws back all attempts by the vast German Army Group "B" to break out from the Ruhr pocket.
Hegyeshalom	On April 2, Soviet forces reach the Austrian border here, less than seventy miles from Vienna.
Nagykaniszka	Bulgarian troops capture the town (April 2).
Aschaffenburg	Surrenders on April 3.
Berlin	Released from Ravensbrück, Norwegian Gerda meets amidst chaotic scenes with Wanda Hjort and Arup Seip in a Berlin café.
Schloss Holte-Stukenbrock	The US 2nd Armoured Division frees the POW camp Stammlager Vik (Stalag 326), liberating 7,890 malnourished prisoners.
Bad Orb	On April 3, troops from General Patch's and General Patton's armies liberate an Allied POW camp north-east of Aschaffenburg. 7,000 prisoners are freed.
Krems	Missy Vassiltchikov's friend leaves a parcel containing the entire cash fortune of the Wilczech family on a train. It is safely retrieved.
Wetzelsdorf	Allied parachute agent Friedrich Berliner, after torture, is taken to a quiet range, and shot.
Marktredwitz	The Klemperers are unlucky with accommodation and (again) improvise.
Zuyder Zee	Field Marshal Montgomery's forces are only twenty-five miles from the Zuyder Zee.
Münster, Osnabrück, and Hamm	are taken by Allied forces.
Bielefeld	is surrounded by Allied troops.
Gotha	General Patton's 4th Armoured Division, pressing on from Eisenach, reaches the outskirts of Gotha.
Zossen	On April 3 the Canaris diaries are randomly found in an office move by a general who was positioned near the exploding bomb on July 20, 1944, and survived.
Buchenwald	Around 11:00 pm, on April 3, Bonhoeffer's hostage convoy departs in a southerly direction.

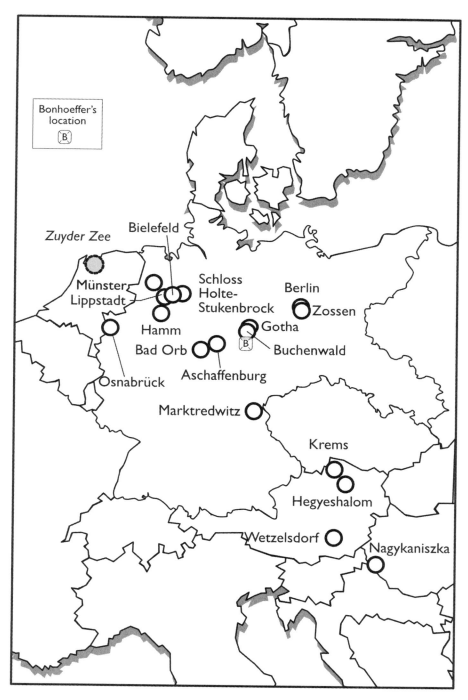

Map 2 of Bonhoeffer's Germany: Chapters 12–16
Staatsbibliothek zu Berlin-Kartenabteilung/Bruce Bovill

12
Buchenwald: Rumbles of Departure

In the camp outskirts, the rumble of artillery in the distance was already audible. The tension was palpable. It was a question of waiting. For Bonhoeffer supplies of high-quality reading material were a comfort and a solace. It is unthinkable, according to Bethge, that he was not also making notes and writing throughout these days, but we have no record of this. By this stage in April, he had finished reading Kurt Leese's *Protestantism in Modern Times*, as we know he exchanged it for Pünder's *Julian the Apostate*. In this instance Bonhoeffer may well have felt he got the better end of the bargain. For Pünder reading such a text as that received from Bonhoeffer was scarcely imaginable under any circumstances.[1] For Bonhoeffer, who had received it from his family on February 7, no doubt upon request, it was of great interest. Not only was it written as a contribution to a specialised area with which he was familiar, but also the author was at the time a controversial figure in Germany. The author, Kurt Leese, was elected professor in 1935 at a time when only those favoured by the regime could obtain posts, yet in 1940, while preparing this publication, which appeared in 1941, Leese had his right to teach rescinded by the authorities. In its field the book is a notable achievement. It sets out to present selected texts and characteristics of the spiritual and religious history of Protestantism, typically (and, for the modern reader, bizarrely) confining its choice of male authors to those whose medium of operation was exclusively within the German language. Notwithstanding this, its ambition and scope made it a text of choice for Bonhoeffer. It aims to engage with the legacy of Martin Luther, a theologian whom Bonhoeffer in his writings cites 870 times, almost always approvingly.[2] Most if not all of the fifty or so theologians whose thinking is discussed in some detail, some better known, and some very obscure, as well as the many others alluded to, would have been familiar names to him. The readability of the 384-page volume, despite the dense printing in the Old German typescript of the

1941 Kröners Taschenausgabe edition,[3] would have afforded him, by contrast with Hermann Pünder, little trouble.[4] His detailed reading may even have reminded him of the title of his own poem, written from prison in July 1944, "Stations on the Road to Freedom" ("Stationen auf dem Weg der Freiheit"), when he re-read the words of his former tutor Adolf von Harnack (1851–1930), at whose funeral he had been invited to speak at the time by the great man himself. "Honest [real] mistakes are stations on the road to understanding [awareness]" ("Ehrliche Irrtümer sind Stationen auf dem Weg der Erkenntnis").[5]

Through Leese the reader is offered many insights, some of which have stood the test of time rather better than others. On the positive side, Leese makes some judgement calls that continue to resonate, even eighty years later, with the modern reader. He undoubtedly captures the spirit of protest that is part of the birthright of the Protestant tradition. Clearly Leese empathises with the tradition of "earnest doubt," which holds the process of striving for truth in the highest esteem. In a preface to chapter 3, he writes,

> Critique of Luther and old Protestantism is truly Protestant in the sense that it stands in the service of a relentless [unerbittlich[6]] and passionate search for a deeper understanding of truth. . . . There is talk of a "Luther Renaissance." New research on Luther can for Protestantism prove fruitful, and promising only if it without reservation affirms the destiny of religious [gläubig] freedom at both a personal and a historical level.[7]

For Leese, Luther is the founder of modernity's freedom of religion and of conscience, in a Protestant faith characterised by a commitment to learning, questioning, and freedom of thought and (related) criticism, with its associated rejections of authority. For example, he cites Tzschirner (1778–1828), the teacher of von Hase, Bonhoeffer's great-grandfather on his mother's side (1800–1890):

> Only an immature race, one that is alienated from independent thought, can believe something because it has been believed in the past, and hence allow it to have validity, because it was valid in days gone by.[8]

The reader is left in no doubt about the Enlightenment's positive impact on Protestant thought. Schleiermacher's contributions, too, are held in high regard: his phrase "the Reformation continues" is mentioned more than once. Leese's reader is soon convinced that the Latin phrase *Ecclesia reformata semper reformanda*[9] holds true. Also highly esteemed are the thoughts of Paul Tillich (1886–1965). Leese notes with approval his critique that

> middle-class society . . . has banished the divine to the fringes of life, made the divine/eternal into a bearer of ethical or logical world-consciousness: it has made God the destroyer of time and the temporal, into a conclusion, or an expression, of the self-sufficient finite.[10]

Leese quotes Bonhoeffer's own doctoral supervisor, Erich Seeberg (1888–1935), highlighting Seeberg's insight that "the Luther Renaissance we are experiencing has awoken our sense of the uncomfortable 'otherness' [*unheimliche Jenseitigkeit*] of God."[11]

On the downside, Leese (seen especially through the lens of hindsight) makes some surprising omissions. He excludes Feuerbach (1804–1872) and Holl (1866–1926) from detailed commentary, and (yet more strangely) in his introduction pointedly dismisses the "so-called, wrongly named 'dialectical theology' of Karl Barth, Emil Brunner, and [*sic*] Friedrich Gogarten as simply 'invalid.'"[12] This dismissal appears particularly questionable in the light of Leese's citation of Seeberg in the words above, given that this awareness (of the uncomfortable "otherness" of God) was at the time most closely associated with the theology of Karl Barth. In a similar vein, Leese's citation of Seeberg in castigation of those who would apparently deny the Christian doctrine of the incarnation, in Seeberg's view a recurring event, as a "heretical tearing-asunder of time and eternity [by so-called dialectical theology]" provides a convoluted and unhelpful ending to a remarkable project otherwise so full of insight.

It was a world Bonhoeffer knew and understood well. That he continued his reading in such a specialised and rarified field, even in Buchenwald, tells us something. But events would soon overtake them.

Somehow aware that advance troop units were already at Eisenach, less than ninety kilometres away, Léon Blum could hardly sleep. He writes,

> For a week already day and night had been spent in a blur of hyper-vigilance. At any moment advance troop units could reach the camp, its garrison already much reduced in strength since the Russian attack on the Oder, and now only guarded by a few hundred SS troops. . . . At night, were the grinding noises we were hearing in a haze between wakefulness and sleep the sounds of the tracks of advancing US tanks? When would they arrive? Tonight, even?

Above all, would they get here in time, before the Gestapo order to
relocate us came, dragging us from our imprisonment so as to place
us far, far away, beyond the reach of the Allied advance? We knew
that what was at stake for us was a matter of life or death. In truth,
the order could already have been issued. But perhaps the Gestapo,
in the chaos and disarray we began to perceive around us, might
have forgotten about us? In which case, our deliverance was only
a matter of time, and we would see France, loved ones, and friends
again. But if the dreaded order arrived, if we were transported south,
to the mountain redoubt where the last stand would play out, oh!
Then we knew what would befall us. We would be crushed in the
final collapse. Hitler would perish, but as with Delacroix's despots,
frenetically dragging with him onto his own funeral pyre his companions, his slaves, and his hostages.[13]

The accuracy of Blum's intuition about the collateral damage to Germany
that Hitler would relish inflicting in defeat is exceptional. At the same
time, there is no doubt that the desire not to be dragged under, along with
the disintegrating wreckage of the Third Reich, was a shared wish among
the hostages as a whole. But the "dreaded orders" had in fact already been
issued, just as Blum feared. The group had indeed not been forgotten.

Tuesday, April 3, 1945

13

Sigmund Rascher

In Buchenwald the prisoners had the whole day to pack and prepare for departure, a process that would have taken the majority of them a very short while indeed. Included in the number of those "travelling light" was Sigmund Rascher. Rascher was born in Munich on February 12, 1909, making him three years younger than Bonhoeffer. He was the youngest of three red-haired children born to Hanns and the beautiful Rosa Rascher. His siblings were Sigrid (1906) and Sigurd (1907). His arrival came just around the period when his father, Hanns, was leaving the church and committing most decidedly to the theosophical and anthroposophical society of Rudolf Steiner. This was a society with occult connections that drew on a mix of Indian and Buddhist ideas and combined influences from the Bible, Pythagoras, and Paracelsus. Hanns soon became an apostle for anthroposophy who, in addition to prescribing alternative medications—he believed, apparently, in trying things out on people[1]—indulged in spiritism, hypnosis, natural healing remedies, and homeopathy; studied Paracelsus; and became an advocate of vegetarian food. During World War I—between 1915 and 1919—he threw himself fully into the work and service of an army doctor. Soon his father left the family. Sigmund was twelve. The effect was profound. Father Hanns then enjoyed a brief spell in a leadership role at the Monte Bre Sanatorium in Lugano before being asked to leave in view of the notorious uncertainties surrounding his work. Sigmund's mother, Rosa, left unsupported to fend for herself and the three children, moved to Dornach in Switzerland with a relative.

From a young age Sigmund's older brother Sigurd started taking on financial responsibility for his mother and siblings where possible—a pattern that would continue long into adulthood.

Meanwhile, during his time in Lugano, Sigmund's father had come substantially under the influence of new and poisonous ideas: he had teamed up with Freiherr Rudolf von Sebottendorf (1875–1945), founder in 1919 of the Anti-Semitic Society, whose members came to include Alfred Rosenberg, Julius Streicher, and Rudolf Hess, with meetings often attended by Adolf Hitler. Sebottendorf was editor of the *Münchener Beobachter*, which in 1920 became the *Völkischer Beobachter*, between 1920 and 1945 the official organ of the Nazi Party. Father Hanns was also declared bankrupt within two years of leaving Lugano but, moving to Hamburg to join with his brother Fritz, and now divorced, found a suitable and convenient solution by marrying a patient/client, Hanna Lampe.[2]

Perhaps unsurprisingly, Sigmund did not succeed in passing his end of school Abitur examinations at the first or second attempts, but only at the third. At this time Sigmund had been attending the Zeppelin-Oberrealschule in Konstanz. When the somewhat delayed moment came, at age twenty-two, for leaving school with his Abitur—needed for onward progression to medical training—Sigmund's school rector wrote in his valediction, "With silent sadness I release you from school, because your future fills me with anxious apprehension."[3]

Perhaps less than the conscious influence of his father or that of his school, one influence that was deeply formative for Sigmund was anthroposophy. An especially profound influencer from his teens onwards came in the shape of anthroposophy adherent Ehrenfried Pfeiffer, who, like Steiner—according to Bär—was a dilettante and a fraud. Anthroposophical websites have him as a professor of biochemistry, which he was not; nor was he vice-president of the American Academy of Nutrition, as he died before it was founded in 1985. Pfeiffer is said to have won over the Rascher family and was always on the lookout for new cures and experiments or homeopathic treatments. He was an explorer of the influences of cosmic rhythms on life processes and developed a (falsified) methodology to show their effectiveness. This purported that crystal images formed during the crystallisation of $CuCl_2$ crystals could indicate the "vitality" of wheat and help diagnose cancer, pregnancy, and tuberculosis. In scientific terms his central thesis was, like anthroposophy, what Bär memorably describes as a "universal flapdoodle machine"—but persuasive enough, somehow, for Sigmund to choose to invest much of his early professional life in the fruitless pursuit of its veracity. Indeed, in his quest for truth, Sigmund, fed up with living off the patronage of his saxophone-playing brother, turned to the legal profession and sued his father—successfully—for some support. He won the case—much to the credit of the legal system extant in Germany in

1932—but his father never paid over anything, so his precarious financial circumstances continued to prove challenging.

By now Sigmund was 4,000 Reichsmarks in debt for his medical studies to his long-suffering older brother. Sigmund moved back home to his mother in Dornach, joined the Nazi Party—according to Bär without conviction—for career reasons in the first half of 1933, and linked up with Basel University to become a disciple of Pfeiffer. He did obtain sponsorship for his medical doctorate in this research area, especially focussing on pregnancy, supervised by a Josef Trumpp, and this process lasted until he somehow passed and became a doctor in 1936. In that same Olympic year of 1936, Sigmund hooked up with a widow, Nini Diehl, rumoured to have formerly been in a relationship of some kind with Heinrich Himmler, to whom she had apparently offered shelter back in the early Munich days. Nini formed a loyalty to Sigmund that she never relinquished. Sigmund too remained true (almost) until the end of their lives in 1945. Thanks to Nini's influence, Sigmund was able to obtain a German Research Foundation (DFG) scholarship. This was awarded to Sigmund in his (doomed) attempt to prove that Pfeiffer's $CuCl_2$ crystals were suitable for cancer diagnosis. Unsurprisingly this in turn launched a project that, as a fraud, would involve multiple layers of complicity on the part of those involved.

An introduction to Heinrich Himmler—who declared a nebulous interest in a broad range of cancer-research-related topics—effected by Nini in April 1939 produced a five-point plan for the (by this time impecunious) Rascher to embrace. Again for career reasons, Rascher, although already in the Luftwaffe, then resigned from the SA and swiftly joined the SS and the Ahnenerbe.[4] Sigmund and Nini had their first child, Peter, on November 25, 1939. Although seemingly incredible, this caused genuine surprise to (Dr) Sigmund himself, as well as to many others, including Himmler, who had been convinced—due to her age—of Nini's infertility. Equally incredibly, a wholescale Gestapo investigation process into the genuineness of this birth, hotly contested by Nini, followed, and was also dropped. Peter would be the first of four children essentially legally procured by Nini—in all probability without Sigmund's knowledge—the ramifications and complexities of which would over time prove contributory to their eventual undoing.

But apparently, despite their bizarre antics, the Rascher couple provided a happy home for these children for the relatively short duration of their Himmler-sponsored—and correspondingly well-resourced—period of grace; one of these would later even contact author Siegfried Bär in 2011 claiming to be the eldest, and stating that those five years were among the best of his life.[5]

Once war broke out, the demands of a war situation upon a harassed researcher attempting to support his masters in the Luftwaffe prevented Sigmund from conducting any worthwhile research along the lines Himmler envisaged—but Rascher was at least rewarded with the title of chief physician of the Luftwaffe by December 1940. Yet still, he was painfully aware of the complete lack of progress in the areas required, and paid for, by his patron. So it was that necessity proved the mother of invention for Sigmund during a course given by the Luftgaukommando (Air Command) in May 1941 in Munich. This took place just after the "birth" in April of their second son, following which Himmler even permitted their marriage in July. (A requirement of any serving member of the SS wishing to wed was the personal approval of the Reichsführer-SS.)

The stimulus for Rascher's creativity was twofold. First, it was hearing Munich's associate professor of aviation medicine Georg Weltz, an individual who had been working on the reheating of hypothermic guinea pigs. Weltz mentioned that the Luftwaffe's new planes could operate at an altitude of 21,000 metres—for example, the rocket-powered ME 163. He went on to state that knowledge was lacking of how pilots behaved when their machine received a direct hit in the pressurised cabin at such a height. The next speaker, Heinrich Kottenhoff—an associate professor and the surgeon general, who had been experimenting with rhesus monkeys at great heights or down to ultra-low air pressures—remarked that "it would be interesting to know whether similar phenomena can be found with flyers." At this point Sigmund had—according to biographer Bär—the single idea of his career, that of using prisoners. When, upon speaking with both, the two expert speakers demurred, Rascher wrote to Himmler, who swiftly accepted Rascher's idea to use prisoners. In this he was pushing on an already open door, as a wide range of criminal experiments using prisoners was underway at a variety of locations: already in May 1941, Himmler had begun the process of engaging a gynaecologist with a previous history of violence to conduct vile experiments on women in Auschwitz-Birkenau.[6] As it was his wife's habit to write to Himmler on an almost weekly basis, and as Rascher himself was also an avid "denouncer," he simply decided to milk the opportunity that was presenting itself for what it would deliver in terms of personal prestige and a possible *Habilitation*.[7] Of course, it also offered financial well-being and standing among other medical colleagues.

Accordingly, when Rascher continued to encounter repeated refusals to cooperate from the likes of colleagues such as Weltz and others, he dug his heels in. He ordered a special and suitable experimental contraption to be made anyway in anticipation of his desired outcome. He also became active in manoeuvring two workplace reassignments, the second with Himmler's help, so that by March/April 1942, he was posted to Dachau. That January, around the time of Rascher's imminent arrival, the Dachau commandant, Piorkowski, noted the news of Rascher's posting there with dismay, "since orders came from the very top." The Luftwaffe vacuum chamber itself arrived via a carefully arranged circuitous route on February 22, 1942. So with the world war by then at its most engulfing, the stage was fully set for Sigmund Rascher to achieve his ends, and he was not slow in commencing. Indeed, he quickly scheduled two hundred experiments, and those chosen were not volunteers, as had been previously agreed. In each case the apparently genial Rascher led a subject into the chamber, applied the ECG electrodes, and closed the chamber door. Outside Rascher turned to the window, watched the prisoner, and turned the wheel to control the chamber pressure. As the simulated altitude increased and the pressure decreased, nitrogen bubbles formed in the subject's blood vessels, causing unbearable pain, and the ECG informed Rascher when the subject of his "terminal experiment" was dead. The process was then quickly to summon an aide and dissect the victims, and then with an underwater autopsy method to photograph for research and career advancement purposes the fatal nitrogen bubbles.

In the first month of operations, April 1942, when one fatality occurred, Rascher was challenged by a colleague that what he was doing was wrong. "Herr Rascher, this has to stop!" said the Luftwaffe's Romberg, after witnessing a second "accidental" death. To this Rascher's reply came: "Mind your own business—or I'll have your passport confiscated." Romberg travelled to Berlin to report him, but this proved inconsequential in the light of Rascher's determination to press on, and so the process continued. Around sixty to seventy prisoners were murdered. On April 5, 1942, Rascher provided a secret report to Himmler:

> 37 year old Jew in good condition. Breathing continued for up to 30 minutes. After 4 minutes the VP [experimental person] began to perspire and wiggle his head, after 5 minutes cramps occurred,

between 6–10 minutes the breathing speed increased and the VP became unconscious. . . . From 11–30 minutes breathing slowed to 3 breaths per minute, finally stopping altogether. Severe cyanosis developed in between and foam appeared at the mouth. Dissection was started about half an hour after breathing had stopped.

This report Himmler "noted with thanks" on April 13, and he paid Rascher the notable compliment of an official visit to Dachau on May 1. Understandably this visit aroused resentment among other colleagues, but overall the visit was a small triumph for Rascher, with the significant exception that Himmler was hot with anger about the discovery that the despatches of coffee and cognac he had expressly sent to "volunteer" participants had not, he discovered, in fact reached any of them. An offence of this nature given to the Reichsführer-SS could all too easily prove to have fatal consequences for many people, in either the shorter or the longer term. Himmler's missing deliveries were not the only non sequiturs on hand. Around this time a medical colleague commented that what Rascher wanted to clarify was unclear, because he asked a lot of questions, then interrupted that project and moved to a different question, in what was an unsteady jumping from one idea to the next. This was indeed Rascher's established pattern. By August 1942 Rascher had already let the vacuum chamber project go and moved on to yet another project. This one was a series of hypothermia experiments connected in part with the experiences of pilots he had heard about in the severe cold of Russia complaining, "We cannot fly," and those of others shot down over the North Sea. In the water bath phase of these experiments, the subjects were wired with electrodes and dressed in flight gear. Offered a comforting (and misleading) cigarette, they were then put into a tub filled with cold water. Sigmund and a colleague, Holzlöhner, sat on the side and watched their human guinea pig. A rectal probe measured the core temperature, and blood was drawn every fifteen minutes. Kindheartedly Sigmund would enquire if the subject was well. Ice was added until the water reached 3°C. The lowering of the body temperature to 32°C was terrible for the experimental subject: at 32°C the subject lost consciousness. They were frozen further down to 25°C. When Rascher took charge, a large number of people were frozen to death in the bath. Between August 15, 1942, and May 1943, Sigmund had cooled down nearly 300 test subjects, of whom between 160 and 180 died.[8] After the cold bath, different types of reheating were tested: heated sleeping bags, liquor, massages, application of an electric arc, towelling, and a hot bath (the runaway winner). The majority of deaths would occur in the reheating phase of the tests such that one could interpret the death as an accident, not as a murder. In a subsequent phase, Rascher took advantage of a period of particularly bitter late winter weather to freeze Dachau subjects outdoors. For the participants it was sheer torture. In the warped logic of Himmler-pleasing, Rascher and Nini, among others, seem to have reasoned somewhat along the lines that "while German soldiers risked their lives for the Fatherland, vermin, unworthy to bear arms, remained sitting in warm concentration camps, and it was only fair that these people make their contribution to the war effort."

Emboldened, Rascher sensed that his "medical" claim to fame was that while others experimented on mice, he did so on men. Sigmund applied for a conference podium slot at the meeting on "Distress and Winter Cold" to be held at the Deutscher Hof Hotel by medical professionals on October 26–27, 1942. It did not work out well for him. But at least he had the boost of another visit on November 13, 1942, from Himmler, who, like sister Pia,[9] was interested to attend in order to watch frozen subjects being warmed up by the sexual attentions of women forced to work as prostitutes, brought over for the purpose from the brothel of KL Ravensbrück.[10] Rascher's ensuing "report" for Himmler's benefit that "intercourse greatly accelerated the subjects' temperature rise" has no ring of credibility whatsoever. Yet this "illustrious" phase of patronage was not to last. The final unravelling of the Rascher household began in March 1944, just before the "birth" of their fourth child. It came when Sigmund fell out definitively with his best friend and groomsman, Erich Schnitzler—who, significantly, was on Himmler's staff.

On Thursday and Friday, March 23 and 24, the *Völkischer Beobachter* reported that week's kidnapping and return of a three-week-old child at Munich station, giving a description of the perpetrator that matched Nini's appearance. What had prompted the mother to change her mind and go with her story to the paper(s)—and thereby cause Nini's undoing—was Nini's revealing body language. In handing over her child for a better future into Nini's safekeeping, the birth mother had received an overwhelming impression from the way the new mother moved when she departed that she was—indeed—a fraud. The birth mother, Rosina Theiss, stated, "I have a bad feeling. That woman ran as if she had stolen money." Despite Nini's having displayed an almost miraculous level of skill and speed in arranging a substitute in the timing needed to continue with the duping of her husband, the mere fact of having an enemy on Himmler's staff was to prove decisive.

Schnitzler connected the "birth" announcement with the story, brought it to Himmler's notice, and then took a full and brutal part in Nini's arrest.

Following tragic, part-comic, and histrionic scenes, Sigmund was also arrested. Both he and Nini were released on April 15, 1944, but, for once, this time they were not rehabilitated. Crucially, spending time with Nini had re-persuaded Sigmund that he really was the children's father. Following on from this, he was foolish enough to disclose this heartfelt conviction "in confidence" to three of his most trusted Dachau colleagues, who (together with sister Pia) lost no time in denouncing both Raschers to the police. Sigmund was rearrested on May 11 and taken to the SS barracks in München-Freimann. This time he was subjected to a raft of investigations that included irregularities in his travel expense accounting and in the acquisition of a potato mash business, a possible extortion involving his employee Pacholegg, a connivance in Pacholegg's "escape" from Dachau, and ambiguities in the child foistings.[11] On all charges, in Sigmund's case, nothing was proven. But innocence was not the only measure by which things operated in the Third Reich. The accusation that he had borrowed 100 Reichsmarks (a very small sum) from Pacholegg in Feldkirchen and had not yet returned it was to prove definitive. It was an illogical, but very real, Himmler "hot button." On the subject of the children, Rascher finally stated on May 17, "I had not the courage to look into the matter—I just wanted to keep up an illusion." The Gestapo—who by this time had extracted a confession from Nini and also established that her own year of birth was in fact 1893, not 1903—agreed with Sigmund, concluding by June 25, 1944, "It can be said, with respect to the child acquisitions, that the wife of Rascher was the driving energy, and the husband was the mindless tool and the sufferer."

After conducting a thorough study of Rascher's life, Siegfried Bär offers the disturbing conclusion that

> Sigmund Rascher was not a monster. His Nazi conviction was not deep. Apart from ambition, he had no outstanding mental or emotional gifts—nor even a disposition for cruelty. Rather, this author finds him to be kind and helpful. If he were alive today, he would probably be a popular physician in alternative medicine. He was not forced to do any of these experiments on living humans. He initiated and performed them of his own free will.[12]

Rascher's disgrace in Himmler's eyes was marked by his expulsion from the SS on August 5, 1944. Nini, imprisoned in Munich's Ettstraße prison, where she was bored and childless, unravelled entirely, attempting to trick and murder a prison warder (and almost succeeding in the attempt) on July 11. She had suffered a full nervous breakdown by October and in the process incurred the deep hatred of Gestapo and prison staff alike. In early November 1944, the Raschers were allowed to see each other for the final time before, on Himmler's orders, Nini was sent to Ravensbrück. She arrived there in the *Zellenbau* on November 24 as the camp population rose abruptly.[13] Rascher was sent to Buchenwald, where, in due course, he would come to be included in the group of hostages being assembled.

Rascher's utter complicity in bringing about and profiting from the worst excesses of the Third Reich places him in stark contrast with the courageous and defiant resistance of others. His incongruous presence amid a group of such (broadly) high-calibre individuals presents at one level an unsettling paradox.

14
Murderous Thoughts—and Many Reports

Okinawa, Japan

As the varied group of Buchenwald prisoners packed their very differing amounts of belongings, the war raged on in the Far East, where the story was also one of profound contrasts. The BBC's Sydney correspondent, R. W. Robson, reporting in what would prove to be the lull before the storm, remained puzzled by the apparent lack of resistance encountered by troops landing on the beaches. While he speculated about a "fatalistic resignation" on the part of the Japanese to their fate, Allied losses at sea from the period April 1–3 jumped to the alarming rate of almost five vessels a day, with 190 lives lost at sea and 410 injured in that period alone. The Japanese tally in those three days, almost exclusively claimed by kamikaze attacks, amounted to 4 destroyers, 4 attack transport vessels, 3 tank landing craft, and 3 other types, a total of 14 vessels sunk or damaged beyond repair. Of these, the only vessel not from the US Navy was the British destroyer *HMS Ulster*.[1] For naval combatants the idea that the Japanese were resigning themselves to their inevitable defeat would have appeared ludicrous.

World Leaders

At a world level, the relentless deterioration in Germany's military situation was also matched by an almost daily deterioration in the relationships between the "Big Three" Allies. April 3 was no exception. In public the BBC assiduously awarded prime-time coverage to "Marshal Stalin" and also lauded the achievements of Soviet generals Tolbukhin and Malinovsky, who "have taken close on three hundred places in a day." In a similar vein, and with masterful understatement, the BBC reported from America that

> negotiations over the representation of Poland were still going on. . . .
> Mr Stettinus in a White House statement presumed that President
> Roosevelt, Mr Churchill and Marshal Stalin were working to iron

out some of the difficulties that recently had threatened the unity of the three nations.[2]

But behind the scenes, the reality was one of relationships at a low ebb. Churchill had written to Stalin on April 1, stating that "we have not retained in the Moscow discussions the spirit of Yalta, nor indeed, at points, the letter."[3] On April 3, in a dramatic escalation, Stalin wrote to Roosevelt excoriating the silence of the British and advising the American president that he was clearly misinformed about the nature of the discussions that had taken place between the Germans and the Anglo-Americans. He presumed the same about the agreements that had been reached, and from which the Soviet command had been (pointedly) excluded, and which were of course in complete violation of the agreed policy of "unconditional surrender." "You are absolutely right," he continued, "that in connection with the affair regarding negotiations of the Anglo-American command with the German command, somewhere in Berne or some other place 'has developed an atmosphere of fear and distrust deserving regrets.'"[4] Roosevelt was furious at Stalin for impugning his integrity and instructed Admiral Leahy, chief of staff, to draft an immediate reply,[5] which, when it came, did not lack in vigour. But fears of Soviet preponderance in Europe did not stop the signature on April 3 of a final vast package of British and US aid to Russia code-named "Millpost."[6]

Berlin, Germany

On Tuesday, April 3, Hitler ordered that the V-weapons be armed with new explosives.[7] The campaign had already inflicted much loss of life over its duration. The name of these weapons is revealing. "V" stands for *Vergeltung*, meaning "retribution," a word in the common currency of the Nazi hierarchy.[8] As a further example of its use, from 1941 onwards in public broadcasts in Germany, the word *Sieg* (victory) was gradually supplanted by *Vergeltung*.[9] For the Allies it was anathema that Germans would use the language of "retribution" in a war they had so clearly initiated. But such thinking was part of the DNA of the German leadership. In a similar vein, on April 6, 1941, Hitler had given the name "Operation Punishment" to a three-day operation designed to destroy the Yugoslav capital, Belgrade, because he had taken offence at Yugoslav conduct. Flying at rooftop height, the German pilots systematically bombed the city without fear of intervention. More than seventeen thousand people were killed.[10] Hitler's desire for retribution also worked itself out powerfully in other ways as well, not least in orders for destruction of German infrastructure. At one level Hitler ordered that nothing should be left behind: a Germany that had lost the war was not worthy of any future. In an edition of the *Völkischer Beobachter* dated September 7, 1944, Hitler had commanded, in what became known as a "scorched earth policy," "Not a German stalk of wheat is to feed the enemy, not a German mouth to give him information, not a German hand to offer him help. He is to find every footbridge destroyed, every road blocked—nothing but death, annihilation and hatred will meet him."[11] This was made even clearer in the "Nero Order" of March 19, 1945. When challenged on this, Hitler would concede that what he meant by the destruction orders was that no military advantage should accrue to the enemy. Virtually the sole person in a position to provide such a challenge and not be sentenced to death for disobedience was Hitler's minister of armaments and production, Albert Speer. He stayed closer than ever to Hitler, always suggesting that lost terrain would swiftly be won back in a counteroffensive: so bridges, power installations, and factories should merely be disabled on a short-term basis to prevent Allied military advantage. Accordingly, at every level, chaos abounded. The military line of command was ordering one thing, at Hitler's behest, and the civil authorities, often with Hitler's consent, another. On April 3 Gauleiter Uiberreither from Graz wrote to Speer requesting detailed instructions concerning which armament plants in his Gau were not to be destroyed in any circumstances. Speer replied the same day,

> According to the Führer's orders of March 30th, 1945 there is to be no scorched earth. All installations and plants are to be crippled [meaning expert crippling by engineers] . . . so that the enemy will derive no military potential from them. . . . Destruction is therefore permissible only if crippling would not achieve the desired effect.

In the nineteen days between March 18 and April 7, 1945, no fewer than twelve contradictory decrees were issued on this question.[12]

Yet Hitler was by no means alone at this stage of the war in thinking murderous thoughts. When the likelihood of German surrender must have been known to most, Hitler's most loyal lieutenants continued with no small efficiency to facilitate the functioning of the Nazi machinery of death. "Working towards the Führer"[13] was in many quarters still alive and well. Among the foremost of such zealots was SS-Major Horst Kopkow, who had made a name for himself deceiving the British by using captured parachute agents and their radio codes. When no longer needed, they were executed without trial. The month of April saw the Gestapo continue to exert its power and murder four more captured agents: two SIS men, one from MI9, and one from the SOE. New research has suggested that the modus operandi in Berlin for such matters was for Kopkow to prepare the documentation and for RSHA IV chief Müller to sign it off, informing Himmler and Kaltenbrunner of his actions.[14] This is a revealing hint in seeking to understand and frame the events of April 5 concerning Bonhoeffer that would very soon take place.

London, England

April 3 was the day on which South Africa's field marshal Smuts—seen by some as the designated leader of the UK should any misadventure befall Churchill—arrived in the UK by air to take part in the British Commonwealth talks, due to open in London the next day.[15] In London the midnight BBC news was read by Joseph Macleod. In the style of the hour, bulletins were produced in the first-person plural form, using "we" and "our" for descriptions of British Allied progress:

> After another good day Field Marshal Montgomery's forces are only twenty-five miles from the Zuyder Zee. In north west Germany we've captured Münster; we're in Osnabrück and Hamm and have surrounded Bielefeld. Today's main news from General Patton's front is that in the south the 4th Armoured Division, pressing on from Eisenach, has reached the outskirts of Gotha, at the summit of the forest of Thuringia, less than one hundred and fifty miles from Berlin.[16]

The BBC saw clearly the role it could play in boosting morale, and not just at home. Extraordinary choices of phrasing were made. At one point, the report states that "the German remnants east of Danzig are being gradually mopped up. Over two thousand prisoners have been taken in two days."[17] Elsewhere the BBC correspondent Robert Barr reports from Hamm,[18] in Germany, that "Ninth Army gunners have already dealt with two long trainloads of troops and armour which tried to race out from the Hamm marshalling yards. Both trains were spotted and the gunners blasted the carriages from the rails at point blank range." In another section the report states that "it's now possible to count up the disasters facing the Germans all along this northern flank of the West front." The upbeat, at times only hazily accurate,[19] and motivational style of reporting was not confined to

Anglo-American reports of progress; detailed and fulsome accounts of Russian advances, as indicated above, were scrupulously afforded similar treatment. As the Soviets exacted on a daily basis an horrific and much-merited revenge on all things German, with scenes of rape and pillage an everyday occurrence, the BBC reported with enthusiasm that "their armies have collected twenty three thousand prisoners and rich booty."

Aschaffenburg, Germany

Finally, on April 3 the German leadership in Aschaffenburg surrendered to Captain Felix Sparks. The German combat commander, who had over-seen the hangings of other civilians and soldiers who attempted surrender, gave himself up. His sense of honour did not extend to self-sacrifice and he walked safely into American captivity. In their defence of the town, the Germans had suffered more than five thousand casualties. At least a thousand were killed. It was a heavy price to pay for useless ground. The US regiment had lost two hundred men, ninety from Sparks' battalion alone. Eleven officers had been killed. When the Americans entered the town, they saw civilians still swinging from lamp-posts above the bodies of twelve- and thirteen-year-old boys on the ground below.[20] The fanatical resistance shocked the American High Command. No less than secretary of war Henry L. Stimson told reporters, "Nazi fanatics used the visible threat of two hangings to compel German soldiers and civilians to fight for a week." Many of the soldiers felt they had passed a point of no return. "I didn't feel sorry for any Germans after Aschaffenburg," recalled Ser-geant Rex Raney, who had fought all the way from Sicily. "When women and kids hold you off, war takes on a different atmosphere." But even amid such trauma, there were some hopeful indicators, signs that a return to common sense, despite orders to the contrary, was slowly beginning to take hold. As the soldiers pressed onwards through villages, from every window there seemed to hang crisp white sheets.[21]

Gotha, Germany

In Germany itself the exuberance evident in the BBC news reports was largely absent. On April 3, among one American armoured division approaching the town of Gotha was a war correspondent, the Jewish novelist Meyer Levin. He later recalled how he and his companions came across some "cadaverous refugees" along the road. "They were like none we have ever seen," Levin writes, "skeletal . . . feverish sunken eyes, shaven skulls." They identified themselves as Poles and asked Levin and the others to come to the site where they had been prisoner. They spoke of "people buried in a big hole" and a "Death Commando."[22] Much more was to be revealed. A radio message decrypted by Bletchley Park on April 3 from Mauthausen concentration camp talks of a "surprise change in the situation" and reports 8,976 prisoners as marching back to Mauthausen from the Vienna area, with 3,147 Jews already arrived from the south-eastern area and another 3,500 to follow.[23] The death marches proliferated.

Bad Orb, North-East of Aschaffenburg, Germany

People were marched and starved in their hundreds of thousands, but some were saved. Troops from General Patch's army, as well as those under the command of General Patton, liberated another Allied POW camp, reported to hold twenty thousand prisoners. By April 3 nearly seven thousand had been freed, about half of them Americans.[24]

Mainz, Germany

Only some twenty kilometres further west, SS-Brigadier and General-major der Polizei Walther Hille and his ranking equivalent in Hannover received clear orders on April 3 from RFSS Himmler for the operations of order police in their respective areas:

(1) At this stage of the war, only a stubborn unyielding will can persevere.
(2) Severe measures are to be taken against the hanging out of white towels, opening of anti-tank traps, non-appearance of the Volkssturm and similar phenomena.
(3) From any house which shows a white flag, all male inhabitants are to be shot. There will be no delay.[25]

But this apparent decisiveness was not the only message Himmler was transmitting that day. Others received orders that to any recipient must have seemed, at best, bewildering. One example of such a command was sent on April 3, 1945: "Do not constantly ask for orders, but act."[26] A string of Bletchley Park decrypts of commands sent by Himmler from the period April 1–9 leave a conflicted, schizophrenic impression on the reader.[27] Meanwhile murderous deeds continued apace. On April 3 in Graz prison, Michael O'Hara, an undercover Allied agent captured on his second mission whose German name was Berliner, was collected and driven to the SS rifle range at Wetzelsdorf and shot, after torture.[28]

Münster, Germany

Outside Münster the BBC's correspondent Wynford Vaughan Thomas was assigned to report from alongside front-line troops. His report, much redacted prior to broadcast, captured a sense of the tragedy of war and the desperate dilemma engendered by orders such as those being issued by Himmler that now faced both civilians and soldiers.[29]

Kiel, Germany

But, at least for the Allies, there was genuine cause for hope. The tide was truly turning. In the war at sea and in the air in Europe, Allied losses continued to be distinctly lower than those sustained by German armed forces, as Allied air power in particular continued to prove overwhelming. The BBC reported that "Kassel has been occupied. . . . Our Lancasters bombed troop concentrations to the east of Kassel today and hundreds of American heavies attacked U-boat yards at Kiel." The broadcast explained that "submarine building yards at Kiel were attacked today by about seven hundred and fifty Flying Fortresses escorted by more than six hundred and fifty Mustangs. One bomber and three fighters are missing." In a recent and more detailed analysis of this latter encounter, it is now calculated that the respective numbers on this occasion did indeed prove decisive: approximately seven hundred aircraft from the US 8th Air Force dropped 2,200 tons of bombs on Kiel's harbour infrastructure.[30]

Hela, Germany

In the light of this onslaught, German forces who obtained safe passage (if anything could be considered so) to the West knew of their great good fortune. Soldier Guy Sajer wrote,

> On the evening of April 1st [Ed: must be April 3] we boarded a large ship—my eyes gaped at all the magnificent and barely-faded details inside that elegant ship. In the darkness, our boat pressed forward. We scarcely dared think of the good fortune that had saved us—and that troubled us. For two days [Ed: must be April 5] our boat slid across the sea, toward the unbelievable West, which we had dreamed of for so long, where we could not imagine the war. We learned that our ship was the Pretoria, and although we were only allowed a small space on the bridge, lashed by wind and rain, the sweetness of the moment made us forget food and drink.[31]

Dorf an der Enns, Austria

But in the "unbelievable" West, millions were fleeing the advance of Soviet troops. In her diary that day, Missie Vassiltchikov, travelling with her friend Sisi Wilczek, wrote about the rigid station controls they underwent before boarding the last train to leave Vienna, before all remaining rail communications were severed:

> [It] was, naturally, packed. We departed punctually. The train crawled. At noon, shortly after Krems, we crept into a tunnel and remained there 6 hours while enemy bombers battered Krems to pieces.[32]

Vassiltchikov writes of her friend,

> In addition to her rucksack and other odd bags, Sisi hugs to her bosom a parcel the size of a shoe box. It contains a million marks and as many Czech Kronen—in fact, the entire cash fortune of the Wilczech family. . . . It is bound to be a headache all the way. . . . At 2 a.m. a freight train pulled up alongside us. Sisi learned that it would be leaving ahead of us, so we decided to switch. We scrambled down, forgot the money-parcel, returned for it and boarded the freight train. . . . Our former train puffed into the station and groaned to a halt. In a jiffy we were back on it again and presently we were on our way to St Valentin, on the river Enns, the terminal station of this line.[33]

The young companions finally arrived exhausted, after travelling for more than twenty-four hours, sick with hunger, at a friend's house, half an hour's walk from the station, to breakfast and a bath. They were truly fortunate. Back in wartime Britain, the news reported that the minister of food, Colonel Llewellin, had been pleased to sign an agreement with the Canadian minister of agriculture in Ottawa. The hard-pressed nation agreed to take all the beef, bacon, ham, and eggs that Canada could supply up to the end of next year.[34]

Marktredwitz, Germany

After a fitful night in anticipation of the next day's early start, Victor and Eva Klemperer succeeded, while it was still dark, in catching a train via Falkenau, onwards to Eger.[35] There had been low-flying aircraft everywhere. At one point in their journey, they saw a suitable train about to depart almost immediately. But then Eva pointed to the anti-aircraft guns on the last car: "We would have been more at risk there than here." By 6:00 that evening, they were on the train to Marktredwitz, arriving there by 7:00. Klemperer writes,

> Terrible squeeze. A fat woman with a well-informed little boy was thrilled by the deeds of the Werewolves. They had shot thirty horses somewhere, and "killed three officers" added the boy. The woman sitting beside them asked, doubtfully, whether this would not also bring harm to other civilians. The Nazi cow said nothing.

For the Klemperers the dominant memory of these days was the constant torment of hunger. On arrival at their destination, they were refused accommodation at every hotel, so returned to the station, where they found lots of people, like them, begging for lodgings:

> We got soup . . . led to the Josefa convent. An infernal hall. Many beds one above the other. Crying children, drying nappies, the air blazing hot and quite suffocating, dirty, cursing women. One complained that her infant was starving, there was milk only up to six months! Another: it wasn't true that she had scabies, it was only a rash. At that, we said we preferred a night in the station waiting room.[36]

15
A Chance Find in Zossen

A chance find, with devastating consequences for the circle of resisters around Admiral Canaris, occurred on April 3 in close proximity to the German capital. Only an hour's drive south of Berlin lay the vast military complex called Zossen. It was the location of OKH headquarters. The base had experienced a particularly heavy air attack on March 15.[1] German infantry general Walther Buhle[2] was in the process of moving offices, possibly as a result of the ensuing disruption, in Zossen, when he, or his officers, made a significant find. He had heard of the links between some of the plotters and Canaris, the former Abwehr chief. The associations with the July 20 bomb added visceral substance to the dislike for Canaris that Buhle had already formed upon first acquaintance. Now, in a turn of events both remarkable and unfortunate in its timing, he came across a *Panzerschrank* (a safe reinforced with steel to a tank-like strength), which was found to contain a thick dossier of Canaris' diaries, volumes 1–5, and six files entitled "Travel Reports." In all there were between eighty and two hundred sheets of paper in each volume, handwritten and dated.[3] Knowing a little of their likely significance, instantly he had them despatched to SS-Gruppenführer Johann Rattenhuber. Rattenhuber was the head of Hitler's personal protection unit, the Reichssicherheitsdienst, in central Berlin, and would make as certain as possible that the files discovered were accorded the full attention that such a traitor merited by the injured Führer himself.[4] For his part, Rattenhuber is likely to have known well enough the consequences that would flow from handing these long-sought-after diaries to Hitler. At this moment,[5] the incarcerated writer of the diaries, edited and harmless enough as they may have been, together with Bonhoeffer and the close associates who dared with him to believe in a different Germany, had less than a week left to live.

16
Departure from Buchenwald

As Buhle was making his momentous discovery in Zossen, the hostage convoy, which included Bonhoeffer, was preparing to leave Buchenwald, around 280 kilometres south-west of Berlin. Just before he and the others in the group allocated to travel on the Grüne Minna were finally instructed to gather outside, Hugh Falconer made sure he achieved a further satisfying act of subversion of the murderous doctor in cell 5. The cell doors were finally opened around 8:00 p.m., and they were instructed to go upstairs to the entrance hall. Falconer hung around to make sure he was the last to proceed upstairs. A fleeting glance to his left told him what he needed to know: the camp doctor was asleep on the bed. Falconer tiptoed in and pinched his ceremonial dirk as a souvenir, then gently closed and locked the door, taking out the key. As soon as he was outside he threw it away as far as he could into the darkness. He wrote, "I like to think they had a lot of trouble getting him out."[1]

The Departure Orders Are Issued

Many of the *Prominenten* who travelled in buses transporting forty or so hostages captured impressions around the experience of departure. One of these was Fey von Hassell.[2] She expresses the tensions they all felt, resulting from both the rumours surrounding the Allied approach and also the agony of being given orders to prepare to be moved (no doubt further away from the liberating Allied troops) and then being asked to stand and wait—for what felt like interminable periods:

> April 1st—circa. Once again the rumble of guns is coming close. According to our resident "expert" they cannot be more than 25 kilometres away. We become intensely anxious. Will we be rescued by the Americans? Or will we be whisked once more out of their reach? At 3.00 in the afternoon of April 3rd the dreaded order comes; "Pack your bags! Bring only what you can hold on your laps!"

A fellow member of the *Prominenten* group, Marie-Gabriele Stauffenberg,[3] agrees with Hassell about the timing of the departure order: she
writes, "Tuesday 3rd April. Large loads of washing. At 3.00 told to be ready
to leave in an hour. Great stir. Americans only 43 km away." But the afternoon passed slowly. The actual time of departure came late into the evening.
She later notes the time of departure as "11.00 pm: drive off in a convoy
comprising 2 buses, one Grüne Minna and one car." In agreement with her,
Hassell notes,

> The afternoon comes and goes, but there is still no sign of our immi-
> nent departure.[4] It is already nightfall when the SS troops in charge
> of our transport march into the courtyard. Three grey buses pull up
> outside. Out of one steps a tall slender figure, a man of about thirty-
> five, dressed in SS grey, wearing black boots and black leather gloves.
> He screams at us to stop complaining. The other officer seems more
> human. We are pushed violently into the three buses, in the most
> contorted positions. . . . The buses move off slowly through the camp
> amidst the ranks of hollow-eyed, emaciated Buchenwald prisoners.[5]

Isa Vermehren[6] was a cabaret singer who, as a known opponent of
National Socialism, had been set to work with the outbreak of war by the
Nazi authorities to provide musical entertainment to serving soldiers.
She became the (reluctant) Vera Lynn of Germany. When her family
were arrested under the *Sippenhaft* measures, she too was incarcerated.
Like Stauffenberg, Vermehren also noted the actual departure time, and
includes it in her book *Reise durch den letzten Akt*, which was published in
Germany in 1946 and which became an instant bestseller. In it she offers
insightful commentary on the moment:

> At 11:30 in the evening, from out of a dozy, half-awake state of waiting,
> the shrill blast of a military whistle shocks us back into the present. . . .
> Suddenly distinguishing itself from the crowd of armed SS men emerges
> the figure of our new transport leader, a true prototype and embodi-
> ment of his species . . . slender, long-legged, with narrow hips and broad
> shoulders. His face is tanned, his jaw strong, two sharp creases hover
> around his tight-lipped mouth, his leathery skin is stretched a little too
> tightly over high cheekbones, and from beneath the peak of the pushed-
> back cap he is wearing at a tilted angle, below black eyebrows, dart two
> piercing, small, dark eyes. His whole appearance reconfirms the often-
> made observation that these young SS officer types, imbued as they
> are with their sense of being the new superior class, are also intensely

concerned to make their own all distinguishing features of the old, including particularly carrying oneself elegantly and in a natural, self-assured manner, second nature to those who truly have it. As in most cases, his attempt is a comprehensive failure, for he too proves unaware that in order to achieve true elegance, above all intelligence and particularly modesty are prerequisites, and not merely a well-tailored uniform. His unpleasant face has a callousness that knows what killing is. As so often in these recent weeks and months, we are seized in this moment of our departure by an awareness of quite how much fear human beings can engender in one another, simply by the sheer level of disdain with which they treat others. These encounters with serving SS invariably smack of something profoundly and shockingly unnatural—or is someone doing what comes naturally, if they act as though another person is non-human? The phrase "non-human" does not remotely do sufficient justice to the level of disdain and contempt in question: the other is not only non-human, this other can purely and simply not be communicated with, and that which is now definitively beyond reach. I can even speak with a dog, with an animal, and as I address it, I make it part of a dialogue, I draw it as something that relates to me into the circle of connection with my person, and in so doing I acknowledge and recognise an ultimate bond. In meetings between prisoners and SS, absolutely none of this was present, and it is almost as though one needs to speak of an "ultimate contempt" [*Zerachtung*] to illustrate the annihilation of the other brought about by this attitude. For our departure by night, considering the circumstances, an extraordinary contingent of troops is assembled: right from the door all the way behind the wall to the street through to the buses, at two-metre intervals on both sides of the path stand guards with loaded machine guns. We are called forward individually by name and have to present ourselves to the transport leader. The intermittent light of a covered torch guides us along the bumpy path to the vehicle. Everything happens quietly, with hushed voices, so that the hum of enemy aircraft and the rumble of the approaching front become even more audible. There is scarcely room in the vehicle for all the luggage, the many prisoners, and the numerous guards. The squeeze in the vehicle is accentuated by the fact that on the outside the windows have been painted over, so that no one can see in. Thank God for bribery![7] Under such circumstances it almost becomes a virtue, and where on earth would we have been if it had not come to our aid! A couple of hours and a few cigarettes later we know that Regensburg is our destination—where an SS weapons training school is supposed to receive us. How good as well that there are rumours! Because we can't see out, such snippets help us pass the time, and then in the end we get the agreeable surprise concerning whether or not they are false. In fact we arrive in Regensburg after a twelve-hour journey.[8]

Léon Blum,[9] displaced from the luxury version of Buchenwald's prisoner accommodation, wrote an account of the journey, describing it as an "exodus under the cover of darkness":

On April 3—Easter Tuesday—the final departure order comes down, even though I had been exempted from it on Easter Monday. It is already evening when my wife and I are summoned. At 8:30 p.m. the SS come and carry me to the car, which is waiting some metres from the house. It is already dark and raining. The car is neither an ambulance nor a big car and has only four seats. It is impossible for me to stretch out. The problem is solved by putting me on the seat and lying me there. I am really suffering but will not mention it again. After a short way we stop in a clearing. Shadows equipped with lanterns give off a mist and circle around us beneath the rain. One large bus emerges from the shadows, its lights dimmed, then another, then a third. Shadows gather around each bus. Our driver, SS of course, stays at the wheel, and while the buses are filled up the other drivers come over to confer with him. They step out of the buses, discussing the route. I overhear the name Jena, then Nuremberg. Of course: the southern redoubt. But who are our fellow travellers? We know that two to three weeks beforehand, Buchenwald had hosted some evacuated civil servants from among SS staff, but quickly we learn these are other prisoners emerging after long months from the depth of the cells of Buchenwald. It's 11:00 when we depart. We drive slowly through the night, headlamps extinguished. We stop at every junction. At every stage the convoy separates and reforms, after interminable delays. We advance through Weimar, half-flattened by bombing. As soon as there is any glow of light in the sky, we discern moving shapes: it is an exodus under cover of darkness. Alone or in groups, weighed down with bags, dragging child-sized shapes behind them, these spectres reach the road—and vanish.[10]

As these accounts indicate, the hostages, depending upon their category and fitness, were spread across a variety of vehicles. The *Sippenhäftlinge*, or *Prominenten*, were fitted into the buses. The Mercedes took Bader, the *Kommandoführer* (transport leader), and the Blums. Bonhoeffer found himself in the group allocated to the Grüne Minna, whereupon they all crowded into a prison vehicle equipped with a wood burner, and had to share what limited room there was with their combustible fuel. Sixteen[11] prisoners and their luggage were crammed into the vehicle, one designed for at most eight people. The discomfort felt by all the occupants was no doubt mixed with irritation at the conduct of the former British spy, Payne Best, whose contribution towards travelling light and space-saving worked in precisely the opposite direction: he would not be parted from his suitcase, a typewriter, and three large cartons.[12] Aside from Bonhoeffer, and the further twelve mentioned in the introduction, the other passengers at this stage were Josef Müller, Ludwig Gehre, and Franz Liedig. All had been in Buchenwald. Payne Best clearly spent much of the cramped journey keeping a detailed diary. His account has the Grüne Minna party setting off earlier, which in view of the slower speed of the vehicle may have been the case:

> It is 10 in the evening before we get the order to move. . . . We have just got settled when the alarm sounds, and all the military personnel bolt for the wide open spaces leaving us securely locked in. After the all clear the engine starts and we moved a hundred yards or so and then come to a standstill with the engine still running. Fumes fill the van and Rascher calls out "My God this is a death van, we are all being gassed." Opposite me a glimmer of light appears through a ventilator and I ask Rascher whether they had such things in gas chambers, and he replies No—and in that case we are probably all right. After a time we start moving and gradually some of the fumes clear from the van, though they remain pretty bad throughout our journey. . . . It proves a hell of a journey. . . . The wood generator does not seem able to propel the car at more than an average of fifteen miles per hour and every hour we have to stop while the flues are cleaned and the generator refilled with fuel. . . . We jog and joggle along through the night, running an hour and stopping an hour, stiff, tired, hungry, thirsty. . . .[13]

Bonhoeffer's party had a very uncomfortable time of it, presumably cursing Best and his luggage, so much so that even Hassell, who was in the (separate) bus with the *Prominenten*, comments, "This group had a dreadful journey to Regensburg. The van was divided into tiny cages in which one could barely sit without bending over double. There were no windows or openings, and every lurch of the van flung one uncontrollably around the cage. How comfortable our journey had been by comparison."[14]

An Awkward Conversation

Josef Müller's account of that night's uncomfortable journey includes the harshest criticism we have on record of Bonhoeffer's prior conduct under interrogation. As outlined in the prologue, both men had been imprisoned and repeatedly interrogated since April 5, 1943, without recourse to any external support or colleagues at this point. The criticism comes as part of the following (almost equally) uncomfortable conversation, which Müller records:

> Vasily Kokorin and I take turns sitting one on top of the other. The wood-smoke generator has to be replenished every hour, so that the space available to us gradually increases, even though it is still an oppressive squeeze. . . . The jail vehicle trundles south at a speed of about 30 km/hr. Although the intensity of supervision by the guards has been increased, we still succeed in having whispered conversations during this nocturnal trip. Of course I use the opportunity and work my way towards ending up sitting next to Bonhoeffer. . . . Bonhoeffer had linked up via his brother-in-law Hans von Dohnanyi with Oster, Canaris, and Beck,[15] and with my agreement was assigned to Abwehr duties at the Munich office. In reality Oster's prime concern was for Bonhoeffer to facilitate links with churches overseas and afford him freedom of operation in the wider resistance struggle of the Christian denominations. Bonhoeffer being an early champion of the ecumenical cause, I saw to it that he was granted admission for long periods in the Benedictine abbeys of Ettal and Metten in order to study and experience monastic life, above all from the perspective of whether Protestant churches should develop such institutions for the formation of the next generation of their clergy. . . . At Oster and Dohnanyi's request he accompanied me several times to Rome. . . . Towards Colonel Beck, Bonhoeffer's journeys were positioned as their purpose being for Bonhoeffer to use his relationships with numerous international dignitaries for gathering information about their views and judgements, thereby acquiring valuable and reliable intelligence for the Abwehr. I recall the searching question of the Admiral [Canaris] in the hallway of the dungeon in Prinz-Albrecht-Straße: "Did Dohnanyi inculpate me?"—I had been unable to provide a clear answer as I had been unable to speak with him since the start of our time in military custody. Now I want to understand from Bonhoeffer what he knows of Dohnanyi's statements. He is of the opinion that his brother-in-law is less adept than myself at dealing with these people, [that] he

does not have the temperament or the knowledge of the terrain they inhabit to indulge their craft. Then I ask Bonhoeffer how he justified his [Abwehr] exemption from military service as "indispensable to the war effort" to the [interrogating] SD. He could easily and simply have referred them to me, as in relation to these henchmen it would have been credible that I had requested him for the difficult work I was undertaking. So I ask, "What did you say?"—"They put me under pressure," he replies. "They threatened me that they would go after my fiancée. So I said I had 'indispensable to the war effort [*unabköm-mlich*]' status to build up an internal reporting service for Oster." Now that was exactly the wrong thing to say [as it was a major violation of the working agreement between Canaris' Abwehr and Heydrich's RSHA]. . . . "Dietrich" I say to my friend, "That will never do. Why did you not use me as your cover—? I could have handled it. I guarantee, Ficht[16] would have covered for me." "They pressurised me," he repeats, "My fiancée . . ."[17]

Curiously, this admission of human frailty on Bonhoeffer's part, published in 1975, was omitted from Bethge's biography, for reasons that are unknown. It works at two levels: first, we see evidence here that Bonhoeffer did not have every right answer throughout the extreme duress of his many interrogations, and second, that when his fiancée, Maria, was threatened, the Gestapo had found his point of vulnerability.

Travelling in Close Proximity

Hugh Falconer writes with wry humour and compassion about the enforced intimacy of the mixed group in such a confined space and his unceasing attempts to undermine this part of the German war effort:

With Heidel [Nowakowski] there are now two women to suffer from the vapours . . . and this keeps our vapour-prone quota of travellers fainting from the fumes up to three [in a separate passage Falconer explains how the only thing to be done when people faint is just to lay them out along peoples' knees].[18] . . . Most of us never get near the fresh air supply at all. . . . At about midnight, at the first refuelling stop on the edge of a wood, we put up a strong plea for the women to travel in the escort car but Stiller, our escort commander, is having none of it. "There is no room" he says. Heidi remarks that she would be perfectly happy sitting on someone's knee, reasonably pointing out that in her profession that was where she is accustomed to sit anyway if there are any men around—but Stiller is adamant. While this argument is going on I try very hard to puncture a tyre with my invaluable six-inch nail, but this time it lets me down. This and subsequent halts are substantially prolonged by a simple procedure involving the exigencies of nature. As we are about to embark, one of us who has previously scorned Stiller's suggestion to profit by the interlude, would suddenly feel a sudden and undeniable urge to step behind the bushes. By the time this incontinence has affected half a dozen of us, a good twenty minutes of additional fresh air has been enjoyed by all.[19]

Fey von Hassell picks up the story of unwanted intimacy from the point of view of the *Prominenten* bus:

> On several occasions the drivers have to ask for directions. During these stops, we are desperate to relieve ourselves, but they forbid us with threats: "Don't act so important! We could just as well treat you quite differently!" But Maria Hammerstein won't let herself be intimidated in that way. Her voice assumes a slightly military tone: "If you don't let me get out right away, I'll give you a stream right in the middle of this bus." The men act as though they haven't heard her. Thereupon, she squeezes herself vigorously between us and the luggage and throws herself against the SS guards with such force that they lose their balance. So they give in. A guard climbs out behind her and aims his gun at her until she is finished. They now allow us to get out, one after the other. During one of these stops we notice that a car is following us with two people under SS guard. We recognize Léon Blum and his wife, who wave at us furtively. Behind them is a Grüne Minna stuffed full of people.[20]

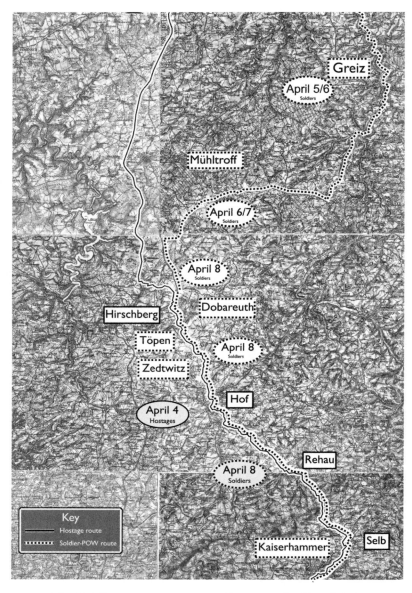

Fig. 17-1. Berga route convergence: Hostages and soldiers/POWs
Staatsbibliothek zu Berlin-Kartenabteilung/Bruce Bovill

17
Unbeknown Companions: US Soldiers Close By

As they travelled onwards, the thought of a possible rescue was never far from their minds. Everyone in the convoy, guard and hostage alike, had heard the sound of the approaching conflict in these recent days. The closest any soldiers came to them before they were moved out of reach was the distance between Erfurt and Buchenwald, around twenty-three kilometres. For many weeks now, the prisoners had been anxious to know how close the Americans were. Unbeknown to them, as they travelled throughout the small hours of this Tuesday night, the convoy passed within a mere twelve kilometres of a substantial detachment of US soldiers, almost 350 men, being kept in a small village called Berga. They are likely to have been the closest any US soldiers came to Dietrich Bonhoeffer.

But these were not the US soldiers the hostages were looking to for rescue, because these soldiers, like them, were captives, and had been so since December, when they had been seized in the initial phase of the German advance in the Ardennes. The "Schwalbe" camp at Berga, a relatively unknown small town in what would soon become East Germany, had now quietly become the scene of the most intense killing of American prisoners of war in Europe. The US military, in their wisdom, saw to it that every soldier was issued with a "dog tag" that, conveniently for the Germans, identified the wearer's religion. The US soldiers in question were mainly Jewish, or perhaps looked Jewish, and had been singled out on the basis of race and actively subjected to the full brutality of the Nazi regime.

The Berga Slave Camp
Since February these POWs had been starved, insulted, tortured, harried, deprived of any rights, withheld medical treatment, and forced to work impossible hours as slave labourers. In a curious twist of fate, as the liberating troops drew closer, this entire contingent, with no rations, were all harried south on a grim death march. Many were shot. Its route

closely matches that of Bonhoeffer and the other hostages, but they were four days behind. On April 3 one of these captured POWs, Tony Acevodo, wrote in his diary, "Excellent news today. Americans are only 100 kilometres from here. Rumours are we are to be moved away." Another POW, Johann Kasten, escaped, was recaptured, and was beaten senseless. In addition to the maltreatments already mentioned, he tells of one day in early April when three prisoners were invited into a room where a large bowl of rice and raisins sat on a table. The Germans asked them to sign a letter saying they had all been well treated at the prison. "In front of this pile of rice, I would have signed anything," Kasten said. They did sign, but using phoney serial numbers, and were regaled not only with rice, but with a bottle of Sekt. Kasten saved the label from the bottle, making a note of the date and where they were.[1]

By way of contrast, at least the more fortunate passengers in the Grüne Minna received scraps of food, and even occasional meals, and had a roof to sleep under. It was not so with these literally starved other captives who, when not being harried onwards at gunpoint, slept in unforgiving conditions, huddled in ditches at the roadside. The soldiers in question may indeed have been American—but for Bonhoeffer and his companions there was no rescue to be had at the broken hands of these skeletal, now unrecognisable, erstwhile troops. Indeed, the plight of these unfortunate soldiers only serves to highlight the relative privilege that the famished hostages were afforded.

18

The Hostage Journey Continues

Peering through slats or cracks between the blacked-out windows, many hostages made an effort to note the route taken by the convoy. Stauffenberg was one of them. She notes,

> Drive all night long. Jena[1]—Hof—Weiden in der Oberpfalz. Convoys and Wehrmacht barricades everywhere. Insolent guards who treat one like a criminal. Outside Hof on the Autobahn. Wait for hours on the outskirts of the city for one of the other buses, then on to Wunsiedel. A longer stop there. Little groups can use an outhouse in the backyard under close supervision. Rest stops in the forest for breakfast and lunch.[2]

Another was Müller. He writes about the subject of the guards' attentiveness, but from a different perspective:

> At first light our prison van nears Hof en route to Bavaria, not far from my home, and I give serious consideration to the possibility of escape. In the Franken woods, in the vicinity of Steinwiesen, was a forester who I would have been able to hide with, but we could not get away from the vehicle.[3] Our guards have a dog, which stands over us with teeth bared, every time we step out.[4]

Léon Blum had a keener sense of orientation than most and also kept a detailed record of the route:

> We pass Jena . . . In order to join the motorway south towards Nuremberg and Munich, we need to take a right turn, but instead continue straight ahead, travelling east. What does this mean? I try to glimpse sight of a road sign as we travel on. The night proves long, and I succeed in getting my bearings only at daybreak.[5]

Payne Best's prolific notes included not only details of the route but also his recollection of a conversation with Bonhoeffer, amid all the claustrophobic discomfort of the Grüne Minna. The exchange may well have been in English, a language in which Bonhoeffer was fluent:

> When we left Buchenwald he sat for a time next to me in the prison van. He told me then how happy prison had made him. He had always been afraid that he would not be strong enough to stand such a test but now he knew there was nothing in life of which one need ever be afraid. He also expressed complete agreement with my view that our warders and guards needed pity far more than we and that it was absurd to blame them for their actions.[6]

In the context of his complete castigation at Müller's hands, Bonhoeffer may well have been relieved to find in Best a more amenable conversation partner. Indeed, despite the cramped conditions and relative privations, there would be some consolations ahead.

Wednesday, April 4, 1945

19

Hermann Pünder and Vasily Kokorin

Throughout the day on April 4, the hostages continued their weary journey towards Regensburg. This chapter introduces more fully two group members of very different ages and nationalities, Hermann Pünder and Vasily Kokorin.

Hermann Pünder

When Hermann Pünder was born on Sunday, April 1, 1888, in Trier, Rhineland-Palatinate, Germany, his father, also Hermann, was forty-seven and his mother, Maria, was thirty-one. His older brother was called Werner. Ten years later his young sister Marianne was also born on April 1; they shared more than a common birthday and would always be close.[1] Hermann attended school in Bad Münstereifel and went on, as had his father and older brother, to study law. He attended law schools in Freiburg im Breisgau, Berlin, and London, graduating as a doctor of jurisprudence in 1911. He served with distinction for the duration of World War I. In 1919 he became a senior official in the Reich Ministry of Finance. On May 8, 1920, he married Magdalena Statz in Düsseldorf's cathedral, the "Bilker Dom." They had four children together—Adelheid, Hermann, Wilfried, and Tilman—between 1926 and 1933. This period of fruitfulness corresponded with one of workplace success: Pünder was promoted to the post of Germany's state secretary from 1926 to 1932. In this capacity he worked in the Reich Chancellery, serving under three chancellors. But things would change. Pünder could not tolerate conduct he considered to demonstrate a lack of integrity. Rather than continuing under the dubious arrangements surrounding Franz von Papen's cabinet, he resigned when the latter took office on May 30, 1932. The regime did not take kindly to the sensed criticism. On grounds of political unsuitability, Pünder was then ousted from his subsequent role as president of the administrative district of Münster. He was forced into early retirement. Pünder took to

farming a smallholding and stood aside from the events of the 1930s. One
upside to this enforced early retirement was that "quality time" with family became associated with the children's formative years. Another was
that the rare distinction of being anti-Nazi without initially experiencing
persecution was achieved. But that could not last.

When war came, as a decorated World War I veteran, Pünder enlisted.
He was assigned to the army reserve in 1939, and was promoted to the
rank of major. But the failure of the July 20 plot in 1944 meant that things
would change again. In the post–coup attempt round-up, Pünder, along
with many others, was arrested. He was apparently deemed by the regime
to be of questionable political loyalty. He was imprisoned in Berlin's
Prinz-Albrecht-Straße building. During his protracted times spent in
interrogations, he was not physically tortured but was constantly threatened. He appeared before the Volksgerichtshof on December 20, 1944,
and, unusually, was cleared of all charges on the basis of insufficient evidence. In a pattern that was also customary for the Gestapo in such circumstances, he was instantly rearrested and returned to prison without
any further charges being brought or any information being provided
about any further hearings or possible release. He was informed that
the Volksgerichtshof ruling did not affect the Gestapo and on January 2,
1945, was transferred to a concentration camp he names as Frostenberg
(Fürstenberg). Pünder believed the location of this sub-camp to be north
of Berlin. During his incarceration here, he could not help but hear at
close proximity the terrible sounds emanating from daily beatings being
administered by camp guards, mostly female.[2] He was moved to Buchenwald a month later. Pünder formed an instant connection with Bonhoeffer and kept some of the most reliable records of any of the hostage group
members. The connection formed was sufficient to inspire the subsequent
provision of copious amounts of information, in due course, to Bonhoeffer's biographer Bethge, and a lifetime of generosity in this respect that
would endure for more than a generation. The reasons for his inclusion in
the VIP hostage party, as with others, are unknown.

Vasily Kokorin

Few others of Bonhoeffer's entourage have been so repeatedly misrepresented, and for so long, as Kokorin. His status as an impostor has become
so well established that the revelation of his deception is likely to meet
with some levels of disbelief. I remain deeply thankful to the generous
Russian colleagues, named in the acknowledgements section, who have

contributed to the project of establishing the information that follows. The story of Bonhoeffer's final week and of his "learning Russian" with Kokorin can now be better understood.

The true nature of circumstances behind and leading up to Kokorin's encounter with Bonhoeffer are set out here (in detail) for the first time in English, following Ian Sayer and Jeremy Dronfield's *Hitler's Last Plot*.

Kokorin was born in impoverished circumstances in 1923 in the village of Moloki, a village situated in the Kumensky District, which itself lies within the Kirov Region of the Soviet Union. Nothing more is known to the author of his early life.[3] While in captivity he mentions an aunt, Tanja Hanonjeko, and having been born in Bronivka, which may be a fabrication. According to the Soviet journalist Leonid Mlechin, Kokorin's story is documented[4] from the moment on March 6, 1942, when the brigade in which he served, the 1st Soviet Air Brigade, was abandoned to the rear of the 16th German Army as those forces pressed on towards Leningrad. The brigade, otherwise left to their own devices, were assigned the mission of retaking the city of Demyansk. This was no small task: the fighting around the town of Demyansk proved one of the longest encirclement battles of the war, stretching from February 1942 to February 1943. In this vast objective they failed, and the paratroopers settled into the woods, leading a guerrilla-war existence. Soon German air raids began, supporting the actions of the Nazi ground units. The fighters began to suffer heavy losses, food and ammunition were running out, aircraft from deeper within Russian territory did not arrive, and for once, Göring's Luftwaffe delivered on a crucial resupply of the German forces.[5]

By the middle of March, Kokorin had developed severe frostbite. With the resulting loss of feeling in both legs, he could move only by shuffling along on his knees. Cut off, he decided to break out and back through to his own people, but in his condition did not want to risk the swim across the Paul river, by now beyond the front line. He crawled about two kilometres into the depths of the forest and crouched alongside the road. On April 9 Kokorin's brigade commander, Lieutenant Colonel Tarasov, surrendered the entire brigade to the Germans, and it was here at the roadside that on April 11 he was captured by German forces. But their surrender brought no relief. It was hardly better than living rough; the conditions in which he was held in captivity were utterly appalling. Medical assistance was non-existent, and Kokorin, by now desperate, and for understandable reasons of self-preservation, soon decided to take a dangerous step. One month later he told the camp commandant that his mother, Olga

Mikhailovna Skryabina, was the sister of the USSR People's Commissar for Foreign Affairs, Vyacheslav Mikhailovich Molotov, whose real name was Skryabin.[6] At the same time, he added three years to his real age and also promoted himself to the rank of lieutenant, and into the position of special officer under the commander of the North-Western Front, Colonel General Kurochkina.

It was a brilliant strategy. Strangely, despite also having in captivity Kokorin's commanding officer, Tarasov, the Germans somehow did not think to check out the story with him. The very next day, he was taken back to Demyansk. There an assembled team of ten German officers peered at Kokorin, comparing his face with a photograph of Molotov. It was the almost miraculous turning point in Kokorin's story. Clearly the Germans were open to the idea and possibility, the concept that they had by great good fortune captured someone special. The conclusion of the "experts" was unanimous—it was similar. However, immediately there were follow-up questions: Where did he live and study? When and where did he last see his "uncle"? Kokorin replied that he had met with Molotov in the Kremlin on March 12, after receiving news of an assignment to the North-Western Front. Referring to this (spurious) conversation, the new "nephew" stated that the military policy of the USSR was to "push the German troops back to the borders of 1941 and then seek peace terms with Hitler." By now waxing lyrical, he continued, "Thereafter, following a period of around 10–20 years, the USSR would re-arm and, in violation of treaty obligations, would attack Germany in order to achieve its destruction." It was a concocted story of sufficient feasibility to sustain and continue the mutually welcome deception of his captors.

Now that he was a prize captive and attracting special treatment as the relative of a high-ranking Soviet leader, Kokorin's wounds were treated. He was provided with fresh clothing and sent to a hospital. There a German officer visited him and, showing him a leaflet with the image of two prisoners of war, asked him to identify them. It was a further golden opportunity, one that could not be missed. Kokorin's reply, hedging his bets somewhat, was that he seemed to have seen one of them somewhere. At this the officer exclaimed, pointing at one of the people in the photograph, "But this is your cousin Gregory. And you must know the other?" quizzed the helpful German. At this crucial moment, Kokorin's intuition kicked in: "I know him and have seen him several times. This is Yakov Dzhugashvili, Stalin's son." This time Kokorin, warming to his theme, despite having lived all his life in a remote Vyatka village, had guessed correctly. At this the officer left, saying farewell until their next meeting, when the "brother" would be present—a meeting that would take place in Berlin.

It took some time, around two months, until July 1942, for Kokorin to be transferred to the German capital. When he arrived there, he fell ill with typhus and hence was left to languish in hospital. During that time, mercifully, his frostbitten toes were amputated, and he was able to recover his strength somewhat. Upon his release from medical care, he was incarcerated in the relative comfort of the small prison in Berlin-Charlottenburg in a section reserved for special prisoners. On January 13, 1943, Kokorin was transferred to Sachsenhausen concentration camp. Kokorin was not immediately placed in the regular prison block of the camp. Upon arrival he was allocated to block "A." This consisted of three eight-room barracks with a barracks for each guard, isolated from the general concentration camp by a high wall and an internal barbed-wire fence. Here the important prisoners were kept in conditions of relative privilege. They were placed in double or single rooms, even unlocked throughout the day, and locked only after dark. After curfew many, with the permission of the commandant, could freely communicate with each other or even walk in the courtyard. Soon Kokorin, wishing to build on his success, and now further improve upon the conditions of his incarceration, turned to the German authorities.

He repeatedly made written offers to cooperate with his German captors in propaganda, intelligence, or counter-intelligence work. In this respect, once he began spying on his own countrymen for the Germans, Kokorin did not make a particular success of "developing" (or befriending with a view to extracting information from) Stalin's son Yakov Dzhugashvili, who (while having his own challenges) clearly knew an informer when he met one, and preferred solitude. By April 1943 the two had begun sharing a room. Dzhugashvili subsequently committed suicide. In December 1943 the SD officer known to Kokorin under the last name "Dedio" informed him that his proposal had been accepted. One other assignment came in June 1944: Kokorin received from the SD the assignment of "developing" the Russian state security captain Alexander Rusanov, who was kept in cell 2. Rusanov, assistant chief of the Ukrainian headquarters of the partisan movement Strokach, had been captured after straying behind enemy lines. Somewhat later, however, Kokorin's information gathering showed that Rusanov had commanded the partisan sabotage brigade near Orel and that his capture by the enemy had come as a result of the information supplied by German intelligence. In his now double agent role with Rusanov, after several days of communication Kokorin "unmasked" himself. He did this in two respects, firstly in relation to the real truth about his "family kinship" identity, and secondly in relation to the assignment he had sought and received from the Germans. Captain Rusanov, having rejoiced at his new-found "ally," then asked him if he would carry out his (Rusanov's) orders. Without hesitation Kokorin agreed, and began writing his reports on the progress of his "development assignment" to the Germans, but this time under Rusanov's direction and dictation. A double bluff had become a triple bluff.

The content of these high-stakes reports was aimed—for example—at discrediting in the eyes of the Germans the leaders of the "Russian Committee"—various future leaders of the Russian People's Liberation Army (RONA). According to Kokorin's account, provided under interrogation after the war, this complex "development" continued until November 1944, when Rusanov also apparently committed suicide. Payne Best documents Kokorin's agonised distress at this event in his cell,[7] recounting in full and at face value Kokorin's fabricated cover story and including the detail (an additional cover story) that his placement with Rusanov was done to cheer up Kokorin after his own suicide attempt. It should be noted that the fact of Rusanov's death, however it transpired, was in some ways life-saving for Kokorin. It would mean that Kokorin's treacherous secrets were still, for the moment, safe.

For all his bluffing, Kokorin still made an overwhelmingly positive impression on the hostage group as a whole. The enduring belief of the German authorities in Kokorin's cover story, despite some doubts they continued to harbour, provides one possible reason for his inclusion in the group.

Map 3 of Bonhoeffer's Germany: Chapters 20–28

Merkers	South Thuringia. Germany's central gold reserves and much more are found hidden in a mine shaft.
Ohrdruf Concentration Camp	Unimaginable scenes are witnessed as the first concentration camp is liberated.
Kassel	surrenders.
Neuengamme	(Hamburg) prisoners rise up in a futile act of resistance. None survive.
Karlsruhe	is liberated.
Kreis Neuruppin	Anton Kaindl, commandant of KL Sachsenhausen, meets with Heinrich Himmler.
Bielefeld	The town surrenders peacefully at 5:30 p.m. to sixty tanks from the 3rd US Tank Battallion.
Gütersloh	On his bicycle, Rev Karl Pawlowski, his clerical robes billowing behind him, pedals between US and German forces. A peaceful surrender ensues.
Hintenberg	Ukrainian SS guards murder forty sick prisoners before evacuating the camp.
Rødbyhavn	Evacuated German troops experience Danish kindness.
Leipzig	297 forced labour prisoners are massacred at the Thekla aircraft wing factory.
Gmunden	Missie Vassiltchikov is fortunate to secure accommodation at the Königinvilla.
Gotha	surrenders.
Weimar	In response to his courageous surrender of Gotha, Lt. Col. Gadolla is court-martialled for cowardice and shot.
Osnabrück	is captured.
Rinteln	Simpson's US 9th Army witnesses an eleventh hour reprieve. The town escapes bombardment. The Nazi regional commander and his wife commit suicide, also killing their daughter.
Harz Mountains	General Patton's 3rd Army moves into the Harz Mountains, bypassing Leipzig to the south.
Regensburg	Bonhoeffer and the hostage groups are accommodated in the local prison.

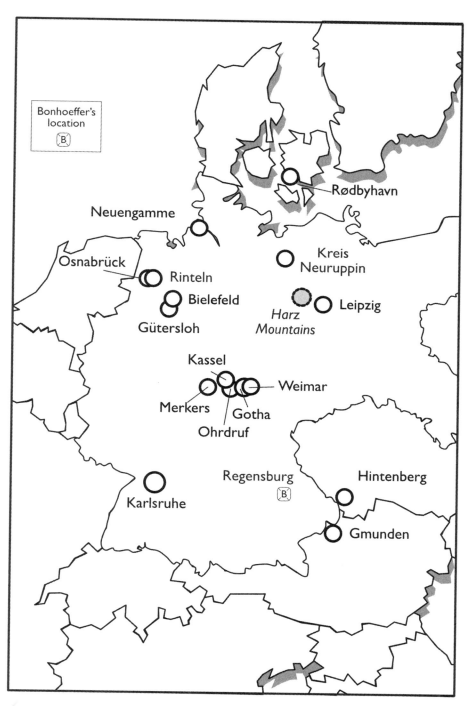

Bonhoeffer's
location
Ⓑ

Rødbyhavn

Neuengamme

Osnabrück

Kreis
Neuruppin

Rinteln

Bielefeld

Harz
Mountains

Leipzig

Gütersloh

Kassel

Weimar

Merkers

Gotha

Ohrdruf

Regensburg
Ⓑ

Hintenberg

Karlsruhe

Gmunden

Map 3 of Bonhoeffer's Germany: Chapters 20–28
Staatsbibliothek zu Berlin-Kartenabteilung/Bruce Bovill

20
A Bankrupt Nation

As the hostage group made their halting way southwards, world events unfolded around them. At one level, Wednesday, April 4, 1945, was surely one of the more memorable dates of World War II. Yet its true significance, for the most understandable of reasons, remained "masked" from public view and was almost entirely unknown at the time. It proved to be the day when Germany transitioned into fiscal bankruptcy. For many years now, Bonhoeffer had held the view that the German regime was morally and spiritually bankrupt. He was proven right, but it was of no use to him now.

When soldiers of the 90th US Division took the town of Merkers in South Thuringia, it must have seemed to them at the time just to be another regular day, another German town—and still a long way to go. But it was not so. They would soon find out that what they had just taken possession of was indeed out of the ordinary, even eye-watering, and represented a shift in world events. Such was its significance that within just three days, when senior officers inspected their find, it would rapidly justify none other than the supreme commander-in-chief of Allied forces in Europe, Eisenhower himself, taking time off from the war to come and behold it with his own eyes.

The background to this set of events was a Saturday bombing raid on Berlin that had taken place on February 3, 1945.[1] Followers of German resistance stories will recall this raid as being the very one in which the notorious Volksgerichtshof was bombed out and its ranting judge Roland Freisler killed.[2] But it was not only the infamous People's Court that was taken out in the raid. So too were the dreaded Gestapo offices on Prinz-Albrecht-Straße, as well as both the Reich Chancellery (Martin Bormann would later write to his wife about his privations) and, most importantly, the German Reichsbank itself. This building received twenty-one direct hits and was demolished. Five thousand employees spent the duration of the raid huddled in the cellar. They emerged to find a scene of utter devastation. Of paramount concern for them was that the presses used for printing banknotes had been destroyed. Equally traumatising for them was the shocking awareness that all the hoarded treasures of Hitler's Reich—the accumulated ill-gotten gains of twelve years' worth of manipulation, theft, and murder; the assets, deposits, reserves, gold and precious metals, cash, currency, and bonds, all of which were urgently needed to continue the war and survive the peace—everything now lay vulnerable and exposed. The smolten contributions from the gold fillings extracted from the mouths of every Holocaust victim now lay open in broad daylight. The strongrooms were all intact, but were vulnerable. One more bomb on target and all would be lost. Foremost among these assets were $2,596,608 that the Nazis had accumulated from the gold reserves of the Czech national bank, plus $32,000,000 from its counterpart in Hungary, as well as $200,000,000 from the respective banks of France and Belgium, together with $100,000,000 from the central bank of Italy. In the light of this devastating news, vastly complex high-security arrangements were swiftly undertaken to deposit the gold and dollar reserves in a mine at Merkers in Thuringia. It had seemed like an ideal solution at the time. Merkers lay in the heartland of central Germany and a safe two hundred miles to the south-west of Berlin. But the speed of events overtook them. In a surprise move, the 3rd Army crossed the Rhine and attacked Ludwigshafen on March 22. Suddenly Thuringia no longer felt safe at all. At the last minute, Reichsbank officials began a frantic race to reship everything they had hidden away deep underground in Merkers back to Berlin. But just as they became aware of the need to act quickly, they found themselves disastrously handicapped. It was not just the speed of the US advance but, of all things, the partial shutdown of their own railway system. Even in a collapsing universe, there are such things as railway timetables, in Germany not least. This was due to the Easter holidays, Good Friday being March 30 and Easter Day April 1 that year. The grief of the Reichsbank employees was complete when out of their 1,000 giant sacks of German marks, only 450 were removed before Merkers fell at 11:00 on the morning of April 4.

Events moved fast. It would take only two days for local and prisoner knowledge to leak news to the Americans about the real-life Aladdin's cave awaiting them 2,100 feet below the surface. When senior military figures duly inspected on April 7, they were not to be disappointed. Descending into the main vault of the mine, they found a full 250 tons of gold ingots, valued at $238,490,000. Not only this, but they also uncovered a huge cache of art treasures from artists including Rembrandt, Titian, Van Dyck, Raphael, Dürer, and Renoir, weighing four hundred tons. On top of all this they learned they were the new masters of a three-thousand-year-old Egyptian statuette representing Queen Nephertiti. Its rescue alone from the realm of thugs, looting, and thievery represented a symbolic triumph of the highest order. The gold itself represented over 93 percent of the Reichsbank's official reserves, its seizure therefore rendering the country bankrupt.[3]

Accordingly, April 4, 1945, was in one sense for the Third Reich—financially—the end of the line. The regime that for twelve years had been morally repugnant and spiritually bankrupt was by the turn of events declared economically and fiscally so. Back in Berlin no one wanted to be the bearer of this Merkers news to Hitler. For his part, upon learning of it, Goebbels wrote in his diary, "One could tear one's hair out thinking the Reichsbahn is having an Easter break while the enemy seize our entire gold reserves."[4] But there was yet more. The day held other surprises, of equal significance, but these were from the realms of nightmares.

Ohrdruf Concentration Camp, Germany

Until this date no Allied forces had yet liberated a concentration camp. On April 4 that would change when US troops from the 4th Armoured Division, led by Brigadier General Joseph Cutrona, and the 89th Infantry Division entered Ohrdruf. It was a sub-camp of Buchenwald, the location from where Bonhoeffer and the other hostages had been *abtransportiert* (taken away) only the previous evening. The soldiers beheld the most terrible scenes, encountering overpowering evidence of starvation, cruelty, and inhumanity towards the powerless. Just inside the camp entrance were hundreds of corpses, all in striped uniforms, each with a bullet hole at the back of the skull.[5] They found bodies piled up like wood, and saw everywhere naked bodies in the last stages of emaciation. Corpses had been sprinkled with lime for the purpose of removing the stench. Colonel Hayden Sears, the commander of the tank force that had entered the camp, spoke with a few survivors. From them he learned about the savage conditions, and the recent removal of most of the inmates. They told him that the SS had shot those unable to walk, but had not finished off everyone. Some had survived. Incensed, Sears had his men round up nearly thirty civilians from the town, including a few dignitaries. They were shown the pits of rotting and burnt bodies. *The Times* reported that the mayor and his wife had committed suicide after they had been forced to view the camp and its victims.[6] When Eisenhower visited the camp, he was so shocked he telephoned Churchill to describe what he had seen, and then sent photographs of the dead prisoners to him. The dreadful scenes accompanying liberations of concentration camps would now come thick and fast. Of all these developments the hostages had little or no idea. But given the resistance that almost all the group had brought to the Nazi regime, the news would have stiffened their resolve.

21
Greatly Exaggerated Rumours

In London the BBC reported in subdued tone the news of Aschaffenburg's surrender from the previous day. It revealed that the British government was starting to give thought to the end of hostilities. The news was that when the end of the war arrived, "Government works and services are to have three days' holiday with pay for the end of the war with Germany—Victory day, the next day, and another later." In a considered appeal to the "make do and mend" generation, clearly now a nation of improvisors, the BBC also reported unwelcome news on behalf of the besieged Ministry of Food. It revealed there was a critical situation on the home front—even in respect of milk bottles. Apparently the bottle manufacturers had produced 144 million new bottles in 1944, but millions of these had disappeared from circulation. The Ministry of Food were convinced that they had "got lost" in tool sheds, cellars, gardens, and cupboards, and issued a dire warning: if these bottles were not found and returned to circulation, it might become impossible to guarantee delivery of milk during the summer.[1]

In mainland Europe the Russian capture of the Slovak capital, Bratislava, with its proximity to Vienna, was the main news of the day, with Soviet Marshal Tolbukhin billed as the hero of the hour. The BBC explained, "Wiener Neustadt is the principal of a group of German strongholds which have fallen to Marshal Tolbukin's forces on a thirty mile front west of Lake Neusiedl. . . . The town itself has one of the enemy's biggest Messerschmitt plants which at one time fed four hundred fighters to the hungry Luftwaffe every month."[2]

Berlin and Rheinsberg, Germany: Himmler's Rumours

Since April 1 Hitler, no doubt largely as a result of the constant aerial bombardments, had remained inside the Führerbunker and the protection of its 3.5-metre-thick roof without venturing outdoors.[3] Meanwhile, Supreme German Headquarters lurched on outwardly unchanged. But there was a discernible shift. While the briefing conferences still took place twice daily, their timings were becoming increasingly orientated around the Führer's own patterns. The midday conference drifted further into the afternoon, the evening conference nearer towards midnight. By the beginning of April, the type of question being discussed at these briefings was, for example, whether it was better to defend the Weser river or to defend the flank in Holland, Emden, and Wilhelmshaven. But with these timings, the speed of events on the ground would at times make any discussions, or resulting orders, soon outdated. In one instance of this, on April 4 a report arrived at Führer headquarters stating that the front at Minden and Nienberg had been pierced, and that the enemy had formed four bridgeheads across the Weser river.[4] The river whose defence they had been discussing was already in enemy hands. On the same day, Hitler ordered the formation of a new fallback line "under the tightest leadership behind the 9th Army," and directed that the Eastern Front was to have priority in the delivery of mines.[5] Such commands, long since unrealistic, were rapidly becoming entirely without meaning. The extent to which the German leadership was irrelevant was almost complete. Germany's armaments minister, Albert Speer, still operating from within Hitler's innermost circle, commented, "It seemed to me that General Staff [under General Krebs] had finally abandoned giving Hitler accurate information and had settled for keeping him busy with war games."[6] RFSS Heinrich Himmler, at whose behest the hostage group was being assembled, may have felt the same. On April 4 at 3:00 p.m., the British ambassador in Sweden, Sir Victor Mallet, sent a top-secret telegram to London, reporting that a third party had received a message from Brand (Himmler's adjutant) through Himmler's masseur Kersten's secretary in Berlin, that on April 2 Hitler had been set aside ("kalt gestellt").[7] But reports of Hitler's death, clearly a Himmler rumour ploy, were, to borrow a phrase once again, greatly exaggerated. Most likely, what Himmler meant by weaving this tangled web was that he was now the right person for the Allies to negotiate with.

While Himmler spun webs of deceit and duplicity, Germany's suffering intensified. On April 4 alone three tactical Allied squadrons flew a total of 3,401 operations across the Western Front, dropping a total of 1,061 tons of explosives.[8] Resistance was in near collapse. Bomber Command's record tells its own story: total effort for the night: 1,172 sorties, sixteen aircraft (1.4 percent) lost.[9] Increasingly aware of how German conduct would be perceived once things were laid plain for all to see, Anton Kaindl, commandant of KZ Sachsenhausen, met with Himmler at Rheinsberg, Kreis Neuruppin, that day and suggested handing over the concentration camp to the International Red Cross. Himmler, however, did not oblige.[10]

Königsberg, East Prussia

In Königsberg the intense Soviet barrage unleashed on the centre of the city, which had begun two days earlier, continued. On April 4 Soviet Lieutenant Inozemstev recorded in his diary that sixty shells from his battery had reduced one fortified building into a "pile of stones." The NKVD[11] was concerned that nobody should escape. "Encircled soldiers in Königsberg are putting on civilian clothes to get away. Documents must be checked more carefully in East Prussia."[12]

Kassel, Germany

At midday, after a hard fight, Kassel surrendered. The BBC reported the following day that the commander had asked for a three-hour truce to evacuate civilians but that the Americans had suspected this to be only a pretext for the Germans to reorganise and reinforce. In the battle for Kassel, two big Henschel works, which turned out aircraft engines, Tiger tanks, and heavy guns, were captured. One of the factories was underground, and unbombed parts were kept running right up to the last moment. Some of the tanks that actually took part in the defence of Kassel and attempted to infiltrate through the American line in the town had rolled off the production line only a few hours before they went into action. Many of these brand-new tanks were found to have less than thirty kilometres on their speedometers. The Americans also seized a truckload of German army rifles outside a small-arms plant, ready to be distributed to scattered troops of Germans sniping in the city. German workers reported for duty at one of the Henschel plants only a few hours before it was captured. On the outskirts of Kassel, a large army food depot was found that included thousands of cases of every conceivable type of liquor plundered from the German-occupied countries.[13]

Hamburg, Germany, and Graz and Styria, Austria

April 4 fell in the midst of a period of unbridled killings. In Neuengamme, one night in April 1945, seventy-one prisoners brought from the Fühls-büttel prison were shot in waves, and grenades were thrown into their cells, when the prisoners rose up in a final and futile act of resistance.[14] Meanwhile a calculated policy of executions continued apace. Farther south, in the Gau of Styria, victims were not confined to those identified as Jewish. During the evacuation of camps in this area, the liquidation of prisoners incapable either of walking as far as Mauthausen or of proving useful on arrival there apparently spread like wildfire. One such incident occurred in the Mauthausen sub-camp in Hintenberg, about two miles (three kilometres) from Lauben. This camp had been established in mid-August 1944 with some six hundred inmates, and held mostly Russian, Polish, Austrian, German, and Yugoslav detainees. By the eve of evacuation, the number had risen to approximately eight hundred. The guard team was composed of about fifteen SD men, Austrians and Germans, and another eighty Ukrainian guards. About forty sick prisoners were murdered by the Ukrainians shortly before the evacuation of the camp on April 4, 1945.[15]

The Wehrmacht in Defeat

For German forces the battle against overwhelming odds was becoming ever more impossible. Seemingly everywhere the speed and weight of the Allied onslaught had broken morale in the German army, who were surrendering at the rate of ten or twelve thousand a day. On one day alone, over forty thousand prisoners were herded into cages. Allied progress was held up by masses of prisoners on the roads and the problem of dealing with them. One aerial picture shows sixteen thousand in a single concentration.[16]

Gütersloh's Vicar on a Bicycle

On April 4 General Student was forced through lack of fuel to cancel altogether the proposed counter-attack against the Allied forces in the Ruhr. There was now no section of the front line in that area through which the Western Allies could not break.[17] In these conditions soldiers and civilians alike were ordered to fight to the last. But at times lives were spared. In Westphalia the town of Bielefeld surrendered peacefully at 5:30 p.m. to sixty tanks from the US 3rd Tank Batallion, as they arrived from Gütersloh. Eyewitnesses described the spectacle of Reverend Karl Pawlowski, on a bicycle, his clergy robes billowing out behind him, waving a cross and prevailing upon defenders to hold fire, and then approaching the Americans in the same manner. Karlsruhe, too, was liberated at 9:00 a.m. that day, with almost no loss of life, prompting a visit from General de Gaulle in person.[18] By this time the trend was inexorable. With the Red Army now fighting in the suburbs of Vienna, in the air the last of Germany's once-dominant air force struggled in vain against the daily mass of Allied bombers and fighters. On April 4, over the Eastern Front, Hermann Graf was shot down: he had to his credit a total of 202 Soviet aircraft destroyed on the Eastern Front, for which he had been awarded the coveted Knight's Cross with Oak Leaves, Swords, and Diamonds. Now he, too, taken eastwards into captivity, was a witness to the destruction of German military and air power.[19]

22

The Hostages: Gradual Progress

Easternmost Saxony, near the Czech Border, Germany

The early hours of Wednesday found the weary *Prominenten* hostages making gradual progress in a generally southerly direction in the diminishing strip of territory still under control of the Third Reich. One of Bonhoeffer's companions, Hermann Pünder, took the opportunity, within a few days of setting off, to record details of the experience. He was not the only traveller to experience mixed emotions as he observed the beauty of the landscape. "Beautiful surroundings," he wrote, "but what good is that?" The travellers in the Grüne Minna were provided with no water to wash, and ablutions were conducted under the so-called "protection" of a machine gun wielded by one of the many SS guards. The van had to halt for refuelling every thirty kilometres, and on one of these stops the hostages received rations for two days: a regular crust of army bread, an end slice of sausage, and a knob of butter. There was no mercy for the unprepared traveller: "If anyone is without a knife, good luck," wrote Pünder drily. To make matters worse, at yet another halt at a roadside hostelry some occupants of the vehicle were able, through the narrow slits in the shuttered windows, to observe the regular habit of the SS guards. This comprised making abundant use of the facilities for their own refreshment. This spectacle served only to reinforce, for the famished hostages, the relative injustice of their lot. The irony was not lost on Pünder. He notes that while the SS enjoy the facilities, "serious criminals pronounced innocent, generals, and holders of the Knight's Cross are left to fester in our dismal, stinking Minna, without a single person bothering to show any care towards any one of us."[1]

Around 9:00 that morning, after another exhausting wait and regrouping[2] of the convoy, Léon Blum, from the back seat of the front vehicle, noted their location as easternmost Saxony, near the Czech border. For him everything had a Bohemian feeling: the landscape, the villages, the costumes of the locals, even the place names. Quite soon their vehicle surged ahead and set the pace, leaving Bonhoeffer and the Grüne Minna party far behind. Despite being flat on his back, he was still able to catch sight of a road sign saying, "Regensburg 200 km," and thereby establish they were headed south. The Mercedes travelled through Neustadt an der Waldnaab and turned on to what looked increasingly like a mountain road through barren and wild terrain, with an adjacent stream thundering along a gorge.

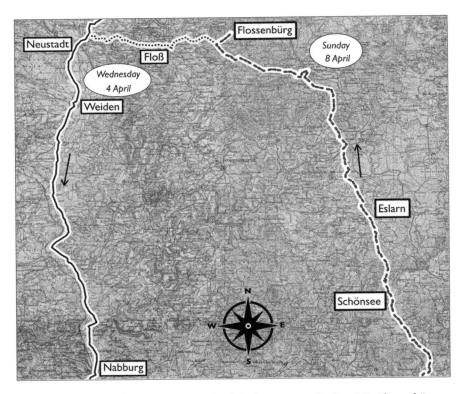

Fig. 22-1. Bonhoeffer waits in Neustadt while the transport leader visits Flossenbürg
Graphic by Bruce Bovill

When suddenly the landscape filled with people and buildings, a quarry, and a small railway, Blum recognised their likely proximity to a camp and the dreadful striped clothing of slave labourers. He records the moment they parked outside the entrance to the camp:

> Our officer, wordless, leaves us alone with the driver. We wait for three hours. It is a sinister place: the prisoners we see returning from the work detail look even more wretched, more skeletal, more ravaged than those of Buchenwald, dragging the carts filled with stones. Everything in this place exudes misery, suffering, and death.

The long wait ended for Blum when the officer emerged, still without a word, and they set off again, leaving Flossenbürg behind. Just as they departed, a strange vehicle, a high-sided lorry, entirely closed up, without openings or flaps, went past them, so they fell in behind and retraced the route back to Neustadt. Blum's conclusion was that they had gone there only in order to collect this vehicle and add it to the convoy.[3] As they arrived back in Neustadt, the other buses from the party also arrived and stopped in the square.[4]

Back in the Grüne Minna, some hours beforehand, the coming of daylight, combined with the added space liberated by burning fuel and better storage, had much lifted the travellers' spirits. Off to their right lay the Fichtelberg im Erzgebirge. A couple of loaves of bread, a large sausage, and something to drink also contributed to an added sense of cheerfulness, which vanished entirely when a consensus emerged that their destination was now Flossenbürg. It was a place widely known and feared as a death camp. Around noon that day, they reached Neustadt, where they halted at the police station.[5]

But while the Grüne Minna had been joggling along at a snail's pace, transport leader (Bader) in the Mercedes had forged ahead at speed to Flossenbürg and spent three hours there, as recounted above. In this interval the transport leader had clearly taken advantage of the abundant food and other provisions available in the SS canteen facilities, and indeed in subsequently speeding back down to Neustadt judged to perfection the time taken for the wood-burning Grüne Minna to catch up.[6]

For Blum the reassembly of the convoy in Neustadt provided a glimmer of real refreshment. People were allowed to stretch their legs. Provisions were distributed to the group. The Blums were overlooked to begin with, but then, just before setting off again, received some *Schwarzbrot* and *Wurst* through the window. The interlude brought out the reflective artist in the French politician. In fine weather he warmed to the sight of a peaceful, undamaged small town, with traders gossiping happily, and children playing. He writes,

> How calm and contented everything is! How far away the war feels! On the pavement, just beside us, a poorly clothed lad of around 7–8 years of age is skipping with the grace and agility of a dancer and the inner elegance of a little princess.[7]

In Neustadt the convoy had now taken on larger proportions. Indeed, leaving Neustadt, with the dreaded Flossenbürg now disappearing behind them, proved a significant boost in morale not only for the hostages, but also for their captors as well, making this journey into the unknown feel more of a shared experience. For a precious moment, the grimness of war had receded. But that relief proved transient; within moments of setting off, brutal SS reality broke in again, for most of the convoy, and especially for Bonhoeffer and his companions in the Grüne Minna.

It seemed as if a mistake had been made connected with the visit of only the lead vehicle to Flossenbürg; the special prisoners Franz Liedig and Josef Müller had not been removed from the convoy. Given that these prisoners had travelled no further than Neustadt, this is readily understandable. This omission, if indeed it were so, was now corrected as quickly as possible.[8] Müller's account captures the intensity of the moment from both inside and outside the police vehicle:

> Towards midday they stop our vehicle in Neustadt an der Wald-naab, the doors are thrown open and somebody screams, "Liedig with luggage, out! Müller with luggage, out!" . . . We jump from the vehicle and—without being asked—Captain [Ludwig] Gehre clambers along behind. He has recognized the voice of Criminal Commissioner Stawitzki, a friend of his, who had treated him well during his interrogation, and had even given him wine to drink.[9]

In a rare moment of humanity, the SS guards allowed a brief but emotional farewell moment to take place between hostages. Vasily Kokorin clearly surprised them by bounding out onto the road in one leap, and his disarming warmth melted the reserve of even the normally reticent Müller. Kokorin clambered back on with lowered head, while Liedig, Gehre, and Müller were loaded into an additional Grüne Minna, one from which emanated the stench of death. Müller had wanted to say farewell in addition to Bonhoeffer, but was unable to do so as Bonhoeffer remained as though "nailed to his seat" inside the Grüne Minna.[10] While this episode took place, elsewhere in the convoy other vehicles had, in solidarity, also come to a sudden stop. Hassell's record indicates that a further passenger in the police van also stepped out briefly in the farewell scenes and concurs that three left the convoy.[11] Shocked into silence, the buses and the now (sadly) rather more spacious Grüne Minna continued their trip with the remaining prisoners. Bonhoeffer, not attracted by the idea of Flossenbürg, remained with them. But now, three prisoners bound for Flossenbürg, at least one of them a Gestapo informer, would know, if pressed or simply asked, exactly where to find him.

Fig. 22-2. Neustadt an der Waldnaab, 1945
The police station in question is visible centrally in the background, as is the square,
and its sense of community, as described by Blum.
Courtesy of Willi Steger, Riedlhütte. Used with permission.

Nabburg, Germany: A Moment of Beauty

In the other vehicle now driving briskly onwards at the head of the convoy, a transient sense of the war being far away was also felt and swiftly disrupted, although in a different way. In the light of the civilian populace's near-famine conditions in Germany, Blum was struck by the sight of the heavy parcels, a loaf, sausages, cigar tins, and bottles of liqueur now crammed at the feet of the transport leader. He found himself noting with sarcasm how essential it was that an "SS officer must enjoy abundance in all things." But the reflective observer in him was still captivated by the fresher air they were breathing, and the mellow light. As they descended through a winding valley, for him even the trees and meadows took on a more delicate and more tender green hue. The landscape as a whole in its lines and colours seemed to gather itself into a perfect harmony. On a ridge beyond the river nestled a picturesque small town, romantically encompassed by its ancient walls.[12] Jeannot Blum whispered, "It's really beautiful." The officer turned abruptly towards them with the words, "It will be more beautiful when the war is over."[13]

A Woman's Generosity

During the day, at least for the Grüne Minna party, there was a welcome stop outside a small house standing alone beside the road. Falconer records that a prim and correct little old lady, with a back stiff as a ramrod, whom he took to be a retired schoolmistress, came down to her garden gate to investigate during a moment when their vehicle had halted. Clearly shocked by the famished appearance of those she surveyed, she stood for no nonsense from the soldiers. She declared herself happy to offer refreshments to this unfortunate and motley crew, pushed one guard out of the way, and ushered the hostages into her house. General von Falkenhausen—with his impressive uniform—was deemed to be the most suitable to be the first one through the door. When the transport leader attempted subsequently to place guards in her kitchen as milk and bread was being miraculously served up to the hostages by this good fairy, she acidly told the SS soldiers to "get out." They complied, confining themselves to guarding the outside.[14] In a transient interlude, providing a minor victory for common sense, a woman's courageous humanity stood sovereign over the authoritarianism and darkness pervading the Third Reich. It was to prove among the last few instances of receiving welcome nutrition that Bonhoeffer would experience.

Regensburg, Germany

Judging by the standards of the time, in Regensburg Wednesday, April 4, 1945, was an ordinary Bavarian day, just like any other. In fact, despite having a Messerschmitt factory and oil refineries, Regensburg had thus far remained comparatively unharmed by the main thrust of the Allied strategic bombing offensive. The battles of the closing stages of the war were happening at quite some supposed distance away in the regions of Main and the Teutoburg forest, as the *Regensburg Chronicle* reported next day. The newspaper, condensed onto two sides of print, reports that the food distribution allowance for the seventy-fourth allocation period amounted to 125 grams of apple purée and that darkness fell at 8:04 p.m. The publication also made members of army units aware that during periods of service for the NSDAP, they were permitted to wear the party uniform in place of their military attire. As they had for twelve years, branches of the party held their regular gatherings and functions.

Victor and Eva Klemperer in Regensburg

On this uneventful Wednesday, at 1:30 p.m. on the train from Marktredwitz, an elderly couple arrived: Victor Klemperer, accompanied by his wife, Eva. The diarist, though his time in Regensburg was short-lived on this occasion, was taken aback by the picture of destruction the station made on him. He describes the shock of seeing "craters, ruined buildings, destroyed railway trucks and carriages, like destroyed ships which had been run aground, just like a ship's bow, the railway station itself largely a ruin." Klemperer's detailed account provides what is likely to be the most accurate information we have on the timings of air raids, which his record shows were in a pattern of continuing well after darkness fell. He writes,

> An alert during the third plate of NSV[15] soup. Possible to continue our journey at 5.45 pm. To a nearby hotel. An air-raid warning while drinking the first cup of coffee. . . . The landlord reports the situation minute by minute. . . . After a while the preliminary all-clear. Wireless (without another siren) repeats three times: extreme danger from low-level attack.

The Hostages in Requisitioned Accommodation

The Klemperers returned later that evening to the station. But as the various vehicles of the prisoner convoy converged on the nearby prison, they were not seen by the diarist's exceptionally sharp and attentive eye. Of course, there was nothing to indicate anything unusual as hostages arrived, exhausted, in dribs and drabs, at the end of a long and uncomfortable journey. Perhaps least likely to attract any attention at all would have been a regular closed police van, with prisoners on board, whose identities were concealed from sight. Among the wider group, Anneliese Goerdeler was the only *Sippenhaft* hostage to recall details of the later

arrival of this police vehicle.[16] Her companion Hassell recalls the journey time and the Regensburg arrival time a little differently, but adds a
note about climbing down from the buses "in the drizzling rain."[17] Goerdeler writes that, as evening fell, all the convoy's vehicles halted a little way north of Regensburg while the accommodation issue was being
sorted out, which took hours. The Grüne Minna was last to arrive, park-
ing at some distance away from the others in the convoy, and she records
that on this vehicle, in addition to its having no windows, the sections
where windows might have been were overlaid with grilles. While the
guards drove around Regensburg making arrangements, leaving a correspondingly reduced number of guards, hostages from the buses were,
as time stretched on, mercifully allowed to disembark in small groups.
Even those in the Grüne Minna were accorded this freedom. Seeing and
recognising him emerge from the confinements of the van, Anneliese
took advantage of a suitable moment to engage General von Rabenau
in conversation, also enquiring about the other occupants. The general
named various people, including, unsurprisingly, Dietrich Bonhoeffer,
who had long been his cellmate in Buchenwald. At first, the word among
the hostages was that a nearby SS weapons school would accept the convoy. But this proved not to be so. The transportation leader then tried
to accommodate the prisoners in Regensburg's concentration camp, but
was again refused. In the meantime, prisoners had, at least initially, to
stay put in the vehicles. "Waiting until they know where to put us," notes
Stauffenberg in her records. But the transport leader had little success.
"Camp overcrowded," she observes.[18]

A wave of uncertainty now overtook the SS guards. Discipline began
to break down. Stauffenberg also records being eventually allowed outside
the bus to stand in the street as they waited and one of the party even
bumping into two acquaintances.[19] It was evidently becoming challenging
even for SS authority structures to remain intact. No one knew where the
prisoners could find lodgings for the night. Even the SS transport leader,
who arrived in Regensburg in the passenger car with the Blum couple
as twilight gathered that evening, was faced with the same problem. He
asked police headquarters to advise him via Regensburg Gestapo in relation to further instructions for the convoy. Leaving the two French VIP
hostages with his SS driver, he set off on foot to sort out arrangements
for the group. But the moment the transport leader absented himself, a
curious conversation arose.

A French Dilemma

Léon Blum records the scene as dusk fell that evening in Regensburg. It was a moment that precipitated a particular moment of *angoisse* for him and Jeannot. During the long wait for the officer in charge, they found themselves engaged in conversation, in their halting German, by their normally completely silent driver. This individual now explained that he (apparently) knew them really well from Buchenwald. He had, on two or three occasions, at night, come to fetch them from their lodging to drive them to the dental surgery. Somewhat nonplussed by this baffling declaration of familiarity, Blum enquired whether they were going any further that night than Regensburg, stating, presumably with slight exaggeration, that it was now over twenty-four hours since he had moved from his spot and that he was at the end of his tether. The reply was that they were not. As to the other vehicles and the precise location of stay, the suddenly talkative driver could offer no further comment, before disappearing for a stroll.[20] The exchange captured here provokes the question: had the SS driver sought to ingratiate himself with his VIP captives in the light of the imminent end of hostilities? By subsequently walking away while leaving the keys in the ignition, he was, it would seem, gifting them with a chance to escape and, presumably, speak well of him. It may be a revealing insight into the fragility of SS willingness in the moment to continue to obey orders issued by the representatives of the fast-crumbling regime, or even as an act of simmering resistance. For Jeannot Blum, it was too good a chance to pass up. In the now-deserted square, she turned instantly to her husband, asking how far it was to the nearest American lines. The immobilised, and correspondingly cautious, Blum replied that with Patton somewhere between Würzburg and Nuremberg, the likely distance might be, say, twenty or forty kilometres. Jeannot immediately offered to drive, confident that they would be long gone by the time the driver returned. As an observant hostage, she knew that that there were already maps in the glovebox and petrol in the boot. At this juncture Blum pointed out that they would not get very far and that even if they did get to the front line, they could not cross. Undeterred, Mme Blum declared that, in staying with this convoy, they were doomed. At this point Blum was torn, given his wife's track record for wisdom. But, moments later, their captors reappeared, now accompanied by a policeman, to show them the onward route . . . to what turned out to be, unnervingly, Regensburg prison. Briefly, the couple were separated and suffered great distress. But this was soon followed by overwhelming and tearful relief at being reunited.[21]

A Prison Bed for the Night

The prisoners' cells were on the second floor of the prison, where they now had to spend the night of April 4, and most of the following day, one that included air raids. But with the distance from Berlin now much increased, combined with the innate self-confidence of many of the *Sippenhäftlinge*, a perceptible change came over the group. For example, only a resilient hostage could initiate a stand-up confrontation with a prison warder demanding that no prison cell doors be locked. Stauffenberg did, and had a long and unsuccessful fight with the chief warder about being locked in for the night. Her recompense was a great night's sleep. She notes, "We are dead tired and sleep like logs."[22]

Stauffenberg was by no means alone, after travelling all that way throughout the previous night, in sleeping very well in her stay in Regensburg prison. Nor was she alone in her assertiveness. Hassell also recalls a confrontation incident.[23] These accounts make clear that the arrival, in stages, of this collection of prisoners provided an unexpected challenge to the prison warders. Initially the hostages as a group were addressed in a very rough manner. But at this stage of the war, the hitherto unruffled National Socialist life of Regensburg was fast approaching its demise. Prison life and prisoner conduct did not proceed in the accustomed manner. An intervention from the regular guards also helped explain to the prison warders that these people were of VIP status and needed treating with more courtesy. Things then improved, although not in every respect. The famished prisoners in Best's cell protested, joining in a loud chorus of "We want something to eat," which was picked up by others. Initially the response came back, "Impossible, the kitchen is already closed." But after much back and forth, some sustenance finally appeared late in the evening: a big bowl of quite passable vegetable soup, a thick piece of bread, and a cup of "coffee."[24]

It was a case of those who complained the most loudly receiving something to assuage them. Bonhoeffer and his cellmates went to bed with almost nothing: after much pleading they were provided with no food, but with a quarter of a beaker each of water.[25]

Notwithstanding this, here in Regensburg prison the hostages were at least able to choose their cellmates. We learn from Pünder's letter that Bonhoeffer billeted with Pünder, Hoepner, Rabenau, and Falkenhausen.[26] As for the others, Best notes that Heidel Nowakowski and Margot Heberlein shared one cell.[27] This arrangement would appear to have satisfied at

least a modicum of decency. It was a pattern that was to be repeated later
on during the week, and helped the fellow hostages close down on Heidel's
flirtations with Rascher. This is likely to have been well received by the
group, as fondness towards Kokorin was much evident. The young Russian
was clearly heartbroken about the withdrawal of Heidel's apparent affec-
tions. The detailed accounts of both Best and Pünder have also omitted
the widely unpopular Sigmund Rascher. His being either forgotten or left
out would seem eloquent testimony relating to how he was perceived: presumably the reverse logic would also apply to the reports that Falkenhausen stayed in more than one cell. Meanwhile, in evident contrast with the
better experience of Falconer's cell, the whole evening's conditions for and
treatment of Bonhoeffer and his companions were tolerable, but far less
comfortable. Hermann Pünder records that despite the presence of strict
guards, there was still much gawping from bystanders as they reached
the local prison. His letter notes not only that two buses from Weimar[28]
arrived, with apparently around fifty to sixty *Sippenhaft* prisoners, but
also that they seemed instantly to be treated much more favourably than
were the Minna contingent. Pünder lists a few of them—the Goerdeler
family relatives, Fritz Thyssen and his wife, the wives of Colonel Generals
von Hammerstein and Halder, and members of the previous Hungarian
government. Despite the narrow confines of the cell containing Generals
von Falkenhausen and von Rabenau, Bonhoeffer, Dr Hoepner (brother of
the general shot by firing squad), and himself, he was able to thank God
for the fact that the cells were clean. On the floor they shared three straw
sacks and two blankets between five. But not every aspect of the intimacy
was easy. Pünder confesses,

> Of course, throughout the day, washing is out of the question. Our
> "evening ablutions" we have to perform one after the other on a rusty
> can that stands in our cell. The whole business [is] utterly disgrace-
> ful and vile. After the day's dreadful journey, finally we sleep well.
> Since the cell window is missing as a result of the many air raids on
> Regensburg, we five in our cell have fresh air. We avoid the cold by
> huddling up close to one another.[29]

By combining the diary of a local chemist[30] with Klemperer's testimony
about raids happening at 5:45 p.m. and continuing until midnight, we
may be confident of what happened upon arrival at Regensburg prison. It
is Falconer whose account describes the arrival of the Minna party at the
prison as being disrupted by air raids taking place in the evening itself, a

version also suggested by Stauffenberg's "Voralarm" diary entry. Falconer's vivid account captures the scene in the cell he shared with Best, Petersdorff, and others:

> We are escorted up to the top floor where, in a very large corridor with doors along each side, we are housed five to a cell. [Stiller] and his men, having handed us over to the prison warders, go out on the town and we see them no more today. . . . Some sort of food is then doled out, and very shortly afterwards there is an air raid. The target is the railway marshalling yard and, as this is only separated from the prison by a wall and our cell window looks straight down on it, we have a splendid view of some very good precision bombing. Our interest cools considerably, however, when a large lump of metal whizzes in through the window, breaking the glass and clanging against the opposite wall.[31]

At this point Falconer records that he made such a racket banging on the door while the air raid was in full swing that the harassed warder appeared. Despite protesting the impossibility of letting anyone out of their cells, he relented, and was then rewarded by being almost trampled underfoot in the ensuing rush to get out into the corridor. It seems for the prison guards that treating prisoners as VIPs was complicated. Indeed, the complications deepened, as once they were in the corridor, the group proceeded zealously with the project of letting out almost everyone else whose door was only bolted shut from the outside. At one point Falconer peered cautiously into a cell through the usual food supply hatch window that is built into doors in German prisons, expecting to catch sight of some dreadful criminal, but instead was taken aback by the sight of three women and two small children, whom he immediately liberated. To add to the general effect, once in the corridor, the emerging hostages were greeted with cries of amazement by Bonhoeffer's cellmate General von Rabenau: it turned out they were old friends. As this impromptu reunion party gathered momentum, the new arrivals prevailed upon Falconer to open many other doors, in which endeavour he was swift to comply, overlooking tremendous protestations from the by now distraught head warder, to whom he gave short shrift. Undoubtedly Falconer's understanding of the dynamics of German prisoner life from time on the inside had informed his sense of how to engender an appropriate sense of authority. He brusquely invited him to shut up, mind his own business, and stop making a pest of himself to his betters. At this the crestfallen guard retired into a corner and sulked.

In this ensuing new-found freedom, Falconer found they had a great deal to talk about with these new companions: all of them were either known to Falkenhausen, Rabenau, or Bonhoeffer, or else had mutual friends.[32]

From Falconer's comments, and those of others, it appears that despite receiving meagre rations, Bonhoeffer benefitted greatly from the social interactions made possible by the air raid episodes, the greater part of which are likely to have occurred the next day. Falconer reported on first impressions gleaned from the Regensburg exchanges with all these—for him—new acquaintances. Weighing by this time only six and a half stone,[33] around half his normal body weight, Falconer was struck by how well-fed and healthy they all looked, even with reserves to spare (by obvious comparison with himself). Earlier he described Bonhoeffer as "a man of about 35, fair-haired and chubby in spite of his incarceration." Falconer himself was thirty-five at the time of writing, and this note is a testimony, despite the contrast engendered by Bonhoeffer's well-nourished appearance, to the extent to which he identified, and got along, with Bonhoeffer, at this point aged thirty-nine.[34] Falconer was also deeply offended—and not just at first impression—by the manner in which the *Sippenhäftlinge* appeared to consider themselves a cut above the rest. He was unimpressed at the way in which, at repeated intervals, they refused to interact with other prisoners or to share food supplies and reserves with others. This was a pattern that continued throughout the convoy's travels. In seeking to grasp how they functioned, he observed that Heberlein was socially acceptable to them because he was a diplomat, although his name was not embellished with a *von*, noting their respect for himself as an officer. But Falconer also took great offence at their treating one of his own Grüne Minna travelling companions with obvious contempt, and took steps accordingly:

> It is with considerable—and perhaps malicious—pleasure that I go to some trouble to show ostentatiously to Heidi all the respect due to her sex if not her profession. In this I am joined by General von Falkenhausen, who is a gentleman in anybody's language. It is late before we go to bed that evening.[35]

Thursday, April 5, 1945

23
Horst Hoepner, Payne Best, and Horst von Petersdorff

On Thursday the hostages spent one of the most agreeable days of their captivity to date. In Regensburg prison they were able to create an unprecedented mingling with fellow prisoners of very different hues for much of the air-raid-interrupted day. In reality their captors were awaiting the cover of darkness in order to be able to continue their onward journey. Long periods of quiet were interspersed with bursts of lively conversation. With this in mind, the characters introduced here represent the quietest and least well-known of the hostage party (Horst Hoepner), together with the most "present, loquatious, and well-known" (Payne Best) and one of the "most striking" (Horst von Petersdorff).

Horst Hoepner

(Dr) Horst Hoepner served in World War I and was wounded on April 11, 1916. He spoke fluent English, no doubt a business asset in the 1920s and 1930s. In 1940 he was living in Berlin. Although he was by this time well beyond normal call-up age, the exigencies of the war's progression meant that he was finally obliged to re-enter military service. After the July 20, 1944, bomb plot, Horst's well-known older brother General Erich Hoepner, who in the latter part of the war became a defiant resister of Hitler's commands, was seized on the basis of his involvement with the plot and executed shortly thereafter, on August 8. Horst himself was also arrested on the basis of his own non-pro-Nazi sentiments[1] and under the *Sippenhaft* clauses in Paris, where he was serving with the army, on July 24. He was taken to Fresnes prison and kept there, mainly in solitary confinement, until August 1, 1944, when he was transferred to Buchenwald. Following Erich's execution on August 8, their sister Margaret was released, along with many other *Sippenhäftlinge*, on October 4, 1944, but as of January 2, 1945, Erich's wife, Irma, was still in Ravensbrück,[2] and Horst remained in custody in Buchenwald as well. In confinement here he was banned from washing and caught scabies as a result. Horst, a serving German officer innocent of any crime or complicity, received extreme inhumane treatment at the hands of the Gestapo. One method reported to have been used in applying physical and psychological torture to him was to keep him awake in darkness below ground while threatening him for almost endless periods. Even the small privilege of a daily exercise routine he was initially granted was withdrawn when the VIP prisoner group, which included Bonhoeffer, arrived in Buchenwald in February 1945. In Payne Best's 1953 account of the hostage experience, Hoepner's (by now) broken mental health provides material for mocking comment by the author, who repeats the judgemental scorn of Vermehren. The reasons for his inclusion in this elite VIP and political hostage group as opposed to the wider *Sippenhäftlinge* group, to which he more logically belonged, are unknown.

Payne Best

Sigismund Payne Best was born on April 14, 1888, to George and Catherine Best, née Allison, in Cheltenham, England. His father was an alumnus of Downing College, Cambridge. Sigismund's birth was followed in 1889 by the arrival of half-brother Leonel and in 1890 by that of half-sister Sybil, by which time the family were living in Clapham. All three children were christened in Twickenham on July 22, 1896. Payne Best's paternal grandmother was reputed to be the daughter of an Indian maharajah and a British woman; one source, which could not be verified, stated that this was kept a closely guarded family secret. Family secrecy may perhaps have been a harbinger of a future life, one soon to be devoted to the often troubling and costly secrecies necessary in espionage work. After initially studying science in London, Best began work as a businessman. In January 1908 he married the independently wealthy Dorothy Stallwood Adams, in Chertsey, and together they set off to Lausanne, where Best studied the violin at the Music Academy. Best went on to study economics and musicology at the University of Munich, graduating in both in 1913. From his time in Munich, Best acquired an excellent knowledge of the German language, a fluency that would prove to be of immense value in future years. Back in England he went as a volunteer into the army.

In World War I, Best served as a captain, first as a member of the Intelligence Corps—owing partly to his poor eyesight and also to his command of French, German, and Flemish—and later as the second officer of General Headquarters' Wallinger London bureau, led by Major Ernest

Wallinger. In 1917 Wallinger sent him to Rotterdam in Holland to establish intelligence networks in German-occupied Belgium. Wallinger's bureau was linked to several Belgian resistance groups. In Rotterdam Best came into conflict with Richard Tinsley, the local station chief of MI6. In November 1917 he was recalled to London after he was caught sleeping with the wife of a Belgian resistance leader—for someone in his profession not, on the face of it, a heinous crime. He was reassigned. Best later accused Tinsley of scheming against him. Schemes or not, the merits of Captain Best's war services were such that he was appointed Officer of the Order of the British Empire (OBE). Given Best's relatively lowly rank, the award is exceptional. He was also awarded the Belgian Croix de Guerre.

Back in Bournemouth the young and fabulously wealthy wife to whom Best had been unfaithful, Dorothy Stallwood Adams, died in 1918.[3] Following the war, after an interval of three years, Best married Dutch high society's Maria Margaretha van Rees. As a consequence the now independently wealthy Best spent the interwar years moving in the highest social circles. He continued to put his Swiss-trained musicality to good use and played the violin in a string quartet with Prince Hendric, consort to Queen Wilhelmina. By now a larger-than-life character, sporting a monocle, he also ran a legitimate import-export business, specialising in pharmaceuticals, which also provided a cover for his second profession: more espionage. Indeed, the network of contacts he afforded were ideally suited to exploitation for spying purposes. As a result, although he had apparently been deactivated through lack of funds by MI6, Best was soon approached by an old acquaintance from the Great War, Colonel Claude Dansey, who asked him to recommence spy operations. There may have been a link between the UK government's lack of funds and Best's apparent lack of need for excessive remuneration. But Best was concealing a highly significant secret: he had incurred a debt of bankruptcy proportions by 1931. He did not disclose this to his latest employers. Soon a network was set up that was based on the passport control offices in British embassies. During the course of the 1930s, one of the many individuals of varying hues whom Best met and charmed was Heinrich Himmler. By the time war was declared, Best was responsible for espionage conducted via the British SIS throughout Holland.

But in the autumn of 1939, perhaps inevitably, things went awry. The circumstances leading up to Best's capture with another agent at the Café Backus on the outskirts of Venlo in November 1939 were outlined in the introduction. During the run-up to this incident, serious misjudgements were made by SIS headquarters and Whitehall as a whole.[4] It ranked (and rankled) among the most notorious and humiliating episodes in the history of British espionage. Richard Stevens, disastrously, was carrying on him a plain-text list of SIS agents in Europe. Both men readily divulged copious quantities of information to the enemy, of which quite possibly little had any real intelligence value.[5] No doubt as a result of this (and his efforts either to fool or to please his captors, or possibly both), after an initial short period of harsh treatment, Best was awarded prisoner conditions of exceptional luxury for the duration of the war in Sachsenhausen. As one example of this, the German authorities arranged for him a special shipment from his home address in occupied Holland direct to his cell in Sachsenhausen. It contained copious amounts of his requested clothing and personal effects, a privilege that makes him virtually unique in the history of Germany's World War II concentration camps. He was even visited in person there by Himmler in 1942, after which his VIP prisoner status increased still further, an event that readily accounts for Best's presence among the group of VIP and political hostages. He was, no doubt as a result of this flattering treatment, poorly regarded by SOE operative Falconer.

Horst von Petersdorff

Horst von Petersdorff was born in Posen,[6] Prussia, to parents Axel and Elisabeth on December 30, 1892. He had two brothers, Egon and Helmut, and was baptised in the military garrison church of Celle on March 9, 1893. He joined the German army when war broke out and was distinguished in the highest degree. In one incident in October 1914, Horst lost his right arm, and over the course of the war was wounded a total of six times. He was honoured with many decorations for valour, one of which he was awarded by Kaiser Wilhelm II in person. He was promoted to colonel. Clearly a larger-than-life character, he survived the war, only to join up with one of the Freikorps units when hostilities ended in 1918, and during this period had a number of hair's-breadth escapes. At one stage in his Baltic campaigns, he crossed his superior officer, Major Bischof, whose tolerance of plundering by troops in Riga he considered excessive. In addition to these escapades, Horst was independently wealthy and in 1918 purchased a plot of land on the Obersalzberg, where the climate was believed well suited to effecting recovery from illnessess such as malaria and amoebic dysentry (both of which he had picked up during a campaign in Syria). At his home, called Dürreck, on the Obersalzberg, Horst entertained founders of the Nazi movement, including Hitler and Eckart, from 1919 onwards. He joined the Nazi Party in 1922 and the SA in 1923 and became much associated for a time with several key, colourful,[7] and dubious characters. He helped reorganise the Berlin SA at Hitler's behest, and in the process objected to the inclusion of Josef Goebbels. He was active in raising funds for these activities, and at one stage secured 2 million Reichsmarks from Siemens for the SA. In this period lasting impressions were formed; he did not like all that he found. Horst left the Nazi Party in 1932. He had become involved with the SA under the leadership of Röhm and, like Alvensleben, with whom he would later share a cell in Buchenwald,[8] only narrowly escaped with his life in the Night of the Long Knives in June 1934.[9] On a happy note, and continuing to move at the pinnacle of Germany's highest social circles, he married Irene, Countess of Bismarck-Schönhausen, divorced Countess of Einsiedel, on June 29, 1935. Over the coming years, he steadfastly rejected Nazi Party secretary Martin Bormann's approaches to buy his property in service of accommodation needs for the Führer's entertainment purposes. Petersdorff said that he would agree to sell only if directly ordered to do so by Hitler himself, which did not happen. He thereby achieved entirely the opposite effect, very dangerous in Nazi Germany, of having "friends in high places." When war came in 1939, Petersdorff quickly volunteered for service and was reactivated to military duties. He took part in the Polish campaign. During the battle for France in 1940, he commanded the armoured reconnaissance unit, which was the first to reach the coast on the English Channel near Abbeville. For this action he was awarded the Knight's Cross of the Iron Cross, one of Germany's highest awards for bravery or leadership in World War II.[10] It was presented to him in person by Hitler, who at the time of the award said, "Finally Petersdorff gets to do something he likes."[11] Petersdorff continued in active service but was specifically denied leadership responsibilities because both Hitler and Göring considered him "mentally unfit." In the course of his duties, Petersdorff was wounded a further four times and, in a sideways move, was posted to industrial commission responsibilities in Slovakia and Hungary. Meanwhile Petersdorff had come to loathe Hitler and abhor the Nazis. Following the July 20 plot, in solidarity with the resisters, he accommodated the fugitive General Fritz Lindemann in his furnished room in Potsdam on July 28, 1944. Petersdorff's arrest, along with those of hundreds of other army officers, quickly ensued. As part of his general falling from favour with the regime, Petersdorff was expelled from the General Staff of the SA on October 18, 1944. Also in that same month, Petersdorff's nine-year marriage to Irene ended. Petersdorff was tried by the Volksgerichtshof but, unusually, found innocent—and yet, like so many, was reimprisoned without charge or right of appeal. During his imprisonment his cell in Berlin's Lehrterstraße prison was hit by the raid of February 3, 1945. He was buried under debris in his cell, suffering injuries to his lungs and kidneys, for which he was given no treatment of any kind. His indomitable spirit continued to shine through, and despite his being very unwell, Best describes him as a likeable, wild adventurer of a man, and reports that during the time of the hostage convoy, he never shirked danger or responsibility. In particular, Margot Heberlein singles him out within the hostage group as being "always cheerful." The actual reasons for his inclusion in the VIP hostage group are unknown.

24
Far from Over

As the hostages mingled in hopefulness that day, talk was of an approaching Allied victory. But the war was far from over.

Okinawa, Japan

After four days that had proved a mixture of anticlimax and euphoric relief for the two marine and two army divisions that had landed on the island, on April 5 combat troops reached the limestone hills. There natural and man-made caves had been linked up with tunnel systems. In addition, the stone of traditional Okinawan funeral vaults, which abounded in the area, served as excellent machine-gun nests. American infantry found themselves being separated from their tanks, which were attacked by concealed teams who jumped out and ran up to the Shermans with Molotov cocktails and satchel charges. Tank crews who abandoned their blazing vehicles were shot down. Now the Americans understood what a battle awaited them.[1] Elsewhere in the Far East theatre, Marshal Stalin was now supremely confident, even in the now-unlikely event of being able to countenance a war on two fronts. So it was that at 3:00 p.m. on that cold and sleety day, Soviet foreign minister Molotov summoned his Japanese counterpart, Naotake Sato, to the Foreign Commissariat in Moscow. He curtly informed him that the Soviet Union was denouncing the five-year neutrality pact that had been agreed with Japan in 1941. The repercussions within Japan, although not only triggered by this news, were both swift and shattering. The BBC reported, "The Japanese Cabinet held a special meeting at nine o'clock this morning to discuss the general state of affairs. At ten thirty General Kuniaki Koiso, the prime minister, went to the Imperial Palace and told the Emperor that he and all his Ministers were resigning, to 'make way for a strong Government.'"[2] The prime minister was replaced by seventy-year-old Admiral Danshaku Suzuki, who secretly asked the Soviets to help negotiate peace between the United States and Japan. In this he was, unsurprisingly, rebuffed.

World Leaders

It was also on this day, in some senses a day of unravelling, that the low point of relations between the "Big Three" was reached. In the light of Stalin's acid words of that Tuesday, a deeply angered and weakening Roosevelt wrote back to him refuting the allegations, which he took personally:

> It is astonishing that a belief seems to have reached the Soviet Government that I have entered into an agreement with the enemy without first obtaining your full agreement. . . . The recent advances on the western front were due to "military action" and the "terrific impact of air power."[3] Frankly, I cannot avoid a feeling of bitter resentment towards your informers, whoever they are, for such vile misrepresentation of my actions or those of my trusted subordinates.[4]

That same day Churchill, in copy of Roosevelt's letter, wrote on the one hand to the US president, advising him that His Majesty's Government cordially associated themselves with Roosevelt's reply, and on the other expressing disappointment that Eisenhower's telegram about priorities was actually sent to Stalin without anything being said to the British chiefs of staff, or Air Chief Marshal Tedder, or commander-in-chief Field Marshal Montgomery. Churchill signed off by stating that the issue was now closed, and included a gauche and inadequate quotation in Latin about quarrels between lovers.[5] For the world leaders of Allied cooperation, it was not their finest hour.

Berlin and Leipzig, Germany

In Berlin the city prepared itself for the coming onslaught. Hans-Georg von Studnitz wrote in his diary, "Now the government really is leaving Berlin. Six-tenths of the staff from major offices has been dismissed. The men have to serve in the Volkssturm and the women are left to decide whether to slip away. One in ten, including myself, make up the so-called command staff and stay in Berlin."[6] Their tasks included destroying incriminating files. The behaviour of many Nazi functionaries provoked outrage: the party officers vanished, mostly to Bavaria, the better-connected ones going to Landshut and Berchtesgaden. Anybody who could get a travel permit, whether through official channels, bribery, or forgery, went westwards. Yet more than 2.5 million civilians stayed behind. On April 5

Ursula Kleinmichel went to the hairdressers for the last time in World War II: she treated herself to a new-style haircut with tinting.[7]

In Führer headquarters that day, Martin Bormann noted in his diary, "General Patton's 3rd Army into the Harz mountains, bypassing Leipzig to the south—Bolsheviks near Vienna, Americans in the Thuringian Forest." The speed of Patton's advance had an unintended side effect. In the courtyard of Leipzig prison, over one hundred Allied prisoners—mainly French political prisoners—were executed. Two kilometres north-east of Leipzig, a column of 6,500 women of many nationalities from the HASAG factories were marched towards Dresden. At the Thekla factory, which manufactured aircraft wings three kilometres north of Leipzig, SS and Volkssturm auxiliaries forced three hundred prisoners into an isolated building. All windows were fastened, then the SS threw in incendiary bombs. Those who managed to break out of the building were machine-gunned. Three Frenchmen survived.[8]

25
A New Low Point

In another sense, too, quite apart from the nadir reached in international relations between the Allies, April 5 represented the reaching of a low point for Germany. It was the day on which the arbitrary decisions were taken to dispose of some of Germany's finest servants. In recent days Bormann and Keitel had been making background preparations to move Hitler's headquarters to the south. His special train stood ready in Munich. Hitler's *Fliegerstaffel* was fuelled and ready at Gatow airfield with fifteen Focke-Wulf 200 and Junkers 52-type craft twenty kilometres west of Berlin. But the Führer displayed no interest in leaving Berlin. There his absolute power, fragmented though it was, remained intact. April 5 was the day on which Hitler had sight, in some measure, of Canaris' diaries. Quite how Hitler came to see the diaries is unclear. Based on the testimony of SS-Sturmscharführer Franz Sonderegger, provided at the post-war trial of Walter Huppenkothen, Chowaniec[1] proposes (credibly) that SS-General Rattenhuber received the diaries from General Buhle late in March or early in April, certainly before April 5, and then, with or without informing Kaltenbrunner, gave them directly to Hitler.[2]

It is a matter of record that Hitler was able to receive in public only documents that had been especially retyped for him in large script, as he was by this time long-sighted and felt that the role of Führer was incompatible with a wearer of spectacles.[3] He was also known to dislike the study of documents.[4] However, if he received and studied these items in private, he may have perused them more fully. At least, it is not believed that there had been sufficient time between the finding of the diaries and their being seen by Hitler for any retyping or summarising to have taken place.[5] Even more important than the extent to which Hitler actually read and assessed them, however, was the fact that the diaries had been found at Zossen. It is important to explain at this point the fact that Hitler's long-standing dislike towards, and disrespect for, the German Reichswehr, which he commanded, was also circumstantially and emotionally linked with the military complex at Zossen. .

The Background to the Zossen Find

In a meeting on November 5, 1939, with Field Marshal Brauchitsch, Hitler had exploded with rage, stating he was near the end of his patience with the "spirit of Zossen," which some fine day he would ruthlessly stamp out.[6] A year later, in October 1940, two young Nazified officers had roused Hitler's fury by reporting to him directly a conversation they had overheard in the officers' mess in Zossen. At this Hitler had shouted that he "knew the spirit of contradiction and defeatism which reigned at Zossen. At the right moment he would take hold of and brutally expunge all these malicious elements in the Army once and for all."[7] On September 21, 1944, the vast "Chronicle of Shame" documenting Nazi war crimes and lies, which Dohnanyi had, as editor-in-chief, been meticulously compiling since 1938, was gifted to the Gestapo by a willing informer.[8] The files contained extensive details of plans for a new post-Hitler Germany, and the wide-ranging support for them, encompassing almost all walks of life. The information contained in these volumes was so far-reaching in substance and implication that Hitler instantly forbade their use in any prosecutions.[9] These files were brought to Hitler by Ernst Kaltenbrunner.

Kaltenbrunner

Any study of the circumstances surrounding the death of Dietrich Bonhoeffer, and the "Canaris group" he was associated with, has to acknowledge the role played by Kaltenbrunner. Yet among the publications of historians and former SS colleagues who survived the war, his role receives scant attention, and academic literature before 1984 affords him insufficient treatment. Even Joachim Fest left Kaltenbrunner off the "face" of the Third Reich.[10] But with the passing of time, and as more information has emerged, there can today be little doubt about the pivotal nature of his contribution. On April 5 Kaltenbrunner was the "Auslöser," the prime mover, together with Gestapo chief Müller, of the confluence of processes leading to the deaths of the Canaris group, including Bonhoeffer.

Ernst Kaltenbrunner was described by one of Hitler's valets as "a tough, callous ox . . . [with] small brown eyes . . . bad teeth, some missing."[11] To this intimidating appearance can be added the fact that Kaltenbrunner was nearly seven feet tall, and his face was scarred.[12] He had a tendency to overindulge in alcohol and had a reputation as a womaniser. Both the

Gestapo and the concentration camps were under his authority. Millions perished on his signed orders, a responsibility he would later astonishingly deny at Nuremberg.

In the hostile world of the Third Reich, Reinhard Heydrich had openly despised Kaltenbrunner, mocked him, and suspected him.[13] For the purposes of his new role, the string of ruthless cruelties attached to his name would have been pleasing to Hitler, and indeed there is evidence that both Hitler and Nazi Party Chancellery chief Martin Bormann pressed for Kaltenbrunner's appointment. Kaltenbrunner was someone in whom the trait of allowing burning hatred to simmer, and later erupt, featured strongly. For example, one of his children, who experienced him as a warm, albeit absent, father, someone who would pick up hitchhikers out of kindness, recalled that he would also suddenly and inexplicably be found shouting violently at people on the telephone. In a further revealing example, he later fell out publicly and irretrievably with his own defence lawyer at the Nuremberg war crimes trials in 1946. He did so in a way that seemed curiously to re-energise him. More pertinently for Bonhoeffer, once Kaltenbrunner was appointed as Heydrich's successor, he did not hesitate to reveal his hostility to Canaris. Only three weeks into his new role, upon meeting the Abwehr chief for the first time in Munich on February 22, 1943, he rebuffed Canaris' friendly greetings and launched into an explosive tirade, publicly attacking Canaris' Abwehr head based in Vienna, making accusations of regime disloyalty.[14] It is fair to say that Kaltenbrunner's dislike of the admiral and his organisation was *à la fois* personal, professional, and visceral.

Kaltenbrunner's Independence of Himmler

Another related and significant development was that from the moment of his appointment in 1943, Kaltenbrunner had soon begun conceiving of ways to please Hitler, or himself, from which his line manager, Himmler, was excluded.[15] But Kaltenbrunner remained consistent in single-minded pursuit of those in his sights. For example, in his reports he would pointedly refer to Canaris as the "former Admiral."

On February 7, 1944, Kaltenbrunner had presented Hitler with a crucial report on Canaris' dramatic shortcomings, without any apparent initial reaction. But the subterranean explosion was building up. For Hitler this latest addition to the ongoing saga[16] represented a toxic cocktail of disloyalties. For this latest fiasco he blamed Canaris personally. On February 11, 1944, Canaris was summoned to the Führer; according to one report, during the stormy meeting that followed, there was a physical confrontation between the two men: Hitler, out of control with anger, leapt at Canaris, grabbed him by the throat, and accused him of defeatism. Canaris was relieved of his duties, given three hours to vacate his office, and banished to Lauenstein castle.[17] At this point SS-Brigadeführer Fegelein, Himmler's representative at the Führer's headquarters, deftly suggested that "the Führer ought to transfer the whole box of junk [the Abwehr] to the Reichsführer-SS."[18] This Hitler did the next day, creating a unified secret service that (at long last) Himmler was to head up. The long-standing dream that Heydrich had held was now to be realised, and it fell to his successor, Ernst Kaltenbrunner, to reap the harvest. Upon handing the transfer order to Kaltenbrunner the next day, Hitler facetiously asked him whether he was now satisfied. But what it meant for the already imprisoned key resisters, including Bonhoeffer, was that now, with Canaris sidelined, their already imperilled lives were even more in jeopardy.

Not only this: Canaris' fall from power did not by any means halt Kaltenbrunner's efforts to eliminate him. Things would take a further turn for the worse for non-compliers and resisters when, after surviving the July 20 bomb, Hitler appointed Himmler to exact retribution. Himmler in turn entrusted Kaltenbrunner with the task of leading all investigations. From then on, Kaltenbrunner's low-key supervisory role in the process of genocide would come to stand in sharp contrast to the ruthless zeal with which he conducted this new and most important wartime assignment: the direction of the commission that investigated the attempt on Hitler's life and exacted retribution. Perhaps inevitably, given the certain death sentences arising in the nature of the subject matter, and the project as a whole, the submitter of those reports would, especially with Bormann's help, rapidly gain direct access to Hitler. Bormann arranged for what came to be known as "the Kaltenbrunner reports" to be seen by Hitler and *not* via Himmler. As a consequence, by January 1945 Kaltenbrunner had begun to appear regularly at Hitler's situation conferences. A Hitler adjutant recalls how Bormann "slowly and discreetly" edged Kaltenbrunner into Hitler's sealed-off world, with the result that RSHA chief Kaltenbrunner could take orders directly from Hitler without the obligation to inform Himmler. This Bormann alliance was crucial in the balance of power: it enabled Kaltenbrunner to ignore Himmler when he saw fit and to obstruct those plans of the RFSS with which he did not agree.[19]

By as early as December 9, 1944, when Kaltenbrunner was awarded the Knight's Cross of the War Merit Cross with Swords, it was merely a symbol of the very real power that he now wielded. One might well count him among the five most powerful men around Hitler in the last six months of the regime, in company with Bormann, Goebbels, Himmler, and Speer. In the light of that privileged status, the soil for taking a direct Führer order and implementing it without so much as involving or even notifying Himmler was already being nurtured and cultivated from the very first days of Kaltenbrunner's arrival in Berlin. The crop from this fertile soil would be momentously harvested on April 5, 1945.

There can be almost no doubt that when Hitler was handed the Canaris diaries, Kaltenbrunner informed him that they, like the earlier cache from the previous September, had just been found at Zossen. Whatever their contents, Hitler would not have needed very much substance to transition from having sight of them to concluding that now the right moment had indeed come. It was time for him to act towards those whom he regarded as traitors as he had always stated he intended to. In the same way, his treatment of the Jews while in power was consistent with what he had stated in *Mein Kampf*. It was also a feature of Hitler's persona that he was able to sustain a resolve, over a long period, to overlook his desire to have a person sidelined or removed. For example, one author reports that Hitler's break with Röhm came in 1925, as opposed to 1934, the actual year of his murder.[20] Along similar lines, Speer observes that "even in the early period" Hitler sometimes shied away from the wearisome business of explaining reasons. An example of this came in relation to architect and Berlin mayor Julius Lippert.[21] Speer concludes,

> After four years of this sort of thing, and right after a walk from the Berghof to the teahouse, during which he once more brooded over Lippert's stupidity, he telephoned Goebbels and categorically ordered him to replace his Mayor.[22]

Hitler in general showed great deference towards architects. In much the same way he had in the past, and for a long season, greatly respected the skills and spycraft of Admiral Canaris. But that was now behind him. Only the day before, Goebbels noted in his diary that "at the moment it is very hard to elicit any decision from the Führer."[23] But this clearly did not apply to the Zossen/Canaris find. Accordingly, upon sight and inspection of the Canaris diaries, Hitler issued an order for the liquidation of "the conspirators."[24]

Indeed, Hitler's mood seems to have been much lightened by this decision. Also present in Berlin that day were his personal SS adjutant,

Günsche; his chief adjutant, General Burgdorf; Himmler's adjutant, Fegelein; General Ferdinand Schörner; and his deputy, von Trotha. Knowing this would please Hitler, Schörner proposed a plan for the relief of
Breslau, currently surrounded by the Russians. Hitler laid his hand on
Schörner's shoulder, naming him his "best general," and was set by this
in the highest spirits. It was for this reason, those present were to understand, that he had the Goldenes Parteiabzeichen (Golden Party Badge),
which signified exceptional service to the Nazi Party or state. Hitler con-
versed with him for a further three or four hours, in the presence of three
Gauleiters he had summoned from Austria to Berlin to discuss the creation of an "Alpenfestung" in the high mountains of Austria: Hofer from
Innsbruck, Eisgruber from Linz, and Uiberreither from Graz. He then
promoted Schörner to general field marshal, also entrusting him with the
command of this final bastion, hitherto little discussed.[25]

26
Interpreting Hitler's Commands

Meanwhile, for the RSHA team, there was now much to be done. The order for the elimination of the conspirators was a blank cheque of the most colossal proportions. Kaltenbrunner said as much that very day. Emerging from the Führer bunker, he bumped into the very person who had set the process in motion, SS-Gruppenführer Johann Rattenhuber. After his return from Soviet captivity in 1955, Rattenhuber met up with his "beer brother in black,"[1] his term of affection for Josef Müller, and reported that Kaltenbrunner had that day greeted him in haste with the news that "the Führer has (literally) just handed over to me the decision about the political prisoners." To this Rattenhuber responded, "Well in that case please render me the service of taking my friend Josef Müller off the list!" to which Kaltenbrunner, also in haste, nodded his agreement. Given that Kaltenbrunner and "Gestapo" Müller were now at liberty to do entirely as they pleased with any number of the people they deemed regime opponents, one person more or less in the scheme of things made little difference at this point of impending general collapse. From their standpoint the issue of the Canaris *Komplex*, or group, was an unresolved case that they had doggedly been pursuing for a very long time. In their own minds, they were fully persuaded of the guilt of the whole group. Throughout the duration of the war, Heydrich and his department chiefs Müller and Schellenberg had begun to bear down hard on the Canaris organisation. Notably, Sonderegger was also numbered among those who had been thwarted from 1943 onwards by the close-downs from Himmler.[2] Compounding the ever-present jurisdictional and personal rivalries of Heydrich and his associates had been three enduring convictions. These were:

(1) In 1940 someone in the Abwehr had leaked invasion information.
(2) Canaris had given the British documentation of German U-boat construction between 1922 and 1935.

(3) With Canaris' tacit approval, Abwehr agents had via the Vatican sought to establish "peace feeler" discussions.[3]

In relation to the first and the third of these points, the suspicions of the RSHA were entirely correct. In the latter instance, they were right even to the extent of intuiting the "tacit approval" working style of the Abwehr. On the first, Oster had indeed repeatedly done this, essentially without Canaris' knowledge or approval. On the second, it seems improbable that this charge could be taken seriously. On the third, as has been alluded to earlier, the team from the RSHA had been incensed at being "closed down" by the trio of Canaris, Keitel, and Himmler. Now Heydrich was dead, a victim of British assassination. His successor, Kaltenbrunner, as outlined above, made no secret of his extreme hatred for, and disgust towards, Canaris. But Canaris himself was less unsettled by Kaltenbrunner and more by "Gestapo" Müller, a man of utter ruthlessness and cold cynicism.[4] Regardless of who was the prime mover, what is known is that at this point the lethal structures that the RSHA controlled, and which still supported and enacted such arbitrary measures, leapt into action, at breathtaking speed. It is not known at what point the team made the decision to appoint a summary court.[5] However it came about, on the basis of the RSHA's loyal "working towards the Führer," a number of orders were issued that day.[6] In the case of the one we have, which concerns only a single liquidation directive, an original copy fell into the hands of Payne Best after the war and is now in the Walter Leschander Collection, Hoover Institution, Stanford University.[7] It is written in the polite formal German style. The phrase "Ich bitte" appears seven times. It begins, "By order of the RFSS" and "After consultation with the highest authorities." This was the euphemistic Prinz-Albrecht-Straße language for a Führer order. The Müller order was addressed to the commandant of KL Dachau, sealed in a brown envelope franked in red ink with "Secret: State Business" and marked for his personal attention. The order, signed by Müller, closes, for readily understandable reasons, with the phrase "Upon absorbing and carrying out of this order I request that you please destroy it."

The letter contains detailed instructions for the handling of ten prisoners and gives clear orders for the liquidation of special category prisoner Elser,[8] whose bomb in Munich's Bürgerbräukeller had almost succeeded in killing Hitler in 1939.[9] The commandant is also issued with a pro forma for the notification to be issued upon fulfilment of the order. It states,

The following directive [of Hitler] has been issued: During one of the next "terror" attacks on Munich, or the area of Dachau, it will be alleged that "Eller" [*sic*] was also unfortunately killed. I request for this reason that you please liquidate "Eller" in as discreet a manner as possible. . . . I request that steps be taken to ensure very few people are involved, and must be especially pledged to silence. The notification can then be sent to me, worded as follows: "On . . . *date* . . . following a 'terror' air attack on . . . protective custody prisoner 'Eller' was, among others, fatally wounded."

Although each of the RSHA orders began with the phrase "By order of the RFSS," the reality, on April 5, is likely to have been otherwise. In post-war testimony[10] Huppenkothen stated, "Ob Himmler eingeschaltet war, ist fraglich" (Whether Himmler was in the loop is questionable). This statement was a shorthand, and represents another Nazi euphemism, which in this instance we may take as disclosing the likely truth, namely that Himmler was, in this situation, not included. As we have already seen in chapter 3, Himmler consistently protected Canaris. Both in 1945, when the order was issued, and in 1951, when Huppenkothen was called for cross-examination, this was not widely known.[11] Yet in the innermost Gestapo circles in wartime Berlin, Himmler's shielding of Canaris was a commonly shared secret. Müller, Kaltenbrunner, and Huppenkothen understood that if Himmler knew of a *Führerbefehl* to execute Canaris and his associates, that would have placed him in an impossible dilemma. Worse still, Himmler may have sought to delay or defer the matter. It may have even been a factor for the team that in this instance, not carrying out Hitler's wish swiftly could have proven perilous for their own safety. Whatever their deliberations, we may be confident of the outcome. The exigencies of the hour meant excluding Himmler from involvement. In this new situation, however many were to be numbered on the list was now entirely the RSHA's decision. Three, or even four, would have been sufficient. It could easily have been seven. It seems they decided upon five. It was wholly within their power, even after the order had been issued, to remove at least one person from the list.[12] It came down to their collective sense of the extent to which those they had been so ruthlessly and persistently interrogating without success had, in relation to July 20 and the war effort as a whole, been active resisters, and hence, in their view, traitors. Bonhoeffer's inclusion on the list was a case of Müller and Kaltenbrunner's autonomous "working towards the Führer."[13]

From the order we have, and from the other events that followed, we may discern the pattern likely to have been used for those missing and hence imagined orders that concern us here. The responsibility for carrying out the respective execution processes lay clearly with the camp commandant. The orders emanating from Berlin were routed via Gestapostelle Prien, in southernmost Germany. Accordingly, one further order issued that day reached the camp commandant of KZ Sachsenhausen, Anton Kaindl, freshly returned from his frustrating meeting with Himmler the day before. We know he was required to convene a *Standgericht* or similar, to be held the following day, on April 6, to issue the death sentence to Hans von Dohnanyi. Huppenkothen was designated chief prosecutor; he received notification of this by 4:00 on the afternoon of April 5. Police Colonel and SS-Oberführer Otto Somann was allocated an auxiliary role.[14] The other orders also issued that day included one addressed to the camp commandant of KL Flossenbürg, Max Koegel, directing that on April 8 an SS *Standgericht* or *Sondergericht* should be convened. Those to appear before the summary court (and be condemned to death) were Admiral Canaris, General Hans Oster, Judge General Karl Sack, Ludwig Gehre, and Dietrich Bonhoeffer. Huppenkothen was here, too, to be chief prosecutor, supported in Flossenbürg by SS judge Stürmbannführer Otto Thorbeck. Thanks to the careful and wholesale destruction of records, these orders, together with all the surrounding documentation, have never been found. For these reasons it has not been possible to ascertain what the charges were, what type of proceeding was mandated, and in that respect what evidence was submitted.

27

The Wheel of History Turns

Buchenwald, Germany

On April 5, according to Elie Wiesel, at that time a sixteen-year-old in Buchenwald, the "wheel of history turned." The phrase makes an auspicious link with the timing of Hitler's decision. Of course, Wiesel was not referring to the execution orders issued by Hitler and his subordinates. Nor was he referring to the execution at German hands of the former camp commandant of Buchenwald, Karl Koch, for corruption. Of this he had no knowledge. But it was a phrase that proved accurate and spoke at multiple levels across many locations. Wiesel was in the children's block in the KL, only metres from where Bonhoeffer had been staying until two nights beforehand. What so stunned Wiesel was that the SS orderly due to oversee the counting of inmates in his barrack was late. It was a moment unprecedented in the history of the camp. Wiesel knew something must have happened.

> Two hours later, the loudspeakers transmitted an order from the Camp Commandant: all Jews were to gather in the *Appellplatz*. This was the end! Hitler was about to keep his promise [to kill every Jew]. The children of our block did as ordered. There was no choice: Gustav, the *Blockälteste*, made it clear with his club. . . . But on our way we met some prisoners who whispered to us: "Go back to your block. The Germans plan to shoot you. Go back and don't move." We returned to the block. On our way there, we learned that the underground resistance of the camp had made the decision not to abandon the Jews and to prevent their liquidation.[1]

Ravensbrück, Germany

Finally, tortuous negotiations via Himmler delivered the smallest sign of actual cooperation. In Ravensbrück a group of prisoners had been in the process of being selected, and then deselected, and then reselected, for days on end. Now one group, all in terrible condition, were allowed to board the buses that were to transport them to freedom. They stared at the men in khaki. "I thought it was a dream," said one. "I think they were Canadians, and they cried when they saw us. When I saw them crying, I began to think it was real." The Canadians helped the women climb on to the buses. Inside they were each given a piece of cake and a large piece of cold sausage. The vehicles started up and drove away. The women were told they were heading to Lake Constance and the Swiss border.[2]

Caserta, Italy

On April 5, the day after Generals Lemnitzer and Airey had arrived back in their Caserta headquarters following the talks about a possible cease-fire, units of General Truscott's 5th Army advanced northwards. Within a few days they took both Massa and Carrara. For the Germans, prolonging resistance was not only becoming more costly; it was also a sacrifice increasingly devoid of meaning.

Rødbyhavn, Denmark

After a sea crossing from Danzig fraught with anxiety, Wehrmacht soldier Guy Sajer arrived safely in the "unbelievable West." He writes,

> We arrived in Denmark, where we saw things we had almost forgotten, like pastry shops, which we devoured with enormous eyes, forgetting our filthy faces ravaged by misery. We scarcely noticed the looks of mistrust fixed on us by the shopkeeper. . . . We had no money, and the wares on display were not free. For a moment, we even thought of our machine guns.[3]

In this standoff, one soldier could not resist temptation. He held out his big hands, and begged for charity. Finally, the baker put a stale cake into them and the soldiers tasted a substance that had become unknown to them. When they thanked the man, and tried to smile, the rotting teeth in their grey faces must have produced the effect of a grotesque grimace, which made the baker think they were mocking him. The baker turned on his heel and disappeared into the back of his shop.

Nuremberg, Germany

April 5 saw the last great Allied raid on Nuremberg. A total of forty-seven raids were carried out, and 17,115 tons of explosives were dropped on the once-iconic city. In all, 6,120 were killed, and 12,900 seriously injured. The number is itself an approximation, since the records were destroyed on that day.[4]

Gmunden, Austria

For Marie Vassiltchikov the day began at 4:00 a.m., when it was still dark. On the walk to the station to catch a train for Linz, she and her companions ran into two drunken German soldiers who had walked all the way from the Hungarian border, a distance of some three hundred kilometres, without being stopped once. To Marie it spoke volumes about the state of the German army as a whole. At 2:00 p.m. that day, Marie went off in search of a butcher and returned, quite proud, with half a pound of sausage. But both her companions were convinced that it was made of horse—or worse, dog—meat and refused to touch it. Amid much confusion they finally arrived at Gmunden, where they were, in a much-appreciated respite, accommodated at the Königinvilla.[5]

Gotha, Germany

In Gotha the town breathed a sigh of relief, experiencing the fruits of the previous day's liberation at the hands of overwhelmingly superior forces in the shape of the 4th Tank Regiment of the US 3rd Army. Surrender conversations had been started, in defiance of orders to hold Gotha to the last man alive, by city commander Lieutenant Colonel Gadolla. He was arrested and driven to Weimar, where he was court-martialled for cowardice. At 7:00 on April 5, he was summarily shot. For him the wheel of history turned. Fully cognisant of the likely consequences of his own courageous actions, he commented, "I must die so that Gotha may live."[6]

Osnabrück, Germany

In Osnabrück the BBC correspondent Chester Wilmot reported from among the debris in the heart of the city, which British Commandos had captured that morning. He testified to the change throughout the day, from total stillness, and no civilians in sight, to a situation where hundreds, thousands of them had been coming out of the houses and cellars where they had been hiding all day long. He stated that they had been coming up to the Commandos and shaking them by the hand and thanking them. They had been pressing into their hands beer and cake and giving them a real liberation welcome. The survivors had many questions for the troops. But in each case, in their voice there was a note of extreme gratitude, as they packed up their belongings, into handcarts and onto bicycles, to begin heading westwards on the way home. Wilmot added,

> If you remember how in Britain we destroyed all the road signs and planned to mis-direct any German who arrives, you'd be surprised to find that every road sign here is intact and the Germans are only too anxious to tell you the name of their village and the quickest way to get to the next one. You'd find hordes of German soldiers anxiously obeying General Eisenhower's instructions to come forward into our lines and give themselves up. . . . Having heard about Werewolves you'd drive cautiously in case it was an ambush, but after a while you'd no longer believe in Werewolves.[7]

Wilmot counted between 1,200 and 1,600 trained soldiers being driven through a no man's land in their own country and wondered, because of stories he had heard of Allied troops, why they did not just try to escape. He concluded, "But you look at them as you pass and the answer's written on their faces. Germany is beaten already."[8]

Rinteln, Germany

Around eighty-five kilometres farther east of Osnabrück, the town of Rinteln, situated on the Weser river in Lower Saxony, found itself confronted on April 5 by divisions of Simpson's US 9th Army, who were racing towards Berlin. For the town it was indeed a day on which the wheel of history turned. The troops from the US 5th Tank Division were commanded by Colonel Leroy Anderson, who had issued a surrender ultimatum to the authorities the previous evening. They were in no mood for prevarications. Others in the 9th Army were rapidly pressing ahead. Major General Isaac D. White commanded the 2nd Armoured Division—dubbed "Hell on Wheels"—the strongest in the US Army. His principal rival in the race for Berlin was the 83rd Infantry Division, known as the "Rag-Tag Circus" because of its extraordinary assortment of captured vehicles and equipment sprayed olive green and given a white star.[9] Both of these divisions also reached the Weser river on April 5. In Rinteln the tension had been exacerbated still farther: no sooner had the US negotiators reached the town centre than the bridge they had crossed was blown. They had not yet been granted safe passage back to US lines next morning when the 9:00 deadline expired; it was extended for an hour. An entire town held its breath. At 10:00 Rinteln's local doctor, Dr Krukenberg, and the town's acting chief councillor, Fritz Schlame, were able to announce the momentous news: the bombardment had been called off. By mid-afternoon town dwellers were able to emerge from their hiding places. But even that out-come met with a mixed reception. In their home in the Hinter-der-Mauer alley, the blood-soaked bodies of the town's NSDAP regional commander, Franzmeier, and his wife were found on the marital bed, covered with a swastika flag. They had killed their daughter and committed suicide together. Only days beforehand Franzmeier had stated, dismally, "They are preparing a gallows for me in the town square."[10]

Munich, Germany

That day, newly arrived in Munich, the Jewish diarist Victor Klemperer and his wife, Eva, shared the midday meal table with a married couple from Berlin. Klemperer noted,

> He said: People were saying, Hitler had shot himself; she: They were saying, the "turning-point," the new weapon, the new offen-sive, was coming in four days.

Unfortunately for the hostages, Hitler had not shot himself. Worse still, he had issued orders for the liquidation of others. As we have seen above, these would be so interpreted as to include Bonhoeffer; and within those same four days, the fantasy of a "turning-point" miracle weapon for Ger-many would not appear. On April 5 the much-vaunted V-2 rocket offen-sive, which since the end of March had been targeting only Brussels, Ant-werp, and Liège, came to a hushed end.[11] Within four days nor would Bonhoeffer be alive. He had been included on the Flossenbürg list.

Flossenbürg, Germany

In Flossenbürg's VIP prisoner section, the former chancellor of Austria Kurt Schuschnigg remained imprisoned in almost total seclusion with his wife and their daughter "Sissy." Schuschnigg's wife, Vera, had chosen internment voluntarily throughout the duration of the war, and their child had been born in captivity. Now four years old, she knew of no other world or uni-verse than that of confinement with both parents in a concentration camp. But, despite their isolation, in Flossenbürg she was still able to hear some of the dreadful screams that emanated from less fortunate prisoners in their sufferings. She understood enough of life to guess at what some of those sounds implied, and asked if they might move back to their earlier "home," the concentration camp in Sachsenhausen, which she had preferred. On April 5 Schuschnigg wrote in his diary, "The tension reaches fever pitch—the Americans in Nuremberg—they could be here in a few days."[12] But in Bon-hoeffer's case, those "few" days would prove to be too many.

28

The Hostages: A Better Day

Regensburg, Germany

In overall terms the day, apparently unmomentous, proved to be a better one for the hostages. Being actually confined to a prison had been much offset by the fact that most of them had actually slept well. Léon Blum was one among a number who did so. He noted, "Lying down without undressing on this grubby pallet of a bed, my tiredness proves such that I rediscover the sleep that has evaded me these many long nights." At the same time, the cell containing Bonhoeffer and his companions continued to receive virtually no sustenance. Hermann Pünder wrote that morning, "Again, washing is impossible. Of course we have not removed our clothes overnight. After many requests we receive a bowl of coffee, although it is not enough to go round."[1] The less preferential treatment afforded to Bonhoeffer's cell was also felt in other ways. On this day it seems that most prisoners, other than those in the cell with Bonhoeffer, were allowed to walk around the corridors freely. It was, according to Fey von Hassell, the most sensational event in the history of Regensburg prison. In the case of Falconer's cell, Best reported that next morning their cell door was opened and a warder informed them they could go out and wash. Doing so, they found the whole corridor crowded with a mass of people: men, women, and children. Small wonder that Blum writes, "In the morning, from outside in the corridor, the silence of the prison is broken by the sound of footsteps and the melody of chattering voices." For Best it was not just a few voices:

> Falkenhausen and Petersdorff seem to know everybody, and soon I am being introduced right and left, and the atmosphere becomes more that of a big reception than a morning in a criminal prison. . . . Every now and again one of the warders shouts "Everybody go to their cell" but the only result is laughter and loud cheers.[2]

Falconer reports a rare, most welcome, and decent meal being brought to them around lunchtime. Stauffenberg's record also speaks of sustenance: "Cell doors open. See the Grüne Minna van people. Morning in cellar air raid alarm. Midday soup provided."[3] In classic fashion the food was obviously distributed selectively. There was none for Bonhoeffer. Pünder reports that in their cell the five of them received neither any food nor even a sip of water.[4]

A Small Act of Regensburg Defiance

But while the randomness of treatment afforded to the different categories of hostage may seem disconcerting, there were still some interesting, and more hope-filled, exchanges that happened among the hostages and behind the scenes on that day. One of the prison guards in charge of the hostages was Austrian Alois Keindl. His occupation, prior to his own incarceration, had been in farming-related work. He had been arrested in the autumn of 1944 for a comment made on a bus journey, overheard and reported to the Gestapo, about the events of July 20. He had offered the opinion that it was a shame that the attempt on Hitler had not succeeded, because if it had, the war would by now be over. This constituted a crime known at the time as *Wehrkraftzersetzung* (undermining military morale). Although Keindl was a member of the NSDAP, he had also previously drawn attention to himself through comments deemed to be critical of the regime. The municipal authorities initiated proceedings against him on the above charges, but these were unable to be progressed because of the difficulties in communication channels between Nuremberg and Berlin. He now found himself not in a concentration camp, but in the relatively favoured role of Regensburg prison's general warder, dogsbody, and odd-job man. At the time he met the hostages, Keindl was imminently due to appear in court in Berlin, where he would, if the session were not once again delayed, almost certainly be sentenced to death. He chose to use the remaining time he had to share kindness and went to great lengths to do what he could to help. It was Keindl who carried Léon Blum downstairs to the shelter. It was he, next morning, who allowed access for Anneliese Goerdeler and her daughter Marianne to the cells where some of the Grüne Minna prisoners were still locked in. Anneliese, like all the hostages, was deeply conscious that all their lives might end at any moment. Keindl, with no small courage, agreed to assist Goerdeler in the project of "leaving a trail" behind in case of execution.

Learning of this, several other hostages took up Keindl's offer. These included interned members of the former Hungarian government, as well as prisoners of Polish origins. Goerdeler's thankfulness to him for his genuine kindness extended after the war to quite a regular exchange of correspondence between them. Included among the letters are some from fellow *Sippenhaft* prisoner Markwart Schenk von Stauffenberg, a cousin of the July 20 bomb plotter. These testify to the gratitude of the Stauffenberg family. At the end of his life, via his family, he bequeathed the letters to a local historian, Prof Dünninger, and it is thanks to him that this litany of Regensburg defiance is now more widely known.[5] Given that so much of what became the corpus of Bonhoeffer's writings were smuggled out of prison in the 1943–1944 period by other jailers equally prepared to expose themselves to great risk,[6] it would seem a fitting testimony to the often unnamed courage of so many ordinary and good-hearted Germans amid the darkest of days that this interlude in Bonhoeffer's final week should not go unrecorded.

A Precious Conversation

Because of this small act of subversion, some good work could be done. Goerdeler's daughter Marianne reported excitedly to her mother that Dietrich Bonhoeffer had made a wonderful impression on her. She recounted a precious conversation she had had at length with Bonhoeffer, albeit through an opening in the cell door, on the subject of her father, Carl. The family had had no news about him, and here she found herself talking to someone who had actually been there with him, his cell neighbour in the dreadful Prinz-Albrecht-Straße building, in his latter days of suffering. Aware that her father had finally been taken away for execution on February 2, Bonhoeffer reported that it was unlikely her father was still alive. But he added that whenever he had seen him, he had been steadfast, albeit very emaciated and suffering, and as a result it had been a double pleasure to pass on to him supplies from his own substantial provisions—especially at Christmas. Bonhoeffer spoke so little of himself that Marianne wondered if her own hunger for news rather dominated over properly asking Bonhoeffer about his own welfare. But to Marianne, only six years older than his fiancée, Maria, he did express the hope that he was now out of the greatest danger zone, with future prospects looking better. He revealed that dearest to his heart was getting news of his ageing parents and his fiancée from Pomerania, about whose whereabouts and well-being he was completely in the dark. In the snatched moments of communication and connection, Bonhoeffer clearly felt he was talking to a kindred spirit, one to whom his fiancée would have related well. Marianne reported that a severe air raid interrupted this conversation but that thereafter throughout the day, understandably, she and her family took opportunities off and on to converse with the Grüne Minna group, especially Pastor Bonhoeffer.

An Interrupted Day in Prison: A Curse on the "Contagion of Hatred"

Best reports that in an intelligent attempt to restore a semblance of order, one of the guards lured the loquacious group back into their cells by serving food. This initially proved a successful ploy, but was soon undermined by the sound of a further air raid alert, necessitating (once more) the accompanied return of the entire group to the basement. Here, in Best's words, "the fun started again." One of the *Sippenhäftlinge* reported that planes roared over Regensburg for three hours that afternoon.[7] The impact of the air raids was by this time shocking. Best writes,

> I had been able to look out over the railway marshalling yard, which was next to the prison, and really I have never seen such a mess in my life. Engines and coaches lying on their backs with their legs in the air, burnt-out coaches in long rows, and railway lines sticking up in great loops like pieces of wire.[8]

Even the temporarily disabled Blum was able to benefit from lively conversations with other VIP prisoners of differing nationalities. For the French couple, periods of quiet were interspersed, even when the door was locked again, with the sounds of chatter. The intermittent air raids meant Blum had to be carried downstairs, where from a camp bed he would hear the loudspeakers recounting the progress of the current air raid. According to one of these, the Allied target for the four-engined bombers for that day was not Regensburg but Neustadt. This information was, for Blum, most distressing to hear: in his mind's eye, he could see the peaceful village, the square where the convoy had assembled, with the children playing on doorsteps, the little girl who was dancing with such grace on the pavement. He thought of children torn from their parents' arms ahead of departure on sealed concentration camp trains. Silently he cursed those whose cruelty had unleashed on this world what he calls "the contagion of hatred."

An Interrupted Journey Onwards

Best reports that at 5:00 one of their old guards from Buchenwald came to tell the group that they must be moving off again. The Englishman was by this time feeling quite cheerful after this day with friends, and having received food both on the evening before and during the day. The sentiments of those who had received nothing, including Bonhoeffer, are likely to have been more measured. When they got outside and found the same Grüne Minna waiting for them, despite its being a contraption of extreme discomfort, Best described it as an "old friend," and they climbed back inside. Setting off, they hardly made it out of town before a major breakdown of the Grüne Minna occured. Most of the other vehicles soon pressed on ahead. Stauffenberg noted, "Leave late afternoon. In fact 19:45 departure. Almost right away: breakdown of Minna, but [other] *Holzgas-omnibus* carries on. We have to stay and wait there until 1:20 a.m. in the morning."[9]

29

An SOE Sabotage Operation

The hostages had a very long and cold night ahead of them. In his account, which captures correctly the impression of all those in the hostage party, Best writes that Falconer, as an engineer, was "called upon for an expert opinion, and he decided there was no way of repairing it there."[1] But Falconer, completely unbeknown to Best, was a highly trained saboteur, in this case, SOE. The raison d'être of the SOE was to undermine any aspect of the German war effort that was in their power to subvert. Falconer picks up the (real) story.

When the vehicle broke down, the hostages were, for once, mercifully allowed to step outside it, to their intense relief. As they stood there in the darkness and the cold, the driver complained audibly that he was not a mechanic, and that it was bad enough having to drive this thing without being expected to mend it as well. At this point a line of inappropriate familiarity between captive and soldier was crossed. Thereupon the (deputy) transport leader enquired about whether one of the hostages happened to be an engineer who could deal with the situation. For Falconer this was too good a chance to miss, and although feeling extremely ill, he volunteered at once. The cause of the trouble was, to him, obvious at first glance: the drain plug on the steering box had become loose, all the oil had escaped, and the box was seizing up. However, having been presented with a bag of tools, it seemed a pity not to use them, so he took the top off the box and admired the aged and now gently smoking contents. Falconer writes,

> At this point, as I contemplate how best to sabotage it good and proper, the driver, who has been watching suspiciously, says he has a tin of oil we could put in and goes to rummage for it. This, of course, is no good at all; with a refill of oil the thing might go on running for miles. Fortunately we are parked on the hard shoulder of the road

and it is the work of a moment to scoop up a handful of grit and dump it in the box while the driver is away looking for the oil. When he comes back he pours the oil in and I obligingly put the cover back on, even conscientiously tightening up the drain plug. In we all climb and off we go again. But not for long. A few miles down the road there is a sickening lurch as we career across the opposite verge and pull up just short of the ditch. One glance at the steering box is enough. The grit has done its job and it is beyond repair.[2]

Best reported from the vehicle that it was by now a raw cold night to spend sitting cramped in a police van with no suspension or heating of any kind. It soon began to rain. There was no food, drink, or even tobacco to be had. Any form of rescue was long in coming. A passing cyclist unfortunate enough to be coming from the other direction in the last fragile moments of daylight was halted, and charged with instructing the Regensburg police to send a replacement vehicle. With his objective achieved, Falconer was quick to point out to the deputy transport leader that one of the benefits of waiting was that it afforded the rapidly approaching and nearest Allied troops time to liberate them, and that under the circumstances, it might be wise for him and his men to withdraw. At this the guards themselves wavered, dropping any appearance of hostility and beginning to conduct themselves as though they were the hostages' comrades in adversity. Best at this point describes the guards as appearing lonely, miserable, and frightened, especially as the stretch of road they were all stranded on was an open one where there lay the burnt-out skeletons of many vehicles. Even the nearby field, visible in the moonlight, between where they were broken down and the railway, was thickly pitted with bomb craters. However, it also seems that the change that had been coming over these men, clearly apparent to both Englishmen, was not hidden from the transport leader.

There was only one occupant of the vehicle who knew what he had done, and the real cause of the standstill, and the squadron leader kept the information to himself. Given what he had just done, he might well have smiled inwardly at the knowledge that there was one occupant of the vehicle in Bonhoeffer whose direct superior in the Abwehr, Colonel Oster, had a favourite maxim that he was fond of citing at every opportunity. It applied to all possible applications of resistance to, and in respect of, everything that Nazi Germany stood for. Oster's favourite resistance phrase was "More sand in the machinery."

A Replacement Bus, with New Guards, Is Arranged

With things at a standstill, Léon Blum, with the transport leader, was driven back the way they had come, to Regensburg, where his vehicle waited while a new bus was requisitioned. He thus found himself waiting again for hours outside the Gestapo Hotel at precisely the same spot they had arrived at the day before. It was 2:00 the next morning before the new vehicle appeared in Regensburg.[3] What still lay ahead of the occupants of the Mercedes even then was the time needed for the recruiting of an entire new team of guards, the driving back, followed by the process of transfer of hostages from one vehicle to another. The rump of the now-separated convoy would finally get underway once again at the second or third attempt, in fits and starts. Blum's take was that Germany as a nation was jammed, unworkable, and broken down, like the vehicles in the convoy. For once the usually accurate observations of the French prime minister did not apply. The replacement vehicle and new guards, taken together, were a sign of an exceptional and ruthless determination to carry out orders. The chaos they were experiencing was due to a deliberate act of sabotage by an undercover Allied agent, one so effectively camouflaged that no one even suspected his presence. It was a brilliant manoeuvre, and one that so nearly saved Bonhoeffer's life. It was not to be.

Friday, April 6, 1945

30
Hugh Falconer, Heidel Nowakowski, and Alexander von Falkenhausen

It would be a very long night for the hostages, thanks to the endeavours of Falconer. So who was this undercover operative, chivalrous in showing respect, together with the ever-courteous General von Falkenhausen, towards the young Heidel Nowakowski?

Hugh Falconer

The future squadron leader was born in Carlisle on October 12, 1910, to Hugh and Edith Falconer. By the time of the arrival of Hugh Mallory (Mallory was the name used by some family members), a younger brother to Agnes, his father, ordained in 1882, had been minister in the Fisher Street Presbyterian Church in Carlisle since 1908. Hugh's father was also a writer of considerable literary ability and the author of many poems.

His family were internationally minded, and Falconer accompanied his mother to France when he was aged only eleven, spending a year in a French *lycée* in Poitiers. One consequence of this was that Falconer's language ability in French was complete: he became a native speaker. Back in the UK, he attended Cheltenham College, was trained in wireless telegraphy, attended the Royal Military Academy in Woolwich, and was commissioned into the Royal Signals.

His affinity with France and all things French, together with a healthy dose of boredom, led to his handing in his papers and joining the French Foreign Legion in 1932. Here he considerably extended his already high levels of competence in wireless telegraphy and in organising radio networks. It was a happy stint spent mainly in French North Africa, when plenty of rugby was played. Sadly a knee injury brought the five-year term to a premature close at the halfway point. Returning to the UK, Falconer married his French fiancée, Simone, and settled into life as a cement engineer in Kent and a special army reserve officer. When war came, Falconer found that his status as one "ineligible for active service owing to being in a reserved occupation" was not much to his liking. He was able to sign up with the RAF (VR) only by April 1940. At the same time, imagining, like so many,[1] the Maginot line to be secure, his wife, Simone, and baby daughter settled in France, first in Touraine, then in Péronne. Once he was in the RAF, Falconer's specialist expertise in radio communications developed still further.

In a curious quirk of fate, he was posted with the RAF's No. IV Squadron to Péronne, and billeted at a small village at a distance of only five kilometres from his young family. Here he was able to participate in both a personal and operational capacity in the traumatic events that ensued. At one stage he was even able to provide a jerrycan of petrol to his father-in-law for the family's southward-bound escape journey. At another, while himself taking charge of the road transport operation leading north towards evacuation at Dunkirk, he witnessed first hand the deliberate Nazi machine-gunning of fleeing civilians, filling him with a lasting hatred of the enemy.

Once he was back in the UK, the quiet days of war exercises that ensued were for Falconer, like his previous stint in the British Army, a period less to his liking. Nonetheless he rapidly achieved the rank of squadron leader, and on July 5, 1941, was released by the RAF and posted to the SOE.

Three days later Falconer, given the agent number 007, was sent to Arisaig in Scotland for a refresher course (in his case, hardly needed) in wireless telegraphy and "thuggery." His unconventionality and sense of humour were much in evidence. His response to the question "Can you box?" was "Not if I can help it!" His training report also notes, "Speaks perfect French and could pass as a Frenchman: capable of 25 words a minute in Morse Code para-sets." Falconer could do the work, or he could train and enable others. By now he was ideally cut out for developing codes of practice for SOE operators working in perilous conditions behind enemy lines. In this spirit, within his own family, he devised a secret system of postcards to keep in touch with his wife right up until at least February 1942. Communications were dangerous and the whole family needed to be vigilant. Both parties needed to rely on their wits to evade censorship. His daughter, Evelyn, aged only two when she said goodbye to her father, later recalled,

> When we got back to Péronne from Touraine my mother had some previous letters from my father. The Nazis had started searching all the houses so she took my beloved Teddy Bear, slit his stomach and

put the letters in there. Then she roughed him up to look like a del-apidated worn out toy and threw him into the attic which, French style, was on the same floor as the first floor of the house—at the top of the T part of it. Every night I remember going up the stairs to bed and popping into the attic to say goodnight to my teddy. Eventually the danger passed off and my French grandmother patched him up as he was a sorry sight. He acquired a light fawn head and ears with embroidered eyes and mouth, fawn legs but the body was a very French looking rather elegant black and white check. He stayed like that for many years until in the end he had to be patched up again.[2]

The spirit of improvisation was no doubt passed down through the family genes. A detailed document, written in French and discovered in the wartime files of the Iberia Section of the SOE, and which came to light only in 2017, reveals a great deal about Falconer and his considerable contribution, not widely known, and hitherto somewhat unrecognised, to the Allied war effort.

In this personal account, deemed compromising because of its detail, Squadron Leader Hugh Mallory Falconer tells how he established a secret wireless network covering the western Mediterranean and linking Gibraltar with North African cities including Casablanca, Tangier, and Oran. This network did not only help pave the way for Operation Torch, the Anglo-American invasion of Vichy French North Africa in November 1942. More pertinently, when the US armed forces went into combat, it was Falconer's improvised radio network, persuasively created out of rudimentary materials, that held up when the other Allied communications systems failed. The undertaking was the biggest amphibious operation in history. What this meant was that for three days it was only Falconer's low-level radio post housed in a cave in the Rock of Gibraltar that kept the Allied commander Eisenhower in touch with his ground forces. In an increasingly challenging situation, Mallory's network (as it was referred to by the authorities) helped ensure this pivotal moment in the war did not turn into a disaster. It is no exaggeration to state that this contribution helped change the course of history. Downing Street, in a memo of May 19, 1943, described the work of Mallory and his team in glowing terms. "It is abundantly clear that the operators handling the signals . . . were as essential to the operations as the organ blower to the cathedral organist." Falconer's own assessment of what transpired is, characteristically, understated: in his post-war debrief, he simply wrote that following Torch "I was out of a job."

Being out of a job that November did not slow Falconer down for long. January 28, 1943, saw Agent 007 being dropped with two companions in a fast motor torpedo boat (307) near Hammamet on the coast of Tunisia, equipped for Operation BEAR with wireless receiver and transmitter, complete with an entirely erroneous briefing about the absence of any curfew in Tunis. Sensibly taking the precaution of hiding the incriminating devices and other items before proceeding, they quickly (the next day) and unsurprisingly fell into the hands of the guards on curfew duties.[3] Upon capture, and appreciative of being given time to think, Falconer created an excellent cover story about being a Frenchman, replete with accurate North African references.

After some weeks the credible story was sadly exploded. This came about thanks to the discovery of his suitcase, complete with radio. His real identity as an enemy spy became known. Despite the grudging respect the Germans afforded him for his prior ability to sustain a cover story, his life was now in genuine and severe peril. Prolonged further interrogation at all hours of the day and night were to follow. One source of mystification to Falconer was how relaxed the enemy seemed when he would not disclose anything about the secret service they assumed he was working for. He later wrote, "It was when I forced open a cupboard in Berlin after the war I discovered the reason: they knew it all already!"[4] In Tunis Falconer's stubbornness duly culminated in his being driven out to an execution site to be shot, on the basis that he had not been willing to reveal anything other than his name and rank, and especially his wireless operator code.

It proved to be a (classic) German bluff. But when this procedure happened for the second time, his tactical move in revealing the code was effective, and was in line with the SOE protocol he had helped develop. The safety net was that all genuine messages contained an intentional coding error; if this were omitted, home friends would at once know he was acting under duress, and could then take the opportunity to feed the Germans false information.[5] In Falconer's case, history does not relate whether any mistake was made, as other events took over and by May 1943 what remained of the German Army Group Africa had evacuated Tunis. In these final hectic moments, Falconer was provided with a haircut, bundled aboard a Ju 52 transport plane, and hastily flown to Naples. When only half the departing planes arrived, and being aware his SS interrogator "Max" was nowhere to be seen, Falconer quickly saw that this turn of events meant that he was being presented with a new opportunity. It was the moment to create a new identity for himself, that of a downed pilot. Under this now entirely different category, he was duly transported by rail via Florence and Berlin to Sachsenhausen concentration camp.

Once he was there, his instinct for insisting on respect paid dividends: he harangued an orderly for not addressing him suitably as an officer of senior rank. He also threw his first evening's bowl of soup at the wall in protest at its not being sufficiently hot to consume. In taking a high-handed line and presenting himself as someone with copious quantities of "blue blood" in his veins, he grew sure he had unwittingly picked the surest way of staying alive. Over the next twenty-two months, on SS rations, even VIP ones, his weight fell by half to 6 ¼ stone. He occupied himself throughout this time by learning German, which he then used to create a resistance newspaper, entitled the *Oranienbürgische Zeitung*, on scraps of paper sized six inches by three inches. An even more effective application of his new-found German-language skills was their employment for the necessary work of blackmailing the guards by threatening them with the disclosure of secret information he had unearthed. Falconer also observed what was no secret: the murdering of 4,600 Russians by camp commandant Kaindl's systematic maltreatment and cruelty. Falconer was also subject to Kaindl's personal malevolence, which extended in his case to the withdrawing of entitled supplies of cigarettes, matches, and exercise privileges from him.[6] But for the committed, there were highlights. On Christmas Eve 1943, the squadron leader's telegraphy skills came in handy when he facilitated a Sachsenhausen Morse code midnight mass, attended "virtually" by twenty-two people connected by heating pipes. It was led by Władysław Goral, the auxiliary bishop of Lublin, in what proved a moving interlude of Christian hope and defiance that was, tragically, to be among the bishop's last acts. That same night one guard was rash enough, under the influence of inordinate quantities of alcohol, to reveal to Falconer that he and others in Sachsenhausen were being kept as hostages for some later undisclosed purpose. When the right moment arose, Falconer was able to update Bonhoeffer with this accurate information. The reasons for his inclusion in the hostage group are unknown.

Heidel Nowakowski

Heidel was born Johanna Nowakowski on August 18, 1914, in Brzeźnica, Poland. Heidel was the fourth of five children born to Ludwig and Aloisia Nowakowski, and the only girl. Despite the ten-year age gap, she was close enough to her oldest brother, Johann, to report after the war that she shared an address with him in Dortmund for over five years. After Germany's conquest of Poland in World War II, Johanna applied for German naturalisation through the Einwanderungszentralstelle, which regulated the resettlement of ethnic Germans from occupied territories.[7] In her application it was noted that she had some teeth missing. She declared her occupation as factory worker. Prior to her appearance at Buchenwald concentration camp in March 1945, Heidel is listed among other displaced Poles as a worker in a pottery owned by Paul Schreier, possibly in Bischofswerda, on October 31, 1941, having arrived there in July of that year. She is also (in an apparent confirmation of the location of the pottery) named in documentation issued by the mayor of Bischofswerda in November 1941 as someone of *Volksdeutsche* status unwilling to wear the identifying badge of a Polish civilian labourer.[8] Another earlier record suggests she may have misrepresented her age in 1928 in order to be married in a Protestant church in Neubartelsdorf, Prussia, at age fourteen.[9] No evidence has been found of Gestapo informing. The reasons for her inclusion in the hostage group remain unknown.

Alexander von Falkenhausen

Alexander von Falkenhausen came from a long line of Prussian nobility with an international military tradition. A second son to Baron and Baroness Alexander and Elisabeth (née von Schuler-Senden) von Falkenhausen, he was born in Blumenthal, Silesia (now Nysa, Opolskie, Poland) on October 29, 1878.[10] In all, over a twenty-year period, ten children were born to the family. On January 7, 1884, when he was six, the family were living in Bad Warmbrunn. Tragedy struck when his new baby sister, Elisabeth, died when only just over six months old. Eight years on, the family had moved to Breslau, where Falkenhausen attended the local *Gymnasium* (grammar/secondary school). He was a professional soldier from the start; his military career was furthered by attending the cadet school at Wahlstatt. From his early days, Falkenhausen showed an interest in East Asia and its societies. In 1897 he was commissioned as a second lieutenant into the 91st Oldenburg Infantry Regiment of the Imperial German Army. In 1900, by now in China, he participated in an eight-nation alliance created to quell the Boxer Rebellion. He travelled and studied widely in the Far East, serving as a military attaché to the German embassy in Tokyo from 1900 up until World War I. But the family could be under no illusions about the cost of military service. On January 13, 1904, his older brother, Friedrich, was killed at Otjituezu while serving in the Imperial German Army in Namibia. Friedrich's widow, Anna, was left with three children under the age of four. But Falkenhausen, now Baron von Falkenhausen,[11] remained loyal to his choice of career. On a return trip to Germany, also in 1904, he married Paula von Wedderkop, a fellow member of the Prussian aristocracy, in the military garrison church in Oldenburg. The couple returned to Asia for what proved a formative period that took in working not only in Japan, but also (from 1909 to 1911) in northern China, Korea, and Indochina. He continued his military service throughout World War I, serving in the 31st Infantry Division in 1914, and rose through the ranks. In 1916 his youngest brother, Hans-Joachim, who had already lost a leg, was wounded. In the late spring of 1916, Falkenhausen was deployed to the Turkish Army Group Caucasus at a highly sensitive time in relations between Germany and her ally. Within three months of his arrival there, following an official request from the Turkish ambassador, the publication of documentation by Dr Johannes Lepsius on the Armenian genocide carried out by the Turkish government was prohibited by the military censors, and existing copies were requisitioned.[12] Falkenhausen became chief of the General Staff there in 1917. Also in 1917, a further two of his younger brothers, Ernst and Konrad, both also serving in the German army, were wounded. It was as a ranking lieutenant colonel, serving in the Ottoman army in Palestine at age forty, that Falkenhausen was honoured with Germany's highest award for military valour, the Pour le Mérite in 1918, for courage in combat.

After World War I, he became one of the few who remained with the German army. He was involved with border negotiations between Germany and Poland, and then in 1927 he headed up the Dresden Infantry School. There one of the bright young officers he had responsibility for training was the twenty-year-old Claus von Stauffenberg, who would subsequently become the leader of the anti-Hitler resistance.[13] A lasting relationship of mutual respect was formed. Across his lifetime Falkenhausen received a total of twenty-four awards and decorations for bravery. Following his eighth promotion—to lieutenant general, an infrequent and high honour in that day, unlike the era that followed—he took early retirement in 1930. He apparently found retirement little to his liking, and was also outspoken in word and deed about the Nazi regime. In doing so, he clearly made enemies. In 1934 he succeeded General von Seeckt as head of the German military mission in China, just in time to avoid being murdered by the regime in the Night of the Long Knives killings of June 30,

1934, a fate that befell his youngest brother, Hans-Joachim. He remained in China for over four years, training the army of Chiang Kai-shek and helping to develop a modern Chinese arms industry. During this assignment his achievements were so profound that they gained world attention.

In 1939, following Hitler's pact with Japan, Falkenhausen was coerced by the National Socialists into returning to Germany, under duress of the blackest threats. These included expropriation of his property, seizure of his assets, revocation of his citizenship, and the *Sippenhaft* arrest of his family. Before leaving, he gave his grateful hosts his word of honour that no Chinese secrets would be disclosed to the Japanese. A highly cultivated nobleman, he detested all that Nazism stood for, and travelled home much against his own will and sense of obligation. He made little effort once back on German soil to hide his sentiments and was never to receive a front command. His contacts with the opposition began, accordingly, in early 1939. The coming of war found him working on his fellow generals and encouraging them towards resistance insofar as his limited contacts would allow (he was based in Dresden at the time). By 1940 he had become so incensed about the prospective attack on the Netherlands that one of the many warnings that filtered through to Belgium emanated from him.[14] On April 3, 1941 (while holding another role), he was enlisted by the Hitler opposition whilst acting as military commander of District IV at Dresden. His role was to embark on a western circuit and mobilise a select group of the most opposition-minded commanders, proposing they go with him to Field Marshal Brauchitsch and urge him either to act or to allow others to.[15] But, rather like Canaris, he was swept along by events and, inexorably, was compromised. In September 1940 he was appointed a full infantry general and to the post of military governor general of occupied Belgium and northern France—a post also held a generation earlier by his uncle. In this post Falkenhausen was charged with maintaining law and order in an occupied military territory on behalf of a corrupt regime. He had accepted a poisoned chalice. An example of this may be seen in his opening decree on taking office. Falkenhausen issued the following signed statement to the nation, dated April 12, 1941:

> For centuries Belgian territory has lain at the cossroads of political tension between Central Europe and the Western powers. The one-sided political approach of the former Belgian Government has once again thrust the country into war on the side of the Western powers. Military operations were intense: the resulting conse-

quences for the nation were harsh. With all available resources the re-building of what was destroyed has immediately commenced and economic life re-set in motion. Accomplishing this great task is not only the will of the German Military Government but above all the sacred duty of the Belgian nation and economy. Only the one who stands ready, in clear-sighted recognition of historical events, to work together and sow seeds for the future, earns for themselves and their nation the right to participate in the harvest in the new Europe and hence the world.[16]

This briefing, issued in Falkenhausen's name, and presumably also signed off by the highest authority in Germany, represents the chilling statement of an aggressive invader severely warning its new coerced citizens into compliance. The statement is irreconcilable with a free and sovereign Belgium.

Despite this, during his four-year tenure in this role, Falkenhausen, ever the diplomat, initially sought to protect the populace from the worst excesses of occupation.[17]

In keeping with the resistance links he had established in April 1941, Falkenhausen soon met with a key resister of the highest calibre, German ambassador Ulrich von Hassell, who himself formed a good impression of the general. Referring to his trip to Brussels at the end of June, Hassell wrote,

> I had a good impression of Falkenhausen, who sees very clearly indeed, as does his chief of staff. Physically Falkenhausen is a phenomenon. He is able to drink enormous amounts in the evening without ever having the slightest hangover, and he is at his office shortly after eight every morning. Eleven years in China have stamped out any drill-ground tendencies in his mentality or dull mechanical obedience he might have had, and pumped some adventurous blood into his veins. It is a pity he is not at a more central spot. I shall remain in contact with him.[18]

It was hence in the summer of 1941 that Falkenhausen became still more involved with resisters. Bethge reports that "after a meeting Hassell, Oster and Dohnanyi had with General von Falkenhausen, he and General von Rabenau went again to Brauchitsch but were [still] unable to persuade him to make any move at all against Hitler."[19]

But after Germany invaded the Soviet Union, Berlin's demands for reprisals against acts of resistance became dramatically more severe. It became an issue where Falkenhausen's military obligations would continue to provide a circle that could not be squared. In August/September of 1941, the military commander of occupied France, Otto von Stülpnagel, issued what became known as the "hostages order." This stipulated that all Frenchmen held in custody by the German authorities on their own behalf or on behalf of the French authorities because of communist activities were to be regarded as hostages responsible with their lives for the impeccable conduct of the entire civilian population. It continued, "In cases of an incident which necessitates the shooting of hostages . . . the district leader in whose territory the incident happened is to select from the list of prisoners [hostages] persons whose execution he wishes to propose to me." A similar code was issued by Falkenhausen in Belgium and by Seyss-Inquart for Holland. It was the type of regulation the SS were infamous for enforcing in occupied territory. The impact of such directives might well be imagined. Falkenhausen wrote a most soldierly protest on the subject to his superior, Field Marshal Keitel:

> In the attached document is a list of hostages shot in my area, and the incidents which gave rise to their being carried out. In a majority of cases, especially the most serious, those carrying out the incidents were only caught and sentenced later [by which Falkenhausen means sentenced post-execution]. This showing is unsatisfactory in the highest degree. The effect on the population's sense of justice and safety is not so much to discourage as to destroy: the gap between the sector of the population open to Communist influence and the remainder is shrunk, at every level people are filled with feelings of hatred, and enemy propaganda receives an inflammatory boost. Military danger derives from this policy and in general thoroughly undesirable political repercussions.[20]

The effect on Keitel, someone not renowned for his ability to deal constructively with those who adopted a similar robust stance, of receiving such a protest is not recorded. But what is known is that since the "hostages order" policy did indeed prove counterproductive, a new policy of "Nacht und Nebel" was subsequently devised by Hitler and promulgated in all Western occupied countries. Under this, hostages simply disappeared without the public or relatives finding out what had happened to them, or where they had gone or been spirited away to. This was carried out by all German authorities, not only the Gestapo and SD, and hence even Falkenhausen was inculpated.[21] Accordingly, even though he was a correct, chivalrous officer who profoundly disliked the methods of the

SS, Falkenhausen nevertheless approved the deportation order for all foreign Jews in Belgium and ordered the execution of 240 Belgian hostages.
The concept of hostages was a perilous one.[22] Of these Belgian hostages,
40 men, who had not faced a trial, were executed on January 7, 1943, in
"atonement" for several attacks that had taken place in occupied Brussels; some were not facing serious charges. In a similar vein, Falkenhausen himself later admitted that among the ten executed in Liège on January 4, 1943, there were several doubtful cases. The reason for their arrest
appears to have been their participation in a strike organised to protest
about the forced deportations of some other workers to Germany; they
did not belong to resistance movements and had not committed crimes
deserving the death sentence.[23] Every time a new act of sabotage occurred,
the SS leadership took vicious advantage of the opportunity to complain
to Hitler about the weakness of the military administration in Belgium.
Falkenhausen was accused of having overly hesitated before conducting
hostage arrests, and of blurring the issue about the real concept of reprisal executions by executing only those actually condemned to death. Still
further, Berlin castigated Falkenhausen constantly for lack of vigour in
reprisal measures against "terrorists." Although he initially opposed the
imposition of the wearing of the yellow star for Jews in Belgium, Falkenhausen was inevitably obliged to yield to pressure from the RSHA. Hence
eventually under Falkenhausen's administration, Belgian Jews were
deprived of their employment, their firms were "Aryanised" without compensation, and they were obliged to undertake compulsory labour service. Thirty thousand were deported from Belgium to Auschwitz. A recent
study tracked the number of death sentences that were handed down to
Belgian civilians and carried out each year over the approximate duration
of Falkenhausen's tenure in office. From zero or almost zero in 1940–1941,
the number rose to 200 in 1942, rose again to 423 in 1943, and fell back
to 290 in 1944.[24] No amount of soldierly charm could or would ever make
recompense for these horrors. But the inner disgust Falkenhausen was
experiencing at these choices had another decisive effect. Presumably
once he was made aware, after 1943, that the leadership of the anti-Hitler
resistance was now in the hands of Stauffenberg, Falkenhausen threw in
his lot with the conspiracy and agreed to provide the needed military support following Hitler's death.[25] With these levels of rising fury within him,
it became only a matter of time before Falkenhausen would move to outright non-compliance with a particular demand placed upon him. That
moment came in 1944. On June 7 resisting Belgian military groups killed

three Gestapo officers in the city of Écaussinnes. The next day German
military authorities took their revenge on civilians by arresting ninety-
seven young men and threatening the people of the city with a deadline
by which to hand over any "suspects," failing which, all the hostages would
be executed. Once again Falkenhausen would receive a visit from the Chinese scientist he had helped in 1940, Qian Xiuling.[26] Falkenhausen was
not surprised when Xiuling walked into his office next morning. He knew
instantly what she would ask, and she was well aware of the difficulties
involved in extending clemency. Three days later her request was granted.
All ninety-seven people were released.[27] Events moved fast. On July 12
Falkenhausen was summoned to Berlin to explain his behaviour and discreetly replaced in post. His contribution to the conspiracy could now
not be counted on. Given that there were already suspicions about his
links with resisters such as Hassell and Goerdeler, not to mention General
von Rabenau, once the round-up began after July 20, Falkenhausen would
spend the remainder of the war in prison. In light of the fact that he was
an active supporter of the conspiracy, it is a resounding testimony to the
bravery of tortured fellow resisters that Falkenhausen was not, apparently,
named and put on trial for his role. It would be in these tenuous circumstances that he would become part of the hostage convoy that included
Dietrich Bonhoeffer, with whom he was much more closely linked than
could be shared.

Regensburg

Stuck in the cold bus outside Regensburg, the very different hostages,
Bonhoeffer among them, could only wait in silent discomfort. From this
there would eventually be relief. For those suffering the consequences of
the war Germany had unleashed, a lasting relief was still some way off.

31
Events Cascade: Hitler Hibernates

Okinawa, Japan

While Churchill had sensed that April 30 might be a possible date for the end of the war in Europe, it was already clear that the war in the Pacific was going to be a far longer struggle. Despite this, on April 6 the British government announced the distribution of five million booklets called *Release and Resettlement* among men and women in the forces. The authorities wanted to make combatants sure that they knew what their rights were, what was being done to help them, and that they knew all the plans for "releasing you from service and getting you back into civilian life." In these booklets the plans for the interim period between the defeat of Germany and the defeat of Japan were brought together for the first time. It was announced that the first consignment—twenty-five tons of them—with all that "help and advice waiting for you when you do return"[1]—was already on its way to the Far East.

It was a bizarre moment. The expectation that the remaining war in the Pacific would be exceptionally violent and bloody was heightened when on April 6 it became apparent, if it had not been so already, that the suicidal determination of the Japanese to conquer or resist was not confined to the ground troops deployed in Burma, in China, or among the Pacific Islands, but extended also to Imperial High Command and to the Japanese navy. The last Japanese naval offensive during World War II began on April 6, 1945. Named Operation Ten-Go, the operation was designed to drive out the Allied forces at Okinawa, utilising kamikazes as the weapon in ten different attacks. The Japanese gave the name Kikusui to the kamikaze attacks, which, when translated, means "floating chrysanthemums." In this instance, instead of single suicide pilots, the operation used 355 such pilots at virtually a single stroke. To support the attacks, the Japanese battleship *Yamato*, along with the light cruiser *Yahagi* and eight destroyers, were sent to complete the destruction begun by the suicidal missions. So successful was the initial attack, in which a total of eight US destroyers were hit, that two were sunk, as well as two ammunition ships and a tank landing ship, with a further two destroyers permanently disabled; but this success came at a cost. In this instance it involved the loss of 355 Japanese aircraft and pilots.[2]

World Leaders

Because Stalin had cast aspersions on the British in his letter of April 3 to Roosevelt, Winston Churchill was, on April 6, obliged to respond. He replied in a long message to Stalin, reviewing the developments of "Sunrise" (the possibility of a German surrender in Italy) and pointing out that an American group (the OSS) had been handling the contacts. At this, Stalin's level of outrage over the circumstances surrounding the talks was somewhat mollified.[3] It was not the only instance of mollifying Stalin that was transacted that day. Up to this date, Churchill had still been saying "Berlin" to military commanders. But now, outnumbered two-to-one in troop numbers, he was obliged to back down.[4]

London, England

In London the first BBC news of the day was read by Alvar Lidell. It followed the by now familiar pattern of the week, offering a general sense of motivational Allied news on progress towards victory, while at the same time providing a background lesson, or even a course, in European geography. Even the most diligent listeners would have needed a marked-up wall map to be capable of following the thread of the major stories. There were so many. The summative headlines, continuing to use the pronoun "we" for Allied troops, explained, "Our tanks went forward another twelve miles yesterday along the Dutch-German frontier; we're along the River Weser on a fifteen mile stretch and are less than forty miles from Bremen." It was quite some "stretch" indeed: by the end of that day, the news stated that the Allies had nine more bridges over the Rhine than the Germans had had in peacetime. The BBC continued, "Third Army forces are now less than seventy miles from the Czechoslovak border. The Russians have only two and a half miles to go before they're inside Vienna's city limits."

The BBC devoted several minutes of coverage to the achievements of Russian forces across Central and Eastern Europe, some under the command of the name now familiar to the British public, Marshal Tolbukhin, and also introduced other names. Among these were Marshal Malinovsky, who had "reached the Morava and the Austrian frontier beyond Bratislava on a broad front," and Generals Petrov and Yeremenko, the latter being dubbed "one of the heroes of Stalingrad and one of the victors of Riga last autumn." In respect of the Soviet advances, one of the most revealing remarks was made by one of Zhukov's divisional commanders, General Maslov. He described German children crying as they searched desperately for their parents in a blazing town. "What was surprising," wrote Maslov, "was that they were crying in exactly the same way as our children cry." Few Soviet soldiers or officers had imagined, or could conceive of, the Germans as human beings. After Nazi propaganda had dehumanised the Slavs into *Untermenschen*, Soviet revenge propaganda (Ehrenburg) had convinced its citizens that all Germans were ravening beasts.[5] It was not an unmerited response to Germany's aggression. It would also not be the first or only time the Russian nation as a whole would be collectively blinded through propaganda.

Reporting the news of Soviet advances within Yugoslavia prompted the BBC's transmission of a reflective piece in relation to the ordeal experienced by the population there. April 6 marked the four-year anniversary of the Nazi attack on the open city of Belgrade. It thus proved a date suitable for the publication by the Royal Yugoslav Government in London of the first of six reports issued by the commission set up under Marshal Tito to investigate the crimes committed by the enemy and those who had helped them. The report, it was stated, contained gruesome details and photographs captured on German or Italian prisoners of the methods used by the enemy. Broadcasting to his countrymen the previous night on the BBC Serbo-Croat service, the Yugoslav chargé d'affaires in London had said that "the hour when the aggressors will have finally to settle the account" was now at hand. In his view the peoples of Yugoslavia had "full right to look back with pride to their contribution to victory and to insist on full allowance being made for the lives they have given and for their sufferings."[6]

Berlin, Germany

In Berlin the architect of much of the world's suffering was himself now a broken, sick, and fanatical dreamer hidden in a bunker 7.6 metres below the city's surface. On April 6 Hitler's physician, Dr Morrell, reflecting that Hitler had not yet been outside during the month of April, wrote in his diary, "The Führer generally only leaves the well ventilated and lit bunker for short periods of time . . . and goes into the garden of the

Chancellery. . . . He is very sensitive to light, and dusty winds. Orderly treatment is very difficult because of the irregular way of living and constant pre-occupation with reports and so on."[7] But unfortunately for Bonhoeffer, the orders issued by Hitler were still being carried out. The top-priority teleprinter messages issued on the previous day by the RSHA had alerted concentration camp commandants and the SS central court to the requirement to act instantly. One of these included the order to transfer Bonhoeffer's brother-in-law Hans von Dohnanyi, who had been extremely unwell for some time,[8] some thirty-five kilometres further north from his hospital bed in the *Staatskrankenhaus* in Berlin to KZ Sachsenhausen for a court martial. Already that evening, the supportive Dr Tietze, consistently unable to gain Dohnanyi's consent to escape plans, had responded by dosing up Dohnanyi with two tablets of Luminal and a further supply of five-gram morphine tablets so as to render him suitably *non compus mentis*. But he would simply be sidelined. Between 4:00 and 6:00 a.m. on April 6, SS-Sturmscharführer Sonderegger arrived at the hospital and debarred Tietze from any further access to the patient. Together with two helpers, Sonderegger proceeded to pick up the unconscious resister on a stretcher and convey him to Sachsenhausen for the proceedings. The so-called trial was (at least in theory) conducted by Walter Huppenkothen throughout the day and included a recess for lunch.[9] According to post-war statements—almost all of which derived from the SS members concerned, and which must therefore be regarded with a level of distrust—Dohnanyi is supposed to have been bright-eyed and fully alert at the key moments, understanding the charges of high treason and treason in the field brought against him. In a dress rehearsal for the events of April 8, no reference was made to the supposedly incriminating recent find of the Canaris diaries; the prosecution case was instead based on a 160-page dossier drawn from the previous set of Zossen documents, first issued as the October 1944 "Führer report."[10] The case arguing for the death sentence hence related to a series of events that had taken place up to seven years previously, and in no small measure to the attempt on Hitler's life on July 20, 1944, which had taken place fifteen months after Dohnanyi's arrest and incarceration. Previously Dohnanyi had also been, according to the subsequent testimony of his wife, Christine, wilfully misled by Huppenkothen about the identity of the "officer" who had led the Gestapo to the Zossen find, and who was in fact a military driver. For the SS it proved a successful ruse, in that Dohnanyi was evidently influenced by the particular betrayal that had been purported, which was so shocking that even when faced with ultimate consequences, he never revealed the name given to him.[11] Procedurally it remains unclear whether Hitler, in his capacity as army supreme justice, ordered the proceedings or whether Hitler appointed Kaltenbrunner or his subordinates to represent him at them, or in the validation of any sentence. At the so-called trial, or court martial, there was no court stenographer. Dohnanyi, debilitated by the effects of his grave illness, was unaided by any state council and had no access to any court records. By evening the grim farce was over. His predetermined sentence, conveniently left in the hands of the death machinery at Sachsenhausen, was issued that evening, typed up by Huppenkothen's secretary, and hand delivered by him by 11:00 that evening back to Berlin for "ratification."[12] When Huppenkothen arrived there, Müller was still in the office, awaiting him with the finalised list for a rerun of the same process booked for April 8 in Flossenbürg. Bonhoeffer's name was on the Flossenbürg list.

Lahde, Westphalia, and Kiel, Germany

Hitler's hibernating underground existence left Germans still loyal to him in a nightmarish vacuum. It was up to people in each situation to make up their own minds about how to conduct the war. In the overall meltdown, among the populace an intense culture of fearfulness took hold. Particularly at risk were any dishevelled, hungry prisoners who might be seen in public. The situation intensified. One author wrote, "Across the Reich, in the Nazis' last days of power over life and death, many of the dictator's fearful adherents sought to ensure that the joy of liberation was denied to all those within their reach." An instance of this occurred only a few kilometres north of Rinteln, when the approach of US forces unleashed a wave of killing of captives entirely unable to resist. In another instance, in Lahde, on April 6, with surrender coming up in just four days' time, guards marched 154 mainly Soviet prisoners of war from the AEL (*Arbeitserziehungslager*) the short distance to the cemetery in Seelhorst. Here the captives, most wearing civilian clothes, were forced to dig their own graves before being machine-gunned by members of the Hanover Gestapo. Only one, Piotr Palnikov, survived. In a further example, in Kiel, the same fate befell a further two hundred prisoners.[13] The total number of victims of the selective massacre of forced labourers in AEL camps was estimated at one thousand.[14]

Map 4 of Bonhoeffer's Germany: Chapters 32–38

Hamm	Liberated on April 6 by US forces.
Bad Sulza	Troops from the US 3rd Army liberate 4,000 British prisoners from Stalag IX-C and its nearby sub-camps.
Hammelburg	On April 6 soldiers from the 14th Armoured Division of the 47th Tank Battalion liberate the prison camp Oflag XIII-B.
Heilbronn	Incandescent at the sight of white flags, Kreisleiter Richard Dranz and accomplices arbitrarily shoot dead a number of civilians.
Alt Wriezen	A Luftwaffe base sixty kilometres east of Berlin is still in German hands.
Sarajevo	Tito's partisans liberate the city.
Schönberg	Bonhoeffer and companions are provided with warm accommodation.
Zutphen	On April 7 Zutphen is taken, together with its launch site for the V-2 rockets.
Bromskirchen	Around 275 kilometres farther east of Zutphen, the US First Army captures a trainload of nine V-2 rockets. Pictures make the front pages of a number of UK newspapers.
Leese	Allies capture the town, including a number of V-2 scientists still in their white coats.
Stein/Krems	A mêlée of authority figures undertake to protect the local population by initiating a shoot-to-kill "rabbit hunt" for released prisoners. 374 die.
Pfaffenhofen	The Klemperers access an ingenious milk churn transport system.
Lippoldsberg	Soldiers from the US Company G, 413th Infantry fight across the Weser river, attacking Lippoldsberg. Private W. James' conduct wins the US Medal of Honour.
Braunschweig	A group of young Werewolf enthusiasts detain and kill in cold blood both the local mayor and the local doctor.
Lüneburg	An air raid on April 7 also strikes a (locked) train containing 400 concentration camp prisoners. 71 perish.
Hanover	The American 9th Army is only fifteen miles west of Hanover.
Czech border	The US 3rd Army is within sixty miles of Czechoslovakia, but making the border will take a further eleven days' fighting.
Hammelburg	5,000 prisoners of war of differing nationalities are liberated
Plukktjønnfjellet mountain	A plane carrying a top-secret combined ski-parachute team tasked with blowing up the Nordland railway in Norway crashes with the loss of all twelve team members.

Map 4 of Bonhoeffer's Germany: Chapters 32–38
Staatsbibliothek zu Berlin-Kartenabteilung/Bruce Bovill

32
Deceptions and Killings Abound

Hamm, North Rhine-Westphalia

On April 6 US forces liberated Hamm, setting up command in the police headquarters on Hohe Straße.[1] There had been resistance, but Nazi units had withdrawn the day before. Also on April 6, the Allied radio station Neues Deutschland, broadcasting on wavelength 1212, intentionally over-reported the extent of the resistance there. The background to this was that Operation Annie (also known as "1212," the frequency on which it broadcast) was a covert Allied "black propaganda" radio station conceived by Sefton Delmer and based in London that had begun broadcasting in late 1944 from a secret location in Luxembourg, and which purported with great subtlety to be pro-German, playing patriotic traditional German songs. It provided an extraordinary blend of up-to-the-minute accurate information and disinformation. Over 127 broadcasts the station had built up a loyal following of both German civilians and soldiers. It was careful, for example, to use Goebbels' language of "der Feind" (the enemy) for Allied troops throughout, but also wove into its news—as it did, for example, on April 6—important reports designed deeply to undermine Nazism. On that day the subject of hypocritical demands of Nazis demanding sacrifice and then using their own seniority to flee was mentioned. There was also a report purporting to come from General Guderian, with which—in the black propaganda—Himmler was said to be in complete disagreement, that it was considered that the presence and contributions of Volkssturm units had hindered rather than helped overall military performance, and that the units should be disbanded. By this stage of the war, with the Allied forces rapidly advancing further into Germany, under direct instruction from General Dwight Eisenhower, the radio station had also begun including in its broadcasts false information about Allied positions, and thereby added to the impression that the major assaults deep into Germany were even more underway than was sometimes the case. This had the intended effect of making German civilians flee from their homes, which in turn hampered the operational retreat of the German army.[2] It was a different resistance from that which had been undertaken by Dietrich Bonhoeffer, but was nonetheless one with which he had a connection: a pivotal contributor to the London project was Otto John, a key resister, obliged to flee Germany after July 20, 1944, whose extensive contribution to the resistance up until that point had been made alongside that of Bonhoeffer's brother Klaus while working for Lufthansa.

Mülhausen and Buchenwald, Thuringia: Marches across Germany

Across Germany further ramifications of the obedience to Hitler's will, which Bonhoeffer had defied, continued to have tragic consequences. On April 6, in Bavaria, soldiers from the 14th Armoured Division of the 47th Tank Battalion liberated the prison camp Oflag XIII-B in Hammelburg.[3] Those who had remained until that point were fortunate in that they had not been included in the renewed forced evacuation marches that had been issuing forth from the camp since March 29. For example, there were American officers there who had arrived in the camp only on March 10 after an eight-week 400-mile (640-kilometre) forced march from Oflag 64 in Szubin. It was just one part of the widespread mass movement tragedy of that period. One estimate states that some 113,000 concentration camp prisoners in all had set out on the death marches in January and February alone,[4] with the numbers increasing throughout March and continuing in April. Over three hundred kilometres further east of Hamm, troops from the US 3rd Army moved on from Würzburg to liberate four thousand British prisoners from Stalag IX-C at Bad Sulza and its sub-camps near Mülhausen in Thuringia. Those liberated were at least spared the death marches. In Buchenwald on April 6, according to Elie Wiesel, the *Lagerkommandant* announced that the camp would be liquidated. Ten blocks of inmates would be evacuated every day. From that moment on, there was no further distribution of bread and soup. The evacuations began. Every day a few thousand inmates passed the camp's gate and did not return.[5] On such marches as these, a terrible madness prevailed among those charged with responsibility. On so many of them, prisoners were despatched without a thought on a daily basis by guards to whom they were totally anonymous, lacking all identity. In one instance of this, one blond SS guard, only about twenty years old, casually shot a thirteen-year-old boy on a march from Sachsenhausen because he could not keep up with the fast pace, almost running speed. In their anger and despair, the boy's elder brother, a Jesuit priest, and his father tried to jump on the SS man, but he simply "fired a few volleys from his machine gun at them." The three died together. The machine guns rattled unceasingly as many prisoners were mown down on the first two days. When, after a night in a barn, one prisoner refused to continue the march, the young SS brute simply shot him dead, then a few minutes later turned his gun on the prisoner's distraught brother-in-law, who had lagged behind. At this point the SS man "simply pulled out prisoners who, in his opinion, did not walk fast enough and shot them on the spot."[6]

Heilbronn, Germany, and Stein/Krems, Austria

One particularly extreme case of madness was the arbitrary shooting dead of four civilians, among them a pastor, in the suburb of Heilbronn. The local Kreisleiter, Richard Dranz, and a group of local fanatics (three of them in the Volkssturm) were fleeing in a car together as the Americans approached, and drove across a street in which white flags hung from several houses. In a rage, he stopped the car and ordered his men, "Out, shoot, shoot, everybody!" Dranz's accomplices arbitrarily shot down their victims, men and women, within a frenzied few minutes, narrowly missing several others, before driving off.[7] But worse was in store. In Stein and Krems, such "berserker" behaviour was, if possible, multiplied many times over, and even sustained beyond the heat of the moment. It was as if obedience to the Nazi regime that Bonhoeffer had resisted were "followed through" to an unprecedented degree. Here a single alarmist telephone call asserting, without substance, that a riot was underway unleashed a cascade of events that resulted in an unprecedented killing spree.

Stein prison held about 1,600–1,800[8] inmates, around 30 percent of them political prisoners. Those in this latter category had been incarcerated for various crimes such as the distribution of leaflets for a banned organisation, or the making of a critical comment about the regime. People were locked up, or had terms extended, for a variety of actions deemed criminal, or subversive, by a subjective approach. These included, for example, listening to foreign news bulletins on the radio, belonging to a sect such as the Jehovah's Witnesses (Bibelforscher), or acts of simple kindness such as the collection of donations for other prisoners. In Stein the inmates were of a whole variety of nationalities and included prisoners who were Greek, Polish, and French, as well as Austrian. As the enemy approached, those in authority in the prison asked for clarification on how to proceed. Loosely worded legislative guidance directed them that regular prisoners could be freed, but that "politicals" should be relocated under guard to alternative locations, or killed. Accordingly, when food supplies ran out at the start of April, the prison governor in Stein, Franz Kodré, began by releasing eighty to a hundred "regular" prisoners on April 5, and the next day advised the "politicals" that they were also to be freed. Attempts to reunite prisoners with personal effects engendered scenes of disarray, but by lunchtime hundreds had left on foot peacefully. One local child, Joseph Streibel, was thirteen at the time. He recalled seeing the doors of the prison being opened and the first wave of prisoners setting off on foot.[9]

In the late afternoon, a report was made to the Nazi Kreisleiter in Krems, Anthon Wilthum, about a "revolt" in Stein prison, to which he responded by ordering to attend at Stein prison the Schutzpolizei, the Volkssturm units, the army garrison, and the Waffen-SS. Knowing that certain annihilation at the hands of the Russians was only seventy kilometres away to their east, they responded with alacrity to the idea of being ordered into active service to represent the restoration of "Order and Discipline" by travelling two kilometres in exactly the opposite direction. They found the situation calm when they arrived, with order in part having been restored by the issuing of firearms to trusted former prisoners. But not for long. Quickly arrests, street blocking, court martials, and disarming began, at which point many prisoners still on site took fright and barricaded themselves inside the inner courtyard of the prison. At this juncture the SS and army opened fire and threw in hand grenades, forcing their way in, and killing dozens as they stood, including one guard. They then moved throughout the prison building cell by cell and continued the murders, even pulling out those from the prison hospital and shooting them dead. Quick thinking by some guards in locking a few prisoners back into their cells prevented some loss of life. Five prison staff, including the governor, were shot without trial. Tellingly Joseph Streibel also recalled the sound of machine-gun fire on the street.[10] A total of 255 died in Stein.[11]

Not satisfied with this, SS mobile units and others then set off in pursuit of those who had been freed earlier, who were of course unaware of recent developments. They had not got far, were unarmed, and saw no reason to hide and so were an easy target for what became known, because local civilians also participated in the process, as the "Krems rabbit hunt." Groups of prisoners, three or four at a time, or in larger groups of twenty-five or twenty-six, were hunted down at a whole array of locations. People were shot as they stood, or fled, and their bodies left unburied. With no small courage, in a few instances locals showed kindness and rescued people. This extended phase of killing brought the total deaths that day to as many as 386 people.[12]

Seventy years later, Robert Streibel, Joseph's son, after several years of research into the events of that day, published *April in Stein*. He chose to substitute alternative names for those who had been involved.

Braunschweig, Germany

On April 6 the *Braunschweiger Tageszeitung* carried the local Gauleiter's call for "fanatical resistance." A group of three or four young Werewolf enthusiasts had been on a training event in Cremlingerhorn. Seized by the idea of "death to traitors," they equipped themselves with weapons and drove in a motorcycle colonnade to Schandelah, where they forced the local mayor to accompany them a short distance before murdering him with a pistol shot to the back of the head. The young people then returned to the village, took the local doctor, and murdered him also, the next morning reporting their Werewolf activities to their company leader, being fully persuaded that they had done the German cause a good service.[13]

Alt Wriezen, Pomerania

Sixty kilometres east of Berlin, the Luftwaffe could do little to help the soldiers and civilians fleeing west. On aerodromes and dispersal airfields scattered across the shrinking Reich, hundreds of German aircraft were unable to move for want of fuel, spare parts, or a pilot—or all three. Among the few pilots still able to get up into the air and at least make some attempt to help his comrades on the ground was Norbert Hannig. He took off on April 6 and shot down a Russian plane, an Ilyushin-2. It was his forty-second and final kill of the war.[14]

Gmunden, Austria

In Austria, but around 150 kilometres further west of Krems, Marie Vassiltchikov turned to the local Kreisleiter on April 6 to obtain official permission to stay at the Königinvilla. He proved very unfriendly. Undeterred, she sought out the mayor, who gave permission when he heard their names. Taking lunch that day at the Hotel Schwan, Marie was informed by a recent arrival from Vienna that already the day before the Russians had been hanging Nazi Party members from the trees in Florisdorf, a suburb of Vienna.[15]

Pfaffenhofen/Schweitenkirchen, Germany

But there were also those whose spirited defiance of Hitler's will remained undetected. In southern Germany survivors of the Dresden fire bombing Victor and Eva Klemperer were able to take both breakfast and lunch that day at the Bräuhaus Müller. They were also able to discover and access the benefits of an ingenious Bavarian transport system. "Somewhere in each district there is a central dairy, each day the farmers have to supply the bulk of their milk to it . . . and get back butter, 'skimmed' milk, etc. . . . The dairy vehicles convey passengers from village to village free of charge." The diarist explained that "one clambers up with difficulty and crouches on the massive milk cans, one gets down when the cans are loaded and unloaded at the milk platforms of the various places; these stages in front of large farms now constitute a kind of station; the timetable is only very approximate." The Klemperers waited a long time for this provision, one for which their thankfulness can readily be imagined. On arrival in Schweitenkirchen, they experienced a heartwarming kindness: it was only for one night, given fears of a Nazi in the same house, but it meant the luxury of dry shoes and socks, coffee, and a plentiful warm supper.[16]

33
The Hostages: Arrival in Schönberg

The Road from Regensburg to Schönberg, Bavaria, Germany

For the Grüne Minna hostages, it was, following Falconer's successful sabotage, a memorably long and uncomfortable night. The only sound was the drumming of rain on the roof. The stench in the cramped vehicle, according to Pünder, was overwhelming.[1] The complete absence of food or drink continued. At dawn the guards at last let the hostages out of the vehicle to stretch their legs. The road seemed completely quiet and no one came by . . . until finally another truly unfortunate passing cyclist had their bicycle requisitioned. Thereupon a guard was despatched back to Regensburg on the bicycle in question to sort things out. He returned around midday with an extremely smart coach and an explanation for why the wait had been so long: a replacement vehicle from Regensburg had in fact come out, but had not been able find them, stopping and turning around only two hundred yards short. Less celebratory for all of the Buchenwald guard contingent was the news that they were now all deemed superfluous to requirements, as the new coach not only had shining upholstery, it also contained a gleaming new replacement detail of around ten SD guards, complete with sub-machine guns, for the next stage of the journey. Somewhat crestfallen, the now redundant guards watched as the prisoner luggage was transferred from the Grüne Minna to the new vehicle. For them it was a moment of farewell to Bonhoeffer and the other hostages, and their brief association with the international *Prominenten* was no more.

For the hostages any feelings of sadness were generally not reciprocated. Settling in to the new coach, Falconer noted that the new and splendid vehicle not only had seats, but also had, by contrast, proper windows that could actually be opened and shut. Having a wood generator as well, it still advanced slowly, but this time there was no inconvenience for passengers as the generator was on a small trailer at the back. They were able to lie back in comfortable seats and admire the scenery. Margot Heberlein wrote in her diary, "For the first time, we see beautiful scenery." Their route followed closely the winding contours of the Danube. A reconstruction of their journey made with the help of local historians indicates that they passed through Barbing, Geisling, Pfatter, and Schönach, before coming (once more) to the Danube at Straubing. As they drove past local airfields, Falconer, while noting the occasional Allied aircraft passing overhead, concluded that the German fighters were grounded through lack of fuel. In Straubing the group discovered that the bridge, like many others, had been bombed, so the search for a pontoon crossing continued. They eventually succeeded in finding one around Deggendorf (see appendix 2), likely to have been the Maximilian Bridge.[2] Crossing there, Bonhoeffer would have recognised their proximity to the monastery at Metten, with its (for him) resistance associations. Now they were into the Bavarian forests they had glimpsed from the other side. The sunshine that afternoon was delightful, trees were in bud, and the daffodils were out. Noting how strong the locality was on poultry, Best spoke up:

> I suggested to one of the guards that perhaps we might stop and see
> if we could beg some eggs at one of the farms, and the idea received
> immediate approval. But when the guard returned with a capful of
> eggs—we got none.[3]

They travelled on past quiet houses and fields with every now and again a stretch of dark pines; it was beautiful. The hostages had a very pleasant journey through the rolling countryside. Being actually able to see the landscape they were being transported through was an entirely welcome new experience. From here onwards the next section of the route wound along narrow country lanes, through a landscape that became increasingly hilly and forested. At one point some village girls asked for a lift, which, remarkably, they were given, and when they were curious to know who this group were, the soldiers told them that they were members of a film company on their way to make a propaganda film. Given the presence of such a large contingent of heavily armed guards, it was for the girls a dangerous topic to pursue, and the account in question does not record their response. But for the hostage group experiencing the new vehicle, this story illustrates how on that afternoon a fresh sense of hope began to emerge. Until now they had been political prisoners, treated entirely differently from the *Sippenhäftlinge*, travelling under hopelessly cramped conditions in a prison van. Now, although still under guard, they had been granted a new status: they were being afforded the same class of travel as the others. In this respect the unknown sabotage work of the SOE had wrought a miracle of hope. Also, as a part of this, for Bonhoeffer and his companions, a sense of being in some sense insulated—and hence shielded—from the tragic scenes they passed through became discernible. Pünder noted,

> In the towns and villages there was a great flurry of people fleeing, as well as smaller groups of Volkssturm units building tank defences. On the other hand, we saw nothing of larger military units, or of more concentrated columns of troops, as we had been given to understand was the case around 100 km or so behind the front lines.[4]

It was the sort of trip, Falconer reflected ruefully, that in more settled times tourists would pay money to enjoy. Having crossed the Danube, their route took them along the Landstraße I. Ordnung Nr. 133, the same route used by the postal service, through Scheuering, Schaufling, and Gerholling, then via Lalling and on today's Bundesstraße 533, to Freundorf and Innernzell, before they arrived in Schönberg itself. One writer noted that the air smelled of pine and hemlock. It was picture postcard territory, and notwithstanding his continuing hunger pangs, it proved for Falconer altogether the most agreeable journey he had made since 1942. No doubt his secret satisfaction at having disabled the prison van, thus securing a better class of travel for the hostages, contributed to his good humour.

Arrival in Schönberg

The former Grüne Minna party were the last vehicle of the convoy to reach this interim[5] destination in the early afternoon. Pünder noted the time as 3:00.[6] When they halted, they noted two other buses parked under the trees,[7] which had travelled overnight, and had been waiting throughout the day. From that group Stauffenberg records that they had already arrived there at 6:35 a.m., and that the warmth of the welcome, after a long wait, stretched to the provision of hot coffee in the Gasthof Dorfner. She also noted, "Once we explain we are prisoners, people are friendly towards us. We wait until 7:00 p.m., and are provided soup. Children are stuffing straw mattresses."[8] To those sitting and waiting, it looked at first as though the villagers had not been expecting them. Indeed, Pünder notes that the locals "gawped"[9] when they saw the weapons their guards were bearing. Of course, news would only filter out gradually to the local community about the *Prominenten* status of the group, although one account suggested that some locals emerged from their houses and began to wave as the hostages were finally marched up to their new quarters. But in fact, considerable preparations, which Hassell later described as "miraculous,"[10] had been undertaken.

The building being made ready for those travelling with the hostage convoy had been the location of an auxiliary hospital and had been authorized for that purpose only on March 15, 1945, by Schönberg mayor Johann Reinsberger. On April 6 the mayor had just received instructions from the NSDAP local branch leader to close the hospital, since it was to be used for other purposes. His orders also announced that the second schoolhouse at the church was needed and would have to be prepared. The orders spoke of generals, prime ministers, and counts with their entourages who would be arriving in Schönberg. Roughly roused from his bed at 6:00 a.m. in the pitch darkness to receive these orders, the mayor wrote in his diary that

> I was outraged on behalf of my new hospital, which was my secret pride and joy. I felt so sorry for the sick and wounded, there were tears and more tears when they had to be so abruptly displaced. Certainly April 6 is a significant day, as [additionally] it was the last day beer was brewed: the order prohibiting it has been issued. My heart was sick indeed, hearing for the last time the familiar sounds of the brewery machinery, a sound I have come to trust over the course of many decades. In it I always discerned the hard work, the energy, and the pride of my father. I too was proud in what I had, even if I never showed it. Beer has been brewed here for 300 years and to think that today it has been brewed here for the last time! In these moments I curse this wretched war, which brings such nameless suffering upon all people, and I am filled with hatred towards the dreadful [*unselig*] people who unleashed it.[11]

With a heavy heart, also thinking of the beer supply drying up, the mayor had to dismiss ten nurses who had been caring for the patients in the hospital. The nurses were transferred to the hospital in Zwiesel. With these premises freed up, the majority of the *Sippenhaft* prisoners were accommodated that evening in the boys' school on the Kirchplatz, while the remaining *Sippenhaft* prisoners and the "special" prisoners, including Bonhoeffer, were billeted in the girls' schoolhouse at 2 Regener Straße.

By this stage all the hostages, both those who had travelled somewhat faster and waited all day and the Grüne Minna party, who had spent the night in the broken-down vehicle, were completely exhausted. But the change of circumstances, combined with the impression the room made on them, helped put this latter group into an excellent frame of mind—they developed a rapport that was clearly evident to all observers. Falconer's first comment was that the room, on the first floor of the village school, gave "every indication of having been prepared in advance as a staging post," an observation in which he was entirely correct. He continues,

> We were soon established in a large airy room, with big windows in two of its walls, beds all round the sides, and a table and benches in the middle. . . . We had a bed each and with sheets, pillows and proper bedding, very comfortable they were too. . . . It seemed we were going to be a great deal more comfortable than we had been before.[12]

Best's account also mentions the welcome high quality of the bedding provided, and that after the door was locked, and the group were left to their own devices, an almost hysterical feeling of relief and happiness swept over the group. He writes,

> After the many hours we had spent cramped up in stuffy vans it was a godsend to be able to move about freely . . . where, moreover, we felt ourselves for the first time for many months out of sight and hearing of our enemies.[13]

He was not alone. Pünder also mentions the wonderful spirit ("viel gute Luft") that prevailed among the hostages. He wrote, "Here we can cope!"[14] He was also particularly struck by the joy of no longer being kept in isolation, since they were now billeted together in a large, sunny room, one that, to their delight and relief, had no bars on the windows.

I include below a possible room layout, which takes into consideration the three published accounts,[15] including a note from Falconer that insists that "Heidi was put firmly in one corner against the wall with Frau Heberlein next to her as chaperone, [ensuring that] all prospects of philandering were firmly thwarted."[16]

According to Falconer,

> The rooms were even heated by a typical Bavarian wood-burning stove centrally placed to warm all the rooms on the floor and stoked from our room. . . . Being in the middle of a forest there was no shortage of wood and we stoked lavishly, for the nights were still cold and our resistance was low.[17]

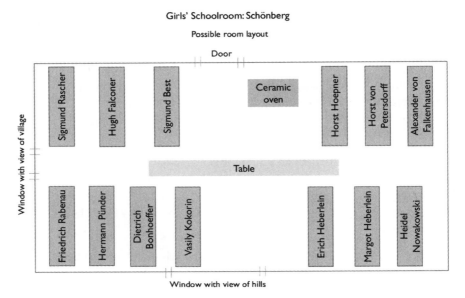

Fig. 33-1. Schönberg schoolroom, possible bed allocation

Some of the other hostages billeted in the rooms above also commented on the wonderful local views, and the connected heating. Clearly the local welcome, in terms of supply and resupply of fuel to burn, continued to be warm. Once they were settled, as had been the case in Regensburg, much banging on the door in the fervent hope of being provided with food succeeded in securing the attentions of their guard. However, on this occasion the only fruit, when the transport leader duly appeared, was the (politely explained, and apologetic) news that there was none to be had.

But that was the official story. Schönberg's mayor had, with the Gestapo, taken the firm line that the authorities had brought the hostages, and they must provide food for them. However, behind the scenes, local villagers were actively making plans to defy the Gestapo, without courting the danger of being seen as wilfully uncooperative. The draconian, arbitrary, and quite possibly fatal penalties prevailing at the time for disobedience as well as for acts of kindness towards "enemies of the Reich" were no doubt prominent in all their minds. That same evening, the former Grüne Minna party found an excellent emissary in the form of the warm, but commanding, personality of Margot Heberlein. Leaving the room under the pretext of needing access to the lavatory, she was able to make contact with someone who appeared to be the housekeeper, whose response was straightforward and refreshing. Within half an hour, two large bowls of potatoes boiled in their jackets arrived. In addition, there were some jugs of coffee for the famished group. The group began thinking of ways to address the food scarcity. Margot Heberlein suggested that if one only knew where to look, some sort of nourishment could usually be found in the fields and hedges even this early in the year. Most of the group were quite ignorant on this subject. From Poland, Heidel Nowakowski was, also, essentially a city girl. Falconer writes, "Surprisingly, Dietrich Bonhoeffer appeared to be well clued up on herbal lore."[18] The group proposed to the sergeant on guard duty that next morning they should all go for a nature ramble along the road outside the village and gather what they could. At first he would not hear of it, saying he needed the authorisation of the transport leader, who was away. But the group pointed out to the guard that none of them was in a fit state to run away, even if there were somewhere to run to, and that the resulting soup would be shared with him, at which point he softened and agreed to the proposal for the next morning—for the occupants of the schoolroom only. As a result, the sense of celebration continued to prevail among the group. Sigmund Rascher made small humorous name signs for every member of the group and placed them above each bedspace. No doubt the regular summoning chime of Schönberg's church bell,[19] clearly audible from just across the road, also contributed to the clear sense of being, for the first time in months, "outside the concentration camp system." Pünder wrote,

> At least we could see, out of the window, views of the beautiful Bavarian mountains, the verdant green of the meadows, farm workers going about their business, children playing, hear the birds singing, and above all, mornings and evenings, the bright sound of the bell from the small village church being rung. What a source of unimaginable life and joy these were to us, we who had been excommunicated from human society![20]

The sense of joy and even adventure that pervaded the group continued as they settled down for the night in this unaccustomed comfort. Best reports that decencies were strictly observed:

> The ladies retired behind a big screen which Mrs Heberlein had induced the houskeeper to lend, whilst we men disrobed in the open as we could. Of course "Heidl" very clumsily knocked over the

screen just as Mrs Heberlein's clothing had reached an abbreviated stage and her own had practically ceased, while General Falkenhausen evened up for our sex by modestly covering his nudity with a kimono, keeping his back carefully turned to the ladies, unconscious of the fact that his only garment was ripped open from top to bottom.[21]

Finally the hostages said a cheery "Goodnight" to one another. Falconer soon fell sound asleep, and awoke refreshed next morning, assuming all the others, in their relief and exhaustion, had done the same. They had, but with one minor (and hilarious) early interruption. The slats of wood used in the hastily improvised construction of the camp beds were a little too small. When the hostages turned over, as Horst Hoepner soon did, they were liable to pop out of their slots, several at a time, resulting in a loud "bang," similar to the sound of a gunshot, and depositing the sleeper on the floor. Best was startled awake at the loud noise, and then laughed with relief at establishing what it was, before precisely the same thing happened to him.[22] The laughter was good medicine for the weary hostages. Sleep overcame them.

Saturday, April 7, 1945

34

Erich and Margot Heberlein

When the hostages awoke after a pleasant first night in Schönberg, arrangements for improving their conditions were taken in hand by Margot Heberlein. Her diary notes report that primitive washing and laundry facilities were installed just outside their room that very Saturday morning. The group had more than one reason to be grateful to the diplomatic couple.

Erich and Margot Heberlein

Erich was born in Cranz, Danzig, on September 26, 1889, to Nikolaus and Julie. He attended the *Gymnasium* school in Danzig and went on to study law in Breslau, Munich, and Berlin. He was employed in the Prussian judicial service from 1912 and added further to his qualifications in 1913. He was an active combatant during World War I but was still able to marry Käthe Wegner on January 2, 1915. They had a daughter together, Gisela, who was born in 1916. Shortly before the end of the war, he was deployed as a reserve lieutenant to the German consulate in Zurich. The marriage ended. In August 1919 Erich was drafted into the diplomatic corps. From 1920 to 1925, he was posted to the embassy in Madrid, where he moved in elite social circles. In a photograph from a picnic taken around the time, in a group that includes the founder of the Herrero Bank, a smiling Erich radiates an assured confidence. He met Margot Camilo Calleja Enright, a member of the Spanish aristocracy; her father was a doctor whose abilities were highly appreciated by the Spanish nobility. She became his lifelong partner. Although Margot was born in Valladolid, in Spain, the family at the time of their encounter was already thoroughly international, with Margot's brother Camilo living in the USA. On February 2, 1922, they were married at the Egglesia San Jeronimo, and they had a son, Oskar, born in 1923. From 1925 Erich became the German Foreign Office representative at the Reichskommissariat for occupied Rhineland territories in

Koblenz. In 1928 he was posted to Athens, and in 1934 to Buenos Aires. From 1937 onwards he was deployed to the German embassy in fascist Spain during the period of the Spanish Civil War. In 1941 he held the role of ambassador. In February 1943 he was summoned to Berlin to take on the role of head of station for Spain and Portugal, but by this time Erich had become increasingly uncomfortable with the conduct and ethos of the regime he was serving. At some point his position moved to one of unwillingness to obey the regime. After much difficulty he was granted a short period of home sick leave around the time of the Berlin funeral of his grandmother Maria, which took place on February 28, 1943. He travelled home to Spain and from that presumed safe distance began what became a protracted process of declining to return to Berlin, ostensibly for health reasons. The Nazi government quickly took a dim view of his conduct and began issuing a series of increasingly stern warnings. Finally, in June 1944 his superiors could tolerate his non-compliance no further and arranged for his return by force. This duly took place on June 17.

The couple made separate diary notes as events progressed, recording the story of their capture at the hands of the Gestapo, which have remained unpublished for almost eighty years. This unabridged first-hand account is offered here for the first time. Margot writes, in good (unamended) English,

> Around midnight on Saturday 17th June 1944 two men claiming to be from the Spanish Secret Police came to the house in Toledo and forced us both at gunpoint to accompany them. We were led to a very secluded spot, about a mile from the house, where two German Embassy cars and a group of six German Gestapo men awaited us. The group included *Kriminalrat* Paul Winzer and was led by *Obersturmführer* Georg Vey. I was violently shoved into one of the vehicles. When the same was attempted with Erich, a most unequal struggle between him and several of the men ensued. His shouts for help were heard by no-one. He was badly beaten up and bundled, almost unconscious, after a head wound, into the other vehicle. The vehicles sped off towards Madrid, arriving at the German Embassy's Air Squadron 18 building. We had our passports and other documents confiscated and were placed in separate rooms on the first floor, guarded by several Gestapo agents. At 2.00 the next afternoon Erich was driven by *Obersturmführer* Vey and three agents to Barrajas airport. Here the private plane of air attaché General Krahmer stood waiting in a remote corner of the otherwise deserted airfield.

Krahmer's nephew, Commander Schwarz, was at the controls. Erich was boarded with two of the accompanying agents and the plane took off immediately, flying over the Pyrenees to land at Biarritz between 4 and 5pm, where he was once more locked up.

Still being held in Madrid, Margot was of course unaware of her husband's movements. With considerable dexterity she was able to persuade her guards that it would be in their interests to allow her to write a few lines of reassurance to her family. She succeeded in wording this no doubt scrutinised message so that the family understood the real truth at once: that they were victims of a kidnapping by the Germans. Meanwhile, the police in Toledo had worked out what had really happened and had submitted a proper report. That night, Sunday, June 18, Margot was driven overnight in another diplomatic vehicle, along with four accompanying agents, led by one called Könicke, to San Sebastián. Here there was a change of vehicle. From there on a Gestapo official named Huber, from the SS consulate, took over the driving. They reached the Irun/Hendaye frontier on Monday, June 19, 1944. The border crossing, with Margot under a false name, was easily arranged. Thereafter the diplomatic couple, still separated, were dragged from one prison to another—Biarritz, Bayerne, Bordeaux, Poitiers, and finally Paris—not reaching Berlin until July 12.[1] But they were still kept apart for the next five months. Margot continues,

> There my husband was kept severely incommunicated in the prison of the Gestapo General Headquarters, Prinz-Albrecht-Strasse 8, and I [was held] under the same conditions in Potsdam. During the 5 ensuing months, due to the repeated complaints of my family, and the energetic protests of the Spanish Government through its Ambassador in Berlin, Mr Vidal, both the Embassy in Madrid and Berlin cynically answered with gross and absurd lies:
>
> (1) That having received news of our son Oskar being wounded, we had been given all possible facilities for the journey. The family meanwhile, was receiving letters from our son, in perfect health dated after 17th June.
>
> (2) That our journey had been voluntary. In that case, and no matter what the hurry, how was it that we had not told the guards in our service to let the family know of our sudden journey? How to explain our departure without even the most necessary toilet articles and that we were in Germany perfectly well and free, even our address was there, which my sisters easily proved to be false.

. . . Besides, several good friends of ours being at the Spanish Embassy in Berlin, how could it be that they did not know anything of our arrival? That we were in the country, in Bavaria. How then, either our cousins in Munich, with whom we were always in contact, nor the Spanish Consul, Román de la Presilla, a very good friend of ours didn't know of our whereabouts? Besides, in about the middle of September 1944, my husband was forced to write a letter with the same lies to Barón de las Torres [and] the falsehoods and pressure under which it was written were plain to see. . . . To judge from some of things said to my husband by the Gestapo, it seems the insistent protests of the Spanish Governor had some effect and on 12th Dec 1944 we were both put in the Concentration Camp of Sachsenhausen (came together under better conditions, and even letting us know our son was alive, from whom we were also kept apart). Due to the events of the war, 10 weeks later, part of the camp was evacuated and we were taken to the other Concentration Camps, Buchenwald . . .

It was in Buchenwald that the Heberleins came into contact with Bonhoeffer and the other hostages. Their VIP and political status is the presumed reason for their inclusion in the group.

With the group safely settled a long way from Berlin, their hopes for a decisive Allied breakthrough were redoubled. But elsewhere the hard work of turning hope into surrenders had to continue unabated.

35
World News: An Interim "Parallel Existence"

The Far East

Far from the hostages, but inexorably linked in the global conflict, on April 7 B-29 Superfortress bombers from the US 21st Bomber Command attacked the Japanese capital, Tokyo.[1] It was a watershed moment. In this mission they were escorted, for the first time, by 108 land-based P-51s, which took off from Iwo Jima. Elsewhere in the Far East theatre that day, there was yet another Japanese suicide attack at Okinawa. Gripped by the same death cult as the army, the Imperial Navy despatched its great battle-ship, the 72,800-ton *Yamamoto*, on a suicide mission. The vessel, the larg-est battleship in the world, was provided with only enough fuel to reach Okinawa, and tasked with carrying out an attack against the American TG38 transport fleet. With no air cover, it tried vainly to survive the atten-tions of 280 aircraft from two American carrier groups,[2] and it did not succeed. It was struck by nineteen American aerial torpedoes and sank with the loss of 2,498 crew. In the same suicide attack, the cruiser *Yahagi* and four destroyers were sunk with the further loss of a total of 1,167 men. Of the 376 US aircraft taking part in the operation, only 10 were lost.[3] The further arrival of news that day of the final destruction of the Japanese 15th Army in Burma meant that it was a first day of unrelenting grimness for the new cabinet of Admiral Suzuki.

World Leaders

On April 7 Eleanor Roosevelt wrote to her husband in Warm Springs, "You sounded cheerful for the first time last night—and I hope you'll weigh 170 pounds when you return." It was the last letter that would ever pass between them. It fell to Eleanor not to be numbered among the bevy of females with whom the president was choosing to surround himself at the time. Prominent among these was Daisy Suckley, who captured a revealing and touching insight in her diary at the time, later crossed out, but left legible. To stoke the president's failing appetite, she and cousin Polly had taken to serving him cups of oatmeal—"gruel," she called it—as he rested before dinner and later in the evenings at what was supposed to be his bedtime. This had developed into a game. Franklin Roosevelt, generally deemed the most powerful person on the planet, pulled his covers up to his chin and "relapsed into babyhood," indicating that he wanted to be mothered and fed. In Daisy's words, he "put on his little act of helplessness! It amuses him to be fed, and I love to feed him," she told her diary. On April 7 he halts the game when he is only half-finished with his gruel, sits up, and lights a cigarette. Then he talks earnestly about the San Francisco conference and the prospects for peace. He says that he can probably resign in a year once the world organisation is "well-started." Then he stubs out his cigarette and finishes his gruel. "I kissed him goodnight and left him relaxed and laughing," Daisy wrote. This was on the fifth night before his death.[4]

Stalin, no doubt flattered by the news reaching him from a humbled Churchill and the ailing US president, now replied to Roosevelt with, this time, a more diplomatically worded message, somewhat backing down from his accusations of bad faith. In it he insisted that he had never doubted FDR's "honesty and dependability." But still not retracting his main complaint, which was that the Germans had ceased to put up much resistance on the Western Front, he reminded his ally that

> the Germans continue to fight savagely with the Russians for some unknown junction in the Czech Republic, Zemlienitsa, which they need as much as a dead man needs poultices, but surrender without any resistance important towns in central Germany such as Osnabrück, Mannheim, and Kassel.[5]

Meanwhile he also belaboured the point that the Soviets should have been invited to the possible surrender discussions.[6] There was still more. In a further addition to their bruisings, on April 7 Stalin sent a message to both his allies effectively dismissing any possibility of getting Western observers into Warsaw.[7] The fate of Poland was effectively sealed.

London, England

In London the BBC news that day carried reports that the German Luftwaffe was experiencing losses at a wholly unsustainable rate—with its related and implied message that the war would soon be successfully concluded. The day's newscast stated,

When thirteen hundred American Eighth Air Force Fortresses and Liberators, with an escort of eight hundred and fifty Mustangs and Thunderbolts, flew to attack targets in northern Germany today, the Luftwaffe made one of its now rare appearances—and paid heavily for it. At least eighty-seven enemy planes were shot down.

By contrast, the bulletin noted, (US) 8th Air Force losses were twenty-five planes out of two thousand.[8] In a similar vein, the UK's Saturday newspapers informed their readers that Germans had been told the preceding day by their government that bread rations, gas, and electricity would be cut on Monday; that from now on, Berliners must walk all distances under two miles; and that no one would be permitted to use transport without a pass. It was also realised that one day soon, normal life would need to resume. An interim "parallel existence" was needed. In line with this, the BBC also included in their day's summary the news that

> ninety thousand people went to Wembley this afternoon to see Chelsea beat Millwall by two goals to nought in the South Cup Final. The King and Queen were there with Princess Elizabeth in ATS uniform; so were King Haakon of Norway and Prince Olaf; Allied military leads; several British Ministers; Lord Wavell, Viceroy of India and representatives from the Dominions, from the United States and Russia.[9]

36

Ramming: At Sea and in the Air

Ijmuiden, Holland—and the War at Sea

Elsewhere, and much closer to the hostage group, the unrelenting daily business of war on all fronts continued apace. In the air war, on April 7 fifteen Lancasters from 617 Squadron and two Mosquitoes of 5 Group took advantage of the day's weather conditions, sufficiently better than those that had prevailed on the previous day, when they had been forced to turn back, and carried out an accurate dusk attack on the motor torpedo boat pens in Ijmuiden. In a pattern that was by now becoming depressingly familiar to the Germans, no Allied aircraft were lost.[1] In the North Sea, the German 2nd Motor Torpedo Boat Fleet (captained by Lieutenant Wendler) had been carrying out a mining operation in the Smith's Knoll area, starting the day before, involving six German vessels. On leaving, the fleet engaged with five British vessels, two of which rammed their German counterparts, in both cases leaving the rammer afloat. In one case the German vessel sank, and in the other it was damaged beyond repair, but was somehow able to return to base. One British vessel was sunk by artillery fire. This proved to be the final engagement of the German navy's 2nd Motor Torpedo Boat Fleet.[2] However, it was not the only instance that day of warfare that involved ramming. But the other was a ramming of a much more suicidal nature.

Berlin and *Sonderkommando* Elbe

When Hitler first heard of the idea of trained German Luftwaffe fighter pilots intentionally ramming enemy aircraft, he dismissed it out of hand. Yet such were the bizarre vagaries and machinations of the Third Reich that in these latter days, as the regime staggered towards total collapse, such a scheme could, and did, actually come to fruition. It is a matter of no small irony that in this same atmosphere of confusion and contradiction, the organisational abilities of Berlin's RSHA in arranging the April 9 executions would prove to be so effective. In just one example of chaos, on April 7 *Sonderkommando* Elbe, the Luftwaffe unit specially formed to ram enemy bombers, made its only attack against the US 8th Air Force. Even at this late stage of hostilities, volunteers for the task came forward.[3] Military historian Roger A. Freeman describes one of the attacks, against a Fortress B-17 bomber of 490th Group, captained by First Lieutenant Carrol Cagle, that did not go to plan:

> A German ME 109 fighter was seen to make a diving attack from 8 o'clock and went on to smash its right wing into the Fortress against the waist gun position, knocking over the gunner, who was unhurt. It was the Messerschmitt's wing that disintegrated, twisting the fighter down and under the B-17's fuselage. The impact left a six foot gash, also mangling the bomber's ball turret, before the fighter cartwheeled across the lower surface of the right wing, first damaging the super-charger of the bomber's inboard engine, and then part of the propellor from the outer engine, before the German fighter finally disintegrated. In the four-engined US bomber, which was still able to fly, the ball turret gunner was helped out of his wrecked turret by two other gunners and given first aid—he suffered a broken arm. Despite having two engines disabled, the Fortress was later put down safely on an airfield in liberated territory. It was to prove the only known occasion when organised ramming was performed, with a total of 5 B-17 bombers lost to this tactic.[4]

Goebbels was aware on the appointed day that the *Rammjet* attack was happening. When he received news of the disappointing "results of the trial," he mused that, of course, it was only a first attempt, which could hopefully "soon be repeated with greater success."[5]

37
Berlin's Gestapo: Ruthless in Pursuit

Berlin—and Flossenbürg—Germany

Also in Berlin, but focussed on a particular project, at Gestapo headquarters Heinrich Müller left no stone unturned in pulling together the necessary ingredients for the trials, with related death sentences, planned for April 8. He had met with the nominated prosecutor in Bonhoeffer's case, Walter Huppenkothen, very late on the Friday evening. At this point he provided him with an updated list of candidates, ensuring Josef Müller was omitted, an arrangement to which Kaltenbrunner had assented in his exchange with Rattenhuber on April 5, one of the now-rarer days of his presence in Berlin.[1] However, it was not the sort of issue to leave in doubt, and to ensure that Josef Müller was removed from it, it took the involvement of a teleprinter message sent from Kaltenbrunner's adjutant directly to Flossenbürg. But that had come through as illegible, so a specific telephone call between Kaltenbrunner's adjutant and the camp commandant ensured clarity was achieved, if not on Saturday, then certainly by Sunday afternoon.[2] The finalised form of the list then stood as: Admiral Canaris, General Hans Oster, General Karl Sack, Captain Ludwig Gehre, and Dietrich Bonhoeffer. Captain Theodor Strünck, already condemned to death on October 10, 1944, was simply to be executed when the other death sentences were carried out. Duly briefed, after a very short night's rest, at 3:00 the next morning, Saturday, April 7, Huppenkothen made a successful rendezvous just off the Berlin autobahn with the designated convoy of vehicles. This included at least one motorcycle outrider, and was headed by Oberverwalter Wilhelm Gogolla, whom "Gestapo" Müller had directed to travel to Flossenbürg, with some special prisoners,[3] to facilitate the conducting of proceedings there. Huppenkothen was accompanied by his wife, Erika, who was of course not fleeing Berlin for the safety of the south, an offence likely for ordinary civilians to incur a death penalty, but rather accompanying her husband on important official business.[4] After a journey of some three hundred kilometres, the party made their first stop, presumably during the course of the morning, at Hof, where the prosecutor later claimed he picked up some documentary evidence for the trial.[5] But the early start was to prove its worth. Huppenkothen's first instinct on arrival at Flossenbürg, which happened at some point during the Saturday, was to ensure that everyone selected for death was present. By a complete fluke, given that it was he who had made the spontaneous decision to be transported there on the Wednesday of that week, Gehre was. Sack, Strünck, Oster, and Canaris were, and had been for some while, Canaris in particular receiving the very unwelcome and regular attentions of Kriminalkommissar Stawitski. But Bonhoeffer proved, infuriatingly, to be the only one on the list who was not there. The frenetic search began right away. Fabian von Schlabrendorff, who had arrived only that same evening after dusk,[6] was awoken in his cell and asked for his name. No sooner had he gone back to sleep than he was reawoken for a second time, and accused of pretending not to be Bonhoeffer, which he hotly denied. Franz Liedig was also asked, further compounding the mystery of his own absence from the list. Josef Müller was still another prisoner asked if he was Bonhoeffer. The difference in Müller's case was that he took particular encouragement in his own denial, knowing full well—like Liedig—that Bonhoeffer was by that stage nowhere near Flossenbürg. Amid everything else that was going on, he did not rate highly anyone's chances of finding him.[7] It remains a mystery how Bonhoeffer's location became known to the prosecuting authorities in Flossenbürg.

There are various possible explanations for this. Most likely camp commandant Koegel recalled without difficulty that the hostage convoy whose transport leader had halted outside the camp for three hours, and who had requisitioned the abundant personal food supplies from his canteen only that Wednesday, was headed south. It was, after all, the Gestapo's own project. Failing that, the Regensburg Gestapo knew exactly where to find all the hostages, as they had, already during that day, expressly written to the transport leader at the precise Schönberg school address where Bonhoeffer was located, issuing formal permission for the spouse of one of the *Sippenhäftlinge*, herself in good standing with the authorities, to make a visit to her husband by flying there.[8] The telephone contact number for the Gestapo office is even visible on the memorandum.

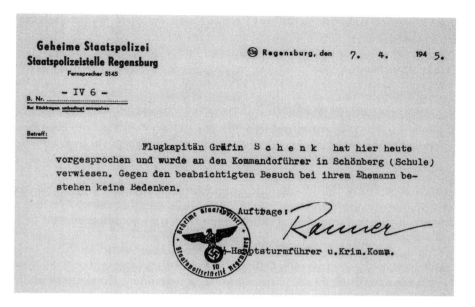

Fig. 37-1. Regensburg Gestapo memorandum
From Richardi, *SS-Geiseln im Markt Schönberg*, 126. Photo: John Hogg.

SS-Hauptsturmführer and Kriminalkommissar Ranner, who issued the warrant, must have been aware of the discussions with the transport leader about the Regensburg Gestapo's inability to accommodate the hostage group overnight (at no notice) on the Wednesday of that week, and was equally aware that the group had departed from Regensburg prison the following evening. It was in Regensburg that the transport leader had requisitioned a gleaming new detail of guards to replace those who had become "soft" towards the hostages during the Thursday night of that week. Another possibility, from within Flossenbürg itself, is that Kriminalkommissar Stawitski may have been approached to renew his deception skills (or fondness for brutality) in relation to the previously compliant Ludwig Gehre and elicit the information from him by whatever means.

Whatever the solution, there was still time. The problem could not be fixed that night and would have to wait till next day. Huppenkothen assented to this, given the late hour, and his own very early start. SS judge Otto Thorbeck had also travelled too far south on a munitions train that night and would need collecting next day from Schwarzenfeld, complete with his bicycle.[9] A driver with a vehicle with sufficient space for the bicycle would have to be sent for him, and a detail of two guards for Bonhoeffer, once his whereabouts were confirmed, in the morning. There were adequate vehicles and fuel supplies in Flossenbürg's well-organised SS garage.[10] There was still ample time for the talented team appointed to make suitable preparations for their wholesale flouting of the multiple legal formalities needed to press ahead. These included a number of needed omissions: the absence of military judges, a defence counsel, a review process, a court stenographer, and a venue considered legitimate for the trial of serving officers. But all of the surrounding documentation and "evidence for the prosecution" would have to be shredded anyway. Back in Berlin, "Gestapo" Müller would simply have to entrust the people on the ground with completing the task.

But in the German capital, Müller could remain confident. Those whom he had entrusted with the Flossenbürg trials leading to death sentences would certainly demonstrate commitment, even in the face of no small level of logistical difficulty. Given the surrounding chaos, the work required for the Gestapo to carry out the Flossenbürg executions would prove a logistical triumph for those committed to it. It remains surprising under the circumstances.

For example, by way of complete contrast, also emanating from the besieged German capital on that same day was a string of seemingly contradictory—and correspondingly irrelevant—messages. This was a stream that continued to flow in earnest, and not only from Martin Bormann. On April 7 Hitler followed up on both his own and Speer's previous directives on the matter of "scorched earth" defence. He issued a statement to the effect that, at the approach of the enemy, all bridge-building facilities were to be completely destroyed, but did rescind the previously ordered destruction of railway and post office facilities and locomotives and rolling stock, as well as the sinking of ships—all that was to cease. However, Field Marshal Keitel, at least nominally responsible for the actual implementation of such matters, failed to confirm operationally this latter positive order and to allow it to take effect. The net effect was to leave people who were asking for direction in a state of suspended animation. At least from Speer's perspective, it was now official policy to do no more than cripple transportation and communication facilities and to postpone destroying bridges until the last moment. But Speer's directives were hardly effective without onward distribution and a chain of command. Speer writes, no doubt with an eye to his plans for credibility in a post-Nazi world,

Once again, 3 weeks before the end, I extracted Hitler's consent to this final statement: "With regard to all measures for demolition and evacuation, it should be borne in mind that when territory is recovered, these installations should be usable for German production."

In line with this, on April 7 Walter Rohland, a steel magnate and senior official on Speer's Ruhr staff, ordered businessmen and senior industrialists across the Reich to report immediately any destruction of industry undertaken without Speer's authorization.[11] But it was all a drop in the ocean. The chaos and confusion continued.[12] Ordinary Germans were simply bewildered.

38
Mounting Chaos

Zutphen, Holland, and Leese and Bromskirchen, Germany

Amid the chaos the bitter graft that was at times being euphemistically and unhelpfully described as "mopping up" operations, at times involving many casualties, still had to continue. On April 7 the ancient town of Zutphen on the Ijssel river was taken, together with its launch site for the V-2 rockets. In coincidental timing, from Germany, that same day, around 275 kilometres farther east, it was reported that the US 1st Army had captured a trainload of nine V-2 rockets near Bromskirchen, another manufacturing site for the weapons, in sufficient time for the picture to make the front pages of a number of UK newspapers. Also on the same day, around two hundred kilometres further north, No. 3 Commando,[1] commanded by Lieutenant Colonel P. Bartholomew, captured the town of Leese. Shortly afterwards the unit captured the V-2 factory there, including a train with V-2s loaded on flat cars, and had the satisfaction of apprehending a number of the scientists from *Kampfstoffabrik* Leese still in their white coats.

In film footage surrounding the event, the combative handwritten message "Nach England" (This one is for the English) can be seen scrawled in chalk along the length of one of the giant rockets. As with the messaging surrounding Germany's aircraft losses, the capture of the rockets was an unmitigated dose of good news for the many towns and cities that had experienced their terrifying destructive power, and it also implied that, for Germany, the end was fast approaching. The myth of the soon-to-be-deployed "wonder-weapon" could no longer be sustained. The seizure included classified technical information on the weapon, which was now "secret no more." Without overtly making the connection with the events described above, the *Western Daily Press* reflected on April 7 that it was "now a week since enemy air activity was reported over southern England—long-range rockets, flying bombs or piloted raiders."[2]

But it was not all one-way traffic. The UK's Saturday papers contained other, unwelcome, messages. The *News Chronicle* ran a sobering article headlined "Why Nazis will fight to the bitter end." Its (accurate) source was a member of the German Foreign Office who did not wish to be named, explaining point by point why "there will be no capitulation."[3]

Plukkutjønnfjellet Mountain, Norway

For this very reason, even at this late stage of the war, hazardous operations were still being attempted. One such was that of the top-secret mission team tasked with disrupting and blowing up the Nordland railway in Norway—the first and only combined ski-parachute operation ever mounted by the US Army. One member of the team was Lieutenant Richard Bosch, aged twenty-five. On April 7, in the bitter cold and fog, the modified B-24 transporting them to Norway crashed into Plukkutjønnfjellet mountain and bounced down the craggy slope, shattering into pieces. Bosch, along with eleven others, was killed outright.[4]

Lippoldsberg, Weser River Valley, Germany

In another instance of the fiercest combat conditions that still prevailed across innumerable locations, soldiers from the US Company G, 413 Infantry, fought their way across the Weser river, attacking Lippoldsberg. Among them was Private Willy James, aged twenty-four. On April 7 his assault platoon was tasked with securing a group of houses on the edge of town. Far out in front, as first scout, James drew German fire, but still offered to go forwards fully to reconnoitre the situation. Furious cross-fire from snipers and machine guns finally pinned down the soldier after he had made his way forwards approximately two hundred yards across open terrain. Lying in an exposed position for more than an hour, he continued in his detailed observations of the German positions, which were given away by the fire that he was courageously drawing upon himself. Then, with utter indifference to his personal safety, in a storm of small-arms fire, Private James made his way back more than three hundred yards across open terrain under observation of the defenders to his platoon positions, and gave a full, detailed report on the German disposition. Using this information, the unit worked out a new plan of assault against strongly held positions, in which James offered to lead a squad of men. In the course of this attack, his platoon commander was shot, and James went to his aid, exposing himself recklessly to the incessant defensive fire. As he was making his way across open ground, James was killed by a burst from a machine gun.[5]

Lüneburg, Germany

On the morning and afternoon of April 7, the town of Lüneburg was bombed by the USAAF. It was a beautiful town to which Bach used to come because it had the most beautiful organ in Europe. Pale sea-green copper spires and a great repose and gentleness characterised the town square, where the old buildings hung together with their curious and lovely facades of twisted stone. High on the wall of the cathedral, the lion and the unicorn on the coat of arms of the House of Hanover, the English coat of arms, proclaimed, "Dieu et mon droit."[6] On the date of Lüneburg's bombing, a twenty-four-year-old master sergeant, Ralph Montavon, was decorated with the Legion of Merit in recognition of the exceptional number of combat missions that had been flown without mechanical failure. A total of 266.9 tons of bombs were dropped. The railway station was heavily damaged, and put out of action. Various installations, including local fuel reserves, were set on fire, and deafening explosions were heard throughout the town. But, as always, there were also unplanned consequences to the strike.

Standing at the station was a train carrying four hundred concentration camp prisoners of French, Yugoslav, Polish, Russian, and Hungarian origin, who had set out from Wilhelmshaven on April 3. The prisoners were locked in throughout the bombing raid. The guards fled to nearby groves of trees in search of shelter. The railway carriages turned into death traps for many prisoners. Seventy-one perished during these raids. Twenty or so succeeded in escaping. Within three or four days, 146 were taken by train to Bergen-Belsen.[7]

The Ruhr Pocket, Germany

With his forces now cut off in the Ruhr, Germany's Field Marshal Model issued an order on April 7 that prisoners in penitentiaries, including those on remand for political offences, should be handed over to the police for "examination." It seems that the unspoken intentions behind his orders were immediately grasped. The execution of more than two hundred prisoners followed. There were also numerous other killings in the final hours before penal institutions were evacuated, or before the Allies arrived. Where an official executioner could not get to a penitentiary in time, prison officials—rewarded with money and cigarettes—carried out the killings. In one subsidiary of Emland camp, a young apprentice chimney sweep, wearing an army captain's uniform, turned up and ordered the execution of dozens of prisoners. Astonishingly, his orders were followed—a sign of the mounting chaos in the collapsing regime. More than a hundred prisoners were executed over the next few days.[8]

Vienna, Austria, and across Europe—a Day of Large Liberations

Across Europe events unfolded rapidly. In its first news edition of the day, the BBC reported that the Russian troops under Marshal Tolbukhin were said to be within a mile of Vienna, but by lunchtime the amended bulletin stated that they had broken into the city itself. Events were progressing so rapidly that news editors attempting at least some measure of verification were hard-pressed to keep pace. For example, several news channels that day already carried stories of anti-Nazi radio broadcasts being made in Vienna late the previous evening with gunfire audible in the background.

Königsberg

But news headlines of surrenders and liberations could not mask the fact that the war was still by no means over. In many places fighting raged with unprecedented intensity. In Königsberg, where the battle for the city was being fought in mortal earnest, Soviet artillery officer Senior Lieutenant Inozemstev wrote in his diary,

> The aviation is very effective—we are using flame-throwers on a massive scale. . . . It is already clear to everyone that the storming of Königsberg will go down as a classic example of storming a big city.[9]

The resulting destruction was terrible. Thousands of soldiers and civilians were buried by the bombardments. There was a "smell of death in the air," Inozemstev wrote, "literally—because thousands of corpses are decomposing under the ruins."

Buchenwald, Germany

At the end of the first week of April, with the sounds of the approaching front line audible to all in Buchenwald, it was still assumed in the camp system that it would be possible to preserve some of the prisoners and that in the southern part of Germany they would continue to be of some use, whether as a labour force or as hostages. In the period between

April 7 and April 10, amid scenes of total chaos, twenty-eight thousand
prisoners were sent out, by rail, or on foot, heading for the concentration
camps many kilometres further away to the south, either Flossenbürg or
Dachau.[10] One rail transport set off on April 7. It consisted of five to six
thousand prisoners of various nationalities being sent south. The first leg
of the evacuation was from Buchenwald to nearby Weimar, six miles (ten
kilometres) away. This brief death march claimed between 300 and 350
victims. Merbach, commander of the transport, subsequently admitted
that he himself had shot to death about ten prisoners who had tried to
escape. On their arrival in Weimar, the remaining prisoners were loaded
onto open freight cars, ninety to one hundred per car. In all there were
between thirty-nine and forty-three cars, some carrying equipment and
food, such as sacks of potatoes, bread, margarine, and canned meat. In the
first stage of the evacuation, the commanding officer lost control of the
situation. One of the French prisoners on the transport managed to jot
down daily impressions of events along the route. The prisoners received
a food ration on average once every two days. It included 7 to 9 ounces
(200–250 grams) of bread, a little cheese, and on some days a few potatoes
or sixteen ounces (half a litre) of soup. Other prisoners in the transport
recalled that the food rations were even smaller.[11]

Eisenerz/Präbichl, Styria, Austria

Throughout the collapsing German Reich, malnourished and often starving
prisoners in the hands of the authorities were intensely vulnerable. In Eisenerz Adolf Schumann had served as senior commander of the Volkssturm
units since November 1944. He was by occupation a policeman, whose main
task was directing traffic and keeping the peace in the sleepy little Alpine
town. On Friday, April 6, he had been appraised that a detail[12] of three to
four thousand Jews, which was on its way from Hungary to Mauthausen,
was due to arrive in his town. (In fact the convoy comprised between seven
and eight thousand prisoners who had left Graz on April 4 and were led
in three columns by a modest detachment of Volkssturm, Gestapo, and
Ukrainian Waffen-SS men.) The police and Volkssturm units at Eisenerz
received orders to be ready to accept this group, which was to cross the
Präbichl Pass, and accompany it onwards to Hieflau. The Eisenerz police
chief, Ernst Bilke, informed Schumann that he had assigned two policemen
to this task, and asked for the assistance of one of the Volkssturm units.
Schumann passed the orders on, as received, to the local Volkssturm unit
chosen as escorts, quite a few of whose members were SA men, emphasising

as he did so that the marchers were Jews and were to be shot only in the event of escape attempts in the town itself.

At 5:00 on the morning of April 7, the additional Volkssturm troops from the locality reported for duty, as instructed, at the unit's assembly spot. The men in question were commanded by Ludwig Krenn, a veteran Nazi and member of the SA since 1933. Aged forty-six at the time, he was too old for active service during the war. The company, which was a fairly typical Volkssturm unit, consisted of sixty-nine men, the youngest born in 1914 and the oldest in 1891. Most of them were between thirty-eight and forty-five years of age. But Krenn was not of the same persuasion as Schumann. It seems that a decision to murder Jews on the march to Mauthausen had apparently been taken by the Kreisleiter of Leoben district, Otto Christandl, who had held the post since 1938, in his capacity as the supreme political authority in the district at the time. The night beforehand Krenn's unit had gathered in the unit canteen for a get-together meal and had received, in view of the coming operation, a half-litre allowance of wine each. Krenn had addressed his men, and the canteen manager had heard him say,

> The Alarm Company [referring to the Volkssturm] has been instructed to take over a transport of Jews on the Präbichl tomorrow. These dogs and swine deserve all to be dead. If among you there is a coward, he must report himself right away, for tomorrow will be too late. If tomorrow anyone goes cowardly on me, I will finish him off personally.

That morning, on April 7, Krenn addressed them again. He told them bluntly that their mission was to kill the Jews. As he put it, if the Jews did not attempt to escape, they should be helped to do so. He also insisted on knowing if any of them felt they were unable to shoot and promised that after the operation, they would all receive schnapps and cigarettes. At 6:30 a.m. they reached the Präbichl Pass. The day passed uneasily. Between 4:00 and 4:30 in the afternoon, the hatred engendered by all that had preceded finally broke out into the open. One of the men from Krenn's company subsequently described what happened:

> The order given to us by Krenn meant that we had to fire on any Jew who was no longer able to move on. There were, as I have been told, 7,000 Jews in troop order, following one after the other. They started at the Hotel Reichenstein and moved to the Präbichl Pass, very slowly, according to their state of health. Krenn and his assistants

were always after them, pushing them on with the butts of their rifles and with sticks. The distance between the attitudes of the different troop units became greater and greater and when people fainted or fell to the ground, Krenn and his assistants began to fire on them. In heaps they fell, 5 or 10 at a time, often badly wounded. Krenn's assistants rushed with their pistols in their hands to those who were lying on the ground in their death struggles, and shot them.

The prisoners in the convoy were at a loss about how to respond. The death blow being inflicted so suddenly on them as they made their way through the mountain pass was wholly unexpected. They had not been ready for such treatment and did not understand what was happening. Those who continued the march picked their way between the corpses of their comrades as they fell, sometimes at their very feet. One of the women who survived described the scene:

> We had to climb up a hill. I was among the first in the column and since the line had scattered, we had to wait at the top of the hill for those who were lagging behind. . . . When people reached the top, the guards began to drive us downhill and at the same time to fire at us. Those who were firing stood behind trees or bushes and fired from their hiding places but after a short time they came out but continued to shoot. I saw them aiming and firing. . . . Then an SS man arrived on a motorcycle and ordered them to stop shooting.

After fifteen minutes it was over. With the involvement of the local population, approximately 250 Jewish prisoners were murdered.[13]

Pfaffenhofen, Germany

In the vicinity of Munich, on April 7 the diarist Victor Klemperer noted that people everywhere were throwing caution to the winds and talking unceasingly, openly, accusingly, and bitterly, while longing for the arrival of the Americans and the end of hostilities. But at the same time, it also proved the final day on which the diarist recorded hearing a pro-Nazi and bellicose voice. After breakfast Klemperer and his wife, Eva, were dropped by a friend at the entry and exit point of the Munich to Nürnberg autobahn.[14] They had spent much of the morning thumbing for a lift there, without success, while a strong, bitingly cold wind was blowing. Opting to walk the four-and-a-half-mile stretch to Pfaffenhofen, they were shown kindness by a serving soldier. Although at first encounter, while he was repairing his military vehicle, he indicated he would be unable to help by offering them a lift, he evidently decided to leave his fellow soldier with the vehicle and soon caught them up on foot. Despite only having one hand (he had lost the other in Normandy), as a matter of course, the soldier took one of Klemperer's bags. In the long and agreeable conversation that ensued, the big, strong eighteen-year-old recounted that he was originally from the Waterkant, the North Sea coast, and that he had been taken captive in Normandy, shipped to the USA, and then exchanged. He liked things in the vicinity of Munich—he had found a girl there. Klemperer writes,

> Only—did he have any future at all? He was in the SS and what would happen to the SS if . . . But the Führer didn't deserve to be defeated, he had had such good intentions and organised everything so well. The defeats so far had been the result of treachery, there had been treachery long before the 20th July, and now, on the Führer's birthday, on the 20th April, our new offensive would begin and liberate the East. He did not seem quite certain of that, however, and was glad to be consoled by me: as a bricklayer he would always earn a living, and he would surely be able to work with one hand and a prosthesis. I asked him what it had been like in America. "Good," he could not deny it, good rations, decent treatment under German officers. . . . But of course the Americans had only done that for propaganda reasons, so that those exchanged would afterwards say good things about the USA when they got home. So the lad got natural and reasonable things and what had been drummed into him all jumbled up.[15]

As they parted company, the soldier's final words were to the effect that if things went really badly, then he would volunteer for the front again.

Gmunden, Austria

In the relative security of the Königinvilla, Marie Vassiltchikov and her friend Sisi enjoyed a breakfast with their hosts en famille. The subject of food and provisions was uppermost in everyone's minds. But at least, after breakfast, Marie was able to visit the hairdresser. In a curious link with Bonhoeffer (see below), the friends' morning contained a "walk with the children to look for dandelions—they make very good salad."[16]

39

Schönberg: Smuggled Sausages

The morning of Saturday, April 7—a day that would indeed contain a walk, as agreed the previous evening, to look for dandelions—began in agreeable fashion for the hostages. In their day, too, the subject of food remained uppermost in their minds. Unsurprisingly, after the week of travel they had endured, they had slept well. The particularly fine weather continued, and the stunning views lifted their spirits. The sounds of the Schönberg church bell were a most welcome novelty. With only two guards (one on duty and one off), the Gestapo could watch only one side of the house at a time. This meant that without too much difficulty the prisoners could open a window and talk to any passer-by who was prepared to stop and chat. Some were. There was still no breakfast, but the kindly housekeeper brought in some hot water. One of the hostages was Sigmund Rascher, who knew full well, like all the others, that his life might be terminated at a moment's notice. In his case the closer he came to Dachau, where his previous conduct had made him mortal enemies, the greater was the likelihood of this happening. At this point Rascher displayed the generous side of his nature. In Buchenwald Best had more than once observed Rascher's habit of drying out his scanty bread ration and hanging it on a makeshift clothesline. He now proceeded to bring out everything he had somehow squirreled away throughout the privations and cramped conditions of the journey thus far and shared it all out with the group. The meagre rations, an alternative to no food whatsoever, were much appreciated. The group, who had all slept under the respective nickname signs Rascher had put up the evening beforehand, were able to eat bread together thanks solely to the generous-heartedness of a Gestapo informer and mass murderer.

There was further encouraging news. On that morning the occupants of the schoolroom, the political prisoners, were now able, thanks to Margot Heberlein,[1] to access and share the use of a small basin, with a working tap, but devoid of a plug. It was situated outside their door, on the landing they shared with the others, the *Sippenhäftlinge*. Relations in the corridor between the two categories of prisoners being kept hostage were, on the surface, jovial, but the *Sippenhäftlinge* as a group were concealing a guilty secret.

The background to this secret was as follows: As soon as the prisoners arrived, Schönberg's mayor had soon overcome his distress at being forced to close the hospital. From his home in the brewery opposite the girls' schoolhouse, he would drop by each morning and enquire after their wellbeing. The food situation was so desperate that even the SS soldiers were complaining of hunger. Upon establishing that the provisions being delivered via the guards were not reaching the prisoners, the mayor helped activate a courageous group of local townspeople to circumvent official orders. These townsfolk began to provide the prisoners with secret food rations and other acts of kindness. One of these was the covert posting out of letters. This was an immense joy and comfort to hostages—almost all of whom had been kept in total isolation from loved ones for so many months. For this, the idea came from the young schoolteacher Erna Sterlich. Her school-related accommodation was on the ground floor of the boys' schoolroom adjacent to the church (see building 7 on map). Soon after the hostages were allocated rooms, she had been shocked to find a note saying "We are prisoners of July 20, 1944" hung below her window. When she saw the large woodpile provided to keep the prisoners warm, she asked a Gestapo guard if some of the younger male prisoners could be allocated to the needed task of chopping logs. Soon the young *Sippenhäftlinge* Otto Philipp and Markwart Schenk von Stauffenberg were set to work. One of them, quite possibly in response to a signal from Erna, contrived an injury that needed medical attention—thus providing an excellent excuse to be out of sight of the guard for a secure conversation. The results flowed thick and fast. Erna's conversation helped begin the flow of supplies to the hostages. Another outcome was that she sent trusted pupils from her class on their bicycles cycling off with a number of letters from hostages to their loved ones to a variety of letterboxes in neighbouring parishes. Erna was not alone. The farmer Otto Hansbauer, a well-respected villager with a strong Christian faith, who lived immediately opposite the girls' school building, was another who supplied provisions. At times he also turned up his radio when his window was open so that the others on the opposite side of the road were able to hear all the news. Offering support such as this was a highly hazardous enterprise. The crime of *Gefangenenbegünstigung* (offering preferential treatment to prisoners) attracted the most horrific of consequences, of which being sent to a concentration camp was among the less severe. In full knowledge of this, another local resident, Maria Merklein, the wife of the school's head teacher, who himself was also the local NSDAP Ortsgruppenleiter, took a decision. Her main bedroom had been requisitioned for Léon and Jeannot Blum. She chose to help the French couple billeted with her. Sadly she was spotted, and boxed around the ears—but was relieved to be spared a worse outcome.[2] Also numbered among those taking risks to subvert the system and deliver supplies were Emilie Salern and her five-and-a-half-year-old daughter Ingrid. On multiple occasions Ingrid would use a doll's pram complete with mattress, teddy bear, and doll as the perfect cover to smuggle sausages, provided by the local butcher, *Metzger* Hörner, into the boys' schoolhouse.[3] With the help of a large suitcase and a bent curtain pole, these supplies travelled onwards via a ventilation shaft in the toilet of the teachers' house, then on to the school toilets—from whence they could be received by the half-starved prisoners. This group of hardy townsfolk also included the local baker, Franz Pleintinger, who readily provided bread supplies for the project.[4] These were carefully smuggled up in to the first-floor window of the boys' schoolroom, where prisoners were lodged (see diagram; Bonhoeffer was in the *Mädchenschulhaus*, the girls' school building). But the

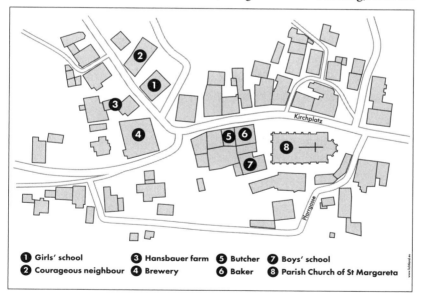

❶ Girls' school   **❸** Hansbauer farm   **❺** Butcher   **❼** Boys' school
❷ Courageous neighbour   **❹** Brewery   **❻** Baker   **❽** Parish Church of St Margareta

Fig. 39-1. Schönberg layout
www.lichtland.eu

successes of such endeavours were patchy. For Bonhoeffer's group it was a case of as in Regensburg, so in Schönberg. His prisoner group was the unlucky one. Naturally the support was given in the assumption that all the prisoners would have access to what the locals were providing. But, overcome with a wave of bitterness, in the girls' school building at least, the *Sippenhäftlinge* made no attempt to share out whatever reached them.[5]

This enforced privation was terrible for the Grüne Minna hostages in the schoolroom, for while they were in prison, no supplies from outside had been received, and Falconer, for one, had never had a Red Cross parcel, so, unlike the *Sippenhäftlinge*, they had no reserves to fall back on, of either food or strength. A specific appeal for food, fronted by diplomat Erich Heberlein, to their hostage neighbours that same morning elicited an offering so paltry that it verged on the ridiculous. Because it would have proven impossible to split what was received into thirteen parts, it was by general agreement shared between Margot Heberlein and her protégée, Heidel Nowakowski. The group were famished. General von Rabenau took some exercise by joining with others in marching around the table. As he did so, the fact that he, like Falconer, had dropped from fifteen stone to ten while in captivity became readily apparent. The discomfiture he felt in continually hitching up his trousers, kept in place by means of a thin piece of string—a Gestapo humiliation so commonplace for any they held in disfavour it was almost universal—was shared by others. Payne Best was moved to raid his vast luggage and present the general with one of his spare pairs of trousers, and insisted he don them at once, but this did not end the discomfiture. Best picks up the story:

> An hour or so later he was still marching steadily round the table, and I noticed that force of habit had led him to neglect certain important buttons. As he passed us, we all made signals and when none of these was any avail, somebody stopped him, pointed, and said "Buttons." Highly indignant, the general retorted: "I have never done up buttons for myself in my life. I leave that to my wife."[6]

But, humour and indignity aside, the painful reality was that the prisoners were at near-starving point. Hermann Pünder wrote,

> Apart from the dried-out daily bread ration, there were some days when we received nothing at all. For the first time in my life, I found myself snatching breadcrumbs away from birds as they pecked at

them on the windowsill, and although they were rock hard, I devoured them greedily.[7]

In the absence of food, there was nonetheless a sensation when the group stirred that morning: Payne Best's abundant supply of useful items also included a working electric razor! The suppressed irritation the group had felt at being inconvenienced by the excessive quantities of Best's personal belongings earlier in the week was no doubt suddenly much dispelled. An orderly queue of eleven men, including Bonhoeffer, formed up to use it, with Best at its head, on the readily accepted rationale of showing the others how the device worked. While the men were shaving, Margot Heberlein and Heidel Nowakowski teamed up—after an initial reluctance on the part of Heidel—and made a start on offering laundry and mending services to the group. Bonhoeffer enjoyed conversations with those allocated beds either side of him. In his conversation with Kokorin, Bonhoeffer did not enquire of the endearing Gestapo informant for too much detail about his life. In Schönberg Kokorin would prove very forthcoming in supplying, to all who asked, the spurious Red Square home address in Moscow, which he had invented in connection with his "Molotov's nephew" cover story and identity. For the astute conversationalist, in a room where comments were by no means private, such matters were best left untouched. Instead Bonhoeffer chose the "safe" topic of the Russian language, demonstrating for the first time, as an internationally aware person, an interest in learning it. He also shared something of the Christian faith with Kokorin, in such a way as would bear fruit the following morning. In his exchange with Pünder, which took place in the warm sunshine at the window, Bonhoeffer was again happy to be engaged in conversation about the Christian faith. It was a friendship that would also bear fruit the next morning. The room was abuzz with quiet fellowship.

While some continued to march round the table and others queued for the razor, Payne Best fell into what was, for him, an agreeable conversation with Hugh Falconer. In this exchange the SOE officer, still under cover in the group as a downed RAF pilot, almost certainly did not disclose to him the real story of his arrest and capture, as Best reports in his book. This information came to Best only at a subsequent date. Worse still, in Sachsenhausen Falconer, already severely malnourished, had got into trouble for stealing onions from the very garden that, as part of his uniquely privileged status, Best was allowed to cultivate. Best's standing as a "special prisoner," with its manifest implications of collaboration with his German captors, was painfully and lastingly seared into the patriotic spirit of the serving officer. But Falconer was sharp enough, and skilful enough, to provide Best with neutral information about the first three or so years of the war, before he was "shot down," and refrained from revealing to an untrusted source any hint of his real feelings.[8] In these agreeable moments, they were joined by the sociable, presumably now clean-shaven, Sigmund Rascher, who in the open dormitory setting was being successfully thwarted in any endeavours to sidle alongside Heidel Nowakowski. His contribution to their knowledge of the war's progression since 1939, which was scanty for Best, and intentionally hazy for Falconer, was appreciated. The VIP captive Best writes disparagingly about the contribution and conduct that day of Horst Hoepner, whose shattering experience of Nazi brutality was way beyond the scope of Best's imagination. Copying Vermehren's cynical remarks, he also notes, "[Hoepner] lived in a perpetual state of panic, but we had all decided to treat him as a joke, and whatever he did or said always drew roars of laughter."[9] Best's account at this point does not ring true of the group as a whole. Not everyone had been afforded ongoing VIP prisoner status. In fact the majority had not. Bonhoeffer, for one, had plumbed the depths of Nazi inhumanity in the dungeons of Prinz-Albrecht-Straße from November 1944 to February 1945.

Still hungry, but by now somewhat more presentable, and strengthened by a flourishing sense of prisoner solidarity, the group then decided that morning to elect Best and Petersdorff as spokesmen. It was a sound choice, given that they had two ranking generals in the room with them, in that it did not overplay the "prior to arrest" implied seniority card, and also reflected the international composition of the group. Best's German-language skills were key. These two demanded of the guards the presence of the officer in charge, with the surprising result that the SS deputy transport leader visited them in person in their room. The group were under no illusions about who they were dealing with. Best wrote,

> This man Bader was a member of the chief Gestapo execution gang and passed his life in travelling from one Concentration Camp to another, like a pest officer engaged in the extermination of rats.[10]

It did not bode at all well for the hostages that their lives were in his hands. But a remarkable scene ensued. The two designated hostages remonstrated with the Gestapo officer about the lack of arrangements for feeding the prisoners, and he showed himself as polite and obliging. He empathised on the subject of food provisions; there were none for his men either. When he mentioned the prospect of a "foraging" motorcycle trip to Passau, some forty kilometres away (hard to achieve because of the ubiquitous lack of fuel), there was a good deal of banter—which the deputy transport leader took in good part—about the idea. It would ensure that he could find a good meal, but hardly do for obtaining supplies for a large group! Best noted,

> In spite of everything, we were all lighthearted and gay; our adventures had knitted a strong bond of comradeship between all of us, and there was a complete absence of jealousy, impatience or fear.[11]

Best felt that Petersdorff made a success of the encounter, one that no doubt contributed to a sense of progress. Their spirits lifted, the group embarked on their own foraging expedition. Falconer picks up the story:

> We set off. Frau Heberlein and Bonhoeffer pointed out to us what edible herbs they could find—mostly sorrels and nettles—and we

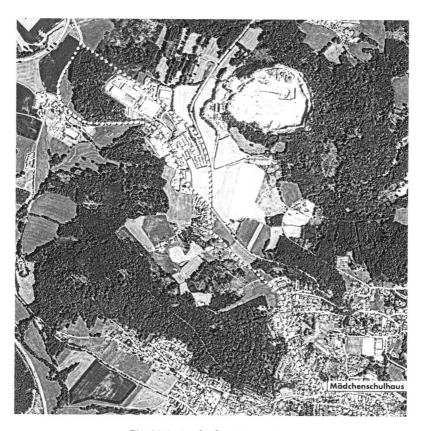

Fig. 39-2. April 7 foraging outing

started to forage. In a surprisingly short time, considering our feeble condition, we had collected quite an impressive heap of rather revolting looking verdure but Frau Heberlein was very pleased with it. It was typical of Bonhoeffer that, adding to the heap an armful of nettles which must have caused him some pain in the gathering, he remarked with his beaming smile and the usual twinkle in his eyes "You see, however bad things may seem to be, God can always help!"[12]

Of course, the sight of this unusual group, accompanied by guards, was impossible to keep a secret from the local population. Schönberg historian Bernd Bachhuber has identified the route that the prisoners from the schoolroom took that day. They were led under guard towards Saunstein along the tree-lined Ostmarkstraße, via the meadow and the river. They then turned left past the old copse. Then, on the way back, taking the bridleway on the right side of the wood, they passed along the road to Spiegelau, finally retracing their steps back along the path to Schönberg.

Upon their return to the schoolhouse, a large pot of water, of which there was no shortage, was put on the stove and the collected items were washed down and stuffed into it. According to Pünder the haul included stinging nettles, dandelion, and sorrel.[13] The items were removed from the pillowcases and items of clothing they had been stuffed into. Falconer reports that the sergeant produced some salt as his contribution, and that the resulting brew was hot and salted, was something to chew, did no harm, and probably did some good. It certainly helped pass the time. Meanwhile the work of the local population came through for the prisoners. The house adjacent to the girls' schoolroom housed the local blacksmith, Josef Duschl.[14] Monika, at age seventeen the second youngest of his eight children, at no small risk, chose to offer kindness. A delicious potato salad was received, together with two large loaves of country bread.[15] This time, thankfully, the distribution for the *Sippenhäftlinge* was arranged by the Grüne Minna group, and there was a satisfying portion for everybody.[16] Provided at the initiative of a courageous young woman, it was probably Bonhoeffer's last meal.

Map 5 of Bonhoeffer's Germany: Chapters 40–45

Klosterneuburg	Russians take the town.
Swedish coast	Seven German aircraft land in Sweden, six of which claim "they were lost."
Haulerwijk	Drenthe, Netherlands. German troops soon discover the existence of 700 French parachutists in the early morning. A firefight breaks out.
Appelscha	One group of Allied paratroopers is discovered by a band of Dutch resistance fighters, who promptly join forces with them.
Spier	A small (successful) party of paratroopers is rescued from imminent annihilation by the timely arrival of vehicles from the 8th Canadian Reconnaissance Regiment.
Osnabrück	A luxurious Mercedes-Benz car, once belonging to Field Marshal Göring, is captured.
Celle	An Allied air raid also strikes a (locked) transport halted at the station with 3,700 prisoners on board. 200 perish in the flames and a further 2,000 do not survive the "rabbit hunt" that ensues.
Between the rivers Mur and Drava in Yugoslavia	Soviet and Bulgarian troops under Tolbukhin's command gain ground, taking nearly 4,000 more prisoners.
Göttingen	is liberated.
Munich	Victor Klemperer is fortunate to eat a "peacetime-size" meal with a friend.
Hof	The 358th and 359th US Infantry Regiments (90th US Infantry Division), the troops who will eventually liberate Flossenbürg on April 23, are still facing fanatical resistance in Hof a week after the assault there began on April 2.
Steyerberg	Weser valley. A warehouse storing (stolen) bottles such as Château Yquem, Margaux and Haut Brion 1929, and Rothschild Château Lafite 1891 is pillaged.
Ravensbrück	Nelly Langholm, included amongst those permitted to travel to Denmark, scoffs at the camp commandant's words of farewell.
Gmunden	Missie Vassiltchikov attends church, noticing the presence of many refugees from Vienna.
Lake Comacchio	Danish/British Special Forces Major Anders Lassen is killed storming against impossible odds. He is posthumously awarded the VC.

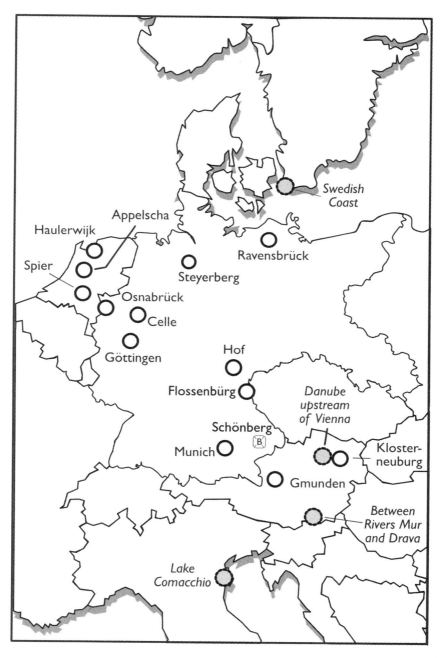

Haulerwijk

Appelscha

Spier

Swedish
Coast

Ravensbrück

Steyerberg

Osnabrück

Celle

Göttingen

Hof

Flossenbürg

Danube
upstream
of Vienna

Schönberg

Kloster-
neuburg

Munich

Gmunden

Between
Rivers Mur
and Drava

Lake
Comacchio

Map 5 of Bonhoeffer's Germany: Chapters 40–45
Staatsbibliothek zu Berlin-Kartenabteilung/Bruce Bovill

40

Bonhoeffer's Reading: Plutarch

Throughout his travels Bonhoeffer had somehow managed to retain in his possession his Bible, a copy of the *Herrnhuter Losungen*,[1] a book of Goethe's works with some illustrations,[2] and Plutarch's history *Lives of the Noble Greeks and Romans*. This latter volume had been supplied to him at his request on February 7 in Buchenwald.[3]

The book sketches a series of portraits with great skill on the part of the writer. The end result is the provision of what amounts to a masterful study on the value and role of ethical behaviour in the seemingly arbitrary universe of the ancient world, a subject of profound interest to Bonhoeffer.

The author provides an account of the lives of eight characters[4] in seven chapters: Tiberius and Gaius Gracchus, being brothers, form the subject matter of a single chapter. In each case the narrative follows a broadly similar pattern. The character's generally illustrious origins and lineage are described, and their (mainly) outstanding qualities, which mark them out for greatness, are outlined. Each chapter charts their seemingly natural path to power and military greatness, rather like the flow of the tide, which at some point will inevitably turn, and will in due course be followed by military defeat and death. The turning point is reached after different lengths of career and campaign, and is attributable to different sets of circumstances. It is most often the case that the leader has eventually overreached himself, whether in a foreign land or simply too far from home, or that a reversal is owing to a combination of circumstances beyond their control. It may be owing to a lack of troop supplies, or sickness, or an insurmountable character flaw, but at some point the moment inevitably comes when their "good fortune" deserts them. One instance of such a development, which would have resonated with Bonhoeffer in the ceaselessly famished final week of his life, particularly on that Saturday in Schönberg, comes in a story from among those soldiers remaining loyal to

Antonius in the latter stage of his campaign aganst the Parthians. Despite successes the army reached a state of near starvation:

> A barley loaf is said to have sold at that juncture for the price of its weight in silver. Soldiers resorted to eating roots and vegetables. But since they found only a few they recognised, they found it necessary to try out some they had never eaten before. In this manner they came to eat a vegetable that caused first delirium and then death. For whoever ate of it stopped caring about normal matters and became entirely obsessed with flipping over and then moving around any stone they came across. The whole plain was teeming with bent-over soldiers digging out stones and laying them somewhere else, after which they spewed out bile and finally died, because there was no wine, which was the only remedy.[5]

There is, hence, in this volume a sober portrayal of human life: a sense of the tragic is never far away. Given what was overtaking Germany at the time, and what was about to overtake him personally, there is no small poignancy in Bonhoeffer's choice of reading matter. The power of Plutarch's writing lies in his ability to observe and narrate in such a way as to enable both profound questions and reflections to shape themselves in the reader's mind.

For example, with particular sharpness Plutarch's account illustrates a number of the complexities of leadership in the ancient world. The degree of sophistication and wisdom required in order to succeed was immense. One area in which these qualities were tested was that of interaction with religious observance. A leader was expected to be fully conversant with the prevailing religious customs and practices. A military commander had as a matter of course to be deeply respectful of the deities. But this on its own was not sufficient. While at times taking heed of the prevailing signs in complete respectfulness and seriousness, he also had to demonstrate the type of leadership that would at times "sit lightly" to omens. Without the benefit of hindsight, this was inevitably a hard judgement call to make. In one instance of such a situation, Tiberius Gracchus stood in some fear of his life, and had accordingly been provided with a guard, which stood outside his home. At daybreak on one particular day, the official whose job it was to provide food for the holy chickens arrived at their enclosure and threw down food. But however much he rattled their cage, they did not emerge; only a single bird made an appearance, and this one did not touch the food but raised its left wing, stretched out a leg, and ran back into the cage. This "warning sign" reminded Tiberius of another he had recently had. He possessed a splendid and beautifully decorated helmet, which he wore in battle. Into this some snakes had crept, laid some eggs, and raised a brood. Accordingly Tiberius was all the more unsettled by the behaviour of the holy chickens. Later that day, amid chaotic scenes, in a large crowd, Tiberius at one point raised his hand to his head in an indication of sensing the threat of danger, whereupon some of his opponents declared he was demanding the imperial crown. One thing led to another, and he was indeed murdered that day.[6] In this instance Plutarch allows the eloquence of the holy chickens to speak for itself. The reader is left to reflect on whether Tiberius may have made a poor discernment somewhere along the way.

The reader discerns that for imperial leaders in general, it was ill-advised to behave casually in relation to the almost innumerable omens that held sway in the prevailing culture. But at the same time, any behaviour-influencing source of foreboding could easily be castigated. In one example of this, Julius Caesar, on what proved to be the day of his own assassination, had been unsettled by a bad dream experienced by his wife, and cancelled the day's senate meeting. Earlier, when at the height of his power, when his friends advised him to engage a personal protection detail, he had dismissed the idea with the words "It is better to die once than to live in perpetual fear of death." At that time he had seen the finest protection for himself and the most secure support for his reign in the love and goodwill (*Zuneigung*) of the people.[7] But on the day in question, upon being ridiculed (by someone planning to do away with him) for holding an entire government to ransom because his wife had slept badly, he reinstated the fateful meeting. Like Pontius Pilate, on a separate occasion, it may be that he paid insufficient attention to a genuine warning reaching him through a dream given to his spouse.

In a further example of the complexities involved in attempting to stay clear of superstition, and the fine line that needed to be walked, the Greek general and king Alexander, at the height of his successes, had been besieging the city of Tyros for quite some while. A soothsayer—Aristandros—brought a sacrifice, and upon reading the signs, boldly assured those present that the city would fall by month's end. At this people laughed loudly, and scornfully, as it was already the last day of the month. However, seeing the soothsayer's embarrassment, the king (given that he wanted to be seen to support these oracles as much as possible) gave the order to regard that day not as the 30th of the month, but as the 28th. All was done. The trumpet blast for the attack was sounded, the storming of the walls was undertaken with stronger forces than had been foreseen earlier—and the city was indeed taken that very day.[8] The writer Plutarch leaves the reader taken aback at the challenging concept of a military leader's being able to change the calendar date at will, and forming a clear sense that this was for Alexander the (familiar) golden phase when everything was going his way.

The dry narrative style of Plutarch's account is such that a direct revelation of the author's own value system is seldom provided. But on rare occasions, it is made clear. One instance of this is worth citing at length. Following Caesar's murder there were great tensions between fellow plotters Octavianus, Antonius, and Brutus. Octavianus now dropped his prior ally Cicero, and sent emissaries to Antonius to propose a settlement arrangement. The three most powerful men were now Octavianus, Antonius, and Lepidus. These three gathered together for the purpose of coming to an understanding on a small island . . . and consulted there for three days:

> They resolved all disputed matters without difficulty and partitioned out the entire Roman Empire between each other like a family inheritance. Only on the matter of those individuals to be done away with were they not able for a long time to come to an accommodation, because each one wanted to know that their enemies would be removed—and their relatives saved. Finally, they offered up their own relatives or friends in order to render their adversaries harmless, and so it was that Octavianus traded Cicero for Antonius' sake, but in exchange Antonius offered up Lucius Caesar, his uncle on his mother's side. Lepidus was required to kill his brother Paulus. . . . There can be nothing more foul, nothing more inhuman than this vile set of bartered arrangements. They traded murder for murder: those whom they offered up, they killed, just as they killed those offered up to them, and of all this the most despairing element of all was that they gave up their friends to death, people who had done nothing to them.[9]

The dark crime of killing for reasons of power and expediency is so commonplace in Plutarch it is virtually assumed as inevitable. It simply forms part of the backdrop of the lives of those in the corridors of power. But it is noteworthy that the author is so outraged on behalf of the victims by the combination of their innocence and the betrayal of friendship that their murders represent that he breaks silence in order to pass comment. In a similar way, the author's openness towards Stoic philosophy is visible via the manner in which the account of the mother of Tiberius and Gaius Gracchus is presented. Her sons, both of whom were exceptionally talented, and rose by turns to dizzying heights, were successively done away with at a young age. Both were much mourned by the people of Rome, Gaius in particular. Plutarch writes,

> Their mother, Cornelia, bore her great misfortune with the calmness of a great soul. She took comfort that their burial places were held in honour. She retired to her farm in Misenum and loved to entertain there, holding an open house, amazing her guests by the way she was able to speak of her sons without grief or tears, and spoke of their deeds and sufferings as of heroes from days gone by. . . . Hence it might appear to many as though her spirit, owing to age or to the excessive suffering she had experienced, had become inured to misfortune and devoid of feeling. But those who might make this judgement know nothing of how faithful a helper in distress and sorrow for humankind are a great-hearted spirit, a noble birth, and being well brought up.[10] Truly, fate favours a bold heart, when it seeks to step away from the path of suffering. But the strength of character needed to endure suffering with steadfastness cannot be withdrawn from such a heart by fate.[11]

Cornelia is seen to be emotionally resilient to misfortune, and to achieve a level of equanimity, or dispassion (*apatheia*), thus promoting a life in harmony with the divine order of the universe, over which one has no direct control. She is spoken of in glowing terms. By way of complete contrast, in the chapter on Marcus Antonius, the relationship between Antonius and Cleopatra is portrayed as being an unwholesome development, and coincides entirely with Antonius' fall from grace. The relationship between the couple is recounted not as a love story but as a tale of ill fortune. Once the formerly revered and mighty Antonius meets Cleopatra, he is "like a dog tied to a cart, and compelled to go wherever it goes"[12]—thus, for Plutarch, flying in the face of reason. Much attention is paid to their extended period of excessive carousing and dissipation, and the material gains extracted from Antonius for Cleopatra's children are clearly enumerated. Finally the ultimate low point of Antonius' military career is reported as taking place when he follows Cleopatra's example in respect of the fleet under her command: during the naval battle of Actium, like her, he turns tail, fleeing in ignominy from the enemy. Death and disgrace follow swiftly.

Throughout his account Plutarch assumes the existence of polygamy and does not pass comment on the institution as such. But even as a writer who inhabits the patriarchal system, he does write with compassion of the galling injustice suffered by Antonius' second wife, Octavia. Her virtuous behaviour (living as a faithful wife to Antonius and serving as a diligent mother to their children) while Antonius is away elsewhere (living in a dissolute manner and under the influence of Cleopatra) ends up having entirely the opposite effect from that which she clearly intends. Because her exemplary behaviour is so evident to all around her in Rome, the nation as a whole are outraged by her ill-treatment at Antonius' hands, with the end result that the more impeccably she behaves, seeking to woo back her husband (at one stage even travelling most of the way to attempt to visit him in Egypt), the more he is driven to distance himself from her. Plutarch's account is hence double-edged: while wanting to convey the philosophy that "virtue is sufficient for happiness," he owns that in this instance, in the face of Cleopatra's jealousy, and Antonius' conduct, Octavia's moral behaviour proves to be of little avail.

Plutarch's Stoic leanings assume a fatalistic and naturalistic pantheism that Bonhoeffer did not share. But Plutarch's scheme celebrates temperance, and clemency towards the vanquished, and towards slaves, out of an ascesis that enables the development of good judgement, and trains attention to remain in the present moment. The prevailing philosophy of the era is known to have encouraged a reflective practice that is alive and well in the majority of Christian churches of the world to this day, and flourishes not only in the Orthodox Church. A sense of the "persistent evil" within humankind is a shared Christian and Stoic awareness, and this is not the only understanding that remains current; a Stoic and a Christian could, for example, readily sing together the first verse of the hymn "It Is Well with My Soul." With reference to the concept of courage, Paul Tillich (1886–1965) once wrote that "Stoicism is the only real alternative to Christianity in the Western world."[13] Bonhoeffer would need every ounce of courage he could muster in the moments that lay ahead. Although a critic of his contemporaries, Plutarch is a creature of his day, and his shrewd eye for detail provides a fascinating companion for Bonhoeffer's final reading and reflective moments.

The remainder of the Saturday in Schönberg was spent quietly in the schoolroom. At least Bonhoeffer could delve into his copy of Plutarch. A second good night's sleep and "White Sunday in the schoolroom" beckoned.

Sunday, April 8, 1945

41

Sunday in Schönberg (I)

That Sunday morning the hostages awoke to the sound of the church bell, accompanied by the now-familiar sensation of hunger pangs, which would go unassuaged. The weather was still fine and the view from their window could not fail to lift their spirits. They were at last able to have conversations with one another without being overheard. With the sense of local civilian life happening around them, and without the sounds of battle being audible, it was possible, for the moment, to feel that the war was far away. In one week—so much had happened. As April progressed, and as the distance from Berlin increased, so too in proportion did the sense flourish for all members of the group of having a better chance of escaping from the persecution being meted out by the collapsing regime. Even the dread feeling of death being visited upon them at any moment, at the hands of brutal captors, or by an arbitrary decision of the collapsing regime, had begun to thaw, just a little. For Bonhoeffer the idea of survival, long since abandoned, may have even been growing. After all, they were now in Bavaria, around 560 kilometres south of Berlin.

There had been real camaraderie and warmth among the group. Hermann Pünder and Friedrich von Rabenau may have soon discovered their shared Münster connections.[1] Soon after they were awake, it being Sunday, from a position in the bed next to Bonhoeffer, Pünder invited Bonhoeffer to lead a service.[2] A man of established and vibrant Catholic faith, Pünder had been much missing the sustaining nourishment of Christian worship. Like Josef Müller he also had a special reason to mark the day, as that particular Sunday was the first Holy Communion day for his niece, and marked an event that he would have longed to be able to attend. His request of Bonhoeffer was in one sense a subversive suggestion, a moment that would bring together the group in the particular collective way that liturgy can enable. Writing about another context, many years later, the Chile of the 1970s, the writer William Cavanaugh highlights the regime's deployment of torture as "an efficacious sign by which the state enacts its power over its subjects' bodies in purest form. . . . The key to this project is: individualisation."[3] By contrast, for those in Schönberg, the chance to hold an ecumenical Christian service behind locked doors was clearly a "coming together" moment, one that worked wholly against fragmentation and individualisation. Bonhoeffer initially demurred, out of respect towards the young Russian, a self-professed atheist, allocated to the bed on his other side. But objections were swiftly overcome, not least when Kokorin himself sided with the proposers. Taken as a group, it was a particularly ecumenical gathering, whose denominational composition reflected the (slight) Protestant majority within Germany as a whole. In the bed next to Kokorin, General von Rabenau was a lifelong committed ecumenist, undoubtedly targeted and persecuted, and soon to be martyred, for the actions that had arisen from his unswerving Protestant faith. Pünder, the Heberleins, and possibly Heidel Nowakowski were Catholic, and the others, excluding Kokorin, were all Protestant, with the exception of Rascher, who, at the wish of his parents, was unbaptised.[4] Bonhoeffer may not have known the detail, but may have sensed some of the ecumenical goodwill and respect towards him (as an internationally aware Lutheran minister) among the members of the group, some of whom had more of a "faith DNA" in their backgrounds than others. From his own bed next to the schoolroom window, the six beds Bonhoeffer was most likely facing included that of Hugh Falconer, a child of the Manse. Falconer's own Scottish father, the Reverend Hugh Falconer, was a Presbyterian minister in England who spoke Latin, Greek, and Hebrew as well as he spoke English.[5] Next to Falconer was Payne Best, who, while clearly in support of the idea of a service led by Bonhoeffer, more likely proceeded out of the mutual friendship that was in the process of being established than out of an active Christian faith. Best had been baptised at age eleven in a "job lot" with his younger siblings in the Anglican Church on July 22, 1896, at Holy Trinity, Twickenham, the Green, suggesting that from the family's point of view, the project was rather an afterthought.[6] On the other side of the schoolroom's green *Kachelofen* were Falkenhausen, Petersdorff, and Hoepner. Falkenhausen and Petersdorff's shared connections with the Protestant faith included their own wedding and baptism, respectively, being celebrated in military garrison churches, and Hoepner, too, the son of a general, was from that same stable. To Bonhoeffer's right were the Heberleins, who had been married in Madrid's Saint Jerome the Royal Church, and whose Catholic faith

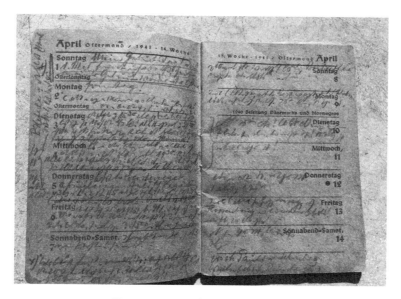

Fig. 41-1. Diary of Hermann Pünder
Author's collection.

had grown increasingly important to them both, and especially to Margot, under the duress of their incarceration.[7]

It would not be a problem. The service time was fixed for 10:00, which Pünder noted in his diary,[8] and Bonhoeffer settled down to do some preparation (see the diary record of fig. 41-1).

Most likely he had already used his *Losungen*[9] earlier that morning. This small, thoroughly ecumenical book of daily Old and New Testament readings, together with a hymn stanza, had come to occupy a significant place for Bonhoeffer in recent years, especially since his incarceration. He had been introduced to it as a child by his governess Maria Horn. In the context of the virtual absence of any paper for printing during the war years, this book was printed and distributed annually without exception by the Herrnhuter Brüdergemeinschaft on special paper. The paper was special because it was specifically imported under the direct auspices of Goebbels and Himmler. The reason for the supportive involvement of both of these individuals was that they were seeking to curry favour with the publication's most influential Swedish advocate, the Hitler admirer and Asian explorer Sven Hedin. So highly did Hitler's paladins esteem Hedin's acclaim, they were prepared to overlook the fact that the primary text for the *Losungen* was always taken from the Old Testament. Of course, under normal conditions, this was a book of Scripture towards which the Nazi Party had sentiments only of disdain and contempt. But with Hitler also in support of the printing of the *Losungen*, no doubt party secretary Martin Bormann could only look on and bite his lip in silent fury. Where this loophole impacted Bonhoeffer was that some years previously, in the light of the increasingly severe constraints under which he had been placed, he had come to an agreement with his former ordinands and closest colleagues along the lines that if it proved impossible to reproduce and distribute their own chosen set readings, which it soon did, everyone would default to the *Losungen*. In this light, reading these faith texts together in solidarity[10] on the same day, which they did throughout the war years, represented a powerful faith- and community-building act.[11] It was also undoubtedly a source of deep satisfaction and joy to resisting believers facing conditions of such intense repression and harassment that simply by dint of their collective daily reading patterns they were also acting subversively, undermining the regime through using a publication centred around a daily Old Testament reading that the authorities themselves expressly permitted and even facilitated.[12] In those war years, using it for quiet times and occasional shared moments must have been a source of great comfort, and may even have felt like a small daily miracle.

The texts for that day, from the 1945 German edition, are shown below. We know Bonhoeffer's preparation included access to a Bible.[13] In addition, at Bonhoeffer's request Pünder was able to offer his *Schott*[14] as a handy resource. In his combined evaluation of the twin resources, Bonhoeffer was likely to have been more influenced by the *Losungen*. In just one of many examples of the importance of these readings to his everyday life, on the equivalent calendar Sunday a year earlier, well before the July 20 assassination attempt, Bonhoeffer had written from the relative comfort of Tegel prison in Berlin to his future mother-in-law, Ruth von Wedemeyer, sharing with her that he had looked up the *Losungen* text for her imminent birthday. This letter also sheds a light on Bonhoeffer's stance towards those "interim" days for Christian believers, the days falling between Easter and Ascension. He writes,

> The time between Easter and Ascension has always been an especially important time for me. We are already looking forward to last things, yet we still have our work to do, our joys and sorrows here on earth, and through Easter we are given the strength to go

März

schon rücken, der auch mein Grab bedeckt; da werd ich den erblicken, der mich vom Tode weckt. 152, 4   Schmolck
M. Matth. 27, 57-66 A. Dan. 3, 14-28 *Luk. 23, 50-56*

APRIL

14. Woche; Ostern
1. Ostertag   Wochenspruch: Offb. 1, 18

1 Sonntag. Herr, zeige mir deine Wege, und lehre mich deine Steige! Pf. 25, 4
Gott Lob! Nun ist der Weg gemacht, uns steht der Himmel offen. Christus schließt auf mit großer Pracht, vorhin war alls verschlossen. Wers glaubt, des Herz ist freudenvoll, dabei er sich auch rüsten soll, dem Herren nachzufolgen. 164, 2   Zwick
Der Herr ist wahrhaftig auferstanden. Luk. 24, 34
Christ ist erstanden / von der Marter alle! Des solln wir uns froh sein, Christ will unser Trost sein. Halleluja! 139, 1 13. Jahrhundert
M. 1. Kor. 5, 6b-8; Mark. 16, 1-8 A. 1. Kor. 15, 50-58
Luk. 24, 1-12

2. Ostertag

2 Montag. Der Herr, Herr hilft mir; darum werde ich nicht zu Schanden. Jes. 50, 7
O Tod, wo ist dein Stachel nun? Wo ist dein Sieg, o Hölle? Was kann uns jetzt der Teufel tun, wie grausam er sich stelle? Gott sei gedankt, der uns den Sieg / so herrlich hat nach diesem Krieg / durch Jesum Christ gegeben! 146, 1   Gesenius
Ich lebe, und ihr sollt auch leben. Joh. 14, 19
Er lebt! dies ist das Losungswort / der heiligen Gemeine. Ach, ruhte sie nicht fort und fort / auf diesem Felsensteine, sie hätte der ergrimmten Macht / der Höllenfinsternisse / und der unselgen Todesnacht / längst unterliegen müssen. 155, 3   Spangenberg
M. Apg. 10, 34-41; Luk. 24, 13-35 A. Apg. 2, 22-32
Luk. 24, 13-27

3 Dienstag. Mein Knecht Mose ist in meinem ganzen Hause treu. 4. Mose 12, 7
Alle Knechte können gleiche Gaben, alle Sterne gleiches Licht nicht

36

April

haben. Eines fragt der Meister, ob man treu / überm anvertrauten Pfunde sei. Gerok
So jemand auch kämpft, wird er doch nicht gekrönt, er kämpfe denn recht. 2. Tim. 2, 5
Es gilt Treue, wenn der Fürst den Kampf soll lohnen. 314, 4   J.
M. Kol. 2, 9-15; Luk. 24, 36-47 A. Apg. 13, 16a. 26-39
Luk. 24, 28-35

4 Mittwoch. Ich danke dem Herrn von ganzem Herzen und erzähle alle deine Wunder. Pf. 9, 2
Gott, unserm Gott, sei Lob und Dank, der uns den Sieg gegeben, der das, was hin ins Sterben sank, hat wiederbracht zum Leben. Der Sieg ist unser, Jesus lebt, der uns zur Herrlichkeit erhebt. Gebt unserm Gott die Ehre! 148, 4   Löscher
Jesus sehen wir durchs Leiden des Todes gekrönt mit Preis und Ehre. Hebr. 2, 9
Die Kraft von deiner Majestät / bricht selbst durch Grab und Steine. Dein Sieg ists, der uns mit erhöht / zum vollen Gnadenscheine. Des Todes Wut, der Hölle Glut / hat alle Macht verloren, und wir sind neu geboren. 150, 3   Böhmer
M. Joh. 21, 1-14 A. Apg. 3, 13-21 *Luk. 24, 36-44*

5 Donnerstag. Deine Sonne wird nicht mehr untergehen noch dein Mond den Schein verlieren; denn der Herr wird dein ewiges Licht sein. Jes. 60, 20
Wird es Nacht vor meinem Schritt, daß ich keinen Ausgang wüßte / und mit ungewissem Tritt / ohne Licht verzagen müßte. Christus ist mein Stab und Licht; daß ist meine Zuversicht. 814, 4   Garve
Die himmlische Stadt bedarf keiner Sonne noch des Mondes, daß sie ihr scheinen; denn die Herrlichkeit Gottes erleuchtet sie, und ihre Leuchte ist das Lamm. Offb. 21, 23
Laß diese Herrlichkeit / das Herz uns ziehen, daß wir in der Zeit / dahin bemühen. Laßt in dunkeln Wort / so Schönes lesen, ach Gott, so zeige dort / uns auch das Wesen. Ev. Pf. 774, 4
M. Matth. 28, 16-20 A. Jes. 37, 1-14 *Luk. 24, 45-53*   Hiller

37

April

6 Freitag. Viele, so unter der Erde schlafen liegen, werden aufwachen: etliche zum ewigen Leben, etliche zu ewiger Schmach und Schande. Dan. 12, 2
Wenn du die Toten wirst / an jenem Tag erwecken / so tu auch deine Hand / zu meinem Grab ausstrecken; laß hören deine Stimm / und meinen Leib weck auf / und führ ihn schön verklärt / zum auserwählten Hauf. 670, 8   Heermann
So wie samt Christus gepflanzt werden zu gleichem Tode, so werden wir auch seiner Auferstehung gleich sein. Röm. 6, 5
Lässet auch ein Haupt sein Glied, welches es nicht nach sich zieht? 1007, 2 1653
M. Joh. 20, 1-9 A. 1. Kor. 15, 1-11 *Hebr. 1, 1-14*

7 Sonnabend. Nicht hat euch der Herr angenommen und euch erwählt, darum daß euer mehr wäre als alle Völker; denn du bist das kleinste unter allen Völkern; sondern darum, daß er euch geliebt hat. 5. Mose 7, 7. 8
O möcht unser Herz auf Erden / nie als in dir erfunden werden! Du hast uns je so sehr geliebt. 611, 3   J.
Welche Gott zuvor ersehen hat, die hat er auch verordnet, daß sie gleich sein sollten dem Ebenbilde seines Sohnes, auf daß derselbige der Erstgeborne sei unter vielen Brüdern. Röm. 8, 29
Gib denn, daß auch meine Seele, Herr, nach deinem Bild erwache. Du bist ja, den ich erwähle, mir zur Heiligung gemacht. Was dienet zum göttlichen Wandel und Leben, ist in dir, mein Heiland, mir alles gegeben. Entreiße mich aller vergänglichen Lust, dein Leben sei, Jesu, mir einzig bewußt. 674, 7   Schröder
M. Joh. 20, 11-18 A. 1. Kor. 15, 35-44 *Hebr. 2, 6-18*

15. Woche; Quasimodogeniti
(Als die jetzt gebornen Kindlein. 1. Petr. 4, 12)
Wochenspruch: 1. Petr. 1, 3

8 Sonntag. Durch seine Wunden sind wir geheilt. Jes. 53, 5
Deine Wunden sinds, die Heil, Ruh und Frieden bringen; da such ich in meinem Teil / auch hineinzudringen. Deine Huld / wird die Schuld / und mein tiefes Grämen / durch sein Blut wegnehmen. 425, 4   Gmelin

38

April

Gelobet sei Gott und der Vater unsers Herrn Jesu Christi, der uns nach seiner großen Barmherzigkeit wiedergeboren hat zu einer lebendigen Hoffnung durch die Auferstehung Jesu Christi von den Toten. 1. Petr. 1, 3
Nun leben, die vorhin Ertötete waren, und eilen, mit Christo gen Himmel zu fahren; er will sie ins himmlische Wesen versetzen / und endlich mit ewigen Freuden ergötzen. 151, 3   Herrnschmidt
M. 1. Joh. 5, 4-10; Joh. 20, 19-31 A. 1. Mose 32, 22b-32
Hebr. 4, 9-13

9 Montag. Leben und Wohltat hast du an mir getan, und dein Aufsehen bewahrt meinen Odem. Hiob 10, 12
Wer hat mich wunderbar bereitet? Der Gott, der meiner nicht bedarf. Wer hat mit Langmut mich geleitet? Er, dessen Rat ist oft verwarf. Wer stärkt den Frieden im Gewissen? Wer gibt dem Geiste neue Kraft? Wer läßt mir so viel Glück genießen? Ists nicht sein Arm, der alles schafft? 28, 2   Gellert
Alle gute Gabe und alle vollkommene Gabe kommt von oben herab, von dem Vater des Lichts, bei welchem ist keine Veränderung noch Wechsel des Lichts und der Finsternis. Jak. 1, 17
Wie preis ich doch den Liebesrat / des Gebers aller Gabe, der immer mehr gegeben hat, als ich gebeten habe. 525, 1   J.
M. 2. Tim. 1, 6-10 A. Joh. 3, 1-11 *Hebr. 4, 14-16*

10 Dienstag. Laßt uns gehen, zu bitten vor dem Herrn und zu suchen den Herrn Zebaoth. Sach. 8, 21
Ach sucht doch den, laßt alles stehn, die ihr das Heil begehret; er ists, der Herr, und keiner mehr, der euch das Heil gewähret. Sucht ihn all Stund von Herzensgrund, laßt euch allein; denn wohl mich sein / dem, der ihn herzlich ehret. 432, 3   Weißel
Er selbst, der Vater, hat euch lieb, darum daß ihr mich liebet und glaubet, daß ich von Gott ausgegangen bin. Joh. 16, 27
Der Vater kann nicht hassen, die seinen Sohn umfassen; mit väterlichen Trieben / muß er sie zärtlich lieben. 824, 7   Woltersdorf
M. 2. Tim. 2, 1-5 A. 1. Tim. 1, 12-17 *Hebr. 5, 5-10*

11 Mittwoch. Sie sollen mein Eigentum sein; und so will ihrer schonen, wie ein Mann seines Sohnes schont, der ihm dient. Mal. 3, 17

39

Fig. 41-2. *Losungen* Texts
Image supplied by Unitätsarchiv Moravian Archives Herrnhut. A matched translation is provided below.[15]

on living. . . . I want to travel [the] road with Maria, of being wholly ready for the last things, for eternity, and yet wholly present for the tasks, for the beauty and the troubles here on earth. Only by keeping to this path can we be completely happy and at peace with one another. We shall receive with open and outstretched hands what God gives us and be wholeheartedly happy with it. And with quiet hearts we shall let go of that which God doesn't yet grant or takes away.[16]

With this in mind, it is sure that the VIP and political hostages began a second day in Schönberg amid favourable signs. Many of them knew what it was to endure adversity. The current circumstances they all faced now called for courage, and patience, from every member of the group, and at multiple levels. Around the world courage and patience were also in high demand as the war continued to rage in earnest.

15. Woche: Quasimodogeniti	Week 15: Like Newborn Children
(Als die jetzt gebornen Kindlein. 1. Petrus 2,2)	(Like newborn children; 1 Peter 2:2)
8. Sonntag. Durch seine Wunden sind wir geheilt Jesaja 53,5	**8. Sunday.** By his wounds we are healed Isaiah 53:5
Deine Wunden sind's, die Heil, Ruh und Frieden bringen; da such ich in meinem Teil / auch hineinzudringen. Deine Huld / wird die Schuld / und mein tiefes Grämen / durch dein Blut wegnehmen. 425, 4 Gmelin	Our sins, our sorrows, Lord, were laid on Thee: / Thy stripes have healed, Thy bonds have set us free: / and now Thy toil is o'er, Thy grief and pain / have passed away, the veil is rent in twain. 425:4 Gmelin
Gelobet sei Gott und der Vater unseres Herrn Jesu Christi, der uns nach seiner grossen Barmherzigheit wiedergeboren hat zu einer lebendigen Hoffnung durch sie Auferstehung Jesu Christi von den Toten 1. Petrus 1,3	Praise be to the God and Father of our Lord Jesus Christ! In his great mercy he has given us new birth into a living hope through the resurrection of Jesus Christ from the dead. 1 Peter 1:3
Nun leben, die vorhin Ertötete waren, und eilen, mit Christo gen Himmel zu fahren; er will sie ins himmlische Wesen versetzen / und endlich mit ewigen Freuden ergötzen. 151,3 Herrnschmidt	Now may the hitherunto dead arise to new life and, with Christ, hasten heavenward: He desires to transport them to the eternal realm / and finally to delight them with everlasting joy. 151:3 Herrnschmidt
M. 1 Joh. 5, 4-10, Joh. 20,19–31, A. 1. Mose 32, 22b–32, *Hebr 4, 9–13, Wochenspruch: 1 Petr. 1,3.	a.m.: 1 John 5:4–10; John 20:19–31; p.m.: Genesis 32:22b–32; Hebrews 4:9–13; verse for the week: 1 Peter 1:3

42

Sunday's Total War

World Leaders

In Warm Springs, Georgia, where the wheelchair-bound leader had arrived by special train on March 29, US president Roosevelt had only four days left to live. He was able to keep the real truth about his failing health at bay, not just from himself and his entourage, but from the wider world. But there was another truth that also eluded him: his inability to perceive the ruthless nature of Josef Stalin. Not for the first, or the last, time, the ability to conceive of just what a Soviet leader could and would actually do would be proven to lie beyond the imaginations of their Western counterparts. Roosevelt was not alone. Despite all appearances to the contrary, both he and Churchill continued to believe and hope in Stalin's promises. Upon Churchill's return from early February's Yalta conference to London's House of Commons, he gave a glowing account of Soviet intentions, stating that the impression he brought back from the Crimea was that "Marshal Stalin and the Soviet leadership wish to live in honourable friendship with the Western democracies." Eight years later Churchill the memoirist would be forced to make the abject confession that "I felt bound to express my confidence in Soviet good faith in the hope of procuring it."[1] For his part Roosevelt persisted in the conviction that winning the cooperation of Joseph Stalin in building a new international organisation would effectively keep the peace, unlike Wilson's League of Nations. Writing in 2017, Joseph Lelyveld documents Roosevelt's belief that if he reached an agreement with Stalin on how to stop future aggression and enforce the peace, other countries around the world would fall in line. In pursuing that plan, Roosevelt painted for himself an image of the ruthless Soviet dictator and his totalitarian regime that bore no resemblance to reality. He wrote to his stormy friend William Bullitt, arguing that Stalin was not the cruel, expansionist despot that Bullitt, the former ambassador, had portrayed him to be: "I think that if I give him everything I possibly can and ask nothing from him in return, *noblesse oblige*, he will not try to annex anything and will work with me for a world of democracy and peace." Bullitt's memorable (and in one sense timeless) rejoinder was that Roosevelt needed to remember he was "not dealing with the Duke of Norfolk, but a Caucasian bandit, whose only thought when he got something for nothing was that the other fellow was an ass."[2]

London, England

In London the morning news was read by Frederick Grisewood.[3] The BBC reported that there had been no overnight news from the Western Front, and hence chose to reiterate a number of identical articles from that theatre as well as from the Far East from the previous day, its carefully crafted phrasing suggesting movement and progress, whether actual or not. With the battle for Vienna raging, the Eastern Front was now in Western Europe. As the day progressed, the bulletins featured more strongly, in relation to this momentous development, a reaffirmation of the Allied/Moscow declaration of independence. For Austria only,[4] the BBC broadcast the news that "no part [of Austria] will be annexed, a democratic way of life will be restored, and the social order will not be changed." For the London listener, the Russians were fully numbered among the heroes of the hour.

Throughout the bulletins there is a distinct sense of good news flowing from almost all fronts, amid an understandable longing for the end of hostilities. Perhaps as part of its role as the nation's flag-bearer, over the course of the day's broadcasts the BBC inflated the reports of German aircraft that had been shot down over Ijmuiden the preceding day from 87 to 100, and then to 110,[5] adding the intriguing detail, by comparison with minimal Allied losses, that some of the downed German fighters were jet-propelled.[6] For the nation news of German defections was invariably "good for the troops"; this Sunday's broadcast included a piece in this genre:

> A German fighter aircraft landed in Sweden today. The crew of three, who have been interned by the Swedish authorities, asked to be treated as refugees. This is the seventh German aircraft to land in Sweden today. This morning six landed there but their crews said they weren't refugees—they merely mistook the Swedish coast for the Danish island of Bornholm. This isn't the first time in recent days that German pilots have professed to have landed in neutral Sweden

by mistake. Among the interned crews was a woman who, according to the Swedish defence staff, is a Russian citizen. Her presence in a German plane is not explained.

Still further, in what the BBC described as a "lighter" piece, it was broadcast that "a British officer is now driving a luxurious Mercedes Benz car with a three hundred horse power engine and seven gears, which at one time belonged to Field Marshal Göring; it was captured at Osnabrück."

But amid the lighter items of news, the unfolding tragedy of Germany's plight was not lost from view. Just behind Allied front lines, near Petershagen, one young BBC correspondent was palpably shocked as he witnessed the extent to which war-weariness and numbness had overtaken and incapacitated German civilians he encountered. Richard Dimbleby writes about one family listening to the news:

> They just picked up what was said, checked it on the map and noted it just as if they were a bunch of neutrals hearing all about somebody else. . . . They seem to have lost the power of passion or sorrow. They show no sympathy for their army, for their government or for their country. To them the war is something too huge and too catastrophic to understand.[7]

Hence in and among the cascade of Allied good news, there was also airtime for a reflective and even compassionate contribution, helping the discerning listener catch a glimpse of what lay beyond the immediate and desperate conflict in hand.

Lake Comacchio, Italy

But the war was not over. Even at this penultimate stage, highly hazardous operations were still essential. In Italy the fighting around Lake Comacchio was conducted against solid veterans putting up a substantial defence. On the night of April 8, Special Forces major Anders Lassen, a Danish citizen who had fought for the SBS[8] and SOE for most of the war in theatres including the Greek islands, and who had been awarded the Military Cross on three occasions, led a team of seventeen men with the task of creating a diversion near the town of Comacchio. They came up against infantry from the 162nd Turkestan Division in three dug-in machine-gun posts on a dike between Lake Comacchio and the Adriatic Sea. The division consisted of battle-hardened volunteers from Turkestan, Azerbaijan, and Georgia, and the posts were situated so that the defenders further back could fire over the heads of the others. As the attack progressed, under cover of darkness, Lassen paid no heed to the five or six machine guns firing down a road fifteen feet wide. Those manning the first two posts were killed or captured as a result of Lassen running forwards and throwing hand grenades. Those on the third seemed to shout, "Kamerad" (indicating surrender), but when Lassen approached, he was mortally wounded and the attack, which had already cost four other British soldiers their lives, was called off. His body was picked up next morning by an Italian priest. He was posthumously awarded the Victoria Cross. He would come, after the war, to embody the spirit of the Danish resistance. His death, representing a different kind of resistance, a different kind of courage, and quite possibly occurring on the same day as Bonhoeffer's, fell on, or on the eve of, the fifth anniversary of Denmark's occupation.[9]

Bad Aussee, Austria

In a similar vein, for hazardous undercover operations, volunteers still came forward. Word leaked out to a select few Allied leaders that a vast collection of looted art was being hidden, or possibly blown up, in Austria.[10] The question of whether it might be saved from falling into the hands of the hungry Russian "Trophy" Brigade no doubt arose.

Almost a day after seven hundred French Special Air Services (SAS) troops were dropped into the Netherlands (see below), at 11:45 p.m. on April 8, on what was a clear and cloudless night, under a full moon, an RAF Halifax with specially adapted bomb doors took off from Brindisi, in Southern Italy. It was destined for the Zielgebiet am Zinken plateau in Austria, about three hours' flying time away. It was the third attempt at making the drop—twice previously the prevailing weather conditions had been unworkable. The "packages" aboard were four "Bonzo" SOE agents: native German-speaking Austrians who had defected or been captured and who had passed a substantive battery of tests in order to establish their genuine anti-Nazi credentials. Albrecht Gaiswinkler, Joseph Grafl, Karl Standhartinger, and Karl Lzicar were trained and equipped by the SOE for undercover operations. Their dangerous mission, code-named "Operation Ebensburg," was to infiltrate the local population and help undermine Nazism by whatever means. Unconfirmed reports suggest they may have had a brief to assassinate Josef Goebbels, then believed to be staying nearby at the Villa Castiglione, Grundlsee, but news of Goebbels' departure for Berlin soon arrived. Under the parachutists' helmets and jumpsuits, they wore civilian clothes and boots suitable for the mountainous terrain over which they would have to make their way. Each was armed with a Beretta 7.65 calibre pistol and fighting knife carried in the pockets of their jumpsuits. Their other weapons and equipment, including of course a high-frequency transmitter/receiver set, were in four containers carried in the aircraft's bomb bay. The inside of the fuselage was unheated, so they would have been cold and stiff. At 3:20 a.m. they jumped from a height of eight hundred feet into deep snow, and regrouped safely. The only container they were able to retrieve was the radio set and that, irreparably damaged, they had to abandon. They were in the wrong place, the Höllengebirge, just above the mountain town of Feuerkogel. The men, anticipating pursuit, lost no time in descending through a local pine forest to Stenkogl bei Ebensee. There they caught the train directly to Bad Aussee, jumping out, just as their British SOE training had taught them to do, a little before their intended destination.[11]

Drenthe, Netherlands

The very early hours of April 8 saw the commencement of activities known as "Operation Amherst," undertaken by French SAS troops, and under the leadership of the highly committed and experienced Brigadier Mike Calvert.[12] Seven hundred combatants with expertise in demolition, harassment, and undercover operations had been parachuted in "sticks" of fifteen men into their drop zones, with greatly varying degrees of accuracy, under cover of darkness the night before. While their general task was the preservation of canal and road bridges on the Canadian 2nd Corps axis of advance, the related aim of this specialist deployment at this stage of the war was to "cause confusion in the German rear areas, help the Dutch resistance . . . [and] raid forward German air bases in order to disrupt enemy fighter cover and to provide operational-level intelligence and battlefield guides to the advancing First Canadian Army."[13] It was a hazardous assignment, and a low-key and injury-free arrival in this sparsely populated rural area did not prove possible in every location for the Allied troops. For example, in Haulerwijk German troops soon discovered the existence of the French arrivals in the early morning and a firefight broke out. In Appelscha, however, the paratroopers were more fortunate. This group were discovered by a band of Dutch resistance fighters, who promptly joined forces with them. At Spier one of the field unit commanders, "having boldly captured the village with a small party, was rescued from imminent annihilation by far superior German forces by the timely arrival, in the best manner of films, of vehicles from the 8th Canadian Reconnaissance Regiment."[14] The SAS units, mostly French and

Belgian operatives, would fight continuously against the Germans and their Dutch Nazi collaborators for the next seven days, preventing the destruction of the vital bridges. A total of 250 Germans were captured.[15]

Berlin, Germany

In the nation's capital, Josef Goebbels was indeed freshly returned from his brief stay in Grundlsee, Austria. Now entrusted with sweeping powers, particularly in relation to the defence of Berlin, he wrote at length in his diary. He described with obvious satisfaction the seriousness with which the Werewolf activity[16] was being taken by the Allies. For the propaganda chief, the fact that the Führer was "extraordinarily satisfied" with this aspect of his work was the reward he craved. But in the privacy of his journal, he recorded his dismay at the Führer's recent retributory removal of the "SS Leibstandarte Adolf Hitler" armbands from the division that bore the Hitler name, following their failure to advance under the most impossible of circumstances. Goebbels notes, "[It] has had disastrous consequences. A whole series of SS leaders have shot themselves out of despair. Punishment for one failure seems too harsh by contrast with the failures of the Luftwaffe." But such journal entries did not deflect him from his primary task. Getting back down to his real work, Goebbels continued in relation to the news from Berlin-Rahnsdorf that two hundred people had stormed a bakery out of desperation at the lack of food supplies: "I will proceed with brutality against these as a sign of weakness and surging defeatism, which cannot be tolerated under any circumstances." Subsequently he condemned three people to death, later reprieving one woman. Goebbels wrote, "It will have a very sobering effect."[17]

Küstrin, near Berlin, Germany

Immediately outside Berlin, on April 8 the 1st Belorussian Front was preparing its assault on the Seelow Heights. For the civilian populations remaining, life was virtually untenable. For the combatants the demands of war were intense. Although the real *frontoviki* were determined to see victory in Berlin, the problem of desertions increased as the offensive came closer. Most of those who disappeared were conscripts from the recent drafts, especially Poles, Ukrainians, and Romanians. An increase in desertions also meant a growing level of banditry, looting, and violence towards the civilian population: "Some deserters seize carts from local citizens, load them with different sorts of property and, pretending they are carts belonging to the Army, move them from the front zone to the rear areas." The potential impact of such behaviour was not lost on the Soviet command. NKVD rifle regiments behind the 1st Ukrainian Front arrested 355 deserters in the first part of April. A report dated April 8 from the 1st Belorussian Front reads, "Many soldiers are still hanging around in rear areas and describing themselves as separated from their units. They are in fact deserters. They carry out robbery, looting, and violence." NKVD regiments continued to encounter small groups of German stragglers trying to slip through Red Army lines after the fighting in Pomerania and Silesia. These small groups often ambushed the odd vehicle for food on the way, and the Soviet military authorities would respond, just as the Germans had in the Soviet Union, by destroying the nearest village and shooting civilians.[18]

Steyerberg, Weser Valley

For a few weeks—before it was stopped altogether—widespread and heavy looting was also carried out by Allied troops. German cars by the hundred were dragged out of garages and hiding places under the straw in their barns, painted khaki, and driven away. Cameras and watches and revolvers were taken automatically from prisoners, and frequently from civilians. Even pictures were stripped from their frames. Wine was fair booty for everybody. In nearly every town, the shops were broached, the distilleries emptied.[19] A particularly poignant moment occurred in Steyerberg, in a warehouse on the main street. The writer who saw it observed that it would have made any thoughtful person weep. Bonhoeffer, with his simple affirming of the good things of life, would perhaps have been among them. Germans and foreigners alike were helping themselves to some of the most beautiful wine ever produced, presumably stolen from France. A case of Château d'Yquem with a very good year was being carried off by a child. Bottles of Margaux 1929 and Haut-Brion of the same year were being haphazardly loaded onto a wheelbarrow. Half-demented children were romping among the really great prizes of the place, Rothschild Château Lafite 1891, in magnum, jeroboam, and rehoboam bottles, with high spillage rates. By evening the floor was awash with claret. By next morning the slush was almost ankle-deep, and nothing remained in the broken cases.[20]

Ravensbrück, Germany

But luxuries such as wine were a thing of the past for concentration camp inmates. After months of tortuous negotiations concerning the release on humanitarian grounds of a number of the women prisoners, and virtually no progress, on April 8 a further milestone was reached at Ravensbrück.

On that day buses stood outside the camp gate. Those fortunate enough to be selected for early release included many Norwegians. One, Nelly Langholm, was among the group that had only learned the news the night before when they were ordered into the (real) showers. She wrote,

> The next day we came out in our new clothes and had to walk to the gate. We saw the buses and there were these Swedish men in grey uniforms with red crosses on their arms. . . . I think they told us "Now you will go to Sweden—now you will be free." Before we left the German big boss[21] came and said "*Meine Damen, Sie sind frei.*—Ladies, you are free." Can you imagine? Here was a German calling us *Meine Damen*. Were they really talking to us? We hadn't been called "ladies" for such a long time. "*Meine Damen.*" A fellow prisoner scoffed: "I would rather he'd said '*Meine Schweine.*'"

Nelly wrote that leaving on the bus was "like a miracle"—and yet, being driven through Germany was terrible. Seeing a large town like Hamburg a month before the end was shocking: not a single whole house could be seen amid the terrible ruins en route to the Danish border.

Meanwhile, as the Swedes made their way towards the Danish border, situated two hundred miles north-west of Ravensbrück, a further 299 French prisoners, who had also been chosen for release, were arriving at Kreuzlingen, on the German-Swiss frontier. They had left three days earlier and had been held up repeatedly, not least by an Allied bombardment that lasted throughout the entire day on April 8 at the town of Hof, through which Bonhoeffer had been inconspicuously transported on the night of April 3–4.[22] At 9:00 that night, the buses slowed to a halt in front of the barred gates and sentry points at the Kreuzlingen border post. After being unloaded for one final *Appell* while German guards checked papers for an hour, the prisoners were hailed with shouts and cheers in the gloom by a gathering that included nurses, doctors, Samaritans, reporters, priests, and ordinary people come to welcome and help. The greetings froze on the welcomers' lips at the sight of so many silent ghosts. Of course, they were unprepared for such proximity to the horrors that Nazi Germany had created. After one more short bus trip, the group stopped for the night and were led into a warm gymnasium, where soup was waiting and much more. Men cried as crumpled figures swathed in bandages were stretchered from the buses. Six women were taken straight to hospital, while others lay on mattresses of fresh straw covered with wool and piled with blankets.[23]

Königsberg, Germany

Far north of the hostage convoy, in Königsberg, the devastation was so complete that even Gauleiter Koch's deputy had urged the abandonment of the city. A counter-attack was mounted to force a way through the onslaught, but it collapsed in chaos on the night of April 8. Bombardment had blocked many of the routes leading to the start line. The local party leadership, without telling the city's commandant, Lasch, had passed the word to civilians to assemble ready for the breakout. It proved a terrible mistake. Their concentration attracted the attention of Soviet artillery observation officers. They were massacred.[24]

Celle, near Hanover, Germany

Elsewhere, the sheer rapidity of the US advance would have unintended consequences. In Celle, a town with a population of sixty-five thousand located thirty-five kilometres north-east of Hanover,[25] April 8 began as an ordinary day. It had been evident for some while to the people of Celle that their town did not stand in danger of Russian occupation. Given that there were no large industrial concerns or army bases in the vicinity, with only a few small army units stationed there, there was no unusual turmoil, no panic-stricken flight of civilians, and little fear of major air raids. But that would change beyond all recognition.

On April 8 several waves of US B-26 bombers first attacked the factories in the nearby Salzgitter concentration camps, and then, at low altitude, turned upon Celle itself.[26] Inhabitants were taken completely by surprise. At least 122 citizens perished in the attacks, but the number of dead was apparently even higher because many were buried under the debris of their homes and others died in giant fires. Among the targets was Celle's railway station. At the time this took place, a prisoner transport was halted at the station. It contained Russian, Ukrainian, Dutch, Polish, Czech, Yugoslav, Italian, Lithuanian, and Hungarian prisoners, some of whom were Jewish, from several camps. The train was carrying around 2,950 male and 750 female prisoners and was eighty-four boxcars long, with forty to eighty prisoners crammed into each car. As well as the prisoners, there were also 232 guards, of whom 200 were male. Instantly the prisoners were caught in a death trap. The interior of the cars was an inferno. The cries of the wounded rose up high. The guards were able to escape and sheltered in a grove of trees half a mile (one kilometre) west of the station. Those who escaped the flames were able to take flight into the nearby woods. As the attack subsided, the people of Celle, panic-stricken already because of the general disorder in their town, watched in terror as groups of starving people in striped uniforms roamed among the bomb-damaged houses and tried to scrounge food. Many townspeople spent the night in cellars and subterranean storerooms in fear for their lives. When one thirteen-year-old boy enquired about the identity of the prisoners, he was told that "they could well be Jews."[27] One officer issued a briefing, stating that a large group of prisoners had escaped from the train during the bombing, and that they had found and donned uniforms belonging to the station firefighting crew. These prisoners were now endangering the civilian population, and a unit of the Waffen-SS was already operating in the forest against them. Of course this briefing was untrue. Almost none of the prisoners were German, and even if some had been fluent enough for some purposes, they could not have concealed their origin because of their wretched appearance and obvious state of malnutrition. In fact among the local residents were a number who had realised with compassion that the prisoners' identifiable clothes put them at risk, and had provided some of them with civilian clothing. But, more generally, a wild fear engulfed the local populace. An officer named Eberhard Streland entered the forest with eighty men from his unit in search of escaped prisoners, together with dozens of other armed men. These were from a mixture of various uniformed personnel and civilians, including boys aged fourteen to sixteen, who did not hesitate to fire at prisoners caught in the forest. A relentless manhunt ensued. An unknown number were caught and shot. Others were beaten to death, while others who had gathered in groups were fired on at random. Many prisoners tried to escape but were too weak to do so, and were eventually caught and shot without mercy. Shooting went on through most of the night without any special effort to conceal the actions from the local residents. No quarter was given to the prisoners, who were being hunted like animals, in an atrocity that continued until midday the following day, by which time corpses of prisoners lay everywhere. Despite this, many civilians tried to assist the prisoners by rendering first aid and supplying refreshments, but were themselves threatened and abused by those taking part in the persecution of the prisoners. Others even hid and sheltered prisoners in their cellars until the British troops arrived two days later. But few were so fortunate. One German prisoner was among a group of about 150 prisoners caught in the forest by several armed Volkssturm men. He appealed to them and asked why they were being handed over to the SS, since the war would be over any day. "We need to cleanse our forest of the communists who are hiding there," the Volkssturm man replied. As punishment for having dared to ask such a question, the prisoner was shot and killed. In all, of the around 3,700 prisoners on the transport that stopped at Celle on April 8, after 200–300 had perished in the air attack on the train, only 1,500 lived to see the day of liberation.[28]

Munich, Germany

In Munich, for the Jewish diarist Victor Klemperer and his wife, Eva, it was another familiar day of the "new normal," a life comprising days spent in the air raid bunker and among the ruins. The cleaners and guards woke them at 5:00. They went to the NSV (Nationalsozialistische Volkswohl-fahrt) room for coffee, then sought out an early-opening hotel, the Excel-sior, in a heavily damaged building close to the station, sitting there qui-etly for a while over breakfast. The Klemperers had by this time acquired sound judgement concerning whom they could trust. The main project of the day was to seek out a work colleague, Herr Vossler. The two couples were soon together, and the Klemperers, noting in admiration that the Vosslers still had "sources," were treated to a princely "peacetime" lunch: soup, a peacetime-size schnitzel with young spinach and fried potatoes, and a dessert, followed by two cigarettes for Eva and a cigar for Victor, amid a most enjoyable catch-up. Later, after much searching for lodgings amid dreadfully shattered, partially collapsed, fire-damaged, and ruined buildings, the Klemperers, by now quite fear-filled, found their steps grav-itated back towards the station bunker. Here they were greeted with the question "Are you still here, people?" and there was only the bare floor for Eva to sleep on. Klemperer noted, "Nevertheless we were glad to be there, because at one o'clock at night there was an air-raid warning, many people poured in, and bombs fell somewhere outside. It would have been no pleasure in one of the pensions."[29]

Gmunden, Austria

In Gmunden Marie Vassiltchikov attended the morning's church service. She noted in her diary the names of some of the many refugees from Vienna who were there. After lunch her hosts drove her and her friend Sisi back to Bad Ischl. She writes, "On the road we were stopped by an SS patrol. Dreadful moment! [Host] Geza produced his fake papers. They asked for ours. Mine say I should be on my way to Schwarzach-St Veit, which is not at all where we were heading, and this immediately made them suspicious. They argued about the dates, wondering why I am still so far from my destination. I explained that I had left Vienna much later than the date of my travel orders. The sergeant in charge ended by saying that if he were not so good-natured, he would haul me out of the car and set me to dig trenches. I answered that I thought that 'in this sixth year of the war' nurses could be more usefully employed. The exchange was not a pleasant one and we proceeded on our way rather shaken."[30]

43
Sunday in Flossenbürg

For some time already, Flossenbürg had been the location of ongoing executions. A comprehensive wave had started a year earlier to dispose of any who were considered to be enemies of the Third Reich, including numerous Allied pilots and SOE agents, and the "normal" daily number was around ninety. This was in addition to the already high numbers who perished as a result of malnutrition or maltreatment, or who were worked or beaten to death en route to the nearby Messerschmitt factory or in the adjacent granite quarry. Compounding the predicament, the camp's geographical location, close to the Czech border, also meant that, whether the KL commandant agreed to it or not, it was by now the "destination point" for a wholly unmanageable number of the death marches. This in turn meant that vast numbers of critically unwell and starving prisoners were flooding into the camp and its sub-camp domain. Given this context, and that the daily processing rate of his special executions simply could not be further extended, it was with sheer incredulity that the beleaguered camp commandant, SS-Obersturmbannführer Koegel, had learned during the course of the week that some of the VIP prisoners being foisted upon him in recent days were not to be done away with.[1] Yet by this stage of the war, Flossenbürg was also a place of feverish "thinking ahead." Preparations for the imminent arrival of the Allies had to be made. Traces of crimes had to be, insofar as possible, eradicated.

On Sunday, April 8, Flossenbürg's camp commandant issued a set of urgent instructions:

- Various important documents and items were to be destroyed by incineration—including the rubber truncheons that the kapos had used for beatings.
- The wooden block used for beatings was also to be dispensed with.

- So, too, was the hanging machinery in the yard of the *Arrest-zellen* building to be dispensed with.

- Above the sawdust—into which the blood of victims selected for death by hanging had flowed—there was to be assembled a harmless-looking pile of wood.

- The gallows hooks that remained in the wall of the execution yard, euphemistically known as the *Arresthof*, were to be torn out.

- The masonry, which was thoroughly blood-soaked, was now to be painted over with white paint.

- For years in this camp, for so-called protective custody, the street light poles that stood at the centre of the *Appellplatz* had been the gallows for public hangings. These were now to be taken away.

Now all these important traces had to be removed.[2] But meanwhile, and paradoxically, regular camp life had to continue. The camp was hosting the trial of senior military figures that day. Proceedings were timed so as to take in the likely arrival of Bonhoeffer and would commence in the SS casino at 4:00. Prosecutor Huppenkothen enjoyed a leisurely lunch in the canteen situated at the same venue with the SS judge, Otto Thorbeck, and took time over the course of the day to bring him up to date. Thorbeck learned that the accused in the SS court martial, over which he would preside, had been expelled from the army by a senior tribunal. Huppenkothen informed him that the relevant judgements were all readily available. A helpful way to frame the event was to consider that the accused were in the custody of the SS, and as they were in a KZ, this could perhaps be equated with an army encampment. Thirdly, it had to be borne in mind that this court martial had been ordered by the Führer. Such a court martial could be called by the senior ranking officer present if combat conditions demanded it and there was a need for instant justice to be dispensed. The proximity and potentially imminent arrival of US forces pertained.[3] It would just be a routine affair, with five defendants. Sentencing would be a formality. Ratification would be taken care of. Huppenkothen laid out all the paperwork on the large table, and Thorbeck had ample time to peruse it, which he did with apparent unconcern.

It has been mentioned earlier that all pertinent contemporaneous documentation was assiduously destroyed before the war ended. However, it is still possible, on the basis of other extant documents, to reconstruct some of what may have been on the charge sheet for all five defendants:[4]

Hans Oster, Ludwig Gehre, Karl Sack, Dietrich Bonhoeffer, and the former Admiral Wilhelm Canaris. In the assumption that such a thing did exist at the time, the wording pertinent to Bonhoeffer within the document is likely to have been along the following lines:

Indictment against Dietrich Bonhoeffer
Berlin, April 5, 1945
Indictment

Against . . .

Pastor Dietrich *Bonhoeffer* of Berlin-Charlottenburg, born on February 4, 1904, in Breslau, single. At the present time imprisoned in connection with the events of July 20, 1944, and previously a pastor of the German Protestant congregations in London.

I bring an indictment against the defendant on the grounds of the following actions:

In 1942 until 1943 on German soil the defendant, Pastor Bonhoeffer, took part in and agreed to cooperate in the operation to overthrow the National Socialist regime, through the elimination of the Führer by cowardly assassination or by another act of violence that included the possibility of his death, and to end the war through ignominious dealings with the enemies. This operation was conducted by the traitor, former Lord Mayor Dr Goerdeler, who, along with officers who had lost their nerve and with other enemies of the state, made proposals for the economic, social, and cultural-political reorganisation of the Reich.

The defendant, Pastor Bonhoeffer, received credible knowledge of the plans of the conspiratorial clique to commit high treason in betraying their country yet nevertheless failed in his duty to inform the responsible authorities of these plans.

The defendant, Pastor Bonhoeffer, as a traitor to his country, has thereby placed himself outside the community of the German people, by disregarding his obligation to tell what he knew in this particularly grave matter.

There is thus sufficient evidence to accuse him of violation of § 5 no. 1 of the Decree of the Reich President for the Protection of People and State, dated February 28, 1933, StGB 73.47.[5]

The indictment would have been backed up with statements from others who had been broken under torture or who had in the end simply acceded to the Gestapo's requests for more names. In Bonhoeffer's instance the prosecution case would argue that the purpose of his 1942 trip to Sweden to meet Bishop Bell was not, as Bonhoeffer argued, to obtain information about key enemies of Germany for intelligence purposes, but to make a high-treasonous contact with the British government. Their evidence for this would have included a statement from Helmuth von Moltke.[6]

In the case of Hans Oster, line manager of both Müller and (one level up) Bonhoeffer, the indictment would have included a section concerned with "revealing military secrets to the enemy in such a way as to prejudice and endanger the lives of German soldiers," otherwise known as *Landesverrat* (betrayal of one's country) or *Kriegsverrat* (military treason). Bonhoeffer was not thought to be involved in this; but as he was someone who reported directly to Oster, it raised the stakes for him considerably. Evidence for Oster's repeated leaks of the May 1940 campaign dates to the Dutch and via the Vatican had been available for some considerable time,[7] but Gestapo progress in bringing forward this accusation had been excruciatingly slow. As it transpired, as of September 1944, the cases against Sack, Gehre, Oster, and Dohnanyi had been ready (*abschlussreich*) to go to court, and after a normal period they would have come before the Volksgerichtshof as accused.[8] Only the Hitler "Stop" order issued following the copious document find in Zossen on September 22, 1944, had, ironically, slowed things down.[9] But now the Canaris diary find of April 4 had changed everything.

All of the presumed indictments, in the formal and measured wording that the regime employed, and which is taken from extant documentation, are likely to have been, at face value, equally as conclusive as the Bonhoeffer example created above. But what even these smoothed phrases could not conceal was the rampant and criminal violence of the regime, which lay just a flicker beneath the surface. In a cruel fashion, a ready illustration of how the system truly functioned was being played out throughout much of the day, only yards away from the so-called courtroom.

Under orders from Huppenkothen, SS-Sturmbannführer Kriminalrat Kurt Stawitzki proceeded on April 8 with his own intensive interrogations of Josef Müller, Bonhoeffer's line manager in the Abwehr. Stawitzki had collected him four days earlier, on the Wednesday of the previous week, from Neustadt an der Waldnaab (as recounted in chapter 22). For the duration of his time in Flossenbürg, Stawitzki had ordered that Müller should be bound with tight manacles on his legs, and handcuffed. These devices were then attached to a bar on the wall of his cell and would not be released at night, and were removed only for interrogations.[10] By dint of opening Müller's suitcase and stealing his prized possession, a cherished letter from his family, Stawitzki had learned that Sunday, April 8, was the date of his daughter's first Holy Communion. Brandishing the letter in front of Müller, he tore it to pieces. The format of these interrogations was that the Kriminalrat would repeatedly strike Müller in fury, driven by the full force of his rage, calling him a dog, a criminal, and a lump (a considerably more violent word in German), knocking over the chair he was bound to and stomping on him, shouting at him again and again, "I'll get you to talk." In this he would not succeed: during the entire period, his subject never provided any information, and never responded with the least resistance, which would have formally supplied Stawitzki with the necessary justification for stating he had been shot for "resisting the authority of the state." In one of these sessions, Stawitzki had confronted Müller with one of the coup plans, specifically the "X-report" that Müller, following a Vatican trip, had composed late one evening with Dohnanyi and Bonhoeffer together. Its first sentence said, "Decent Germans have decided to negotiate with the English via the Vatican." Stawitzki read the text aloud, and every time he came across the phrase "decent Germans," a phrase often repeated in the report, he would deliver a karate chop to Müller's upper lip. Müller's face became bruised and swollen. The prisoner's teeth, already much weakened by malnutrition, were shattered. The three sessions on April 8 were prolonged ones, lasting several hours, until 7:00 in the evening.[11] Finally the Kriminalkommissar yelled, "This show is ending, this is it! The only satisfaction you'll get is to hang one head lower than your friends Canaris and Oster!" Stawitzki's conduct led Müller unashamedly to think in full of the famous words from Goethe's *Götz von Berlichingen*: "Of him, tell him he can lick my arse." He was led outside to the execution yard and left to one side. There, full of faith, he prepared to die. He made his peace with God in final, courageous prayers.[12]

The Trial in Flossenbürg

At 4:00 the court convened. Those present were Koegel, Huppenkothen as prosecutor, Thorbeck as presiding judge, and most likely in part, Stawitzki. Despite the obvious need for great caution surrounding the self-protective post-war testimony supplied by Thorbeck, his post-war assertions (as well as those of Huppenkothen) are virtually all we have as a partial record. Oster he describes as making the most soldierly impression, readily admitting everything, not wanting to diminish his honour by lying, and requesting death by firing squad as a preferred choice. Strünck he omits; his case was not included here. Gehre, he stated, admitted everything. (There may have been an awkward moment if Gehre cited the arrangement he had come to with Stawitzki, that his life would be spared if he collaborated and agreed to help the Gestapo by extracting information from Josef Müller.) Thorbeck recalls that Sack disputed all charges vigorously. Canaris the prosecutors also had "great difficulty" with, as he represented all evidence submitted as having been undertaken as counter-espionage activity. Thorbeck conveniently omits any mention of the degraded physical condition to which the torture and abuse of the Gestapo system had reduced the admiral. Finally, the court resummoned Oster, and asked Canaris if Oster was lying in the version of events that he (Oster) had brought. Canaris, like all the defendants, was found guilty, and sent back to his cell by around 10:00, where he tapped out messages protesting his innocence to his cell neighbour.[13]

44

Sunday in Schönberg (II)

Back in the schoolroom, opening the two texts in Schönberg that day, Bonhoeffer would have been struck instantly by what they had in common. Both had 1 John 5:4–10 as an Epistle; both had John 20:19–31 as the set Gospel, these two printed in full in the *Schott*. Both shared the passage after which the calendar Sunday was named, 1 Peter 2:2. The opening page of the 1940 edition is shown below:

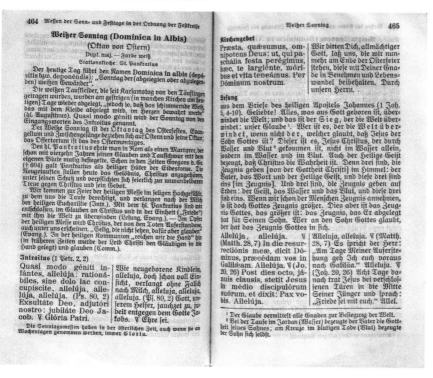

Fig. 44-1. *Schott Messbuch*, 1940
Author's collection. Photo: John Hogg. A matched translation (for the second Sunday of Easter) is provided below.

Messen der Sonn- und Festtage in der
Ordnung der Festkreise
Weisser Sonntag (Dominica in Albis)
(Oktav von Ostern)
Dupl.maj. – Farbe Weiß
Stationskirche: St Pankratius

Services for Sundays and Festivals
(Seasonal Liturgy)
White Sunday (Dominica in Albis)
Octave of Easter
(White)
Festival of St Pancras

Introitus (1 Petr. 2,2)
Wie neugeborene kindlein, alleluja, doch
schon voll Einsicht, verlangt ohne falsch nach
Milch, alleluja, alleluja, alleluja. (Ps 80,2)
Gott, unserem Helfer, jauchzet zu, jubelt
entgegen dem Gotte Jakobs. **V** Ehre sei.

Introitus (1 Peter 2:2)
Like newborn children, alleluja, yet with
wisdom, crave pure spiritual milk, alleluja,
alleluja, alleluja. (Psalm 81:1) Shout for
joy to God our strength, shout aloud to
the God of Jacob! V. Glory be to God.

Kirchengebet
Wir bitten dich, allmächtiger Gott, laß
uns, die wir nunmehr am Ende der
Osterfeier stehen, diese mit Deiner Gnade
in Benehmen und Lebenswandel beibehalten. Durch unseren Herrn.

Congregational prayer
Almighty God, we beseech thee, as we
now stand at the end of the Easter celebrations, grant us in all our doings that your
grace may shape and infuse our conduct
aright. Through Jesus Christ our Lord.

Lesung (1 Joh. 5,4–10)
Alleluja, alleluja. **V** (Matth. 28,7) Es
spricht der herr: „Im Tage Meiner Auferstehung geh Ich euch voraus nach Galiläa".
Alleluja. **V** (Joh. 20,26) Acht Tage danach
trat Jesus bei verschlossenen Türen in die
Mitte Seiner Jünger und sprach „Friede sei
mit euch". Allel.

Reading (1 John 5:4–10)
Alleluja, alleluja. V. (Matt. 28:7) The Lord
says, "On the day I rise I am going ahead of
you into Galilee." Alleluja. V. (John 20:26)
Eight days later, though the doors were
locked, Jesus appeared among his disciples and said, "Peace be with you." Allel.

Evangelium (Joh. 20,19–31)
Offertorium (Matth. 28,25 u. 6)

Gospel (John 20:19–31)
Offertory (Matthew 28:25, 26)

Ein Engel des Herrn stieg vom Himmel
und sprach zu den Frauen: „Er, den ihr
suchtet, ist auferstanden, wie er gesagt
hat", alleluja.

An angel of the Lord came down from
heaven and spoke to the women, "See
the one you seek is risen, as he told you,"
alleluja.

Stillgebet. Wir bitten Dich, o Herr, nimm
an die Gaben der frohlockenden Kirche:
und wie Du ihr den Anlaß zu solchem
Jubel gewährtest, so schenke ihr als Frucht
die ewige Freude. Durch unseren Herrn.

Contemplative prayer. Receive, we
beseech you, O Lord, the gifts of your
joyful people: and even as you give unto
them cause for such rejoicing, grant them
the fruit of eternal joy. Through Jesus
Christ our Lord.

Communio (Joh. 20,27)
„Reiche deine Hand her und erkenne die
Male der Nägel", alleluja „und sei nicht
ungläubig, sondern gläubig!", alleluja,
alleluja.

Communion (John 20:27)
"Reach out your hand, see the mark of
the nails," alleluja, "and do not doubt, but
believe," alleluja, alleluja.

Schlußgebet
Herr, unser Gott, wir bitten Dich: die
hochheiligen Geheimnisse, die du uns
übergabest, um unsre Erlösung zu sichern,
laß uns Heilmittel sein für jetzt und später.
Durch unsern Herrn.

Closing prayer
Lord our God, we pray: grant that the
sacred mysteries you have entrusted to us
for our salvation may be to us the means
of healing now and always. Through Jesus
Christ our Lord.

The service he had agreed to lead had to be conducted hastily and quietly to remain within the bounds of the strict Gestapo prohibitions that prevailed and were being enforced by the patrol of Gestapo "thugs"[1] keeping guard in rotation outside the classroom's locked door. Bonhoeffer began with a prayer, which he followed by (in part) reading out the set texts from the *Schott*, while at times seeming to recite from memory, an area where he had a considerable repertoire.[2] Further prayers followed, most likely some of which were from the above list, and some extempore. Switching back to the *Losungen*, he preached a simple, brief, and moving sermon on the Isaiah passage "By his wounds we are healed."[3] Falconer later wrote that Bonhoeffer described

> the comfort and security which he himself found in complete faith in the rightness of the will of God and the effectiveness of prayer. . . . We must not, he explained, pray to God for what we want, because we cannot possibly know what is best. We must only pray to God to do with us what He wishes for us, even if that leads to our destruction. That is how God is, through us, best served.[4]

Given the passages available to him for the day, and which he is known to have accessed, it is hard to imagine Bonhoeffer would not also have made the link between the hostages' own situation in a locked room and Jesus' appearance to his disciples (in the Gospel reading, John 20:19–31) through doors that were locked out of fear. On that occasion the disciples were "overjoyed when they saw the Lord." The theme of joy, a subject close to, and much present in, Bonhoeffer's heart, presents itself. Given what Falconer reports Bonhoeffer having said, which has a link to Bonhoeffer's love of the Psalms, it is also possible that one of the set readings he also used (from the Introitus, as above) was Psalm 81:2: "Shout for joy to God our strength, shout aloud to the God of Jacob!"

Whatever he chose, the sources on what Bonhoeffer said that day agree that his words were well received. Bonhoeffer had written about preaching back in 1934:

> When a preacher opens their Bible and interprets the word of God . . . a mystery takes place, a miracle: the grace of God, who comes down from heaven into our midst and speaks to us, knocks on our door, asks questions, warns us, puts pressure on us, alarms us, threatens us, and makes us joyful again and free and sure.[5]

It seems that some of this richness was transacted. The role of liturgy is uniquely Christian in that it does not attempt to "fix" things, but rather places human time in the context of eternity.[6] Pünder wrote that the service brought "huge joy" and that "the thin soup we were brought for lunch at midday that day tasted really good."[7] Clearly he had received food for his soul. He was not the only one. Best noted, "[Bonhoeffer] spoke to us in a manner which reached the heart of all, finding just the right words to express the spirit of our imprisonment and the thoughts and resolutions which it had brought."[8] Despite the need for keeping a low profile, word of the service taking place quickly filtered through to the *Sippenhäftlinge* contingent in the adjacent room on the first floor, which instantly conceived the idea of smuggling Bonhoeffer into their room to take a service for them as well, and asked him to do so. It also appears that another effect of the service was to cause at least three[9] of the group in the schoolroom to lose track of time; it is possible they were "given pause for thought" in some unusual sense. The service had begun at 10:00, and even if the singing of "Ein fester Burg ist unser Gott" ("A Mighty Fortress Is Our God") did take place, which must remain unlikely, not least because of the need for circumspection, it would have concluded not long after 10:30.[10] It was in fact some while later, at 3:00,[11] that two plain-clothed Gestapo officials arrived, but it seemed to those present that day as though time had flown. Best wrote that "[Bonhoeffer] had hardly finished his last prayer when the door opened and two evil-looking men in civilian clothes came in and said: 'Prisoner Bonhoeffer—Come with us.'"[12]

Thus summarily instructed, and asked to pack, Bonhoeffer hastily assembled his things, essentially his Bible and an illustrated volume of Goethe's poems, intentionally leaving aside his Plutarch volume to reveal a trail in the subsequent chaos, a book that he had previously marked up for just such an eventuality.[13] It would, only moments later, be picked up from the table in the middle of the schoolroom. Hoping that the two Englishmen might survive the war, Bonhoeffer rapidly asked Hugh Falconer, if he should survive, to get in touch with his twin sister, Sabine, whom he had helped to take refuge in England in 1939. Drawing Payne Best aside, he clasped Best's hand, and speaking with emotional earnestness, asked him twice in the same words to convey a message to the bishop of Chichester:

> [Tell him that] for me this is the end, but also the beginning[14]—with him I believe in the principle of our universal Christian brotherhood which rises above all national hatreds, and that our victory is certain. [Tell him too that] I have never forgotten his words at our last meeting.[15]

It was not an out-of-place gesture of warmth. The very clothes Bonhoeffer was wearing were those provided for him by Best.[16] The room fell silent as

Bonhoeffer took his leave of everyone. There was a flatness to the expressions of goodwill and the various words of hope that they would meet again that were exchanged. The hostages were all by now well accustomed to being transported hither and thither like packages. Yet in the moment, Pünder felt that the sudden removal of Bonhoeffer, someone who had not even yet faced trial, underlined the relative fragility of his own situation, as one who, by contrast, had actually appeared before the Volksgerichtshof. For Pünder it was a wrench: "Thus was I parted from my Dietrich, without him entrusting me with any small request or service."[17] But also, in the schoolroom itself, the departure of one member of the group did not appear as anything untoward, and was certainly not unusual. The very next morning, a further three members of the small schoolroom group would be collected in the same manner and transported to Dachau. As a group those present, including Bonhoeffer, still had some, albeit faltering, confidence in Germany's ability to provide a fair trial. Falconer states, "Dietrich himself confidently believed that he would get a fair trial and probably get some prison sentence, which would of course be cancelled as soon as the war was over and the Allies victorious."[18] By this time word of what was going on had reached the *Sippenhäftlinge* in the next room. The Gestapo vehicle was parked outside the "back entrance" to the schoolhouse, outside the door onto the street, in such a way that a prisoner departure would be somewhat less open to public view, but where it was clearly visible from their window.

Fig. 44-2. Schoolhouse backdoor
Author's collection.

Parked there, facing uphill, the vehicle was also spotted by one local resident, Adolf Häring, from a discreet second-floor vantage point across the
road. From inside the adjacent shared room, despite the locked door, Fey
Pirzio-Biroli,[19] who had heard the car pull up and the sound of boots pounding heavily up and down the stairs, sprang into action. Quickly, under some
pretext, Anneliese Goerdeler was almost able to "bump into" the departing
Bonhoeffer by the shared tap arrangement installed outside their respective rooms as he made his way hurriedly down the stairs towards the black
Gestapo vehicle. She waved farewell, but by now Bonhoeffer's hitherto unruffled demeanour had changed. She wrote, "He seemed to me much upset." Fey
rushed over to the window in time to see Pastor Bonhoeffer being hustled
into the vehicle.[20] From that window another *Sippenhäftling*, Peter Jehle, also
attempted a wave.[21] A sense of apprehension seized Anneliese and others
that there was no hope of his return.[22] Unaware of Bonhoeffer's intentional
strategy with the book he had left behind, General von Falkenhausen had
proffered it to the guards. Their rebuff was revealing: "Bonhoeffer will not be
needing that any more."[23] The remark could also have applied to Bonhoeffer's
urgent need for food. It was not within SS thinking to waste scant resources
on a condemned man. Bonhoeffer was placed in the rear of the vehicle with
one guard, and they set off along the Ostmarkstraße towards Flossenbürg,
climbing out of Schönberg and sweeping round to the right. In the beautiful
afternoon sunlight, a stunning glimpse of the valley where the schoolroom
group, in a transient happier interlude only the day beforehand, had gathered
nettles to make an attempted soup came into view.

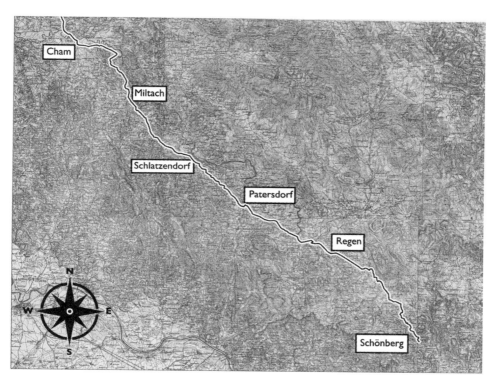

Fig. 44-3. Schönberg to Cham
Route is the one believed, but not known, to have
been taken. Graphic created by Bruce Bovill.

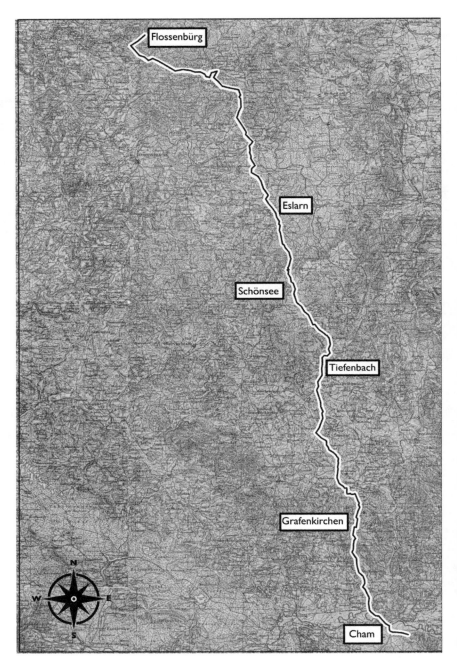

Fig. 44-4. Bonhoeffer's final sunset
Sunset that day was at 19:56. Graphic created by Bruce Bovill

45
Transfer to Flossenbürg

The route (see map) took them north-west to Regen, and onwards via Patersdorf and Schlatzendorf, to Miltach, where they travelled alongside the river Regen for a short while, before Cham, where the bridge was still intact. There, they were able to cross and continue in a north-westerly direction onwards to Grafenkirchen. From there, their route took them north to Tiefenbach and onwards to Schönsee. At some point along the route the sun was setting. The scenery was of an almost incomparable beauty. Then, with darkness falling, they struck north along winding, tree-screened roads to the tiny town of Eslarn. The familiar, almost cosy feel of the lights coming on in the German homes they passed along the way provided a poignant sense of roadside welcome in view of the hostile contrast soon to be afforded by Flossenbürg's dark camp gates, with their "Arbeit Macht Frei" inscription. Bonhoeffer did not know that his fiancée Maria had already walked a full seven kilometres uphill from the Floß station to those very gates, forty-eight days earlier, in search of him, with a rucksack full of clothing, where, after a "believable effort of looking through records for his name" over the space of two hours, she had been politely turned away. By the time they arrived, darkness had fallen. Given that the "trial" of the five defendants had begun around 4:00 p.m., and lasted until at least 10:00 at night, it is possible that Bonhoeffer may have been brought directly from Flossenbürg's main camp entrance directly to the room that his accusers were using.[1]

Bonhoeffer in Flossenbürg

According to SS judge Thorbeck, whose testimony must be treated with circumspection, the trial of Bonhoeffer was different. He made no attempt to lie or misrepresent events, readily confessing his involvement in attempted regime change, through means of removing Hitler by force. Bonhoeffer, he stated, freely confessed high treason, which was already

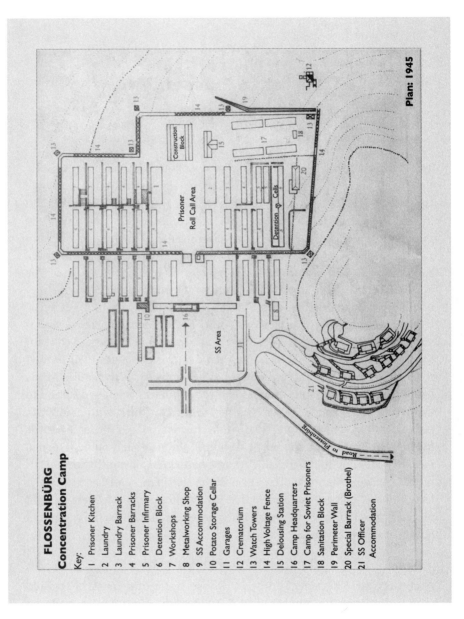

FLOSSENBÜRG
Concentration Camp
Key:

1 Prisoner Kitchen
2 Laundry
3 Laundry Barrack
4 Prisoner Barracks
5 Prisoner Infirmary
6 Detention Block
7 Workshops
8 Metalworking Shop
9 SS Accommodation
10 Potato Storage Cellar
11 Garages
12 Crematorium
13 Watch Towers
14 High Voltage Fence
15 Delousing Station
16 Camp Headquarters
17 Camp for Soviet Prisoners
18 Sanitation Block
19 Perimeter Wall
20 Special Barrack (Brothel)
21 SS Officer
   Accommodation

Fig. 45-1. Flossenbürg plan
Provided by Bruce Bovill

apparent from the documentation submitted to the court, and not least from his own admission. The question the hearing had with Bonhoeffer was whether he had committed military treason. He took the view that it was his Christian duty to attempt via Christian channels to bring about an end to the war. But the panel took the view that a Christian minister in wartime was not justified in taking soundings abroad or in informing those overseas of the existence of a large group preparing a coup. On the basis of the correspondence supplied, which was not disputed by Bonhoeffer, he was sentenced to death for high treason and military treason.[2]

But there is another possibility. Bonhoeffer was readily able to read the "body language" of predetermined outcome surrounding the situation with which he was now confronted. He had thought deeply and had even preached that day on Isaiah's suffering servant (see appendix 7). That servant was one who, before his accusers, remained silent.[3]

Bonhoeffer was allocated a single cell in the 20–40 wing[4] with the other condemned defendants, Canaris being in cell 21 (detention cells in the 1945 plan). The sense of isolation was compounded by the fact that even with such overcrowding, the pattern of having a vacant cell between those condemned to death was the norm. Unlike in Tegel there was no prison chaplain in Flossenbürg. The only late-night visit Bonhoeffer received was from the camp dentist, who needed to perform a check for gold or metal teeth, which resulted in a small thread being tied on the toe of the condemned man.[5]

While all this had been happening, Josef Müller had been shunted from pillar to post. He stood in various spots for hours awaiting his summons. It never came. He was finally sent back to his cell and informed he had been forgotten, or possibly overlooked. He was shattered. Sleep, for him, was out of the question. He wrote,

> The camp seemed shrouded in a harsh light. An unusual commotion reigned; camp guard dogs were barking at someone; I had the impression of constant comings and goings, which was subsequently confirmed as having been so. Some prisoners were tasked with hauling logs, and for that they were using the path up on the ridge which went past the huts of the guard dogs. What was actually happening, I could only guess at, in my cell. I had the feeling of being caught up in a whirlwind of thoughts.[6]

Bonhoeffer was left to spend his final hours on earth with his volume of Goethe's poems and his older brother's Luther Bible, with its twin-verse inscription in his mother's familiar handwriting.[7] His cell was unlit, so the comfort he took from having them with him overnight most likely did not include much opportunity for reading. Only as the executions began early the next morning would the first shafts of daylight filtering through the small window become sufficient for reading purposes.

Monday, April 9, 1945

46
The Administration of Death

Hof, Germany

Hof had been the target of an intense Allied bombing assault on April 2. The US 358th and 359th Divisions, the troops who would eventually liberate[1] Flossenbürg on April 23, were still facing fanatical resistance there a week later. Many of these men had landed at Utah beach ten long months earlier. To the troops, after the crossing of the Rhine, it had seemed as though the whole backbone of the German army was broken. They had travelled through town after town, meeting only very slight resistance, and on some days would take as many as five towns without a shot being fired. However, as they approached the Czechoslovakian border, that would change. Enemy resistance stiffened, and rapid eastward progress stalled. But the US top brass demanded results. A news blackout was imposed on the activities of the 3rd Army for several days. The news-hungry public read newspapers avidly for word of Patton's dramatic drive. It was a thrust that, when achieved, would mean that the 90th Division had become the first unit in the European Theatre of Operations to slice across the German nation, to cut the land in half, to divide Bavaria in the south from the great industrial Germany of the north. But the date of that landmark event would be far too late for the resisters in Flossenbürg. It would take place only on April 18, 1945.[2]

Flossenbürg, Germany

A hundred kilometres south of Hof, the alarm clock went off at a very early hour indeed for Prosecutor Huppenkothen. He needed to supervise the carrying out of the death sentences agreed at a late hour the previous day. He also needed to ensure his wife, Erika, was conveyed onwards in connection with the prisoner transport that left at 4:00 that morning, travelling towards Dachau and, hopefully for her, bound for safety. Certainly it gave him an additional degree of peace of mind knowing that even if the

"Southern Redoubt" never materialised, she would be more likely to be able to surrender to US forces rather than being at the mercy of Russian troops. Just the thought of what might happen to an SS spouse at their hands was enough to make any serving SS officer shudder. That said, there were still some residual perks of being married to an officer in the SS. One was that the circumstances of Erika's southerly transportation would be considerably more comfortable than those of the hostages involved, despite the inclusion on that transport, for example, of Kurt von Schuschnigg, former chancellor of Austria. Another was that all the hostages concerned, including a small child, had already been bundled into the vehicles the evening beforehand and told to sit and wait, in order to facilitate the transport's leaving at the time planned. But in Erika's case, she needed only to present herself in time for the actual moment of departure and could happily spend what remained of the short night in the relative luxury of the SS quarters, comforted in the knowledge that her own prospects of survival were being much enhanced by her journey.[3]

In the prison itself, one fellow resister who survived the war was Bonhoeffer's "almost-family" member Fabian von Schlabrendorff. From his account, cited earlier, we know that in his final moments, Bonhoeffer deposited his belongings, among them a Bible and a volume of Goethe, both with his name inscribed, in the guardroom. Schlabrendorff testifies both about the process adopted in general and also about the events of that morning:

> In the morning at six o'clock I could hear prisoners being awakened in their cells.
>
> [They] had to strip completely. The doomed victim was led naked past our cells into the courtyard. . . . In a diabolical fashion, hanging was arranged so as not to break the cervical vertebrae; the prisoner was slowly strangled until he suffocated. It happened now and then that a prisoner was cut down as soon as he had lost consciousness. They waited until he returned to life, told him jeeringly that now he had a taste of what hanging was like; and then he was hanged in earnest.[4]

This account tallies with that of another prisoner, one who had arrived in Flossenbürg only on the Thursday of the preceding week, Greek general Alexandros Papagos. In his account, published in Greek in 1945, he writes,

> The most vile personality in Flossenbürg Prison was SS-Captain Baumgartner, who was adjutant to the commandant.[5] Superficially,

he had characteristics belonging to a kind and civilized person. But "les apparences trompent," as the French say. Baumgartner, despite his external appearance, was in truth a monster, an incarnation of brutality and inhumanity. He felt indescribable pleasure whenever he found a reason or a pretext to torture a prisoner. Again and again I observed him standing and listening outside cell doors. And whenever he would overhear prisoners criticising the prison regime, he would immediately begin torturing them. It was he, and not SS-Lieutenant Colonel Koegel, who was the real commandant of Flossenbürg concentration camp and prison. Koegel obeyed him blindly; after every bestiality that Baumgartner had ordered was actually carried out, Koegel would officially approve it.

The level of Baumgartner's inhumanity was such that the following tragic scene took place: one of the inmates who had been condemned to death was being transferred to the gallows. He had been whipped and kicked around at the same time. As the hangman put the rope around his neck, the individual wet himself. This may have been out of sheer distress or due to the wild beatings he had suffered. Baumgartner, who was usually present at the executions, ordered the guards to take the prisoner back down from the gallows, to whip him until they drew blood and only then to hang him. This episode is characteristic of the conditions of life in Flossenbürg concentration camp.[6]

In the light of the foregoing and other reports, it is now believed that the hangings of the resisters were overseen by Huppenkothen and the camp doctor, Fischer-Hüllstrung, with Rapportführer Johanni Geissberger[7] administering proceedings. The prisoners were kept in strict isolation from one another, until they were summoned to the washroom, told to strip, and marched along the building on the outside, past the windows, to the canopied place of execution. The order in which the six—Oster, Gehre, Sack, Strünck, Bonhoeffer, and Canaris—were hanged is unknown, but the process of tying their hands behind their backs before they walked, naked, towards the gallows was the same. A noose was placed around the prisoner's neck. One source states that the execution hooks were expressly designed so that when the two-step wooden box, which functioned as a portable platform, was kicked aside, the constriction around the prisoner's neck would tighten to strangulation point. At this point the metal hook would flex just sufficiently to enable the flailing feet of those of average height to bear enough weight to extend the process of suffering.[8] Another source states that Canaris, shorter in stature, was kept until last and hanged until he had had a taste of death, at which point he was cut down, and hanged again.[9] The short-lived inebriated euphoria experienced by the guards, who were plied with schnapps, was succeeded next day by a lasting "high," no doubt at having been part of the profoundly thrilling experience of facilitating such prolonged cruelty (meted out to such senior military figures, regarded as traitors). The abundant measure in which that was handed down, and to which Papagos testifies, was clearly the order of the day.[10]

As dusk fell that evening, the smoke and ashes from the daily pile of burning corpses had cleared. The clack of teleprinter keys was audible in the camp office. An orderly had, at Huppenkothen's behest, encrypted a message, using the Enigma code, for SS-Gruppenführer Müller in Berlin via SS-Gruppenführer Glücks. This message was transmitted at 5:37 p.m. Glücks, in the Central Directorate for Concentration Camps, was to inform Berlin as soon as possible by telephone, telex, or messenger:

Auftrag Befehlsgemäss erledigt.   Task carried out in accordance with
Bestätigung nicht erforderlich   orders. No acknowledgement required.[11]

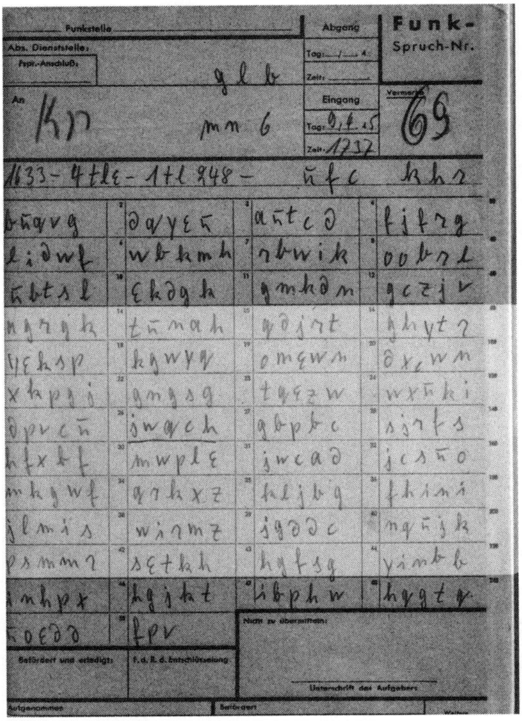

Fig. 46-1. Transcript of message from Flossenbürg to Berlin
From Richardi, *SS-Geiseln im Markt Schönberg.* Photo: John Hogg.

Epilogue

After a further interval of three days, General Friedrich Rabenau was also collected from the Schönberg schoolroom. Rabenau was among those who believed he would get a fair trial. In response to his insistent demands for a hearing, he had been advised via the SS to travel to Flossenbürg, where "a branch of the People's Court was fully functioning." He was entirely misled. Despite Petersdorff's strongly worded advice not to pursue this possibility, he continued to press his demands and was transported to Flossenbürg.[1] Petersdorff's counsel was sound. A second encoded message to the Berlin RSHA, dated April 15, this time from Stawitzki in Flossenbürg, reports Rabenau falling victim to an attack by low-flying US aircraft, the customary euphemism for such murders. Hermann Pünder was kind enough to write to his wife, Eva, with the news in October 1945. Rabenau's brother Karl-Friedrich was subsequently notified by a letter from the Danish consul that he had been executed at between 6:00 and 7:00 on the morning of April 13 or 14. The family's understandable attempts in 1960 to have Ludwig Baumgartner, whom they believed to be the perpetrator, held accountable were dismissed. He was never traced. Rabenau's Christian martyrdom has not been acknowledged, but its consideration is perhaps overdue.

Bonhoeffer's personal effects were picked up in the guardroom by Prince Philip von Hessen. Hessen's thoughtfulness in ensuring they were somehow returned to the family at a later date was deeply appreciated.[2] The news of Bonhoeffer's death[3] was delivered in person to his fiancée, Maria, by senior cleric and family member Wilhelm Stählin on May 4 or 5. She had been summoned to Bundorf. Theologically in a different place from Bonhoeffer, Stählin had always been lukewarm about the relationship between Dietrich and Maria. For her it was a shattering experience. She emerged with the halting words "Dietrich lebt nicht mehr" (Dietrich is no longer alive). Her first thought would most likely have been to contact Dietrich's parents, but with no functioning post or telephones, and post-war Germany divided into zones of occupation, even contemplating such an undertaking was no simple matter. The extraordinary willpower and energy she had shown in January and February was now, understandably, lacking.

Bonhoeffer's parents may have originally heard the news through Hans Bernd Gisevius, who visited them in July. When Bethge and his wife, together with their son Dietrich, attended the Berlin synod on July 29, it is likely that they stayed at the Bonhoeffer family home. Certainly they listened together with them to excerpts from Dietrich's memorial service, held in London, and transmitted by the BBC at 9:45 that evening.

Erich and Margot Heberlein

On April 9, across much of Germany, a German-language newspaper was circulated by the Allies to German civilians with a vivid graphic showing that the gap between the (Russian) Allies advancing from the East and their counterparts in the West was by now only 270 kilometres wide. The hostages still in Schönberg are unlikely to have received this actual propaganda information. But the question, if they survived at all, of whether they might fall into US or Russian hands was truly a burning one. With now only nine in their party remaining, Falconer felt moved to offer support to a fellow hostage. He wrote a carefully crafted and supportive note for Margot Heberlein. Using his RAF squadron leader rank, he requested "all possible consideration" from any Allied forces whose custody she might find herself in.[4]

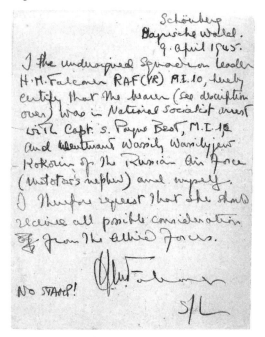

Fig. 46-2. April 9 letter from Falconer
Courtesy of Sofia Ceballos Garcia-Escudero

Margot kept the "safe passage note" with her diary papers. Fortunately it was never needed. Along with most of the other occupants of the Grüne Minna, both Erich and Margot were liberated in a group of 139 hostages at the Pragser Wildsee Hotel on May 4 by the arrival of Lieutenant Melvin Asche's G Company, 339th US Infantry Regiment. The unit had made a forced march through the night to come to the hostages' rescue, having been especially alerted to the presence of the hostages and the danger they were in by Austrian Anton Ducia and great escaper Harry "Wings" Day. These two highly courageous individuals had experienced a particularly hazardous journey to make contact with the Americans after setting out from the Pragser Wildsee Hotel (where the remaining hostages were being temporarily accommodated) three days earlier. The story is ably recounted by Sayer and Dronfield in *Hitler's Last Plot*. The group as a whole were transferred to Capri, where they were all interviewed and, with some exceptions (see below), repatriated in July. Erich and Margot settled back on their farm near Toledo. Both of them were important people in the high-society life of both Madrid and Toledo. Margot dedicated herself to the teaching of English. She kept up a correspondence with a number of *Prominenten* for many years. Their son Oskar survived the war but was killed in a car accident in 1950. Erich accepted a position in 1954 with the Foreign Office under a law passed in 1951 to ensure that anti-Nazi public servants did not experience discrimination. The couple never really spoke publicly about their war story. Margot died in 1967. Erich did remarry; his second wife's name was Margerita de Ceballos Calleja.

One notable exception was Vasily Kokorin. His behaviour towards the group became more emotional as he realised his time as "Molotov's nephew" was coming to an end. Fully aware that Stalin regarded as traitors all who had surrendered to the Germans, he parted company with the (by now much larger) group and by later in May had found his own way to the Russian military mission in Rome. Here he dropped his cover story, simply giving his name and listing the names of the camps he had been in. Soon repatriated, he was, however, immediately arrested on arrival at Odessa and sent for interrogation by the head of SMERSH, the Soviet counterintelligence service, in the infamous Lubyanka prison in Moscow. He was charged on three counts: treason, masquerading as Molotov's nephew, and complicity in the death of Yakov Dzhugashvili. He languished in custody for over six years, and was finally sentenced to death on broadly these charges. He courageously appealed against the sentence on two grounds: (1) his actions had been undertaken when he had lost the use of both legs and was under terrible Gestapo prison conditions of hunger and death, and (2) the injustice he had suffered in post-war interrogations had been unduly severe. On these he was turned down. His inclusion of a sudden last-minute appeal to "family relative" Molotov was also fruitless. He was executed on March 26, 1952.

General von Falkenhausen similarly spent all the immediate post-war years in prison, but in his case in Belgium. He did all he could to care for his wife, who died from cancer in 1950. Despite supportive testimonials from Léon Blum, Hugh Falconer, and Payne Best, he was sentenced in Belgium in 1951, aged seventy-three, to twelve years' hard labour, to be served out in Germany. By now the world was in an entirely different place. Falkenhausen had become such a cause célèbre in Germany that virtually every journalist in the country was calling for his release. He was the very embodiment of the honourable German Wehrmacht officer who had despised the SS and had even resisted Hitler. Almost as soon as he set foot on German soil, having already served one-third of his sentence, he was granted a pardon by Chancellor Konrad Adenauer. Supporters came from far and wide to witness the occasion. Hugh Falconer took time out from running the passport office in the British sector of occupied Germany to be on the spot at Aachen to greet him. In 1960 Falkenhausen remarried. His new wife was Cécile Vent, who had fought for the Belgian resistance.

Hugh Falconer's wartime heroism, and his survival, was much appreciated by the SOE. His honouring included a classic return home "moment": being collected in an enormous black Packard limousine, chauffeured by a FANY (First Aid Nursing Yeomanry) driver who looked as if she had stepped straight out of the pages of a wartime number of the *Tatler*. But not every turn of events worked out to his liking. When Payne Best published his bestselling book *The Venlo Incident*, he sent Falconer an effusively inscribed copy. It was dated December 1, 1950: "As an expression of the author's admiration for his fortitude and gallantry during the years of our common imprisonment at Sachsenhausen and in other places." Given the brutality of his experience and his near starvation in Sachsenhausen, the phrase "common imprisonment" was hard for Falconer to swallow. By comparison Best had enjoyed a private vegetable garden and a host of other VIP comforts. Falconer was understandably furious. He did not reciprocate the greeting. After reorganising German passport control, Falconer carried out a further assignment in Hanover until 1952. Once back in the UK, he returned to his former profession in the cement industry.

From then on all his contracts were abroad in India, Pakistan, and Iran. His work took him to Afghanistan, Kashmir, Bangladesh, and many other parts of the world. In 1954 he received £2,293 from a fund that had been set up for people who had experienced exceptional hardship[5] in World War II. During a two-year contract in Zambia, while visiting South Africa and Rhodesia, he and his wife decided to settle there.

Horst von Petersdorff retired to his property in Berchtesgaden and, in an interview given in 1957, stated that he was planning to extend it. Curiously, he also divulged at that time that he had insider knowledge on systems for contacting former Nazi Party members wanted for questioning. He maintained a host of contacts in industry, especially among lawyers. He dabbled with both the idea of going into politics and the idea of writing up his thoughts on the killings of June 1934 to "set the record straight." His former wife lived between Canada and Frankfurt am Main. In 1954 Horst became a Knight of Honour in the Most Venerable Order of St John Hospitaller of Jerusalem, an organisation to which he had been admitted in 1927.

Heidel Nowakowski, like Kokorin, but for different reasons, was also somehow absent from the May liberation moment at the Pragser Wildsee. She had "hooked up" with another hostage. She lived in Essen after the war and gave birth to a daughter in 1946. In 1953 Heidel married Harold Kaiser but was divorced in 1955. By the time of her death in October 1956, at the age of forty-two, she had married again, to a Hans Gunther Liell, and had accrued eight convictions for fraud under the aliases "Heidel von der Marwitz," "Jensen," "Stauffenberg," and "Smith." She had also been investigated by the Dortmund police for attempting to secure funds set aside for those affected by their involvement in the July 20 attempted assassination plot.

Sigmund Rascher did not survive the war. His prescient sense that being incarcerated in Dachau would mean his demise proved quite correct. Around 7:00 in the evening of April 26, SS-Oberscharführer Theodor Bongartz appeared at the isolated prison cell Rascher was sharing with Falconer, insisted Rascher show his face, and shot him twice in the stomach through the food hatch.[6] Once he had died, Falconer covered Rascher's face with his handkerchief. There were two camp commandants of Dachau that day, so it remains unclear which of them ordered his execution. One source suggested it was a direct order from Himmler.[7]

After the war Payne Best met with his old MI5 boss Claude Dansey, who half-heartedly suggested he write an account of the events leading up to his capture. He responded by writing a whole book. *The Venlo Incident* was published in 1950, and while it not so subtly inculpated his colleague Stevens, its deep subtlety, and success, was that by virtue of its publication it helped exonerate him from the charge of divulging any information of value to the Germans. Another feature of the book was, perhaps understandably, that it afforded him the starring role in the story of the hostages' "liberation moment," alluded to above. This was the wider hostage odyssey (of which Bonhoeffer's final days were a part) that came to its denouement at the Pragser Wildsee Hotel in May 1945. Although Best undoubtedly did play a central and helpful part, this particular version of events was an overstatement.[8] But the tale of adventure and survival against the odds that Best narrated in cheery fashion proved highly popular to avid postwar audiences of both Allied and German persuasions. In his account Best often portrays ordinary Germans as victims of a cruel system, one that they in many cases sought to circumvent. Clearly the process of writing had had a therapeutic effect on Best in relation to his 1945 "hatred of all things German." More significantly the book's conclusion plainly cast troops from the SS in the role of menacing villains, while at the same time casting soldiers from Germany's Wehrmacht as the rescuing heroes. This, for Germans, was an irresistibly appealing storyline, even contributing in some small measure to the growing solace felt across the nation around the "honourable Wehrmacht" narrative. Added to this was the fact that the book's author, Captain Best, a fluent German speaker, was a larger-than-life character who apparently liked Germans and was himself the very caricature of an affable, tweed-sporting, monocle-wearing English spy and gentleman. In his own account, he was represented, possibly quite reasonably, as the victim of the espionage incompetence of senior figures. The impression conveyed was that as a result, Best had (tragically for him) been outfoxed in dastardly fashion by agents of Himmler's unscrupulous Gestapo in 1939. Even more, Best had briefly shared in the incarceration of the lion-hearted General von Falkenhausen. In Germany, in the early 1950s, journalists clamouring for the general's release even began to adduce Best's name in the chorus of favourable advocacy.

In the light of the foregoing, Best continued to be a character inspiring strong likes and dislikes. On the one hand, Best was feted by the West German government in Bonn in the summer of 1952, and even provided with a Mercedes-Benz as compensation for his wartime treatment. He extended his charm offensive to a number of former *Prominenten*, and numbered Bonhoeffer's biographer Eberhard Bethge among the many

Germans on whom he made a favourable impression.[9] On the other, he experienced a highly acrimonious split from his wife, Margareta von Rees, in 1953. She subsequently revealed that Best had been appointed to the board of a British company and fired only eight months later. Best had received five hundred pounds for his book as well as a further five hundred pounds from a newspaper serialization. Sadly the money earned did not help prevent the once fabulously wealthy Best from being the subject of bankruptcy proceedings in 1958 as a result of a debt that, according to his wife, went back to 1931, a fact he had successfully withheld from his wartime employers. But his charm, or his luck, had not run out. In 1968 Best was awarded by some margin the highest payout of any of the fourteen Sachsenhausen Fund claimants, totalling four thousand pounds, almost double the amount received by Falconer. In 1975 he married the recently widowed Bridget Lind, a woman twenty-four years his junior.

Horst Hoepner returned home to his prior occupation, trading in timber out of a base in Hamburg. His homecoming was inconspicuous. The social standing of the family members of any who had offered even limited resistance was at best uncertain. He was not the recipient of a Mercedes-Benz, nor of a handsome payout from a war hardship fund. Following his experience of torture at German hands, he did not feature on Payne Best's networking and follow-up list, and a letter he wrote in May 1946 to Best seeking support in emigrating away from what he dubbed the dull hopelessness of post-war Germany remained apparently unanswered. He died in 1951.

Hence for every individual in the Grüne Minna party, a very different onward path was experienced. Rascher outlived Bonhoeffer only by a fortnight, and the incarcerated Kokorin by just under seven years. Hoepner, ostensibly a free man in Berlin, did not long outlive Kokorin. As mentioned above, Nowakowski, although by far the youngest, and whose untold story still calls out to posterity, died aged forty-two the following year. The poignant intimacy of what the group had experienced together, not widely known, was recounted only in part. But a good number, never forgetful of the experience, and certainly not of Bonhoeffer's part within it, would survive.

Extraordinarily Victor and Eva Klemperer also survived. The shorthand name Klemperer used for their family home, which had been so tragically and unjustly requisitioned from them under the era of persecution, was Dölzschen. The tenacious diarist closes his account on June 10, 1945, almost on a note of disbelief:

> On Sunday [June 10], we were in Dresden. . . . This is when the fairy-tale turnabout came. Tired and hungry we walked to the Neustädter

station—*nada*! We went to the police station opposite . . . very friendly reception. . . . You must go to Dölzschen immediately! I objected that it would take time before I could move into my house there. The officer grinned: You've no idea how quickly that can sometimes happen! And in that he proved to be right. . . . In the late afternoon we walked up to Dölzschen.[10]

APPENDIX 1

Maps of Hostage Dates and Places of Birth

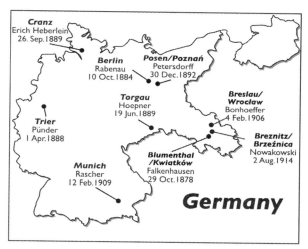

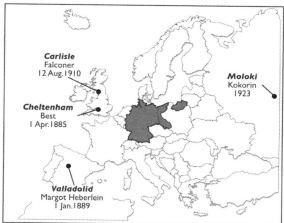

Staatsbibliothek zu Berlin-Kartenabteilung/Bruce Bovill

APPENDIX 2

Bonhoeffer's Route

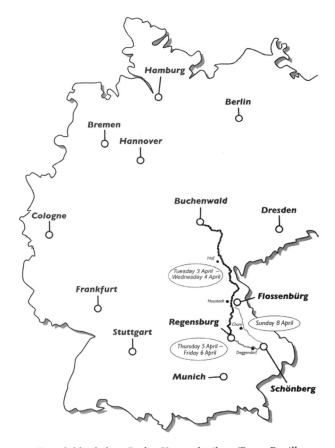

Staatsbibliothek zu Berlin-Kartenabteilung/Bruce Bovill

APPENDIX 3
Specific Primary Literature

Author	Prisoner category	Language	Publication/comments
Alexandros Papagos	VIP	Greek	Δύο χρόνια στά Χιτλερικά στρατόπαιδα συγκεντρώσεως [Two years in Hitler's concentration camps] (1945; not translated into English)
Isa Vermehren	*Sippenhaft*	German	*Reise durch den letzten Akt* (1946; not translated into English)
Léon Blum	VIP	French	*Le dernier mois* (1946; not translated into English)
Payne Best	VIP	English	*The Venlo Incident* (1950)
Hermann Pünder	Political	German	*Von Preussen nach Europa* (1968); unpublished letters to his family (1945; not translated into English)
Anneliese Goerdeler	*Sippenhaft*	German	*Verschleppt* (1969; diary notes from 1945; not translated into English)
Josef Müller	Political	German	*Bis zur letzten Konsequenz* (1975; not translated into English)
Fey von Hassell	*Sippenhaft*	Italian (English)	*Hostage of the Third Reich* (1987 [1989]; diary notes from 1945); Fey's married surname, Pirzio-Biroli, is generally not used here
Marie-Gabriele von Stauffenberg	*Sippenhaft*	German	*Aufzeichnungen aus unserer Sippenhaft* (2010; diary notes from 1945; not translated into English)
Hugh Falconer	VIP	English	*The Gestapo's Most Improbable Hostage* (2018; written 1975)

Notes

There are at least ten first-hand/primary accounts of this short section of
the hostage journey, as well as two letters written at the time by Hermann
Pünder. These latter items, curiously omitted from his memoirs in 1968,
have somewhat languished in the German Bundesarchiv until now, and the
citations from them appear here for the first time in English. In relation to
the above list, it should be noted that Best, a fluent German speaker, had
access to the Vermehren publication, but apparently not to that of Blum.
Following Best's publication date, and the wide distribution of his detailed
account, all subsequent authors knew of his work. In general, all took heed,
in some measure regrettably, allowing Best's account to stand as definitive.
No other primary account references Blum, and the first translation of his
work into German dates from 2008. Consequently the quality of the contributions of Vermehren and Blum has been relatively unmarked and, as
can be seen from the list above, almost entirely unknown in the English-
speaking world. Papagos' work remains inaccessible to English readers save
for the sections translated here.

APPENDIX 4

Schott Messbuch—A Comparison of Editions
Weißer Sonntag—Schott

Jahrgang: 1907

Druck und Bindung

Imprimatur, Friburgi Brisgoviae, die 24 Decembris 1906, + Thomas, Archiepps

Auflage

Freiburg im Breisgau Elfte Auflage—mit einem Titelbild

Vorwort

Der Weiße Sonntag (Octav von Ostern; dupl.) hat seinen Namen von der lateinischen Benennung Dominica in albis (zu ergänzen: depositis): „Sonntag der (abgelegten) weißen Gewänder", welche die Täuflinge von Karsamstag an bis zum darauffolgenden Samstag beim Gottesdienst, um den Altar herumzustehen, jeden Tag getragen hatten. „Die Neugetauften" sagt der hl. Augustinus von der damaligen Feier dieses Tages „wechseln die Kleider, jedoch so, daß zwar die weiße Farbe der Kleider abgelegt wird, die Unschuld im Herzen aber immer bleibt"; und der Bischof betete: „Möge die unsichtbare Reinheit Christi allezeit in deiner Seele sein, möge sie dieselbe nie verlieren". Man sagt auch Sonntag Quasimodogeniti, von den ersten Worten des Introitus.—Die Erscheinung des Herrn vor der versammelten Jüngerschar und der großmüthige Sieg, den seine Geduld und Milde über den Unglauben des Apostels Thomas errang, der seinen Zweifel durch Reue, Demuth und Liebe wieder sühnte, sind der Gegenstand der heutigen Feier.—An den meisten Orten Deutschlands und Oesterreichs feiern heute die Kinder ihre erste heilige Communion.

Der Eingang führt die Worte des hl. Petrus an, die den Neugetauften gelten. Sie sind die zarten Kinder, welche die geistige Milch des Glaubens trinken.

Eingang / Eingangslied / Introitus (1 Peter 2,2)

Wie neugeborene Kindlein, alleluja, verlanget nach der geistigen, unverfälschten Milch (der heiligen Lehre). Alleluja, alleluja, alleluja. Psalm.

Frohlocket Gott, unserem Helfer; jubelt dem Gotte Jakobs. **V** Ehre sei.

An diesem letzten Tage einer so hochfestlichen Octav nimmt die Kirche in der Collecte gewissermaßen Abschied von den vollendeten Feierlichkeiten, und bittet, daß deren unendlich erhabener Gegenstand im Leben ihrer Kinder sich ausprägte.

Gebet/Kirchengebet

Gib uns, allmächtiger Gott, laß uns, daß wir die österlichen Feste, die wir begangen haben, in Sitte und Lebenswandel (als wahrhaft zu einem heiligen Leben Auferstandene) durch deine Gnadengabe immerfort bewahren mögen. D.J.Chr.

Epistel/Lesung

(1 Joh. 5,4–10). Geliebteste! Alles, was aus Gott geboren ist, überwindet die Welt; und das ist der Sieg, welcher die Welt[1] überwindet, unser Glaube. Wer ist es, der die Welt überwindet, als der, welcher glaubt, daß Jesus der Sohn Gottes ist? Dieser ist es, der durch Wasser und Blut gekommen ist,[2] Jesus Christus, nicht durch das Wasser allein, sondern durch das Wasser und das Blut; und der Geist bezeugt,[3] daß Christus die Wahrheit sei. Denn drei sind, die Zeugnis geben im Himmel: der Vater, das Wort[4] und der Heilige Geist, und diese drei sind Eins.[5] Und drei sind, die Zeugnis geben auf Erden: der Geist[6] und das Wasser und das Blut, und diese drei sind Eins.[7] Wenn wir der Menschen Zeugnis annehmen, so ist das Zeugnis Gottes größer; dies aber ist das Zeugnis Gottes, welches größer ist, daß er von seinem Sohn bezeugt hat. Wer an den Sohn Gottes glaubt, der hat das Zeugnis Gottes in sich.[8]

In der Epistel preist der heilige Apostel Johannes das Verdienst und den Werth des Glaubens. Wir wollen aufrichtigen Herzens glauben, uns gegenüber der göttlichen Wahrheit glücklich fühlen wie Kinder, und allezeit bereit sein, das Zeugnis Gottes liebevoll aufzunehmen.

Allelujalieder

Alleluja, alleluja. **V** "Am Tage Meiner Auferstehung, spricht der Herr, will ich euch vorangehen nach Galiläa." Alleluja. **V** Nach acht Tagen, da die Türen verschlossen waren, stand Jesus in der Mitte seiner Jünger und sprach: Friede sei mit euch! Alleluja.

Die ergreifend schöne Erzählung des Evangeliums gibt auch uns die Lehre, daß unser Glaube, um Gott zu gefallen und Belohnung zu verdienen, nicht durch Werstandeshochmuth und *Bernünstelei* angekräkelt sein darf, sondern demüthig und hingebend, von Kindeseinfalt sein muß. „Selig, die nicht sehen und doch glauben!" Welcher Trost für uns und alle diejenigen, welche ohne die Sinneswahrnehmung der Apostel zum Glauben gelangen! Möchte in aller Herzen, besonders in denen der glücklichen Kinder, die heute bei ihrer heiligen Communion eine ähnliche Gnade haben wie der hl. Thomas, alle Zeit ihres Lebens dessen feuriges Glaubensbekenntnis: „Mein Herr und Mein Gott!" lebendig sein!—Am Siegestag seiner Auferstehung ertheilt der glorreiche Sieger über Sünde und Tod jene großartige Amnestie, indem er der Gesamtheit der Apostel die Gewalt der Sündenvergebung überträgt.

(Offertorium) (Matth. 28,25 u. 6) Opferungslied

(none)

Stillgebet

Im Stillgebet bittet die Kirche, daß die Wonne dieser irdischen Ostern *in die ewigen Ostern* übergehen möge.

Nimm auf, o Herr, die Gaben deiner freuderfüllten Kirche, und wie du ihr Grund zu so großer Freude gegeben, so verleihe ihr auch als Frucht die ewige Seligkeit. Durch Jesum Christum.

Präfation von Ostern, S. 42.

Der Apostel legte seine Finger in die Wundmale Jesu—im allerheiligsten Sacramente des Altars legt Jesus sich selbst in unser Herz—heute in Tausende unschuldiger Kinderherzen;—möchten auch wir den Glauben besitzen, den der Herr selig preist!

Communio (Joh. 20,27) Kommunionlied

Lege deine Hand her und erkenne die Male der Nägel, alleluja, und sei nicht ungläubig, sondern gläubig. Alleluja, alleluja.

Zum Schluss bittet die Kirche, daß dies zur Stärkung unserer Schwachheit eingestezte Geheimnis für die Gegenwart und Zukunft ein wirksames Mittel sei, um die Gnade der Beharrlichkeit zu erlangen.

Schlußgebet

Wir bitten Dich, o Herr, unser Gott, daß die hochheiligen Geheimnisse, welche du uns zur Kräftigung unserer Wiederherstellung gegeben hast, ein Heilmittel seien für die Gegenwart, so für die Zukunft. Durch Jesum Christum.[9]

Nota Bene

This edition belongs to the Pünder family, who in a telephone conversation with me in 2017 briefly thought it might have been the one Bonhoeffer used. Upon further inspection the date of July 1945 in Hermann Pünder's writing in the front clearly indicates it could not have been. (The family recalls that this edition was given to him by an army chaplain in Capri and is dated July 1945, Wiesbaden.) However, its printing date may be helpful in estimating which edition Bonhoeffer is likely to have referred to.

Jahrgang: 1936

Druck und Bindung

Volks-Schott, Imprimi permittitur, Beuronae, in Annuntiatione B.M.V., 1936 + Raphael, Archiabbas, Imprimatur, Friburgi Brisgoviae, die 28 Aprilis 1936, Rösch, Vic. Gen., Herausgegeben von Mönchen der Erzabtei Beuron

Auflage

Freiburg im Breisgau 1936 achte Auflage

Vorwort

Weißer Sonntag (Farbe weiß)

Stationskirche zu Rom: St. Pankratius

Heute feiert die Kirche den Oktavtag des Osterfestes. Der Name „Weißer Sonntag" spielt auf die Täuflinge an, die heute zum letzten Male in ihren weißen Taufgewändern beim Gottesdienst erscheinen. Um sie zu heiliger Treue zu ermahnen, fand zu Rom der Stationsgottesdienst in der Kirche des jugendlichen Martyrers Pankratius statt, der als Patron der Eidestreue galt, weil er schon mit 14 Jahren seinen Glauben mit seinem Blute besiegelte.

Das Eingangslied gilt den Täuflingen, die mit der Milch der heiligen Eucharistie genährt wurden. Auch wir kommen in ähnlichem Hochgefühl wie jene zur heiligen Opferfeier und verlangen nach jener göttlichen Speise.

Eingang / Eingangslied / Introitus (1 Peter 2,2)

Quasi modo geniti. (1 Petr. 2,2) Wie neugeborene Kindlein, alleluja, doch schon voll Einsicht, verlangt ohne Falsch nach Milch, alleluja, alleluja, alleluja. (Ps 80,2) Gott, unsrem Helfer, jauchzet zu, jubelt entgegen dem Gotte Jakobs. **V** Ehre sei.

Gebet/Kirchengebet

Wir bitten Dich, allmächtiger Gott, laß uns, die wir nunmehr am Ende der Osterfeier stehen, diese mit Deiner Gnade in Benehmen und Lebenswandel beibehalten. Durch unsern Herrn.

Epistel/Lesung

In der Lesung schildert der hl. Johannes die Kraft des Glaubens an Jesus Christus. Für diesen Glauben bürgt Gott der Vater bei der Taufe Jesu im Jordan („durch Wasser"), der Sohn durch sein eigenes, an Kreuze vergossenes Blut, und der Heilige Geist durch seine vom Heiland vorhergesagte Herabkunft.

Lesung aus dem Briefe des heiligen Apostels Johannes (1 Joh. 5,4–10). Geliebte! Alles, was aus Gott geboren ist, überwindet die Welt; und das ist der Sieg, der die Welt überwindet: unser Glaube.[9] Wer ist es, der die Welt überwindet, wenn nicht der, welcher glaubt, daß Jesus der Sohn Gottes ist? Dieser ist es, Jesus Christus, der durch Wasser und Blut[10] gekommen ist, nicht im Wasser allein, sondern im Wasser und im Blut. Auch der Heilige Geist bezeugt, daß Christus die Wahrheit ist. Denn drei sind, die Zeugnis geben [von der Gottheit Christi] im Himmel: der Vater, das Wort und der Heilige Geist, und diese drei sind eins [im Zeugnis]. Und drei sind, die Zeugnis geben auf Erden: der Geist, das Wasser und das Blut, und diese drei sind eins. Wenn wir schon der Menschen Zeugnis annehmen, so ist doch Gottes Zeugnis größer. Dies aber ist das Zeugnis Gottes, das größer ist: das Zeugnis, das Er abgelegt hat für seinen Sohn. Wer an den Sohn Gottes glaubt, der hat das Zeugnis Gottes in sich.

Allelujalieder

In der österlichen Zeit fällt das Stufenlied weg; es warden statt dessen zwei Allelujalieder gebetet. Das zweite Allelujalied bereitet heute auf das Evangelium vor.

Alleluja, alleluja. **V** (Matth. 28,7) Es spricht der Herr: „Am Tage Meiner Auferstehung geh Ich euch voraus nach Galiläa". Alleluja. **V** (Joh. 20,26) Acht Tage danach trat Jesus bei verschlossenen Türen in die Mitte Seiner Jünger und sprach „Friede sei mit euch". Alleluja.

(Offertorium) (Matth. 28,25 u. 6) Opferungslied

(Matth. 28,25 u. 6). Ein Engel des Herrn stieg vom Himmel und sprach zu den Frauen: „Er, den ihr suchet, ist auferstanden, wie Er gesagt hat" alleluja.

Stillgebet

Wir bitten Dich, o Herr, nimm an die Gaben der frohlockenden Kirche, und wie Du ihr den Anlaß zu solchem Jubel gewährest, so schenke ihr als Frucht die ewige Freude. Durch unsern Herrn.

Präfation von Ostern (in hoc potissimum–ganz vornehmlich aber zu dieser Zeit) S. 42 f.

Communio (Joh. 20,27) Kommunionlied

„Reiche deine Hand her und erkenne die Male der Nägel", alleluja „und sei nicht ungläubig, sondern gläubig", alleluja, alleluja.

Schlußgebet

Herr, unser Gott, wir bitten Dich: die hochheiligen Geheimnisse, die du uns übergabest, um unsre Erlösung zu sichern, laß uns Heilmittel sein für jetzt und später. Durch unsern Herrn.

Nota Bene

This edition has kindly been made available by Pfr. Michael Bauer, incumbent of the Catholic church St. Margareta in Schönberg. His sense is that the 1936 edition is among the most likely to have been on hand at the time of the service in 1945.

Jahrgang: 1940

Druck und Bindung

Imprimi permittitur Beuronae, in Nativitate D.N.J. Chr. 1940 + Benedictus, Archiabbas. Imprimatur, Friburgi Brisgoviae, die 31 Decembris 1940, Rösch, Vic. Gen.

Auflage

Freiburg im Breisgau 1941, Schott 2 48. Auflage

Vorwort

Weißer Sonntag (Dominica in Albis)
(Octav von Ostern)
Dupl. maj.—Farbe weiß
Stationskirche: St. Pankratius
Der heutige Tag führt den Namen Dominica in albis (depositis bzw. Depondendis): „Sonntag der (abgelegten oder abzulegenden) weißen Gewänder".

Die weißen Taufkleider, die seit Karsamstag von den Täuflingen getragen wurden, wurden am gestrigen (in manchen Kirchen am heutigen) Tage wieder abgelegt „jedoch so, daß das schimmernde Weiß, das mit dem Kleide abgelegt wird, im Herzen bewahrt werde" (hl. Augustinus), Quasi modo geniti wird der Sonntag von den Eingangsworten des Introitus genannt.

Der weiße Sonntag ist der Oktavtag des Osterfestes. Evangelium und Zwischengesänge beziehen sich auf Ostern und seine Oktav; das Offertorium ist das des Ostermontages.

Den hl. Pankratius ehrte man in Rom als einen Martyrer, der schon mit vierzehn Jahren seinen Glauben und Taufschwur mit dem eigenen Blute besiegelte. Schon in den Zeiten Gregors d. Gr. († 604) galt Pankratius als heiliger Hüter der Eidestreue. Die Neugetauften stellen heute das Gelöbnis, Christus anzugehören, unter seinen Schutz und verpflichten sich feierlich zur unwandelbaren Treue gegen Christus und sein Gebot. Wir kommen zur Feier der heiligen Messe im seligen Hochgefühle, zu dem uns die Taufe berechtigt, und verlangen nach der Milch der heiligen Eucharistie (Intr.). Mit dem hl. Pankratius sind wir entschlossen, im Glauben an Christus und in der Einheit („Friede") mit ihm die Welt zu überwinden (Lesung, Evang.)—Im Opfer der heiligen Messe wird Christus, der von den Toten Auferstandene, auch unter uns erscheinen. „Selig, die nicht sehen, dafür auch glauben" (Evang.). In der heiligen Kommunion „reichen wir die Hand" hin (in früheren Zeiten wurde der Leib Christi den Gläubigen in die Hand gelegt) und glauben (Comm.).

Eingang / Eingangslied / Introitus (1 Peter 2,2)

Wie neugeborene Kindlein, alleluja, doch schon voll Einsicht, verlangt ohne Falsch nach Milch, alleluja, alleluja, alleluja. (Ps 80,2) Gott, unserem Helfer, jauchzet zu, jubelt entgegen dem Gotte Jakobs. **V** Ehre sei.

Gebet/Kirchengebet

Wir bitten dich, allmächtiger Gott, laß uns, die wir nunmehr am Ende der Osterfeier stehen, diese mit Deiner Gnade in Benehmen und Lebenswandel beibehalten. Durch unseren Herrn.

Epistel/Lesung

Aus dem Briefe des heiligen Apostels Johannes (1 Joh. 5,4–10). Geliebte! Alles, was aus Gott geboren ist, überwindet die Welt; und das ist der Sieg, der die Welt überwindet: unser Glaube.[10] Wer ist es, der die Welt überwindet, wenn nicht der, welcher glaubt, daß Jesus der Sohn Gottes ist? Dieser ist es, Jesus

Christus, der durch Wasser und Blut[11] gekommen ist, nicht in Wasser allein, sondern im Wasser und im Blut. Auch der Heilige Geist bezeugt, daß Christus die Wahrheit ist. Denn drei sind, die Zeugnis geben [von der Gottheit Christi] im Himmel: der Vater, das Wort und der Heilige Geist, und diese drei sind eins [Im Zeugnis]. Und drei sind, die Zeugnis geben auf Erden: der Geist, das Wasser und das Blut, und diese drei sind eins. Wenn wir schon der Menschen Zeugnis annehmen, so ist doch Gottes Zeugnis größer. Dies aber ist das Zeugnis Gottes, das größer ist: das Zeugnis, das Er abgelegt hat für seinen Sohn. Wer an den Sohn Gottes glaubt, der hat das Zeugnis Gottes in sich.

Allelujalieder

Alleluja, alleluja. **V** (Matth. 28,7) Es spricht der Herr: „Im Tage Meiner Auferstehung geh Ich euch voraus nach Galiläa". Alleluja. **V** (Joh. 20,26) Acht Tage danach trat Jesus bei verschlossenen Türen in die Mitte Seiner Jünger und sprach „Friede sei mit euch". Allel.

(Offertorium) (Matth. 28,25 u. 6) Opferungslied

Ein Engel des Herrn stieg vom Himmel und sprach zu den Frauen: „Er, den ihr suchet, ist auferstanden, wie er gesagt hat" alleluja.

Stillgebet

Wir bitten dich, o Herr, nimm an die Gaben der frohlockenden Kirche: und wie Du ihr den Anlaß zu solchem Jubel gewährtest, so schenke ihr als Frucht die ewige Freude. Durch unseren Herrn.

Präfation von Ostern (in hoc potissimum–vornehmlich aber zu dieser Zeit), S. 428 f.

Communio (Joh. 20,27) Kommunionlied

„Reiche deine Hand her und erkenne die Male der Nägel", alleluja „und sei nicht ungläubig, sondern gläubig!", alleluja, alleluja.

Schlußgebet

Herr, unser Gott, wir bitten Dich: die hochheiligen Geheimnisse, die du uns übergabest, um unsere Erlösung zu sichern, laß uns Heilmittel sein für jetzt und später. Durch unsern Herrn.

Nota Bene

In this edition, purchased online, the previous owner has left a slip marking the date of her first Holy Communion received on "Weißen Sonntag" April 25, 1954. (The time lapse between printing date and First Communion is hence fourteen years.)

APPENDIX 5

Bonhoeffer's Ordination Vows

Agende
für die
Evangelische Landeskirche.
Zweiter Teil.
Kirchliche Handlungen
Berlin 1895
Ernst Siegfried Mittler und Sohn
Königliche Hofbuchhandlung und Hofbuchdruckerei
Kochstraße 68–70
Ordination

Die Ordination kann entweder als selbstständige kirchliche Handlung vollzogen oder dem Hauptgottesdienst angeschlossen oder in denselben eingefügt werden. Sie wird vorher der Gemeinde unter Fürbitte für die Ordinanden bekannt gemacht (siehe Teil 1, S. 8, Fürbitte 4 und S. 78, Gebet 74).

Gemeinde*): „Komm Heiliger Geist" oder ein ähnliches Lied.

Ordinator: Im Namen des Vaters und des Sohnes und des Heiligen Geistes.

Wie lieblich sind auf den Bergen die Füße der Boten, die da Frieden verkünden, gutes predigen, Heil verkündigen, die da sagen zu Zion: dein Gott ist König.

Lasset uns vor dem Herrn unsere Sünden bekennen und miteinander also sprechen:

Gott, sei mir gnädig nach Deiner Güte, tilge meine Sünden nach Deiner großen Barmherzigkeit. Wasche mich wohl von meiner Missethat, und reinige mich von meiner Sünde.

Schaffe in mir, Gott, ein reines Herz, und gieb mir einen neuen gewissen Geist. Verwirf mich nicht von Deinem Angesicht, und nimm Deinen heiligen Geist nicht von mir.

Tröste mich wieder mit deiner Hülfe, und mit einem freudigen Geist rüste mich aus. Denn ich will die Übertreter Deine Wege lehren, dass sich die Sünder zu Dir bekehren. Amen.

[*Gemeinde*: Herr erbarme dich unser, u.s.w.]

*) *Der Eingang bis zum Glaubensbekenntnis fällt weg, wenn die Ordination in den Hauptgottesdienst eingefügt wird. Die Handlung verläuft dann bis dahin nach dem Formular für den Hauptgottesdienst. Für den Vortrag des Glaubensbekenntnisses bleibt auch in diesem Falle die Anordnung auf der folgenden Seite 10 in Kraft.*

Ordinator: Also hat Gott die Welt geliebt, dass Er Seinen Eingeborenen Sohn gab, auf daß alle, die an ihn glauben, nicht verloren werden, sondern das ewige Leben haben.

oder:

So man von Herzen glaubt, so wird man gerecht, und so man mit dem Munde bekennt, so wird man selig.

oder eine andere Gnadenverkündigung.

Lasset uns nun in Einmütigkeit des Glaubens mit der gesamten Christenheit also bekennen:

Ordinator und *Ordinanden*, oder einer der *Ordinanden* im Namen aller:

Das apostolische Glaubensbekenntnis

Ordinator: Lasset uns beten: Allmächtiger, gütiger Gott und Vater, der du deinen lieben Sohn uns befohlen hast, daß wir Dich bitten sollen, Arbeiter in Deine Ernte zu senden, wir bitten Dich von Herzen, Du wolltest allen, die Du zu Arbeitern in Deine Ernte berufen hast, Deinen heiligen Geist reichlich verleihen, und sonderlich diesen Deinen Dienern, die zum Predigtamt bestätigt werden sollen, Dein Wort in Herz und Mund legen, daß sie es mit aller Freundlichkeit und Beständigkeit verkünden, auch ihr Amt durch einen gottseligen Wandel zieren, damit eine heilige christliche Gemeinde dadurch erhalten und erbaute werde, durch Jesum Christum. Amen.

Ansprache.

(Hier erfolgt die Verlesung der Namen der *Ordinanden*, wobei auch der Dienst, zu dem sie berufen sind, genannt wird.)

Ordinator: Dieweil ihr nun berufen seid zu dem heiligen Predigt- und Hirtenamt, und bereit, dasselbe anzutreten, so höret an mit Aufmerksamkeit und bewahret in eurem Herzen, was Gottes Wort von diesem Amt und seiner Einsetzung, seinem Segen und seinen Aufgaben sagt:

(die assistiernden Geistlichen lesen abwechselnd vier der nachfolgenden Bibelstellen:)

Matth, 28, 18–20; 1. Tim. 3, 1–7; Joh. 10, 12–15; Apostelgesch. 20, 28–32; Hesek. 3, 17–19; Joh. 21, 15–17; 2. Tim. 2, 8–13; Luc. 12, 42–48; 2. Tim. 2, 1–7 (24,25); Luc 5, 1–11; 2. Tim 4, 1–5; Joh. 15, 13–16; Joh. 20, 21–23; Tit. 1, 7–9.

Ordinator: Geliebte Brüder, aus Gotteswort habt ihr vernommen, daß es wohl ein köstliches, von dem Herrn gebotenes und seine Segens gewisses Werk ist, das ihr begehret, aber daß es auch heilige Pflichten auferlegt denen, die es übernehmen. Es wird euch demnach folgendes vorgehalten:

1. Ihr werdet berufen, die Gemeinde Jesu Christi, die Er durch Sein eigenes Blut erworben hat, mit dem reinen Worte Gottes zu weiden, die heiligen Sakramente nach der Einsetzung Jesu Christi zu spenden, dass Heil der euch anvertrauten Seelen durch Treue Vermahnung mit anhaltendem Gebet zu suchen, die Jugend mit allem Fleiß in der heilsamen Lehre zu unterweisen, die Schwachen zu stärken, den Verirrten nachzugehen und keine Seele verloren zu geben, die Betrübten zu trösten, die Kranken zu besuchen und die Sterbenden zu einem christlichen Ende zu bereiten.

2. Dabei sollt ihr ernstlich beachten, daß es dem evangelischen Prediger nicht zusteht, eine andere Lehre zu verkündigen und auszubreiten als die, welche gegründet ist in Gottes lauterem und klarem Worte, verfaßt in der Heiligen Schrift Alten und Neuen Testaments, unserer alleinigen Glaubensnorm, und bezeugt in den drei christlichen Hauptsymbolen, dem Apostolischen, Nicänischen und Athanasianischen, und in den Bekenntnisschriften unserer Kirche (hier werden wie herkömmlich die symbolischen Schriften genannt).

3. Euer Amt habt ihr dem Worte Gottes gemäß nach den Vorschriften der Kirchenordnung und der in der Kirche bestehenden Ordnung des Gottesdienstes auszurichten, und wie ihr selbst als Christen verpflichtet seid, aller menschlichen Ordnung unterthan zu sein, für alle Menschen, für den König und die Obrigkeit zu beten, so habt ihr auch die euch anvertraute Gemeinde zum Wandel in Zucht und Frieden, zur brüderlichen und allgemeinen Liebe, zum Gebet für alle Menschen anzuleiten.

4. Endlich sollte ihr unablässig darnach trachten, immer tiefer in das Verständnis des Wortes einzudringen, durch einen geistlichen, Gott wohlgefälligen Wandel der Gemeinde in allem guten vorzuleuchten, euch und euer Haus in allen Stücken unanstößig zu bewahren und euch nicht mit Dingen zu befassen, die nicht eures Amtes sind. In Summa, wir ermahnen euch vor Gott, die Kräfte eurer Seele und eures Leibes diesem heiligen Amte aufzuopfern und euer ganzes Leben also einzurichten, wie ihr euch getrauen dürft, es dermaleinst vor dem Richtstuhl Jesu Christi zu verantworten.

Seid ihr nun entschlossen, dies alles zu geloben, und willigt ihr ein, über euch zu nehmen das teure Predigtamt, so antwortet: Ja.

Die *Ordinanden* (antworten jeder einzeln): Ja, ich will es mit Gottes Hülfe.

Ordinator: Der Herr stärke und helfe euch, gewissenhaft zu erfüllen, was ihr vor dem Angesicht Gottes und in Gegenwart dieser Zeugen gelobt habt.

(Der *Ordinator* legt mit den Assistenten den *Ordinanden*, welche niederknien, die Hände auf und spricht:)

Das Gebet des Herrn.

Dieweil wir nun allhier, im heiligen Geiste versammelt, Gott durch unseren Herrn Jesum Christum angerufen haben und nicht zweifeln, daß unser Gebet erhört ist, so übertrage ich euch kraft des mir gewordenen Auftrages das evangelische Predigtamt im Namen des Vaters und des Sohnes und des Heiligen Geistes (+). Amen.

Der Herr segne euch, daß ihr viel Frucht schaffet, und diese Frucht bleibe ewiglich.

(Folgen die Vota der Assistenten unter Handauflegung.)

Ordinator: Lasset uns beten: Barmherziger Gott, himmlischer Vater, wir danken Dir, daß Du das Flehen der Deinen um Sendung von Arbeitern in Deine Ernte nicht unerhört läßt, und befehlen nun auch diese, welche Du wiederum gesendet hast, Deiner Gnade, daß sie als rechte Arbeiter Dir dienen, den Samen, den Du in ihre Hand gelegt hast, ausstreuen, und Dir eine reiche Ernte einbringen helfen für Deine himmlischen Scheuern. Dazu wollest Du sie ausrüsten mit allem Vermögen Deines Geistes, daß sie unter den Versuchungen treu und fest bleiben, damit Dein Name geheiligt, Dein Reich gemehrt, Dein Wille vollbracht werde. Solch unser Gebet wollest Du gnädiglich nach deiner Verheißung erhören, wie wir glauben und trauern durch Deinen lieben Sohn, unseren Herrn Jesum Christum, der mit Dir und dem heiligen Geist lebet und herrschet in Ewigkeit. Amen.

So gehet nun hin und weidet die Herde Christi, so euch befohlen ist, und sehet wohl zu, nicht gezwungen, sondern williglich; nicht um schändlichen Gewinns willen, sondern von Herzensgrund; nicht als die übers Volk herrschen, sondern werdet Vorbilder der Herde. So werdet ihr, wenn erscheinen wird der Erzhirte, die unverwelkliche Krone der Ehren empfangen.

*) [Abendmahls Feier]

Segen

*) Wird die Ordination in den Hauptgottesdienst eingefügt, so tritt vor die Abendmahlsfeier Lied und Predigt.

APPENDIX 6

Losungen Readings for the Period April 1–8, 1945

April 1, 1945 (Sunday)

OT *Losung*: Show me your ways, Lord, teach me your paths.
Reference: Psalm 25:4

NT passage: Christ is risen indeed! Allelujah!
Reference: Luke 24:34

April 2, 1945 (Monday)

OT *Losung*: O Lord God, come to my aid, then shall I never be put to shame.
Reference: Isaiah 50:7

NT passage: I live! And so also shall you live.
Reference: John 14:19

April 3, 1945 (Tuesday)

OT *Losung*: Of all God's people, my servant Moses is faithful.
Reference: Numbers 12:7

NT passage: Anyone who competes as an athlete does not receive the victor's crown except by competing according to the rules.
Reference: 2 Timothy 2:5

April 4, 1945 (Wednesday)

OT *Losung*: With all my heart I will give thanks to you: I will sing praise to your name, O Most High.
Reference: Psalm 9:2

NT passage: We see Jesus now crowned with glory and honour because he suffered death.
Reference: Hebrews 2:9

April 5, 1945 (Thursday)

OT *Losung*:	The sun will no more be your light by day, nor will the brightness of the moon shine upon you, for the Lord shall be your everlasting light.
Reference:	Isaiah 60:20
NT passage:	The city does not need the sun or the moon to shine upon it, for the glory of God gives it light, and the lamb is its lamp.
Reference:	Revelation 21:23

April 6, 1945 (Friday)

OT *Losung*:	Multitudes who sleep in the dust of the earth will awaken, some to everlasting life, others to shame and everlasting contempt.
Reference:	Daniel 12:2
NT passage:	For if we have been united with him in a death like his, we will also certainly be united with him in a resurrection like his.
Reference:	Romans 6:5

April 7, 1945 (Saturday)

OT *Losung*:	But the Lord did not set his affection on you or choose you because you were more numerous than other peoples: for you were the fewest of all peoples: but rather, because the Lord loved you.
Reference:	Deuteronomy 7:7–8
NT passage:	For those God foreknew, he also predestined to be conformed to the image of his son, that he might be the firstborn among many brothers and sisters.
Reference:	Romans 8:29

April 8, 1945 (Sunday)

OT *Losung*:	By his wounds we are healed.
Reference:	Isaiah 53:5
NT passage:	Praise be to the God and Father of our Lord Jesus Christ! In his great mercy he has given us new birth into a living hope through the resurrection of Jesus Christ from the dead.
Reference:	1 Peter 1:3

APPENDIX 7

Notes on Passages for April 8, 1945

Bonhoeffer on Isaiah 53:5 and Isaiah 53

Text/date: 1928
Ref.: DBW 9:575
DB comments/notes/other

In a sermon preached in Barcelona, Bonhoeffer comments in an address on John 19 (on the crucifixion): "Soon Jesus has also reached his destination. An old man passes by on his way to the city. Recognising Jesus, he trembles, and calls out, 'God is with you.' Softly he whispers the words of the prophet: **'He was wounded for our transgressions, crushed for our iniquities: upon him was the punishment that made us whole.'** Jesus' eyes light up. The man was one of those whom Jesus had healed and who had followed Jesus devotedly from that time. A blow from the soldier threw him aside."

Text/date: 1935
Ref.: DBW 4:229
DB comments/notes/other

In *Discipleship* Bonhoeffer writes, "Only by bearing all our infirmities and sorrows in his own body was Jesus able to heal the infirmities and sorrows of human nature. **'He was wounded for our transgressions and crushed for our iniquities.'** He bore our sins and was therefore able to forgive sin: for in his own body our sinful flesh has been 'accepted.' This is why Jesus accepted sinners (Luke 15:2): he bore them in his own body. In Jesus the 'acceptable' year of the Lord had dawned."

Text/date: Bonhoeffer's sermon outline on Isaiah 53 (student notes before July 11, 1935)

Ref.: DBW 14:340–42

DB comments/notes/other

In a sermon outline/lecture on **Isaiah 53**, Bonhoeffer teaches:
"1. Here the OT at its limits. Glimmers of the NT visible. Before unnerving riddle of unnerving prophecy. Here in the middle of the night prophet already awake. Stretches out his hand and points exactly in the direction where the sun will rise. Mystery[ies] disclosed to him that still hidden to others. Which absolutely demands faith. About future salvation, about peace with God. About the vicarious represent[ative] suffering of a nameless one. But who believes the voice of the prophet—to whom is the promise [,] the arm of the Lord [revealed]? Who will believe that redemption is through the vicarious representative suffering of a nameless one?

2. Who is that one? He? Individual, God's people? (Professors) The professors [have] discovered something quite nice: perhaps he is both [:] the individual and the entire people (Adam individual and entire people/entire human race at the same time?) A new Adam? Whether not a good reason that he has no name? He doubtless knew that he would come, had already come. Sees him already as one who has come. But the name that is above all names still remains hidden. But the prophet knows enough about him.

3. From a barren region. Poverty . . . All human form and joy count for nothing; judgement and standards turn him out. Despised so that [people] hid faces. Remains alone. That is who he is. From whom one demands faith. Who believes?

4. What does this picture mean? Be frightened and know: he is your true image. That is us. Everything is heaped upon him, hence so terrible. Faith sees that he is the one who is struck down for us, our punishment, in the place where we ought to suffer. Stands where I and humanity ought to stand. So he is both after all? World order shattered (order: every person advocates for him/herself before God: each one saw his path, that is the order of unbelief) he shatters this law and bears the punishment and judgement of others. This is why none of the laws are valid any longer: noble, rich [,] beauty, honour. That must collapse. Because he no longer seeks to stand for himself, because he suspends this law of the world, we have peace. Only through him, as the most despised of all. If he had not borne everything, we would be in damnation.

5. He offers no explanation, no interpretation; otherwise it would not be proper suffering; that is why it requires faith. Interpretive suffering is already no longer suffering. [Faith] sees the mute one and sees the saviour.

6. Taken through such suffering out of anxiety and judgement (before death) verse 8: Get[h]semane. He lives in eternity. He dies innocent. God's path. God struck him down. Ends such that God tears the servant out of the land of the living. The dead one lives through his sin offering.

7. That now means life for all human beings. Through vicarious representative law he will have those who belong to him. Church-community. God's action always only through his hand. Vicarious representative action now applies to his entire community. Be righteous also through him. Whoever respects the despised one will be righteous through him, will be drawn into the new law of life.

8. The despised one rules among his enemies. [They] must bow. Evil-doers must be his because he prayed for them. Precisely as the most despised of all, he becomes the Lord.

9. Who is the Unnamed? Answer is given. Answer is there: in the New Covenant, [in] Christ as the Crucified, as the anticipated messiah. For whom Israel waits. [Who] already established community in Israel and established community among us. [Who] rules in the midst of his enemies and prays for them.

But today as well: Who believes and to whom [is] the arm of the Lord revealed precisely here?"

Text/date: Lecture on pastoral care at Finkenwalde (March 12, 1936)

Ref.: DBW 14:580

DB comments/notes/other

Pastoral care for the sick and dying.

1. Visitations among the sick should be conducted *regularly*. 1. For the sake of the sick person . . . 2. For the sake of the pastor him/herself. Let the pastor visit the sick often. *See for oneself*: sickness is nothing abnormal in our world, belongs together with being healthy. Sickness and pain are one of the laws of this fallen, sinful world. The person who is plagued by pain or disgusting illness experiences and suffers the world in a special way, resembling the one who bore all our sicknesses and was so despised that people turned their eyes from him. Matt 8:17, cf **Isa. 53[:4]**! This passage quoted precisely in the case of the healing of the sick! Among the sick, we are closer to Jesus' own sufferings on the cross than we are [among] the healthy, here

we recognise the world better. *Spending time with the sick is the proper way for the pastor to spend time.*

Text/date: Letter to Rüdiger Schleicher (April 8, 1936)
Ref.: DBW 14:145–46
DB comments/notes/other

Either I determine the place where I want to find God, or I let him determine where he is to be found. If it is I who says where God is to be found, then I will always find a God who is commensurate with my own nature. But if it is God who says where he is to be found, then it will probably be a place that is not at all commensurate with my own nature and that does not please me at all. This place, however, is the cross of Jesus. And those who want to find God there must live beneath that cross just as the Sermon on the Mount demands. Doing so, however, is wholly incommensurate with our nature; indeed, is wholly contrary to it. Precisely this however is the message of the Bible, not only in the New but also in the Old Testament (**Isa. 53!**). In any event, both Jesus and Paul intended it thus: the cross of Jesus fulfils Scripture, that is, the Old Testament. Hence the entire Bible claims to be this word in which God wants us to find him. It is not at all a place that we find pleasant or that might be clear a priori [from the outset] but a place alien to us in every way, a place utterly repugnant to us. But that is the very place where God chose to encounter us.

Text/date: Outline for a lecture on Confirmation instruction (October 20, 1936)
Ref.: DBW 14:808
DB comments/notes/other

What does Scripture say about the suffering and death of Jesus Christ? Jesus' entire life was suffering (hatred, persecution, privation). In this suffering, Jesus bore and suffered God's curse on our sin. Mark 15:34.

Jesus was crucified by the "righteous" and by the worldly authorities of his age.

In his suffering, Jesus perfectly fulfilled the will of God and perfectly bore the wrath of judgement on our sin.

Jesus Christ thereby satisfied the holiness and righteousness of God and redeemed us from the wrath of God.

Jesus dies as the messiah of Israel promised by Scripture—1 Cor. 15:2.

Isa. 53. With Jesus, our flesh is given over to death, and we are crucified and have died to the world. [-] Gal. 6:14.

Thus are our sins forgiven in the death of Jesus.

We belong no longer to the world but to Jesus.

In Jesus, it was actually God who acted, God who fulfilled the law, God who suffered death; God reconciled us to him, God himself demonstrated his righteousness insofar as he alone is righteous. [-] 2 Cor. 5:20–21. Rom. 3:23ff.

Text/date: 1936–1937

Ref.: DBW 5:85

DB comments/notes/other

It is remarkable that the Scriptures talk so often about "forebearance." They are capable of expressing the whole work of Jesus Christ in this one word. **"Surely he has borne our infirmities and carried our diseases . . . upon him was the punishment that made us whole" (Isaiah 53).** Therefore the Bible can characterise the whole life of the Christian as carrying the cross. It is the community of the body of Christ that is here realised, the community of the cross in which one must experience the burden of the other.

Text/date: December 15, 1943

Ref.: DBW 8:232

DB comments/notes/other

In a letter to Eberhard Bethge, Bonhoeffer writes, "Ever since your sermon on **Isaiah 53** I have been very fond of your language."

Text/date: July 16, 1944

Ref.: DBW 8:533–34

DB comments/notes/other

Days before the failure of the plot, Bonhoeffer writes to Bethge, "We cannot be honest unless we recognise that we have to live in the world—'etsi deus non daretur.' And this is precisely what we do recognise—before God! God himself compels us to recognise it. Thus our coming of age leads us to a truer recognition of our situation before God. God would have us know that we must live as those who manage their lives without God. The same God who is with us is the God who forsakes us (Mark 15:34!). (At three o'clock Jesus cried out in a loud voice, 'Eloi, Eloi, lama sabachthani? Which means "My God, my God, why have you forsaken me?"' Martin Luther in WA 5:602, 25–28 notes that [Jesus] yet names God and thereby confesses that he is not deserted. For no one says to God 'My God' who has been utterly deserted.) The same God who makes us to live in the world without the working hypothesis of God is the God before whom we stand continually.

Before God, and with God, we live without God. God consents to be pushed out of the world and on to the cross; God is weak and powerless in the world and in precisely this way, and only so, is at our side and helps us. Matt. 8:17 (which refers to **Isa. 53**) makes it quite clear that Christ helps us not by virtue of his omnipotence but rather by virtue of his weakness and suffering! Human religiosity direct people in need to the power of God in the world, god as deus ex machina. The Bible directs people towards the powerlessness and the suffering of God; only the suffering God can help."

Text/date: July 18, 1944
Ref.: DBW 8:535
DB comments/notes/other

In continuation of an almost final letter to Bethge, Bonhoeffer writes, "It is not a religious act that makes someone a Christian but rather sharing in God's suffering in everyday life. That is *metanoia*, not thinking first about one's own needs, questions, sins and fears but allowing oneself to be pulled into the path that Jesus walks, into the messianic event, in which **Isaiah 53**[1] **is now** being fulfilled! [Editor's note: 'now' is a later insertion.][2] Hence 'believe in the good news' and in John, the reference to the 'Lamb of God who takes away the sin of the world' (the Luther Bible refers the reader to **Isa. 53**). (By the way, J. Jeremias asserted recently that 'lamb' in Aramaic can also be translated as 'servant.' That's really fine, in view of **Isa. 53**!) This being pulled along into the—messianic—suffering of God in Jesus Christ happens in the NT in various ways: when the disciples are called to follow him, in table fellowship with sinners (Cf. Matt. 9:11b), through 'conversions' in the narrower sense of the word (Zaccheus, Luke 19:1–8), through the actions of the woman 'who was a sinner' (done without any confession of sin taking place) in Luke 7, through the healing of the sick (see above Matt 8:17 [author's note: which refers to **Isa. 53**]), through receiving the children (Mark 10:14–16). The shepherds stand [at] the manger just as do the wise men from the East, not as 'converted sinners' but simply because they are drawn to the manger (by the star (Matt 2:1–12)) just as they are. The centurion at Capernaum, who makes no confession of sin at all, is held up as an example of faith (Matt 8:5–13, Luke 7:1–10) (cf. Jairus, Matt 9:18–19, 23–26, Mark 5:22–24, 35–43, Luke 8:41–42, 49–56). The rich young man is 'loved by Jesus' (Mark 10:21: * in Bonhoeffer's Luther Bible, 'Jesus, looking at him, loved him,' is underlined in pencil). The courtier in Acts 8 (Acts 8:26–40), Cornelius (Acts 10), are anything but persons in desperate straits. Nathanael is 'An Israelite in whom there is no deceit' (John 1:47) and finally there are Joseph of Aramathea (Mark 15:42–46 et passim) and the women at the tomb (Matt 27:61; Mark 15:47; 16:1; Luke 23:55–56). The one thing they all have in common is their sharing in the suffering of God in Christ. That is their 'faith.' There is nothing about a religious method; the 'religious act' is always something partial, whereas faith is something whole and involves one's whole life. Jesus calls not to new religion but to life. But what is this life like? This life of participating in God's powerlessness in the world? I'll write about this next time, I hope."

Text/date: 2010

Ref.: DBW 8:653

DB comments/notes/other

In the editors' afterword, Christian Gremmels writes, "This reversal of a religious disposition into a non-religious and thus genuinely Christian attitude characterises . . . also a whole series of additional 'reversals' expressing the notion of *metanoia* as theologically engaged penitence: the person who follows the call to penitence allows himself or herself to be pulled into the path that Jesus walks, into the messianic event, in which **Isaiah 53** is now being fulfilled."

Bonhoeffer on 1 John 5:4–10

[4]for everyone born of God overcomes the world. This is the victory that has overcome the world, even our faith. [5]Who is it that overcomes the world? Only the one who believes that Jesus is the Son of God.

[6]This is the one who came by water and blood—Jesus Christ. He did not come by water only, but by water and blood. And it is the Spirit who testifies, because the Spirit is the truth. [7]For there are three that testify: [8]the Spirit, the water and the blood; and the three are in agreement. [9]We accept human testimony, but God's testimony is greater because it is the testimony of God, which he has given about his Son. [10]Whoever believes in the Son of God accepts this testimony. Whoever does not believe God has made him out to be a liar, because they have not believed the testimony God has given about his Son.

Text/date: January 17, 1928

Ref.: DBW 17:67

DB comments/notes/other

Dietrich's examination paper on the New Testament concept of baptism, which received a "Very Good" mark, includes the following lines: "John describes baptism in conjunction with communion as founded on the death of Christ. (Ref. John 19:34,35) He names baptism, the Holy Spirit, and Holy Communion as constitutive elements of Christianity." There follows a technical discussion on the differences in meaning obtaining from the different possible placings of the comma in the Greek text of 1 John 5:6, whether the *Zäsur* (split) to the next sentence comes before or after the phrase "and the Holy Spirit."

Text/date: 1934

Ref.: DBW 13:404

DB comments/notes/other

In closing a sermon in London, Bonhoeffer concludes, "You will overcome the world."

Text/date: Circa November 6, 1935

Ref.: DBW 14:473

DB comments/notes/other

In a Bible class, Bonhoeffer's students noted, "We are witnesses to these things," and as a Trinitarian passage, 1 John 5:7 is included.

Text/date: Circa December 6, 1935

Ref.: DBW 14:468

DB comments/notes/other

In a Bible study class, Bonhoeffer's notes on the Holy Spirit include "The Holy Spirit as Person," with "Paraclete" as a subheading, then adducing Acts 15:28. The fifth reference following is to 1 John 5:7.

Text/date: Circa April 1937

Ref.: DBW 14:527

DB comments/notes/other

In a homiletics lecture, Bonhoeffer adduces many Bible passages under the heading "The Witness." Bonhoeffer states, "Witnessing means a. testifying to what I myself have seen; b. testifying in court, speaking in a binding fashion. 1. I do not make myself into a witness. I am made an eye witness and summoned by others to testify. As it pleased God to make the apostles into witnesses." In the section where his student notes, "Apostles are witnesses insofar and because God is the first witness," 1 John 5:9 is on the list.

Text/date: Circa April 1937

Ref.: DBW 14:527

DB comments/notes/other

In the same lecture, introducing the phrase "God testifies to what is true and comes before the court of human beings" is the verse 1 John 5:6.

Text/date: June 20–25, 1938

Ref.: DBW 15:49

DB comments/notes/other

The "Communion and Meditation" text notes, "And this is the victory that conquers the world, our faith. We are not victorious, but we are allowed to participate in the victory of Christ, who has conquered all that causes us such crisis and anxiety."

Bonhoeffer on John 20:19–31—An Edited Summary (Unfinished)

Jesus Appears to His Disciples

[19]On the evening of that first day of the week, when the disciples were together, with the doors locked for fear of the Jewish leaders, **Jesus came and stood among them and said, "Peace be with you!"** [20]After he said this, he showed them his hands and side. The disciples were **overjoyed** when they saw the Lord.

[21]Again Jesus said, "Peace be with you! As the Father has sent me, I am sending you." [22]And with that he breathed on them and said, "Receive the Holy Spirit. [23]If you forgive anyone's sins, their sins are forgiven; if you do not forgive them, they are not forgiven."

[24]Now Thomas (also known as Didymus), one of the Twelve, was not with the disciples when Jesus came. [25]So the other disciples told him, "We have seen the Lord!"

But he said to them, "Unless I see the nail marks in his hands and put my finger where the nails were, and put my hand into his side, I will not believe."

[26]A week later his disciples were in the house again, and Thomas was with them. Though the doors were locked, Jesus came and stood among them and said, "Peace be with you!" [27]Then he said to Thomas, "Put your finger here; see my hands. Reach out your hand and put it into my side. Stop doubting and believe."

[28]Thomas said to him, "My Lord and my God!"

[29]Then Jesus told him, "Because you have seen me, you have believed; blessed are those who have not seen and yet have believed."

[30]Jesus performed many other signs in the presence of his disciples, which are not recorded in this book. [31]But these are written that you may believe that Jesus is the Messiah, the Son of God, and that by believing you may have life in his name.

Text/date: 1927

Ref.: DBW 1:97

DB comments/notes/other

And, after the resurrection, Christ himself restores both forms of community that had been broken: with Peter through Christ's appearance to him as presumably the first to whom this was granted (1 Cor. 15:5), perhaps with an express conferral of office (John 21:55f); and after that with the Twelve through an appearance in their midst (1 Cor. 15:5; John 20:19).

Text/date: August 8, 1936

Ref.: DBW 14:220

DB comments/notes/other

In a pastoral letter to Bethge, Bonhoeffer comments on the power of the word of God to "pass through closed doors." He writes, "A word about your visitations to the sick. I, too, always found it difficult with those with cancer. They are often quite bitter and despairing. But your place is to bring the word of God in both good and bad times. Hence do so cheerfully and confidently. Just like the Lord, it [God's word] can also pass through closed doors."

Text/date: Set meditation on "joy" (Philippians 14:1-9; December 11–17, 1938)

Ref.: DBW 15:346

DB comments/notes/other

A set of student notes on the concept of joy:

"Χαρά. Bonhoeffer states:

1. Joy is the most prominent word on Jesus' birth, his early life, resurrection, ascension. [A list of Bible passages follows, concluding with **John 20:20**.]

2. Joy not only among human beings."

Text/date: Prepared January 24, 1940, for April 22, 1940
Ref.: DBW 15:555
DB comments/notes/other

Sermon meditations on John 20:19–31 for Quasimodogeniti Sunday.

1. Verses 19–20. The miracle happened at morning. In the evening, the disciples are together. And, as night falls, when the shadows of unrest want to cover the disciples, when in the light of the new situation they carefully close the doors to be safe from the agitated Jews, not considering they might close the door to the Lord, "Jesus came and stood among them." Strange that in the hour we most hope for Jesus' presence, we always seem to close the door out of fear of all kinds of other things. But far more miraculous that Jesus does not let himself be hindered by those locked doors. On his way to the people, the Resurrected One does not let himself be stopped by human beings. His new body does not hinder or limit him anymore, as our body does, but Jesus' body has now become the consummate tool of his spirit. The Resurrected One steps among his fearful disciples. He speaks: "Peace be with you." Certainly this used to be the common greeting and an appropriate greeting, for it contains everything that people might say in greeting one another. But even among us, it makes a difference who utters a greeting. The pious greeting of a mother or an elderly Christian has a different weight than if someone simply uses it as a formula. "Peace be with you"—instead of "be" it would be better to add "is" (DBW: In Bonhoeffer's Nestle NT Romans 5:1 has been changed to ἔχομεν in pencil)—on the lips of the Resurrected One, this means: the end of all your fears, the end of the reign of sin and death over you, now you have peace with God, with human beings, and therefore with yourselves. Thus speaks the very one who has won the peace for us, and like a visible sign of the battle fought and the victory won, he shows his pierced hands and his wounded side. "Peace be with you"—that means: He, who himself is this peace, Jesus Christ is with you, the Crucified and Resurrected One. Word and sign of the living Lord give the disciples joy. The community with the Lord is found again after days of fear and darkness.

2. Verses 21–23. But there is no community with Jesus that is not at the same time *a call to service*. The community with Jesus is fulfilled only in service to him. Jesus has always told his disciples this. (cf. John 15:1ff.) Now, as the Transfigured One, he reveals to them the highest charge, namely, the one in which they are to prove and preserve the

community with him. "I send you" (present tense!). The sending of the disciples through Jesus parallels the sending of Jesus through the Father. Jesus places his work into the hands of his disciples before he goes to the Father. The same peace that has been granted to the disciples shall be the force of their service. This is why Jesus speaks to them "again": "Peace be with you." The peace that comes forth from the resurrection of Jesus is the potent force for the commission. Here, too, the word and sign meet. Jesus does to his disciples what the Creator did to the first human being. The breath of new life and of the new commission, the breath of resurrection touches, fills the disciples. The one who has fought with sin and death, the one who comes forth from the battle won, from the resurrection morn, is able to bring to the disciples what no human being could obtain: the Holy Spirit. "Receive the Holy Spirit." There is no dilution or deception here. It is the Holy Spirit himself, the Spirit of Pentecost, that the Resurrected One gives to those who are his and with whom he equips them for their commission. Only in the possession of the Holy Spirit can the work of Jesus be done. That means forgiving and retaining sins in divine authority. This was Jesus' work on earth: this is the task of the disciples and with them all believers (cf. Matt. 16:19; 18:18). The disciples are now charged to do that which had—in the eyes of the pious—made Jesus the thief of the honour that was God's alone, namely, that he forgave sins. Previously, only the one who bore the curse of sin in his own body and yet was without sin was allowed to forgive sins in the name of God; from now on, the disciples do this in Jesus' name and spirit. Yet because forgiveness of sins is a gift of the free and pure grace of God, whatever sin may not be forgiven due to the hardness of heart, sin must be retained; that is, God's judgement must be proclaimed. Wanting to forgive sins but not wanting to retain sins turns divine forgiveness into a human work, a dalliance with sin. The squandering of grace dishonours God and does damage to human beings. Nonetheless, the proclamation of judgement serves the proclamation of grace; the retention of sin serves the future repentance, conversion, and forgiveness. The disciple shall forgive and retain sins with great certainty and joyfulness by Christ's authority, for this is the work of his Lord that has been entrusted to him. He/she may not shy away from it. Both will be carried out in the public proclamation of the word and in personal confession. The breath of the Resurrected One blows through both of them. Divinely authorised preaching and confession exist because Christ lives and has given us the Holy Spirit.

3. Verses 24–29. What good to me is the news of the most glorious miracle if I cannot experience and examine it myself? Dead is dead, and a wish makes people gullible. So speaks doubt in all ages, and this is what Jesus' disciple *Thomas* thinks. From the few words we have from him (John 11:16; 14:5), we know him as a disciple ready for any sacrifice, who openly acknowledged his questions for Jesus and desired clear answers. After the death of Jesus, he had separated himself from the other disciples and also kept his distance on Easter day. He did not want to be drawn into sick fanaticism. "I will not believe it," he says firmly when the news from the other disciples reached him, "before I have seen it and touched it myself." Thomas is right when he either wants to find his faith on his own or is not willing to believe at all. But the way in which he seeks it is wrong. Despite his refusal to believe, Thomas comes to the circle of disciples on the following Sunday evening. This is important since it shows the sincerity of his doubt. Yet it is the free grace of the Resurrected One that now pursues the individual, overcomes the doubter, and creates in him the Easter faith. Jesus comes, again through locked doors. There could be no doubt about the miraculous nature of his presence. He speaks the greeting of peace that is directed to all, but this time it is directed in particular to the peaceless heart of Thomas. Jesus comes for the sake of his doubting disciple. He knows the whole process that has unfolded within him; he knows him through and through. This is shown by his first word to Thomas. Jesus calms the doubtful yearnings of the disciple by granting him what he denied Mary. ([John] 20:17) There is a difference between our wanting to take something and the Lord granting something to us. Mary is rebuffed; Thomas is allowed to hear, see, and touch. To allow himself to be put to the test is an incredible courtesy on the Lord's part for the benefit of his doubting disciple. "Do not become unbelieving, but believe"— Christ woos his disciples; the final decision has not been made yet but is dangerously close. But when Jesus addresses the disciple as one who has not yet decided against him, he gives him the freedom to change his ways. But whether Thomas dared to stretch out his hand remains unsaid. It is not important. What is important is that the Easter faith breaks through in Thomas: "My Lord and my God." This is the entire confession of Easter. No one had spoken in this manner before this doubter. The conquest is complete. Jesus' answer does not glorify doubt, seeing, or touching, but glorifies faith alone. Faith can find assurance in or rest not on that which we see but the word of God alone. Millions of doubters will follow Thomas. Their doubt will be overcome not through seeing or touching but

through the witness of the living Christ. Even Thomas could not trust his eyes and his hands but Christ alone. Hence the silence about what he did and the straightforward narrative about his Easter confession.

4. Verses 30–31. Is less given to us than the disciples, than to Thomas? Did Jesus make access to him more difficult for us? Did we not receive only shards of the deeds of Christ so that the full richness of his miracles as the disciples experienced them is lost to us? John says: it is true that Jesus did many more things than we know today. But what is written is enough for us, enough in view of the one thing that is most important: that we believe Jesus to be the Christ, God's Son, and in his name we have eternal life. He instituted for us word and sign, sermon and sacrament, in order to help us believe. The disciples did not receive more than that either, nor did Thomas. What they saw, Jesus in his poverty, in his death, and his transfigured form, was no less exposed to doubt than what we see. Only when they themselves believed Him was he Lord for them. They could ground their lives only in him, based not on how they saw him but on how they believed in him as the Christ, the Son of God, and not some supernatural appearance, and so they could have eternal life in his name. This is also the reason why word and sacrament are given to us, that we may become blessed by believing, not seeing.

The following three points informally relate to Quasimodogeniti Sunday: that the resurrection of Jesus is our new life, that from now on we live in service to Jesus, and that both only become real for us in faith.

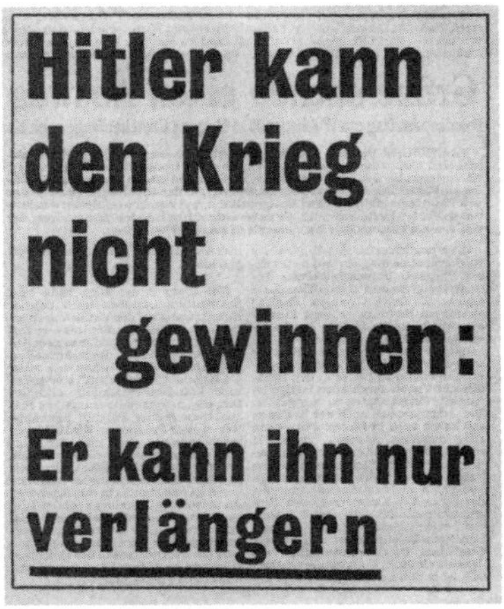

Hitler kann den Krieg nicht gewinnen:

Er kann ihn nur verlängern

Fig. A8-1. Leaflet dropped by Allies
Sammlung Universitats- und Stadtmuseum Rinteln

SIE KOMMEN

mit ihren Stahlkolossen, Jabos und Flammenwerfern.

SIE KOMMEN

denn jetzt kann nichts und niemand sie mehr halten.

SIE KOMMEN

denn jetzt liegen auch Nord- und Mitteldeutschland offen vor den Anglo-Amerikanern und Russen. Der grösste Betrug der Weltgeschichte ist bald vorbei:

WO BLIEBEN die deutschen Wunderwaffen?

WO BLIEBEN die operativen Reserven?

WO BLIEBEN die Parteigenossen und „Hoheitsträger", die immer zum fanatischen Widerstand aufgerufen haben? Die alliierten Armeen nehmen Deutschland im Sturm.

SIE KOMMEN

um den deutschen Militarismus endgültig auszurotten.

SIE KOMMEN

um die Kriegsverbrecher ihrer Strafe zuzuführen.

SIE KOMMEN

um den Rechtsstaat aufzurichten, damit der Weltfrieden nicht wiederum gestört wird.

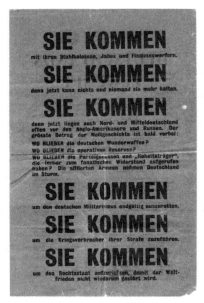

Fig. A8-2. Leaflet dropped by Allies
Sammlung Universitats- und Stadtmuseum Rinteln

DEUTSCHLANDS ZUKUNFT

Die nachstehenden Erklärungen stammen aus dem Bericht, den Präsident Roosevelt am 1. März 1945 dem amerikanischen Kongress erstattete. Er behandelte darin die Beschlüsse, die von den Vereinigten Staaten, Grossbritannien und der Sowjet-Union auf der Konferenz in Yalta getroffen wurden.

„WIR werden in unseren Anstrengungen nicht einen Augenblick nachlassen bis zur bedingungslosen Kapitulation des Gegners. Das deutsche Volk und die deutschen Soldaten müssen sich darüber klar sein: Je eher sie den Kampf einstellen und die Waffen strecken — sei es in Gruppen oder als Einzelne — desto eher werden ihre gegenwärtigen Leiden vorüber sein. Und weiter muss sich das deutsche Volk darüber klar sein: Nur durch restlose Kapitulation kann es den Anfang damit machen, wieder ein Volk zu werden, das die Welt als gesittete Nachbarn anerkennt. Wir haben es in Yalta eindeutig ausgesprochen, und ich wiederhole es jetzt noch einmal:

Bedingungslose Kapitulation bedeutet nicht die Vernichtung oder Versklavung des deutschen Volkes.

Aber wir haben auf der Yalta-Konferenz keinen Zweifel darüber gelassen, was bedingungslose Kapitulation für Deutschland bedeutet. Kapitulation bedeutet: Zeitweilige Überwachung Deutschlands durch Grossbritannien, Russland, Frankreich und die Vereinigten Staaten. Eine Kontroll-Kommission, bestehend aus den Vertretern der vier Weltmächte mit dem Sitz in Berlin, wird die Verwaltung der vier Besetzungs-Zonen koordineren.

Bedingungslose Kapitulation bedeutet ferner das Ende des Nationalsozialismus und der NSDAP mit all ihren barbarischen Gesetzen und Einrichtungen. Bedingungslose Kapitulation bedeutet das Ende aller militaristischen Einflüsse im öffentlichen, privaten und kulturellen Leben Deutschlands.

Für die nationalsozialistischen Kriegsverbrecher bedeutet bedingungslose Kapitulation schnelle, gerechte und empfindliche Bestrafung. Kapitulation bedeutet auch die völlige Entwaffnung Deutschlands, die endgültige Beseitigung des deutschen Militarismus, die Vernichtung allen deutschen Kriegsgeräts, das Ende der deutschen Rüstungsindustrie, die Demobilisierung aller deutschen Streitkräfte und die endgültige Auflösung des deutschen Generalstabs, der so oft den Frieden der Welt erschüttert hat. Den von ihm angerichteten Schaden wird Deutschland in Sachleistungen gutmachen müssen — durch Auslieferung von Industrie-Anlagen, industrieller Ausrüstung, rollendem Material und Rohstoffen. Wir werden nicht wieder, wie nach dem vorigen Krieg, in den Fehler verfallen, Wiedergutmachung in Geldleistungen zu verlangen, die Deutschland niemals aufbringen kann.

Wir wollen nicht, dass das deutsche Volk Hunger leidet oder eine Last für die übrige Welt wird. Die Absicht, die uns bei der Politik gegenüber Deutschland leitet, lässt sich in wenige Worte zusammenfassen: Wir wollen kommenden Generationen den Frieden sichern."

WG 50

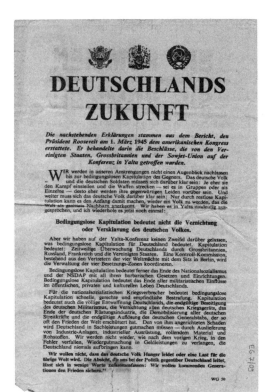

Fig. A8-3. Leaflet dropped by Allies
Sammlung Universitats- und Stadtmuseum Rinteln

APPENDIX 8

Leaflets Dropped by Allied Aircraft, Spring 1945

Fig. A8-1

Hitler cannot win the war:
He can only prolong it

Fig. A8-2

They're coming

with their mega-tanks, fighter-bombers, and flamethrowers.

They're coming

because now nothing and no one can stop them.

They're coming

because now both northern and central Germany are freely
accessible to the Anglo-Americans and Russians. The greatest
deception in world history will soon be at an end:

SO WHERE are the German wonder-weapons?
SO WHERE are the operational reserves?
SO WHERE are the party members and "authority figures" who
have always called for fanatical resistance? The Allied Armies are
taking Germany by storm.

They're coming

to get rid of German militarism for good.

They're coming

to bring war criminals to justice.

They're coming

to create and build civil justice, so that world peace is not
threatened again.

Fig. A8-3

Germany's Future

The following statements are taken from the report that President Roosevelt made to the US Congress on March 1, 1945. It concerns the decisions taken by the United States, Great Britain, and the Soviet Union at the Yalta Conference.

We will not desist for one moment until unconditional surrender. The German people, as well as German soldiers, must realise that the sooner they give up and surrender by groups or as individuals, the sooner their present agony will be over. They must realise that only with complete surrender can they begin to re-establish themselves as people whom the world might accept as decent neighbours. We made it clear again at Yalta, and I now repeat:

Unconditional surrender does not mean the destruction or enslavement of the German people.

We did, however, make it clear at the Conference just what unconditional surrender does mean for Germany.

It means the temporary control of Germany by Great Britain, Russia, France, and the United States. Each of these nations will occupy and control a separate zone of Germany—and the administration of the four zones will be coordinated in Berlin by a Control Council composed of representatives of the four nations.

Unconditional surrender means something else. It means the end of Nazism. It means the end of the Nazi Party—and of all its barbaric laws and institutions.

It means the termination of all militaristic influence in the public, private, and cultural life of Germany. It means for the Nazi war criminals a punishment that is speedy and just—and severe.

It means the complete disarmament of Germany; the destruction of its militarism and its military equipment; the end of its production of armament; the dispersal of all its armed forces; the permanent dismemberment of the German General Staff, which has so often shattered the peace of the world.

It means that Germany will have to make reparations in kind for the damage that has been done to the innocent victims of its aggression. By compelling reparations in kind—in plants, in machinery, in rolling stock, and in raw materials—we shall avoid the mistake that we and other nations made after the last war, the demanding of reparations in the form of money that Germany could never pay.

We do not want the German people to starve, or to become a burden on the rest of the world. Our objective in handling Germany is simple—it is to secure the peace of the rest of the world now and in the future.

APPENDIX 9

Isa Vermehren

Isa Vermehren has scarcely been mentioned in connection with Dietrich Bonhoeffer, and yet she merits a certain pride of place. She was not actually in the Grüne Minna police van with Bonhoeffer for these last momentous days. But she has proven an excellent resource. Travelling with and around fellow prisoner Bonhoeffer in the period April 1–8, Isa was returned home after the collapse of Nazism by the Allies in early July 1945. She quickly began the work of writing up and publishing a remarkable book, *Reise durch den letzten Akt* (A journey as the curtain falls).[1] It is an eyewitness account—a detailed, reflective chronicle of the events she experienced in her period of incarceration in the final days of Nazi Germany. Posterity is much indebted to her for this work. Its high standard of reporting formed a benchmark upon which later authors were able to draw in order to piece together a fuller account of Bonhoeffer's final days. It became an instant bestseller. But perhaps this is unsurprising. Isa, despite her complete disavowal of Nazism and everything it came to represent, was widely known throughout Germany by this time. Not only had she enjoyed a pre-war stage and screen career, but she had also, for much of the duration of the war, been employed under duress (and deployed in many countries) in the role of "Forces Sweetheart." She had, no doubt wholly unintentionally, become the "Vera Lynn" of Germany. Quite remarkably her book spoke truthfully, as well as reflectively, of her experience, and was a landmark publication in terms of the fragile and incipient journey of post-war Germany. Her work certainly contributed at a very early stage to the process of a wider acceptance (as true) of some of the dark things that had actually transpired in the concentration camp system under Nazi rule. In this sense her publication also helped Germany begin to take steps towards a new national self-understanding.

The author herself, having started her work career in musical theatre, was not long after the war in taking holy orders as a nun. She finally ended what became a distinguished career of service at a highly regarded Catholic school in Hamburg as head teacher. By this time Isa was also a respected public figure and broadcaster. It was Isa who wrote these brief words, published in her 1946 book, in a short paragraph about Bonhoeffer:

> The prison warders [in Regensburg] proved to be friendly and amenable, once the SS guards had left. So finally we were able to meet the occupants of the secretive Grüne Minna, which had left Buchenwald with us and had ever since been following in our wake like a secretive small appendage. Among these occupants was Pastor Bonhoeffer, who was shot [sic] a few days later in Flossenbürg. During an interrogation he had seen a memo on the desk of the Commissar that began with the words "Since the demise of General Lindemann . . ." With this information he was able to bring certainty to the general's wife on the fate of her husband, long anxiously feared, and who had succumbed to injuries he had incurred during interrogation. I know that Pastor Bonhoeffer deserves a worthier obituary than these few short words, and I hope that someone may be called to write it.[2]

The word corresponding to "called" in German is "ein Berufener," and it is a word with connotations of faith. As things turned out, the hope was soon to be turned into what might be viewed as an answered prayer. Eberhard Bethge did indeed experience a call to write up his friend's life, devoting much—if not the greater part—of his working life to that cause, and then the projects, thanks to his success, that became associated with it.

Isa's Early Days

Isa was born on April 21, 1918, to Kurt and Petra Vermehren, a younger sister to Michael, soon to be followed by a younger brother, Erich. The family established a happy and musical home in Lübeck; one familiar pattern that they had was attending September's organ concert at Lübeck's Marienkirche. At one point in 1932, they hosted for an extended period an equally musical English exchange student from Winchester. He was staying with them ostensibly to learn German, whereas in practice the children, charmed by his manners, used the time with him that was not spent playing music together to practise their own English. Isa's father and grandfather were both lawyers, and when Kurt Vermehren landed a good legal job with HAPAG in 1924, he bought a family home in the delightful Harvestehuder Weg in Hamburg. Petra Vermehren liked the idea of

Hamburg much less, and soon developed her own career aspirations. Perhaps these might have surfaced anyway. A time began when the children and their mother saw relatively little of their father, with the children staying at school in Lübeck. The children's nanny at the time, Daida, recalls it was a "modern, free relationship—there was not such a tender intimacy between the parents, and whilst never a cross word was spoken, or any hint of marital trouble, there were one or more attractive young women around the house."[3]

A Star Is Born

Isa was a highly gifted and likeable child and was musical from an early age. She progressed rapidly from the recorder to the violin, to the stage where, attracted by the sound of the accordion, aged around ten, she received one for Christmas. It was followed soon thereafter by an even finer instrument, a splendid thirty-two-hole Hohner accordion. This quickly became not only an instrument that she played to her heart's content, but also one on which her level of proficiency was astonishing. In addition to singing in her native German, Isa rapidly developed a repertoire of songs in Italian, French, English, and Russian. Like her mother she was also a free spirit. Within her family, when a school report described her as "immature and arrogant," with the consequent request to repeat a school year, it was seen as a matter of great amusement. But external events would soon overtake such matters in scale and scope. One of these came in 1933, when Isa was fifteen. In the build-up to the May 1 parade, a Jewish classmate was forbidden from joining in. In solidarity with her classmate, she refused to offer the Nazi salute. The consequences for Isa were serious: she was excluded from school. It would not have brought her troublesome repercussions at home. Her mother, an avid reader, was numbered among those who had not just come into possession of Hitler's *Mein Kampf* but also read it in full. This she had done with dismay. The family had many Jewish friends, including Reichstag member Julius Leber, who was arrested in 1933 and finally executed in 1945, and were all intimately aware of the brutality and the modus operandi of the protagonists of National Socialism. By now once again restless, Petra networked an opening for herself as a journalist in Berlin through a Baron von Wedderkop, who had been lodging with them in Lübeck. This Petra linked together with an idea for Isa to audition for Werner Finck's satirical and risqué cabaret show *The Catacomb*. Eldest child Michael, finishing school, was happy to be based around his father, and youngest Erich was sent to boarding school, so Petra, Isa, and Erich found a new base—in Berlin. Isa was hired there that same autumn after a single audition: her blend of singing and accordion playing, combined with her personality, would prove to be of professional standard, and pleasing to audiences. With that, what was to prove a notable career on stage and screen—one of remarkable duration—was launched. Once again Isa was on the fringe of becoming an enemy of National Socialism. The two years that followed saw Isa's musical career throughout Germany reach dizzying heights of fame, particularly with her "hit" shanty song "Eine Seefahrt, die ist lustig." But during one 1936 performance in Hamburg, Isa was catcalled and shouted almost off stage by political objectors. They correctly saw, in the not overly subtle innuendo of the lyrics, a potential undermining of Nazism. Isa would never again perform in public the song that, alongside her recording, radio work, acting, and other activities, had by this time made her a nationally admired figure. Indeed, for what had seemed like an age, Werner Finck's cabaret had appeared somehow to remain able to poke fun at the regime, and get away with it. But one afternoon that same year, in 1936, that would change. That day Isa came home to find the cabaret venue deserted: the show had indeed been closed down, and Werner himself and all other cast members arrested, and sent to a concentration camp. Fortunately for them, most avoided the worst excesses of the system and survived the war. The Gestapo report shows that Isa's name had been included on the original list of those to be incarcerated, but someone—it is unknown who that was— had at the last minute removed it. Apparently she had been spared, at least for the moment.

In 1937 Isa's mother departed Berlin for Athens, where she was installed as a foreign correspondent. At age nineteen, financially independent, Isa assumed responsibility for herself and her younger brother. Both by now had become well accustomed to spending long periods apart from their parents. Isa took advantage of a three-month house-sit in Haffkrug to re-engage with final school year exams, encouraged by her father, while younger brother Erich, after a school falling-out with Nazism, and influenced by his friendship with Adam von Trott zu Solz, aimed for a Rhodes Scholarship at Oxford to study "Ancient Greats."[4] During this time away, Isa entered a period of joyful discovery and personal and spiritual growth, being profoundly impacted by the writing of Catholic theologian Otto Karrer. Isa also met Countess Elisabeth von Plettenberg, a woman of vibrant faith. Elisabeth was a sensation. Her harassment of the Gestapo when her Catholic parents were imprisoned for their faith was so effective that she secured their early release. The "earthquake" experience of meeting the dynamic young countess challenged Isa to find faith for her-self, and it did not take long before she committed her life to Christ. She was joyfully received in 1938 into the Catholic Church and was sure she was on the way to finding her true calling. As a part of this, Isa applied three times to Sophie Barat's Order of the Sacred Heart in Grünewald. She was turned away each time because of her singing career. A trial year in February 1939 was under consideration when the order itself was dis-solved by the Nazis, and the membership of the entire order were forcibly reassigned to nursing duties.

A Time of Romantic Connections

Meanwhile Isa's younger brother, Erich, was not far behind her. He too was being discipled in a new-found faith by the plainly heaven-sent Elis-abeth. The onset of war brought a time of romantic connections: Isa turned down one proposal of marriage from Willo von Moltke, but fell deeply and mutually in love with Karl Beutler. He was a man of strong and sincere faith who was considering ordination before being called up for military service. From early in the war, Isa's singing skills were requisitioned by the Luftwaffe. As part of a quartet, she travelled to entertain and encourage soldiers in Norway, France, Northern Italy, and Pomerania, and in 1943, with two other singers, to Russia. She wrote reports that were published in *Das Reich*, the publication that included her mother and older brother as regular contributors. For his part Erich soon proposed marriage to Elisabeth von Plettenberg, eight years older than him, and they were married in 1941. Her older brother, Michael, working in a non-military role in Rome, became engaged to Countess Elisabeth Rességuier. Karl Beutler and Isa became engaged, and on one momentous occasion while Karl was on home leave from the Russian front in 1943, they exchanged rings. But they gave up their commit-ment under pressure of war. Karl was lost during the Russian campaign. Despite all their endeavours, his family were never able to discover what became of him. Isa would never reconsider marriage.

The reason Isa Vermehren came to be among the fellow hostages accompanying Dietrich Bonhoeffer during his final week was that she—along with her mother, father, and older brother—had been arrested by the Nazi authorities following Erich's high-profile departure from his consular job in Istanbul in January 1944 and his connected "defection" to the Allies. Initially arrested and held together with Isa and Michael, her parents, long estranged in marriage, would be reunited in incarceration.

It was an experience that ranged from the luxury of the Potsdamer Palace Hotel at Easter 1944 to the confines of grim Nazi prison cells in Sachsenhausen and, in Isa's case, Ravensbrück.

The Vermehren Story

The back story to this development runs as follows (largely my adapted translation of pp. 128–31 of Matthias Wegner's *Ein weites Herz*, much of it written in the first person by Erich Vermehren). Erich was twenty-three when he was transferred from Berlin to Istanbul. By now a capable lawyer, he had the job of representing German interests in the international legal proceedings surrounding the Danube fleet interned in the sea of Marmara, assisting and supporting military attaché Paul Leverkuhn in the validation of German ownership claims under Turkish law. He quickly found his feet in the legal arena and was also in charge of "agents," gathering news relevant to the war in the Middle East. But there was a high cost. His wife, Elisabeth, was not considered politically reliable and hence not permitted to accompany him, and was obliged to remain at home under effective house arrest with the family in Bremen.

Erich's daily study of the international press broadened his understanding of the world political situation and revealed to him on a daily basis the extent to which he had been exposed in Germany to falsified information and lies. He perceived that Hitler had long planned this war of conquest to create *Lebensraum* for the German "master race" and establish Germany as a world power. The implication was that the war would become a war of destruction against the "inferior" population in the East. The truth about the "purging of the Jews from Europe" he now recognised in all its grim true colours. In summary, he now concluded that Germany's military undertakings did not at all represent the country's best interests but were instead based on fantasies of unlimited power and an insane racist ideology.

New and Brave Decisions

Since the entry of the United States into the war and the defeat at Stalingrad, the possibility of a German victory could no longer be regarded as a serious consideration. Seen in this light, the continuation of the war meant that the real struggle was against the Germans themselves. This life-changing realisation spurred Erich Vermehren into new decision-making. His options for personal intervention in this unhappy situation were so limited as to be laughable. He was still young and junior . . . but he could see more, and more profoundly, than others, and wanted to put his insight to good use—but how?

His wife lived in Germany, and she was the only one with whom he could speak in freedom and confidence. But first he had to take solo decisions and shape a sensible plan, thinking over every detail with painstaking care. His legal and analytical skills were an advantage. At the start of December 1943, Erich was allowed his first home leave from Istanbul. Once he was alone with his wife, he shared his thoughts with her. She agreed immediately. Provided she was permitted to travel, she would follow him anywhere. Erich gave serious thought to the question of to what extent, if any, he was committing treason. As a patriotic German, he would never have countenanced such a thing as desertion—absconding behind enemy lines—but now he could see no alternative. The couple discussed the matter at length and decided that this step was unavoidable. For both of them, it was unthinkable to let anyone else know of their plans, not even their closest relatives. It would have endangered them—under interrogation they would have been represented as accomplices. The couple vowed silence.

As a lawyer Erich had good friends in the Foreign Office. Via these connections he managed to get hold of a travel permit. His friend Adam von Trott zu Solz was able to arrange things such that Elisabeth Vermehren, a believing Catholic, was given a church/political information-gathering assignment.

A Hazardous Journey

In Istanbul no one had any idea that Erich Vermehren would return accompanied by his wife, because it was known that for political reasons she was not allowed to leave Germany. Accordingly, in mid-December, when the couple boarded the train for Turkey, they were disturbed not a little to find among their fellow passengers in the same sleeping compartment—also sent by the Foreign Office—a representative of the SD. But the journey passed uneventfully—that is, until they reached the passport control point on the border between Bulgaria and Turkey, at Svilengrad. At this point the SD representative emerged from his up to now concealed reserve by requesting the border control official to send Elisabeth back to Sofia. Of course, Erich was able to stay on the train. The Bulgarian border policeman apologised profusely to Elisabeth that something was not in order with her papers, more precisely with her Turkish entry visa, and that it was better to send her back now so as to save her from being turned back at the Turkish border. In Sofia the visa section of the German embassy would certainly help her obtain the correct paperwork, and she would be able to continue her journey in a few days. "This," Erich would later say, "was immediately obvious as being a whopping lie, since the visa in my wife's passport had been issued only a week beforehand by the Turkish embassy in Berlin."

Elisabeth, carefully prepared by her husband for such hindrances, played the part of the naïve traveller to perfection. She enquired about the name of the official she should turn to in Sofia. The couple separated on the platform, not knowing when they would next see each other. The Gestapo agent observed events at arm's length. Erich reboarded the train for Istanbul, where he arrived in good order the next morning.

For her part Elisabeth initially sought refuge with an acquaintance whom she knew would not make common cause with the Nazis. Although, following air raids, the telephone connections between Sofia and Berlin were scarcely functioning, they finally succeeded via a naval telephone line connection in reaching the friends in the Berlin Foreign Office who had arranged her overseas travel papers.

The information she received ran as follows: "There is a once weekly courier flight from Berlin to Istanbul with a stopover in Sofia. The Foreign Office will reserve a seat on board for you. You need to collect the ticket from the embassy in Sofia. Remain in contact with our trusted colleague Councillor H . . . and gird your loins with patience—these courier flights are often cancelled."

What happened next is slightly reminiscent of the closing scenes in the film *Casablanca*. Elisabeth Vermehren left her acquaintance's home, following her advice, after a very brief stay. Indeed, soon afterwards, a Gestapo official called on the telephone asking to speak to Frau Vermehren. When the acquaintance innocently answered that she was in Istanbul, the caller replied—surprisingly under the circumstances—that Erich Vermehren had travelled on alone, because his wife had been turned back at the border, and now the Gestapo in Sofia was searching for her.

Elisabeth had in the meantime found refuge with other Germans whom she had been referred to by the Foreign Office. There she was to await the arrival of the courier plane. She continued to wait in the absence of any contact with her husband in Istanbul. The impending arrival of the flight was announced twice; twice nothing transpired. On Christmas Eve 1943, the moment came: Elisabeth was collected by a car from the German embassy. Erich explains,

> The driver promised to accompany her in person all the way to the door of the aircraft. . . . At the check-in counter, her papers were subjected to intense scrutiny. The airport in Sofia was small and had

only one runway. A single-storey building with glass doors on the longer sides served as a terminal. It lay positioned between the drop-off and collection area for passengers and the runway approach. There was no such thing as space for a waiting area. It was simply a question of standing around between the glass doors until one was called. While my wife was there, a small plane landed. It had obviously brought a "big fish" because she suddenly saw half a dozen young men emerge from vehicles with diplomatic plates parked in front of the "terminal" and hurry towards the taxiing aircraft. As the welcoming committee approached the building with their guest, my wife realised to her horror that this was none other than the very top Gestapo Führer responsible for the Balkan states—the very person who had been issuing search orders for her for a fortnight.

Elisabeth Vermehren did her utmost to conceal her face as well and unobtrusively as she could. The Gestapo leader passed within a hair's breadth of her without shining a torch at her.

Immediately thereafter someone pressed my wife's papers into her hand. Her driver urged her to hurry: the plane was delayed and had to take off immediately. My wife sank exhausted into her seat, ordered a sherry from the attendant, and steeled herself in preparation for a stopover landing in Varna, the final station under German control. "Unfortunately," the attendant disclosed as he arrived with the sherry, "because we are so much delayed, we will no longer be able to make our scheduled stop in Varna, otherwise we will not be granted permission to land in Istanbul." "What a pity," sighed my wife. "I had been told the landing approach over the Black Sea is particularly beautiful."

When the courier flight landed in Istanbul, Elisabeth Vermehren was safe. A married couple, fellow passengers from the flight, drove her to a hotel, from where she called her husband, who was being put up in the German embassy formerly patronised by the Kaiser, at work. The conversation that ensued was, as an understandable precaution, brief and vague.

"Deep breath, Erich—it's me."

"I can't talk now: we're just celebrating Christmas here. Where are you?"

"In the lobby of the Parkhotel."

Only when work responsibilities were at an end did Erich Vermehren appear there to gather his wife in his arms. He took her "to Egyptian friends, who lived in an old Turkish wooden palace, directly on the

European shoreline of the Bosphorus." She was happy—but felt unwell: pleurisy was making its troublesome onset noticeable, and her condition had become serious enough to be life-threatening.

The next day Erich followed the correct protocol in notifying the German consulate general of his wife's arrival. Astonishingly enough—after the journey from Germany she had just experienced—permission was granted.

Operation Flight

A few days later saw the launch of Operation Flight. A spurious kidnap plan was arranged and executed on January 27. It was arranged by an intelligence operative who was unknowingly being exploited,[5] British agent Nicholas Elliott. Including an extended stop in Gibraltar, where the couple greatly feared being arrested, they were duly conveyed safely overland via Cairo to UK shores, where they were welcomed with open arms by the active KGB agent Kim Philby to a "safe house" owned by his mother in Kensington.[6] There they were "debriefed." At the time an internal German report admitted that Vermehren knew details of the Abwehr officers and agents in Turkey and their cover names, and indeed he had in his possession a prepared forty-page treatise on Abwehr personnel and embassy staff. Max Hastings reports that, to the lasting shame of the British intelligence community, "Philby passed to the Russians Vermehren's long list of Catholic Conservative contacts in Germany: all those in the East were liquidated by the Russians in 1945–6, as actual or potential anti-communists."[7]

Meanwhile, as Erich was "debriefed" by Kim Philby, Isa—back in Germany—and her older brother and parents were subjected to a loyalty test for five weeks by a regime that had its suspicions already. Every conversation in every room in that hotel was listened to by the Gestapo. The family did not pass muster. The suspicions of the authorities were confirmed, and they were reclassified as enemies of the state, to be held as prisoners.[8] In this new dispensation, their now-perilous onward journey took them to Sachsenhausen, and in Isa's case, Ravensbrück. Michael and his parents, not spared from the daily anxiety of not knowing if each day would be their last, were kept in a higher standard of accommodation than other prisoners, as was Isa. Somehow she found a way to keep her harmonica with her throughout, even once singing two items with prisoners.[9] Finally the moment came in February 1945, when she, together with Michael's wife, Gisela Plettenberg, who was incarcerated in Ravensbrück with her, would be summoned to join the southerly journey of the diverse group of political, clan custody, and VIP prisoners being assembled at Himmler's behest—to be used as "trading chips," or liquidated, as the Third Reich disintegrated.

APPENDIX 10

Table of Comparative Military Ranks Mentioned

Waffen-SS	German army	Allied
SS-Unterscharführer	Unteroffizier	Corporal/sergeant
SS-Scharführer	Unterfeldwebel	Lower rank than staff sergeant
SS-Oberscharführer	Feldwebel	Sergeant/staff sergeant
SS-Hauptscharführer	Oberfeldwebel	Warrant officer 2/ technical sergeant
SS-Sturmscharführer	Hauptfeldwebel	Warrant officer/master sergeant
SS-Untersturmführer	Leutnant	Second lieutenant
SS-Hauptsturmführer	Hauptmann	Captain
SS-Sturmbannführer	Major	Major
SS-Obersturmbannführer	Oberstleutnant	Lieutenant colonel
SS-Standartenführer	Oberst	Colonel
SS-Brigadeführer	Generalmajor	Major general
SS-Gruppenführer	Generalleutnant	Lieutenant general
No equivalent	Generalfeldmarschal	Field marshal/general of the army

GLOSSARY

Terms with their equivalent or explanation

Abitur	Matriculation certificate for university entry
Abwehr	Germany's military intelligence service
Abwehrstelle	Regional office of the Abwehr
Alpenfestung	Fortress located in the Alps
Arresthof	Detention area
Arrestzelle	Detention cell
Appellplatz	Roll-call area
Aufzeichnungen	Notes
Braunschweiger Tageszeitung	Daily newspaper of Braunschweig
Depositenkasse	Deposit box
Einwanderungszentralstelle	Office for Immigration
Evangelische Konsistorium	Protestant consistory (a regional or national committee)
Führer	Hitler's title as Germany's supreme leader
Führerbefehl	An express order of Germany's Führer
Gauleiter	Regional leader or commander
Gedenkstätte	Memorial centre
Gestapo	Germany's Secret State Police Service
Herrnhuter Losungen	Moravian daily Bible texts
Holzgasomnibus	Vehicle powered by burning wood
Kampfstoffabrik	War production facility
Kreisleiter	District leader or commander
Kriminalkommissar	Detective inspector
Kriminalrat	Senior detective inspector

Luftwaffe	Germany's air force
Mein Kampf	Hitler's published work setting out his views and early ascendancy
Metzger	Butcher (Bavaria)
"Nacht und Nebel"	An established German phrase co-opted by the Third Reich meaning "Night and Fog," the destination of unwanted persons
Nationalsozialistische Volkswohlfahrt	NSDAP welfare organisation
Oberverwalter	Senior supervisor
Oranienbürgische Zeitung	Newspaper in Oranienburg
Ortsgruppenleiter	Local group leader (senior regional political functionary)
Prominenten	VIP prisoners
Rapportführer	Report leader (KZ work detail leader)
Reichsmark	Germany's currency
Reichsbank	Germany's national bank
Reichsbahn	Germany's national rail network
Reichssicherheitsdienst	Reich Security Service (Hitler's personal protection unit)
Reichswehr	Germany's army
Sippenhäftling(e)	Clan custody prisoner(s)
Schutzpolizei	Protective (custody) police
Sondergericht	Summary Court
Sonderkommando	Work detail in KZ
Staatskrankenhaus	Hospital run by the state
Standgericht	Court martial
Stapoleiter	Regional Gestapo commander
Untermenschen	Subhumans
Volksdeutsche	Ethnic Germans
Völkischer Beobachter	Newspaper of the NSDAP
Wehrmacht	Germany's army (Hitler's preferred designation)
Zeitgeschichtsarchiv Pragser Wildsee	Archive of the Pragser Wildsee Hotel (Italian Dolomites)

NOTES

Preface

1 Probably either a Walther PPK or a Mauser HSc.
2 English readers will note the jarring effect of the then-current orthographical fashion, with the old German script's use of a character (exactly that of medieval English) resembling an *f* for the letter *s*.

Introduction

1 I. Kershaw, *The End: The Defiance and Destruction of Hitler's Germany, 1944–1945* (London: Penguin Books, 2012), 208.
2 Chapter 17 includes a note of gunfire audible at a distance of ninety kilometres but which was believed by hostages to be from only twenty-five kilometres away. Prevailing wind conditions may have contributed.
3 E. Bethge, *Dietrich Bonhoeffer: A Biography* (1967; repr., Minneapolis: Fortress, 2000), 930.
4 C. Madsen, "Victims of Circumstance: The Execution of German Deserters by Surrendered German Troops under Canadian Control in Amsterdam, May 1945," *Canadian Military History* 2, no. 1 (1993): 93–113.
5 A. Weale, *Army of Evil: A History of the SS* (New York: NAL Caliber, 2012), 189. They inspected the facility only on July 2, twelve hours after the last adult "patient" died. Falthauser was sentenced to three years in prison in 1949 but pardoned in 1954.
6 H. Pünder, "Pervertierung des Polizeirechts in Nationalsozialismus (Teil 1)," *JURA—Juristische Ausbildung* 1 (2023): 15, n. 69. The textbook was renamed *Dürig/Herzog/Scholz*. Maunz was a leading Nazi lawyer and continued until his death in 1993 to publish articles in the ultra far-right press, especially the *Nationalzeitung*, albeit under the guise of a pseudonym.
7 Bethge, *Dietrich Bonhoeffer*, 22.
8 H. Linge, *With Hitler to the End: The Memoirs of Adolf Hitler's Valet* (London: Simon & Schuster, 2009), 30.
9 N. Davies, *Europe: A History* (London: BCA, 1996), 2.
10 Duško Popov records that prominent Yugoslav prisoners were incarcerated for this purpose in 1942: D. Popov, *Super Spion: Der Doppelagent im Zweiten Weltkrieg* (Vienna: Molden, 1974), 230. This was a commonplace state of affairs across Germany's occupied territories.

11   Clan custody—*Sippenhaft* in German—refers to the Nazi practice of exacting
      revenge on an individual by declaring their families also to be culpable of what-
      soever alleged or suspected misdemeanour they were connected with (or simply
      accused of). It involved siblings, parents, relatives, and children in a litany of
      maltreatment and, in many cases, even death.

12   The project will build upon and extend the work done close to the time by British
      MI6 officer Payne Best, by others in 1968, and by Hans-Günter Richardi in 2010.
      Also referenced is work done in 2018 by Tilman Pünder and, also in 2018, by
      Hugh Falconer's daughter Evelyn Smith on behalf of her father, who was present
      in Schönberg. A book written by Isa Vermehren—herself a fellow hostage, but
      not one of the group who travelled in close proximity with Bonhoeffer—which
      has not appeared in English, is also referenced. (For specific notes on primary
      sources, see appendix 3.)

13   All French and German translations are my own. In relation to those from Rus-
      sian, Spanish, and Greek, see this book's acknowledgements.

14   The period April 1–8 is an octave of days. Bonhoeffer's execution happened on
      April 9. A particularly important reference book for Bonhoeffer, on Psalm 119,
      included this note: eight is the number of regeneration, and the eighth day of each
      week is a recurrence of the first day. Hence baptismal fonts are commonly octag-
      onal. Eight Beatitudes introduce the Sermon on the Mount, the first and eighth
      being in unison. See R. Benson, *The Way of Holiness: An Exposition of Psalm
      CXIX* (London: Methuen, 1901), 109. To make the connection: Bonhoeffer's final
      sermon on April 8 has this linkage back to the message of Easter Day.

15   This tallies with Falkenhausen's recollections in 1952 correspondence with
      Pünder and the diary notes of others.

16   Of course, these cannot be adequately represented here.

17   Marie "Missie" Vassiltchikov (1917–1998) grew up as a refugee in France, Ger-
      many, and Lithuania, after her parents, Prince Ilarion and Princess Lydia Vassilt-
      chikov, left Russia in 1919. Although stateless, she moved among the cosmopol-
      itan set, who managed to maintain a trance-like normality, until as late as 1941.
      Through Adam von Trott, for whom she worked in the Information Ministry, she
      became involved with a hard core of anti-Nazi resisters, herself displaying uncom-
      mon bravery in the face of the Gestapo and the "detestable" Dr Six of the SS. A
      consummate linguist and a compulsive diarist, she wrote in English, and spent
      the last weeks of the war in the company of Countess Elizabeth (Sisi) Andrassy
      (born Countess Wilczech). She finally decided to make her notes available to the
      public only in 1976. See M. Vassiltchikov, *The Berlin Diaries, 1940–1945* (London:
      Pimlico, 1985), 269.

18   The son of a rabbi, Victor Klemperer (1881–1960) was, in 1933, a professor in
      Dresden. Despite being a distinguished combat veteran of World War I, over the
      next decade, in common with other German Jews, he lost his job, his house, and
      many of his friends. The publication of his diaries brought to light one of the most
      extraordinary documents of the Nazi period.

19   Information to the author from Tanya Fichtner, *Gedenkstätte* Flossenbürg, in an
      email of June 7, 2019.

20   The time is noted in a pocket diary entry of Hermann Pünder, which came
      to light only in 2014. See T. Pünder, *Kalenderblätter 1945: Hermann Pünders*

Taschenkalender-Eintragungen im ersten Halbjahr 1945, transcribed from Stolze-Schrey shorthand by Rosemarie Koller from Gossau (Münster: self-pub., 2014), 14.

21 The Special Operations Executive (SOE) was a secret British World War II organisation. Founded in June 1940, it was one of the nine secret services that Britain maintained during the war. Its role was to foster, together with local resistance organisations, sabotage, subversion, and resistance to Nazi rule. "Set Europe ablaze!" ordered Churchill.

22 The Sturmabteilung (SA) was a paramilitary organisation associated with the Nazi Party.

23 P. Best, *The Venlo Incident: A True Story of Double-Dealing, Captivity, and a Murderous Nazi Plot* (1950; repr., London: Frontline, 2009), 196.

24 A sketch layout of the possible arrangement of the beds is included in chapter 33.

25 Bethge, *Dietrich Bonhoeffer*, 1044.

26 H. Bücheler, *Hoepner: Ein deutsches Soldatenschicksal des XX Jahrhunderts* (Herford, Germany: Mittler, 1980), 17.

27 In his interview, conducted in English, in Capri on June 6, 1945, Hoepner describes his subject as "Science and Economy." See TNA, WO 328/14.

28 A. Goerdeler, *Verschleppt*, in W. Zimmermann, ed., *Begegnungen mit Dietrich Bonhoeffer*, 4th ed. (Munich: Christian Kaiser, 1964), 5–7.

29 H. Pünder, *Von Preussen nach Europa: Lebenserinnerungen* (Stuttgart: Deutsche Verlags-Anstalt, 1968), 173.

Chapter 1: Dietrich Bonhoeffer

1 It was to be a significant year for the worldwide Christian church. When the Bonhoeffer twins were just over two months old, on April 9, 1906, in a warehouse on Asuza Street in downtown Los Angeles, the Holy Spirit fell in power. To this and other awakenings of the Spirit around the world around the same time, the Pentecostal church traces its origins. The initial revival in Los Angeles lasted for three years. Within two years the phenomenon had spread to over fifty countries, and by 2010 constituted approximately half the Christian population of the world. See D. Runcorn, *Spirituality Workbook: A Guide for Explorers, Pilgrims and Seekers* (London: SPCK, 2011), 35–37.

2 Bonhoeffer's governess Maria Horn introduced him at a young age to the *Herrnhuter Losungen* Bible readings.

3 R. Jenkins, *Churchill: A Biography* (London: Pan, 2003), 121.

4 The family were regular skiers, good at tennis, and fortunate enough to maintain a regular holiday home in various locations. This included latterly one in the Harz mountains, Friedrichsbrunn, to which they would escape with a degree of freedom and regularity.

5 The station's name remains Karl-Bonhoeffer-Nervenklinik. Perhaps for that reason the Bonhoeffer name is still in some ways more readily connected across Germany with Dietrich's father than with Dietrich himself.

6 DBW 8:132. That said, in 1922, when Dietrich was sixteen, his father was offered a significant career move upwards to a chair in Munich, and declined it. His life pattern was to arrive punctually at work at 8:30 and leave at 1:30 for a blend of other responsibilities.

7   Dietrich's older brother Karl-Friedrich, in his own chosen work sphere, suc-
     ceeded in due course in no less a task than the splitting of the hydrogen atom.
     In 1930, at the very young age of thirty-one, he was appointed to the position of
     chair of physics in Frankfurt.
8   DBW 9:55.
9   DBW 9:3.
10   For a thoughtful consideration of the extent to which Bonhoeffer's faith may have
     been influenced by his time in America, in particular at the Abyssinian Church
     in Harlem, see R. Williams, *Bonhoeffer's Black Jesus: Harlem Renaissance Theology
     and an Ethic of Resistance*, 2nd ed. (Waco, Tex.: Baylor University Press, 2021).
11   DBW 14:113. The editors' afterword in DBWE 3 notes, "For Bonhoeffer the
     knowledge of death and resurrection had become a truth of the utmost certainty
     already at some moment during 1932" (DBWE 3:173).
12   DBW 11:349.
13   Diels himself, as might be inferred from this incident, may have been "too soft"
     to continue in office under Heydrich. He was fortunate to receive and act upon
     a tip-off that he was in fact on the liquidation list for June 1934, the Night of the
     Long Knives. It was thanks to his friendship with Hermann Göring that he would
     survive the war. On the subject of the subsequent vote that Bonhoeffer and his
     colleague were seeking to influence, they were unsuccessful.
14   Without this fateful clergy cooperation, the entire Holocaust could not have taken
     place. Both Bonhoeffer and his clergy colleague Hildebrand were unsuccessful in
     their campaign, but their contribution, which has received little acknowledge-
     ment, should not pass unmentioned.
15   Much later, his great friend and biographer Bethge would agree, in exchange
     for receiving and publishing those weekly sermons, to omit Elizabeth from
     his biographical work on Bonhoeffer. Dietrich Bethge—Eberhard Bethge's
     son—conferred on this point with his sister and confirmed to the author that this
     arrangement had been made (email of July 12, 2018).
16   DBW 15:19.
17   The book is in Ian Sayer's archive. Lutheran images of the Christian as a tree bear-
     ing good fruit abound.
18   *Agende für die Evangelische Landeskirche*, vol. 2, *Kirchliche Handlungen* (Berlin:
     Mittler and Sohn, 1895). A copy is provided in appendix 4.
19   Many would venture that the process of bringing lasting fruitfulness from Bon-
     hoeffer's endeavours is still ongoing.
20   A colleague who made this choice was Hermann Stöhr. He was guillotined on
     June 21, 1940.
21   Liedig, Gisevius, Hans and Christine Dohnanyi, Müller, Schmidhuber, and Bon-
     hoeffer. See H. Deutsch, *The Conspiracy against Hitler in the Twilight War* (Min-
     neapolis: University of Minnesota Press, 1968), 326. Canaris was not included.
22   That year, at the festive season, some of those whose destiny was to be party to such
     grave and life-imperilling secrets sat up half the night together: Fathers Leiber, Zei-
     ger, and Schönhoeffer from the Vatican; Consul Wilhelm Schmidhuber and Cap-
     tain Ickrath; Josef Müller; the abbots of Metten and Ettal; Dohnanyi; and Bonhoef-
     fer. Bonhoeffer, by now on friendly terms with a widening circle of Catholic clergy,
     had often driven over to the abbott Hofmeister's Metten monastery in the Bavarian
     forest. Josef Müller also introduced Bonhoeffer to Canon Neuhäusler.

23   For an excellent recent study, see T. Dunkel, *White Knights in the Black Orchestra: The Extraordinary Story of the Germans Who Resisted Hitler* (New York: Hachette, 2022).

24   Despite extensive warnings of an impending Gestapo raid, the resisters were still caught red-handed. In one instance of this, one particularly incriminating document (for Bonhoeffer) that was seized that day stated, "For a considerable time now, a small circle of prominent clerics in the German Protestant Church have been debating how the Protestant Church can help in this war to bring about a just and lasting peace, and construct a social system based on Christian foundations. . . . Work is already far advanced. . . . It is possible that the Pope enunciated his basic peace aims in his last two Christmas messages. . . . Since it would carry great weight if all Christian churches adopted a concerted approach to the problems of arranging a peace . . . it appears extremely important and desirable that a German Protestant cleric should be enabled not only to hold discussions on the subject with representatives of the Catholic Church in Rome, but also to familiarise himself with the relevant activities of the worldwide Protestant Churches in Geneva or Stockholm" (Indictment against Dohnanyi and Oster, 9–10).

25   The unfortunate story is recounted in full in H. Höhne, *Canaris*, trans. J. Maxwell Brownjohn (London: Secker and Warburg, 1979), 498–515. Recent Canaris biographers have relativised or omitted Höhne's account.

26   On September 21 Felix Kerstenhahn, the hitherto trusted driver of a resister who had taken his own life, arrived unsolicited at Sonderegger's office and told him where the much sought-after cache of documents was stored. The next day he accompanied the Gestapo official to the precise spot in Zossen's Maybach II (Höhne, *Canaris*, 579–81). So fulsome were its contents, revealing the vast extent of conspiratorial activity ever since 1938, that the Gestapo were speechless. Hitler expressly forbade any wider disclosure.

27   After the war, Allied and German interrogators of the torturers and other perpetrators would find they had "no memory or awareness of any ill-treatment ever occurring," and "never heard any sounds." Smartly dressed secretaries who had worked there would testify effusively to the "kindness and consideration which [their line manager] had always demonstrated towards visitors" and that "to my knowledge he never raised his voice." But, in the autumn of 1944, the death cries and gasps of the tortured were known to all. Brave men, when they knew their limits would imminently be exceeded, and that breaking point was near, when they might crack and release the name of someone they knew, would take matters into their own hands. In one instance, on March 10, 1945, Kurt von Plettenberg, while being conducted to yet another interrogation on the fourth floor, sent his interrogator sprawling with a blow on the chin, rushed to the window, and leaped out to his death. In another, Fabian von Schlabrendorff was among the many arrested following the failed plot of July 20, 1944. He was sent to the RSHA and tortured, apparently with no particular agenda in view other than simply to find out what and who he knew. During his subsequent trial before the so-called "People's Court," he related his experience. The torture was executed in four stages. First he was subjected to finger screws, metal mechanisms that inflicted excruciating pain by forcing pin points into the fingers. When this method proved to be ineffective, Schlabrendorff was strapped face-down on a bedstead-like frame. His

head was covered with a blanket while cylinders resembling stove pipes studded with nails on their inner surface were placed around his bare legs. Again, a screw mechanism was used to make the tubes contract so that the nails pierced his legs from ankle to thigh. For the third stage, the bedstead was expanded like a medieval torture rack, gradually or in sudden jerks, painfully stretching his chained and shackled body. Finally, Schlabrendorff was tied in a bent position that did not allow him to move even slightly and was then beaten forcibly with clubs, making him crash to the ground with full force on his face. See F. von Schlabrendorff, *Revolt against Hitler: The Personal Account of Fabian von Schlabrendorff*, ed. G. Gaevernitz (London: Eyre and Spottiswood, 1948), 155. During this process he described the apparent pleasure that his torturers, young, both male and female, took in their actions. None of this barbarity succeeded in extracting a confession out of him, or persuaded him to betray the names of his fellow conspirators.

Chapter 2: One Week Earlier

1   But then the Japanese attacked with all the ferocity of men defending their homeland. The battle would last for eighty-two days of ferocious fighting, causing American combat troops involved to increase to 180,000, with a further 368,000 in support. The number of Japanese soldiers known to have been killed totalled 107,500, with a further 20,000 thought to have perished in caves sealed by American assault teams using flamethrowers and explosives. It has also been calculated that 150,000 local Okinawan citizens were killed, and that in the spring/summer of 1945 a quarter of a million human beings died, including American losses of 7,613 on land and 4,900 at sea. See M. Gilbert, *Second World War* (London: Phoenix Giant, 1989), 655.

2   M. Dobbs, *Six Months in 1945: From World War to Cold War* (London: Hutchinson, 2012), 147.

3   Stalin was in no mood for light-heartedness. Marshal Zhukov, summoned on March 29, had been somewhat delayed in reaching Moscow, arriving in the end by train. That same day a violent storm and ensuing plane crash of the flight carrying all the leaders of the Polish Home Army had necessitated them bravely completing an interrupted journey to the Soviet capital, also by train. Upon reaching Moscow, the designated Polish leaders were all, in total violation of every understanding and agreement reached by the Allies hitherto, conveyed swiftly and directly to the Lubyanka prison and the brutal Soviet system of (in)justice, from whence they would re-emerge only after a desperate interval of many years. By contrast, Zhukov, for the present, was more fortunate: following his meeting with Stalin, the Russian *Stavka* now worked in great haste, fearing that the Allies would be quicker than the Soviet troops in taking Berlin. They had much to coordinate. The operation to capture the German capital involved 2.5 million men, 41,600 guns and mortars, 6,250 tanks and self-propelled guns, and 7,500 aircraft. On that very day, the date of the start of the final assault on Berlin was fixed as April 16. See A. Beevor, *Berlin: The Downfall, 1945* (London: Penguin Books, 2003), 147.

4   That Germans were, via Berne, putting out peace feelers, was quite true: yet it was quite wrong for Stalin to be so suspicious that he was being stabbed in the back. Soviet sources indicated to Stalin that, over a two-week period, negotiations took

place that led to an agreement whereby the German front would be opened to Anglo-American troops, permitting them to advance east, in exchange for the easing of post-war German peace terms. Stalin was quick to accept in full this inflammatory rendition. Ambassador Molotov instantly wrote an insulting note to the Anglo-Americans and withdrew from the forthcoming fifty-nation world conference, due to last a full two months, which was planned to begin on April 25 in San Francisco. (It did take place and became the founding conference for the United Nations Organisation.) Volume 6 of Churchill's detailed account *The Second World War* is, accordingly, named *Triumph and Tragedy*, and the events of April are covered in the chapter entitled "The Polish Dispute." The entry of the United Kingdom and Dominions into the war had been expressly in the defence of Polish sovereignty. When, in what felt like an eternity later, the ensuing world war was drawing to a close, it was crystal clear to Churchill, and to Roosevelt, that genuinely free elections and post-war sovereignty for Poland was the very opposite of what Stalin was intending. Poland would imminently be "lost" to the free world. The ironic nature of this looming failure, which it was now almost impossible to avert, was not lost on Churchill. Never one to abandon hope, he agreed with Roosevelt on March 31 that they would both address Stalin directly on the matter. Meanwhile Churchill also played quite possibly his strongest card: he chose this moment to send his wife, Clementine, on a state visit to Moscow in her role as chair of the Red Cross Aid to Russia Fund, as part of a Russian tour that extended as far as the Urals.

5   Hibberd was the broadcaster of choice for the momentous VE Day bulletin thirty-seven long days later. Listeners thought they could detect the sound of a cocktail party taking place in the BBC studio that day during the one o'clock news. In fact, Hibberd had been at the microphone with all his old medals pinned to his chest. See D. Hendy, *The BBC: A People's History* (London: Profile Books, 2022), 286.

6   The BBC broadcast continued: "The German Government has ceased to exercise effective control over wide areas. The German High Command has lost effective control over many units, large and small, of the German forces." These are the opening sentences of two messages issued the previous evening by the supreme commander, General Eisenhower, "in order to avoid further unnecessary bloodshed and sacrifice of human life." One was addressed to German soldiers, giving them detailed instructions on how to surrender. The other informed all foreign workers in western Germany how best to take refuge till the Allied Armies arrived to finish mopping up German units and put the workers in touch with liaison officers from their own countries. See BBC News HNB Film 128/129, April 1–9, 1945, BBC Archive.

7   On April 1 Lieutenant General Hodges' 1st US Army, advancing from the south, linked up in the area of Lippstadt with Lieutenant General Simpson's 9th US Army, which had advanced from the north. The effect of this was that German General Feldmarschal Model's Army Group B, Colonel-General Harpe's 5th Panzer Army, and Infantry General von Zangen's 15th Army were trapped between the Rhine, the Ruhr, and the Sieg, in the "Ruhr pocket." The initial Allied assessment of 80,000 troops encircled was at first upgraded to 125,000 and then increased again to 150,000. In fact, also included in the huge pocket of some four thousand square miles, in addition to Feldmarschal Model, were 323,000 soldiers,

including twenty-five further generals and an admiral. See J. Trigg, *To VE-Day through German Eyes: The Final Defeat of Nazi Germany* (Stroud, UK: Amberley, 2020), 238.

8   J. Goebbels, *Tagebücher 1945: Die letzten Aufzeichnungen* (Hamburg: Bastei Lübbe, 1977), 478.

9   K. Scholder, *Preliminary History and the Time of Illusions, 1918–34*, vol. 1 of *The Churches and the Third Reich* (London: SCM Press, 1977), 222. At the time a minority, whose number included Bonhoeffer, did see the reality behind the falsity. Léonard Ragaz, the Swiss religious socialist, wrote about the Potsdam Day celebrations of March 21, 1933: "All this had been a lie—the apex of lies, *the* lie—the religious display of the whole demonic swindle, the ringing of bells and organ-playing, everything to the tune of 'God is with us,' this last a grave blasphemy. . . . For quite apart from all the lies, amidst all this . . . singing and praying resound the screams of the sons and daughters of Germany tortured in the barracks of this 'liberator and restorer of Germany'. . . . This edifice of illusion and deceit, crowned by this religious deceit, will collapse horribly, as a symbol of the downfall of all the forces that come together in it" (256).

10   John Conway, *The Nazi Persecution of the Churches, 1933–1945* (London: Regent College, 1968), 16, quoted in M. Burleigh, *The Third Reich: A New History* (London: Macmillan, 2000), 258. As a whole, the Nazis despised Christianity for its Judaic roots, effeminacy, otherworldliness, and universality. It appeared life-denying to those who saw themselves as life-affirming, mobilising entirely unwanted sentiments and values. Forgiveness was not for resentful haters, nor compassion of much use to those who wanted to stamp the weak into the ground. In short, Christianity was a "soul malady." Many other Nazis were also equally visceral in their anti-clericalism as Hitler: one historian has suggested that "one would have to visit the Reformation or the extreme anti-clericalism in the modern era to find anything analogous to their vicious and vulgar attacks on priests" (Burleigh, *Third Reich*, 255).

11   L. Rees, *The Nazis: A Warning from History* (London: BBC Books, 2005), 235.

12   Gilbert, *Second World War*, 657.

13   A charlatan, according to H. Trevor-Roper, *The Last Days of Hitler* (London: Macmillan, 1947), 54.

Chapter 3: Heinrich Himmler

1   Evidence of Himmler's protective stance towards Canaris (and by implication, his associates) abounds. In a deposition by F. X. Sonderegger dated September 9, 1948, Himmler's former colleague stated that he had been instructed to "leave Canaris alone" (A. Kraell, *Akten der Lüneburger Staatsanwaltschaft IX*, 250, cited in Höhne, *Canaris*, 508). Another statement summarising Himmler's approach to Canaris was "Not interested in proceeding vs Canaris" (A. Kraell, *Akten der Lüneburger Staatsanwaltschaft III*, 166, cited in Höhne, *Canaris*, 529). In reference to another similar incident shielding Canaris dating to February 1943, see also W. Meyer, *Unternehmen Sieben: Eine Rettungsaktion für vom Holocaust Bedrohte aus dem Amt Ausland/Abwehr im Oberkommando der Wehrmacht* (Meisenheim, Germany: Anton Hain, 1993), 377. More pointedly, an example of Himmler actively pretending he had authorised something Canaris was involved in, so as to cover

for and protect Canaris, is cited by Mueller: "Himmler refused to read Roed-er's report—he stated he was not interested in prosecuting Canaris" (M. Mueller, *Canaris: The Life and Death of Hitler's Spymaster* [Barnsley, UK: Frontline, 2007], 231–33). In post-war testimony Sonderegger was also able to list three previ-ous cases all involving Canaris' Abwehr departmental head, Dohnanyi, or oth-ers in the Abwehr and concerned with conspiracies to assassinate Hitler where Himmler had stopped the investigation. SS intelligence chief Walter Schellenberg in his (at other points unreliable) memoirs also conveys the same message. He states that when he would report the admiral's apparent betrayal, Himmler would merely say, "Leave the dossier here with me" and "I will bring it to Hitler's atten-tion when the right moment arises." It never did. This happened with some fre-quency. Mueller makes the point succinctly: "Himmler not only showed a com-plete disdain for investigating the suspicions against Canaris, but also ensured that the accusations against him in connection with the prosecution of Dohnanyi and Oster did not succeed" (Mueller, *Canaris*, 243). This theoretical "protection" was known to Dohnanyi and hence Bonhoeffer; see also Christine von Dohnanyi citing Himmler's "surprisingly normal" working relationship with her Abwehr departmental head spouse and Bonhoeffer's brother-in-law, Hans von Dohnanyi (see p. 14, IfZ, ZS 603, fol. 75). For his part Hans von Dohnanyi strategically "kept a line open to Himmler, and more especially to his chief of staff, Karl Wolff" (Höhne, *Canaris*, 510). Along the same lines, in one snatched conversation in the dungeons of Prinz-Albrecht-Straße on October 9, 1944, Bonhoeffer suggested to von Schlabrendorff that if he ever somehow "gets out of here," he should seek a personal audience with Bonhoeffer's father and with Heinrich Himmler (Bethge, *Dietrich Bonhoeffer*, 902). Some resisters had (in their naivety) even counte-nanced allowing Himmler's SS to be part of the military element of ousting Hitler.

2   BAB, NS 19/4005, speech in Alt-Rehse (1938); see P. Witte and S. Tyas, *Himmler's Diary, 1945: A Calendar of Events Leading to Suicide* (London: Fonthill Media, 2014), 114.

3   An example of this is cited in chapter 14, p. 108.

4   Martin Bormann was the Nazi Party's head of chancellery and party secretary. He was a ruthless and self-serving power broker whose influence in the closing days of the Third Reich was profound. At Bormann's suggestion, Hitler had appointed Himmler in November 1944 as a genuine military commander responsible for live situational command. Himmler, initially delighted, quickly found it not to his liking—especially, imminently, on the rapidly collapsing Eastern Front. Here things did not work out well for German soldiers or for Himmler, who rapidly took to his sickbed. By the time he was relieved of his command, his rise in Hitler's esteem—until this point seemingly inexorable—had been halted. By March 15, 1945, Hitler informed Goebbels, who noted it in his diary, that Himmler had been to see him and that he had given him "an extraordinary dressing down" (P. Longerich, *Heinrich Himmler* [Oxford: Oxford University Press, 2012], 723). He was relieved of military command of Army Group Vistula on March 21, 1945. Less than a week later, following the collapse of a Waffen-SS offensive in Hungary under the command of SS-Obergruppenführer Sepp Dietrich, Hitler verbally lac-erated the troops and the SS in general and ordered that the Leibstandarte Adolf Hitler unit wearing armlets in his name be stripped of them. Among the signals

given out by this gesture was the resounding disfavour in which Himmler, the founder of the SS, was now regarded. (The Bormann suggestion was designed to reduce Himmler's standing with Hitler—and this was achieved.)

5   I. Kershaw, *Hitler* (London: Penguin Books, 2009), 224–25.

6   This organisation, whose name translates as "People's Storm," was set up by Hitler in the closing stages of the war, conscripting civilians between the ages of sixteen and sixty. Ill-equipped and under-resourced, its members committed numerous war crimes and made many heroic, often futile, sacrifices.

7   Rees, *Nazis*, 351–52.

8   The gripping story is recounted by A. Dulles in *The Secret Surrender* (London: Harper and Row, 1966). Following World War II, Dulles became head of the CIA, and Wolff, subsequently engaged like so many by the American CIC, received immunity from prosecution for war crimes at Nuremberg.

9   In his case the normal most senior SS rank of HSSPF (Höherer SS- und Polizeiführer) was reconstrued as Höchster SS-Polizeiführer (meaning most senior, or supreme, police commander). His role and function, crucially, also held, from July 1944 onwards, line authority as a plenipotentiary general of the German Wehrmacht for the Rear Italian Front lines. On Easter Sunday afternoon, an exhausted Wolff, after incessant travelling, had an appointment with the Wehrmacht's General Vietinghoff to tell him of Generalfeldmarchal Kesselring's consent to a general surrender in Italy (A. Dulles, *Germany's Underground: The Anti-Nazi Resistance* [Boston: Da Capo, 1947], 133). Over the Easter weekend, the high stakes events continued, and Wolff had to deal, at intervals, with being summoned to Berlin by the Führer, ordered to Hungary at once to stiffen resistance, and harried by Kaltenbrunner and Himmler, whose joint and incandescent sense of being excluded was palpable. So out of sorts with this lack of control did Himmler feel that he found himself obliged to take drastic steps to keep this matter in hand. He "helped" Wolff in early April 1945 by taking Wolff's family into "protective" custody.

10   The Allies were not to be trifled with: as the American Dulles waited in Ascona for further news from Wolff, a British Commando unit broke out of the Allied battle line in Italy, which had been static for three months, and on April 1 surprised the German 162nd Division in the area of Lake Comacchio on the Adriatic coast and took over nine hundred prisoners. See Dulles, *Secret Surrender*, 137.

11   Gilbert, *Second World War*, 657.

12   S. Helm, *If This Is a Woman: Inside Ravensbrück: Hitler's Concentration Camp for Women* (London: Little, Brown, 2015), 565ff.

Chapter 4: The Speed of Events

1   A. Hillgruber and G. Hümmelchen, *Chronik des zweiten Weltkrieges* (Bindlach, Germany: Gondron, 1978), 275.

2   G. Sajer, *The Forgotten Soldier: War on the Russian Front—A True Story* (London: Cassell, 1999), 544.

3   C. Waite, *Survivor of the Long March: Five Years as a POW, 1940–1945* (Stroud, UK: History Press, 2012), 184.

4   D. Blatman, *The Death Marches: The Final Phase of Nazi Genocide*, trans. C. Galai (Cambridge, Mass.: Harvard University Press, 2011), 175.

5   Beevor, *Berlin*, 184.

6   Blatman, *Death Marches*, 228ff.
7   The chosen victim was a lieutenant called Friedl Heymann, a highly decorated combat veteran who had been recovering from serious wounds in the city. When Heymann had not joined a reserve unit as ordered, Lamberth's men had seized him from the home he shared with his young wife, whom he had recently married. He was quickly tried, convicted of *Fahnenflucht* (dereliction of duty in the face of the enemy), and then executed in a public square on Lamberth's orders. A sign was attached to his dangling corpse: "Death to all traitors!" For many, Heymann's conduct was not that of a traitor.

Chapter 5: Surviving Hitler's Demands

1   A. Kershaw, *The Liberator: One World War II Soldier's 500-Day Odyssey* (London: Arrow, 2013), 243ff.
2   In total the US used 14,000 tons of napalm in World War II, two-thirds of which were deployed in the Pacific (Kershaw, *Liberator*).
3   M. Hastings, *All Hell Let Loose: The World at War, 1939–1945* (London: Harper, 2011), 618.
4   Burleigh, *Third Reich*, 785.
5   Kershaw, *End*, 321.
6   A. Joachimsthaler, *The Last Days of Hitler: Legend, Evidence and Truth* (London: Cassell, 2000), 46.
7   Introduced in n. 18 of this book's introduction.
8   V. Klemperer, *To the Bitter End*, vol. 2 of *The Diaries of Victor Klemperer* (London: Phoenix, 2000), 536. In this latter comment, both Klemperer's bravery in keeping in his possession such a journal and his implied respect for those who dared to resist, as did Bonhoeffer, are evident.

Chapter 6: Buchenwald, Bonhoeffer, and the Hostage Convoy

1   I. Sayer and J. Dronfield, *Hitler's Last Plot: The 139 VIP Hostages Selected for Death in the Final Days of World War II* (New York: De Capo, 2019), 18.
2   This "centre" comprised an aviary, a zoo, an equestrian centre, and a large Teutonic hunting hall (built by prisoner labour) with carved oak timbers and huge fireplaces, filled with trophies and furniture to match. It had been lavishly created for the personal use of Hermann Göring, in his capacity as Reich hunt master, but in a characteristic Nazi irony, Göring was never actually to visit (Sayer and Dronfield, *Hitler's Last Plot*, 19). For fuller details, see V. Knigge et al., *Konzentrationslager Buchenwald 1937–1945: Speziallager Nr. 2 1945–1950. Zwei Lager an einem Ort—Geschichte und Erinerrungskonstruktion* (Weimar: Gutenberg, 1998). In relation to Blum, Beevor notes, "Prior to German invasion, French troops were unwilling to fight. All the French High Command did to maintain morale was to organise front-line entertainment with visits from famous singers and actors . . . but more alarming still for the Allied cause were those right-wingers in influential positions who said 'Better Hitler than Blum,' a reference to the socialist leader of the 1936 popular front, Léon Blum, who was also Jewish." Beevor, *Second World War* (London: Weidenfeld & Nicholson, 2012), 50.
3   T. Pünder, *In den Fängen des NS-Staats: Staatssekretär Dr. Hermann Pünder 1944/45* (Munich: Aschendorff, 2018), 126. I am thankful to Dr Tilman Pünder for kindly sending me a copy of the SS daily provisioning sheet.

4   In Piester's logic the larger rooms—if they were in fact larger, which is not
     clear—were not used for two people. Pünder in cell 2, previously alone, was
     considerably cheered up by the arrival and subsequent company of Commander
     Liedig. Piester's decision to allocate Bonhoeffer and Rabenau to the same cell was
     a significant encouragement to them both.

5   H. Falconer, *The Gestapo's Most Improbable Hostage* (1975; repr., Barnsley, UK:
     Pen and Sword, 2018), 111. Erfurt is twenty-three kilometres from Buchenwald.
     US troops were in Eisenach and Creuzburg, not Erfurt, that day.

6   Pünder, *In den Fängen des NS-Staats*, 127.

7   Falconer, *Most Improbable Hostage*, 101. In this observation Falconer is correct,
     as after the war Buchenwald was in the Russian occupied zone and the building
     was indeed demolished at the end of the 1940s.

8   Falconer, *Most Improbable Hostage*, 101.

9   With this diagram, published in 1950, Best captured some of the consensus of those
     who have published accounts. Assimilating other published information, from
     Müller, Pünder, and Falconer, and from Falkenhausen's archive statement, it seems
     most likely that Müller and Gehre were in 7 and Alvensleben and Petersdorff in
     8, and hence Kokorin in 4. A detail for which we are again indebted to Falconer
     (as well as Pünder) is the presence in room 5 (with General von Falkenhausen)
     of one of the SS camp doctors, possibly Dr Gerhard Schiedlausky (H. Stein, ed.,
     Konzentrationslager Buchenwald 1937–1945: Begleitband zur ständigen Ausstellung
     [Gedenkstätte Buchenwald, Germany: Wallstein, 1999], 57), SS Dr Hoven (Best,
     Venlo Incident, 178; and Hoepner, TNA, WO 328/14), or even Dr Wagner, whose
     term in Buchenwald ended prior to these events but who is known to be associated
     with the medical abuse of prisoners mentioned in Falconer's account.

10   In 1952 Falkenhausen described this diagram as inaccurate, stating that the cells
     were all of the same size (Militärarchiv Freiburg, Blatt 16, May 16, 1952).

11   Commander Liedig was a forty-five-year-old former lawyer and friend of Admi-
     ral Canaris. During their investigation into the July 20 bomb plot in 1944, the
     Gestapo had stumbled over the plans for a previous attempt on Hitler's life back in
     September 1938, and Liedig's name and long-term associations had been uncov-
     ered. Although the evidence lacked corroboration, it was true that Liedig was to
     have been one of two assassins assigned to kill Hitler: he was to have been the
     accomplice of Abwehr colonel Hans Oster—but the operation had been shelved
     following the Munich Agreement. Later, in 1940, in Oster's leaking of details of
     imminent offensives to the West, it had been Liedig, acting as Oster's driver, who
     had sat waiting for him in the car while he revealed plans for the invasion of
     Holland to the Dutch naval attaché in Berlin. From the Gestapo's perspective, the
     main case against Liedig lay in his long-term friendship with Admiral Canaris
     and his association with others, such as Oster, now suspected of involvement in
     the July 20 plot. As a result he was finally arrested in Oslo in November 1944.
     As is the case with almost all the other hostages, the precise reason for his initial
     inclusion on the list is unknown. Unlike all the others (except Josef Müller) in the
     close Canaris group, he was omitted from the execution order soon to be issued
     on April 5, for reasons that also remain unknown.

12   Erich Wagner was an SS doctor whose academic furtherance was based on a tat-
     too study conducted in part by murdering inmates of Buchenwald ("Ein Beitrag

zur Tätowierungsfrage [A contribution to the question of tattooing]," dissertation submitted in 1940 to Professor Dr Friedrich Timm of the Medical Faculty at the Institute of Forensic Medicine and Scientific Criminology of the University of Jena; for a description of the crimes involved in this submission see Falconer, *Most Improbable Hostage*, 110).

13 Ludwig Gehre had worked at Abwehr section IIIF and had high-level connections, for example to Rudolf Hess, so had been drawn into preparations for the coup by Oster. He had fallen into the clutches of the SD (Sicherheitsdienst) because he had passed on a warning to someone involved in the plot that he was in danger and should flee. That was enough to put him under close scrutiny. As an officer, he could not be arrested right away, but was taken to Sachsenhausen and interrogated by the SD. There he told his interrogators that he had some excellent bottles of wine in his flat, and, accepting his invitation, they drove there together. The three drank copious quantities. Gehre showed himself the most resilient in relation to the intake of alcohol and, under pretext of fetching another bottle from the cellar, was able to make good his escape. For what seemed like countless weeks on end, he and his wife hid together at a friend's home. Gehre explained to Müller, in their shared cell in Buchenwald, that his wife could not stand the close cellar confinement any longer, so they went for a walk—of all places past Tirpitzufer 78, the Abwehr's office address, his former place of work. At this juncture an employee—unsurprisingly—recognised him, and instantly informed the SD. Only moments later the SD henchmen appeared in a car. Gehre took out his revolver and shot his wife, turning the pistol on himself, but the bullet did not kill him, only tearing out an eye; he remained alive. Gehre was brought to a hospital, and in his despair gave up the names of people who had harboured him or known of his concealment. In a far-reaching revelation, but one that proved contributory for the Canaris group, he also inculpated Admiral Canaris and even Judge General Sack. At this time Gehre was repeatedly asked about Josef Müller, and especially about Müller's relationship with Canaris.

14 Werner von Alvensleben was an independent-minded individual and a thoroughgoing regime opponent. He was disinherited by his father after falling out with him in 1909, and left for Canada. In that same year, he married Alexandra, Countess of Einsiedel. He returned to serve in the German army in World War I and was awarded the Iron Cross, First Class. In 1939, politically a member of the conservative opposition, he refused to swear the oath of allegiance to Hitler. By 1945 he had as a result been under some form of arrest for many years, and had on more than one occasion narrowly escaped with his life, notably on June 30, 1934. In a letter written in 1951, Payne Best describes encountering him in Buchenwald: "It was not the etiquette amongst prisoners to ask questions as to the reasons of their imprisonment, nor even to seek information of this nature. The Gestapo frequently had spies disguised as prisoners and in any case, no one was safe from being called up for interrogation, and therefore, the less one knew and could give away, the better. Old Alvensleben was, however, very talkative, and it was from him that most of my information about my companions was derived" (Best, quoted in F. Schlingensiepen, *Dietrich Bonhoeffer: Martyr, Thinker, Man of Resistance*, trans. I. Best [London: T&T Clark, 2010], 418; Alvensleven was born

in 1875 and hence turned seventy in 1945). His outspokenness is believed to have resulted in his being tortured in Buchenwald.

15   Best, quoted in Schlingensiepen, *Dietrich Bonhoeffer*, 418.

16   J. Müller, *Bis zur letzten Konsequenz* (Munich: Süddeutscher Verlag, 1975), 236.

17   Petersdorff's nine-year marriage to his wife, Irene, a former Einsiedel, ended in October 1944, and Alvensleben had married into the Einsiedel family in 1909 (see n. 14 above in this chapter).

18   Falconer, *Most Improbable Hostage*, 112.

19   I. Vermehren, *Reise durch den letzten Akt: Ravensbrück, Buchenwald, Dachau: Eine Frau berichtet* (1946; repr., Hamburg: Rowohlt, 2005), 192–93.

20   Falconer, *Most Improbable Hostage*, 106.

21   M. von Stauffenberg, *Aufzeichnungen aus unserer Sippenhaft: 20. Juli 1944 bis 19. Juni 1945* (Stuttgart: Haus der Geschichte Baden-Württemberg, circa 2012), 109.

22   J. Bidez, *Julian der Abtrünnige*, 4th ed. (Munich: Verlag D Callwey, 1940). The fact that Pünder was able to be kept so relatively up to date with thoughtful subject matter is testimony to the tenacity of his family.

23   Bidez, *Julian*, 283. See 1 Samuel 16:7: "Humankind looks at the outward appearance, but the Lord sees the heart."

24   Bidez, *Julian*, 284. See Romans 12:1; James 1:26; 3:8; and Proverbs 26:20; 21:23, among others.

25   Bidez, *Julian*, 199.

26   Bidez, *Julian*, 136.

27   Bidez, *Julian*, 351.

28   The phrase (and substance) is from T. Holland, *Dominion: The Making of the Western Mind* (London: Little, Brown, 2019), 408 (see also 119–21, 122–23, 127–28, 143, 200).

Chapter 7: General von Rabenau

1   F. Rabenau, *Die alte Armee und die junge Generation: Kritische Betrachtungen* (Berlin: Mittler, 1925), 84. In this section I acknowledge H.-J. Ramm, *Mich trägt mein Glaube: Friedrich von Rabenau: General und Christ im Widerstand: Tagebuch einer Gestapohaft* (Beau-Bassin: Fromm, 2011) as a primary source throughout.

2   Reichstagsprotokolle, 1924/28,2, 66th session, May 26, 1925, 2051.

3   He was promoted to colonel on March 1, 1932.

4   IMT Zeugenschrifttum, 25:124, cited in Ramm, *Mich trägt mein Glaube*, 33.

5   A phrase coined by Victor Klemperer mocking the pomposity of the language being used in official government communications.

6   A derogatory German term for those functionaries eager to carry out the wishes of the Nazi Party.

7   F. von Rabenau, *Vom Geist und Seele des Soldaten* [The soldier's heart and mind] (Vortrag [lecture] vom 27. Mai 1940; Berlin: Schriftenreihe der NSDAP Gruppe I Deutsche Wehrkraft, 1940; repr., Munich: Eherverlag/Zentralverlag der NSDAP, 1941), 9.

8   F. von Rabenau, *Vom Sinn des Soldatentums. Die innere Kraft von Führung und Truppe* [On the meaning of soldiering] (Bonn, Germany: Bernard and Graefe, 1939; repr., Cologne: DuMont/Schauberg, 1941), 18, cf. 22f.

9   F. von Rabenau, *Buch und Schwert: Rede des Generals der Artillerie Friedrich von Rabenau: Gehalten am 28. Okt. 1940 zu Leipzig* [Word and sword] (Leipzig: Bibliographisches Institut, 1940), 23.

10   F. von Rabenau, *Ernste Laiengedanken* [Serious lay thoughtfulness] (Archiv Rabenau, circa 1940), 111.

11   Rabenau, *Ernste Laiengedanken*, 157.

12   Rabenau, *Ernste Laiengedanken*, 109.

13   Even in 1941, at the height of his involvement in the ruthless extermination of Jews, Himmler wanted to cultivate the image of the reasonable, approachable, considerate deputy. He also had a keen instinct for discerning the link between faith and resistance, and nurtured many such surprising links, which he no doubt anticipated he could later either expose or turn to his advantage.

14   J. von Stülpnagel, *75 Jahre meines Lebens* (Oberaudorf, Germany: Obb, 1955), 379.

15   Eher Verlag was the publisher of Hitler's *Mein Kampf.*

16   Bethge, *Dietrich Bonhoeffer*, 726. No date is indicated.

17   The German branch of the Order of St John has links back to the Order of St John Hospitaller of Jerusalem, which dates back to 1538.

18   Schreiben des Gauleiters Florian an Stellvertreter des Führers v. 3.9.1940, IMT Band XXV, 122ff., Zeugenschriftum 064 PS. Friedrich Karl Florian (1894–1975) was Gauleiter of the NSDAP in Düsseldorf from 1930–1945.

19   F. Halder, *Kriegstagebuch* (Stuttgart: H. A. Jacobsen, 1964), 311.

20   U. von Hassell, *The Ulrich von Hassell Diaries: The Story of the Forces against Hitler inside Germany* (London: Frontline, 2011), 315. It is almost inconceivable that in this meeting Bonhoeffer's name was not mentioned.

21   M. Feuersenger, *Mein Kriegstagebuch: Führerhauptquartier und Berliner Wirklichkeit* (Freiburg, Germany: Herder, 1982), 96.

22   BA/MA, N62 Nachlass Rabenau, F. Rabenau, *Soldat, Krieg, Religion*, unpublished MS, circa 1942, pp. 19, 25, cited in Ramm, *Mich trägt mein Glaube*, 44.

23   BA/MA N62/80, report by A. Büttner, *Der General und Theologe*, October 24, 1950, p. 3.

24   J. Goebbels, *Die Tagebücher von Joseph Goebbels, Teil II, Diktate 1941–1945* (Munich: E. Fröhlich, 1993), entry for January 23, 1943, p. 180f.

25   BA/MA N62/6.2, Nachlass Rabenau, E. Rabenau, *Kürzer Überblick über das Leben meines Vaters*, MS dated 1946/1947, 3.

26   BA/MA, N62/3, W. Vorberg, *Friedrich V. Rabenau: Eine Lebensschilderung*, circa 1955, p. 50.

27   Diary entry for October 10, 1944, quoted in Ramm, *Mich trägt mein Glaube*, 87.

Chapter 8: Double Summer Time

1   During World War II, in order to further the war effort, the UK went on extended British Double Summer Time (BDST). This added two hours to Greenwich Mean Time. The project began on February 25, 1940, and ended on October 7, 1945.

2   Deutsch, *Conspiracy against Hitler*, 260.

3   Meanwhile, the BBC news that day of course continued to report all Allied successes in upbeat language: "When the American troops met at Lippstadt yesterday, they captured an airfield from a thousand Germans who gave in without

a fight. The Americans liberated two thousand five hundred Polish officers and men yesterday—including nine Generals—who'd been in German hands since 1939. Two hundred and forty six Russian officers were also set free" (BBC News HNB Film 128/129). But at the same time, the actual number of German troops now trapped was a considerable underestimate.

4   Dobbs, *Six Months in 1945*, 146.

5   The cost being borne in this respect by the Soviet people was staggering: on a typical day, nearly 800 Germans were killed by the Red Army, compared with just over 60 combat deaths on the Western Front. Conversely, roughly 2,500 German soldiers were reported "missing" on the Eastern Front each day, compared with ten times that number in the West. Reich territory was fast disappearing on all fronts. Also on that Monday, and the following day, the 1st Belorussian Front, under Zhukov, and the 1st Ukrainian Front, under Konev, received their instructions for the final assault on Berlin, while a little farther north, Soviet artillery began its softening-up barrage on the centre of Königsberg. The complete destruction and surrender of the city would be achieved in a week.

6   Beevor, *Berlin*, 190.

7   P. Ashdown, *Nein! Standing Up to Hitler, 1935–1944* (London: Collins, 2018), 252.

8   The pilot was Wing Commander Bill Fraser. The aircraft was a C-54 four-engine passenger lease-lend airliner acquired from the United States. It was the first tricycle type, and the height of the entrance door was nine feet, so no steps were available and had to be hurriedly found so that the arrival in Moscow would not be an embarrassment. The BBC reported, "It will last a month or so, this inspection of Red Cross and medical work in the Soviet Union. One of Mrs Churchill's main objects is to visit Rostov-on-Don, where her Red Cross Aid to Russia Fund is to equip two hospitals at a cost of about four hundred thousand pounds" (BBC News HNB Film 128/129).

9   A. Bullock, *Hitler: A Study in Tyranny* (London: Penguin Books, 1962), 772.

10   W. Churchill, "The Sinews of Peace," March 5, 1946, cited in P. Frankopan, *The Silk Roads: A New History of the World* (London: Bloomsbury, 2015), 397.

11   Gilbert, *Second World War*, 657 (known to the Allies through Ultra decrypt).

12   It was perilous to be among Hitler's entourage. In early April, when Brandt quite innocently told Hitler he had evacuated his wife and child to Thuringia, Hitler thundered to his horror that this was treason, and ordered that Brandt be court-martialled and sentenced to death. See G. Sereny, *Albert Speer: His Battle with Truth* (London: Macmillan, 1995), 505. (Himmler, Speer, and Dönitz contrived his rescue. Brandt was hanged for war crimes in 1948.)

13   Sereny, *Albert Speer*, 505.

Chapter 9: Germany's Leadership

1   A. Mayer, *Why Did the Heavens Not Darken? The Final Solution in History* (London: Verso, 1990), 447.

2   Bullock, *Hitler*, 778–79.

3   An early suggested post-surrender programme for Germany.

4   See chapter 5, pp. 46–47.

5   Goebbels, *Tagebücher 1945*, 476–78.

6   Helm, *If This Is a Woman*, 569.

Chapter 10: Himmler's Hostage Plans

1   Helm, *If This Is a Woman*, 574. Lanckoronska, who grew up in her family palace in Vienna, distinguished herself in relief work in the early war years before being imprisoned in Ravensbrück in 1943. She provides an early example of Himmler keeping a note of VIP prisoners who might be of some use to himself.

2   A. Levy, *Nazi Hunter: The Wiesenthal File; How Simon Wiesenthal Hunted Down the Nazi War Criminals* (London: Robinson, 2002), 126.

Chapter 11: Germany

1   For Germany at the time, Russians were not well regarded, but the label "Bolshevik" was still more derogatory.

2   Kershaw, *Liberator*, 312.

3   Helm, *If This Is a Woman*, 577. Salvequart in fact managed to survive rape attempts, the war, and war crime investigations.

4   Helm, *If This Is a Woman*, 561.

5   A. Beevor, *D-Day: The Battle for Normandy* (London: Penguin Books, 2012), 728.

6   Kershaw, *Liberator*, 244.

7   Of the more than 714,000 prisoners still in the concentration camps at the start of 1945, estimates state that between 240,000 and 360,000 fell victim to the evacuations. See Longerich, *Heinrich Himmler*, 731.

8   Hanke was captured on May 6 by Czech partisans, not initially recognised, and later killed while attempting to escape (Kershaw, *End*, 321). Being nominated RFSS by Hitler when Himmler was stripped of all roles for disloyalty on April 29 may, if he knew, have been of passing solace to him. (Hitler's instruction was ignored by Dönitz.) See Weale, *Army of Evil*, 405.

Chapter 12: Buchenwald

1   Dr Tilman Pünder, conversation with the author, August 2021.

2   M. P. De Jonge, *Bonhoeffer's Reception of Luther* (Oxford: Oxford University Press, 2017), 1. For Bonhoeffer, next (a distant second) is Karl Barth, with fewer than three hundred citations. Bonhoeffer cites Augustine, Thomas Aquinas, Søren Kierkegaard, and John Calvin each several dozen times. "Luther's ubiquity in Bonhoeffer's corpus should be taken seriously" (8). Bonhoeffer's thought in relation to what was then the modern period was also informed by Catholic and Jewish writings, as well as a rich variety of influences from other world religions.

3   The author assumes the copy Bonhoeffer used and exchanged was from the first-edition run, volume 180.

4   Tilman Pünder assured the author in a telephone conversation in June 2021 that there was "no way" his father Hermann would have been at home in the subject matter of the publication in question.

5   K. Leese, *Der Protestantismus im Wandel der neueren Zeit* (Stuttgart: Alfred Kroner, 1940), 234. There appears to be an error in the critical apparatus attributing this Harnack citation to *Der deutsche Protestantismus, seine Vergangenheit und seine heutigen Lebensfragen*, 1846, 48f. It in fact appears in *Religiöse Glaube und freie Forschung*, 1908 (according to K. Nowak, *Adolf von Harnack als Zeitgenosse: Reden und Schriften aus den Jahren des Kaiserreichs und der Weimarer Republik*

[Berlin: De Gruyter, 1996], 829 [271]), and, given this date, may have been current enough in Harnack's thinking for Bonhoeffer to have heard it mentioned.

6   A relatively harsh word much in circulation in Germany at that time, and also used by representatives of the church.

7   Leese, *Protestantismus*, 157.

8   Tzschirner, cited in Leese, *Protestantismus*, 90.

9   "The Reformed Church is always reforming itself."

10   Tillich, cited in Leese, *Protestantismus*, 356.

11   Seeberg, cited in Leese, *Protestantismus*, 361.

12   Leese, *Protestantismus*, xiv.

13   L. Blum, *Le dernier mois* (1946; repr., Paris: Arléa, 2004), 30.

Chapter 13: Sigmund Rascher

1   S. Bär, *Der Untergang des Hauses Rascher* (self-pub., 2011), 18, later published as *The Fall of the House of Rascher: The Bizarre Life and Death of the SS-Doctor Sigmund Rascher* (self-pub., Kindle, 2014). I acknowledge Bär as my primary source throughout this section. Citations are from either the self-published German edition in the Zeitgeschichtsarchiv Pragser Wildsee or the electronic (English) edition. All translations (and, in the case of the English electronic version, adaptations) are my own. At one point in this text Bär comments, in an aside, with no small irony, "As everyone knows, after the war it turned out that almost all Germans were secret resistance fighters or were at least apolitical. Actually there were only six real Nazis: Hitler, Göring, Bormann, Streicher, and Goebbels—although the last is doubtful. In his diaries Goebbels sounds like a leftist student" (*Fall*, loc. 3127).

2   She was the daughter of a wealthy businessman, who paid for the new couple's resettlement in Munich, as well as for his daughter's morphine dependency. He was subsequently very pleased with the arrival of two grandchildren.

3   Bär, *Fall*, loc. 453.

4   A forum established by Himmler with the purpose of providing "evidence" for Nazi racial doctrine and promoting these ideas to the German public along quasi-scientific lines.

5   Bär, *Fall*, loc. 7213.

6   P. Padfield, *Himmler: Reichsführer SS* (London: Papermac, 1990), 333. For a fuller, but not complete, list of crimes, see R. Lifton, *The Nazi Doctors: Medical Killing and the Psychology of Genocide* (New York: Basic Books, 2000), 270–74.

7   The German equivalent of a postdoctoral viva enabling further progression up the academic and career ladder.

8   In Dachau, in broadly the same period, 100 (mainly Polish) priests were used as test subjects in fatal malaria experiments. Rascher's work caused the death of around 200. At Auschwitz more than 12,000 died in medical experiments, as a result of tests and practice operations and amputations. See Beevor, *D-Day*, 297. As late as April 1945, around 100 Australian POWs—some sick, some healthy—were also being used for experiments, receiving unknown injections. In Manchuria 1,485 American, Australian, British, and New Zealand POWs held at Mukden were used for a variety of experiments with pathogens. After the Japanese surrender, MacArthur agreed to provide immunity from prosecution to all involved in "biological warfare Unit 731": a deal that in exchange allowed the

Americans to obtain all the data that had been accumulated from their experiments. See Beevor, *Second World War*, 772.

9   Eléonore Baur—a co-founder, with Adolf Hitler, of the Nazi Party, with a distant connection to nursing.

10 Two and a half years on, in 1945, it was directly from this camp and (possibly) role that Heidel Nowakowski was assigned to join the small party of Bonhoeffer's fellow travellers.

11 In total, ten children were involved, before the four were retained.

12 Bär, *Untergang des Hauses Rascher*, 1.

13 For Nini, in Ravensbrück, food supplies were almost non-existent: Nini was said to have planned a further attack on a wardress and been hanged there in late April 1945.

Chapter 14: Murderous Thoughts—and Many Reports

1   S. E. Morison, *Victory in the Pacific, 1945* (Oxford: Oxford University Press, 1960), appendix 2, 390–92.

2   BBC News HNB Film 128/129.

3   W. Churchill, *The Second World War*, 6 vols. (London: Cassell, 1948–1954), 6:382.

4   Churchill, *Second World War*, 6:392.

5   Dobbs, *Six Months in 1945*, 151.

6   The Soviets did indeed receive more than 1,000 fighter aircraft, 240,000 tons of aircraft fuel, and 24,000 tons of rubber from Britain—and from the United States, more than 3,000 aircraft, 3,000 tanks, 9,000 jeeps, 16,000 weapons and carriers, and 41,436 trucks, plus two thousand million dollars' worth of machinery and equipment (Gilbert, *Second World War*, 658). If the Allied victory was in truth bought with Russian blood, it was wrought by American hardware.

7   G. Janssen, *Das Ministerium Speer: Deutschlands Rüstung im Krieg* (Berlin: Ullstein, 1968), 207.

8   Hence "Vergeltungswaffen" (weapons of retribution).

9   Best, *Venlo Incident*, 104.

10 Bullock, *Hitler*, 636.

11 R. Hansen, *Disobeying Hitler: German Resistance in the Last Year of WWII* (London: Faber and Faber, 2014), 1.

12 A. Speer, *Inside the Third Reich: The Classic Account of Nazi Germany by Hitler's Armaments Minister* (London: Weidenfeld and Nicholson, 1970), 611, 615.

13 The phrase "working towards the Führer" is from a seemingly unimportant speech given by Werner Willikens, State Secretary in the Ministry of Food, on February 21, 1934 (Bundesarchive Lichterfelde, file 43, I/2696).

14 S. Tyas, *SS-Major Horst Kopkow: From the Gestapo to British Intelligence* (London: Fonthill Media, 2017), 130, 182, 170. Kopkow survived the war and, following interrogation, was employed for twenty years as a consultant for Britain's Secret Intelligence Service.

15 Smuts, no stranger on the world stage, would go on to (help) found the League of Nations.

16 Gotha is in central Germany and lies around 315 kilometres (or 196 miles) from Berlin. (The 150-mile exaggeration is repeated later.)

17 BBC News HNB Film 128/129.

18   The BBC explained that Hamm was "the best equipped and most bombed railway centre in Europe; it's reckoned to be as big as twelve Clapham Junctions."

19   See chapter 42, n. 6.

20   Hansen, *Disobeying Hitler*, 245.

21   Kershaw, *Liberator*, 245–47. The book includes a photograph of one of tens of thousands of German boy soldiers captured in spring 1945, this one aged around seven (250).

22   Gilbert, *Second World War*, 658.

23   CIRO/PEAR/ZIP/AT 1726, transmitted April 3, 1945—extract from GPD 4053, TNA, HW 16/71.

24   BBC News HNB Film 128/129.

25   Witte and Tyas, *Himmler's Diary*, 114.

26   Witte and Tyas, *Himmler's Diary*, 120.

27   Witte and Tyas, *Himmler's Diary*, 111–24.

28   TNA, HS 9/134/5, statement by 1st Lt Melvin H. Milbrath, May 25, 1945. H. Fry, *The King's Most Loyal Enemy Aliens* (Cheltenham, UK: History Press, 2007), 112, has April 4.

29   The report continues, "German snipers were shooting from a large red brick building on our left. One of the tanks swung its turret around, there was a flash and a roar, and a great fountain of red rubble leapt out of the wall. Then there was a ping overhead, and we and the American infantry alongside the tanks flung ourselves flat in the roadside ditch. A sniper! The Americans jumped up with a bazooka and they steadied it on a tank and they fired. Again a house wall on the other side of the road erupted with a red splash of powdered brick. And while this was going on, stumbling down the middle of the road past the infantry lying in the ditch and the tanks firing into their houses, more and more of the Münster civilians came out past us. A middle-aged man led on a group of women: he ran from side to side of the road waving his white handkerchief: then ducking his head as the sniper bullets whistled over: it was the queerest sight to see this sudden interruption of the battle by these frightened men and women in civilian clothes. Then, with a last turn, the leading tank turned its turret up the road and rumbled forward. The road block was clear and Münster was now before us. But it wasn't a city we saw ahead—it was just a wilderness of burnt-out houses. Blackened walls, and out of which the remaining church towers lifted themselves like black chimneys. It was impossible to tell, at the distance I was, which spire was which, and to pick out the church of St Lambert and the famous tower on which the unfortunate anabaptist leaders were hung after torture back in those distant days of the reformation; for historic Münster, the Münster of the guide books, is gone. . . . Yet, in the ruins, the Germans were still resisting. When I left at nightfall, our lead tanks were just up to the entrance of the oldest part of the city, and we were still meeting shells and mortar fire. The German solders want to surrender. They surrender in droves when they get the chance, as we saw this afternoon, but it seems as long as they've got someone to give them orders, they just go on firing. But the trouble is that there's now no one in authority who'll risk giving them the order they're all praying for—the order to cease fire. . . . So we're now wondering if we're going to find every town we meet another Münster." See BBC News HNB Film 128/129.

30   Hillgruber and Hümmelchen, *Chronik des zweiten Weltkrieges*, 276. According to the website www.seekrieg.de in 2019, before it ceased operations, the resulting German tally of losses was that U-boats U 237, U 749, U 1221, U 2542, U 3003, and U 3505; minelayer M 802; mine transporter *Irben*; minesweepers R 59, R 72, R 119, and R 261; passenger ship *New York* (22,337 BRT); and hospital ship *Monte Olivia* (13,750 BRT), as well as the still-under-construction freighter *Axenfels* (6,200 BRT) and the tanker *Mexphalte* (2,578 BRT), were either sunk, destroyed, or burned out.

31   Sajer, *Forgotten Soldier*, 544.

32   Vassiltchikov, *Berlin Diaries*, 272.

33   Vassiltchikov, *Berlin Diaries*, 273.

34   BBC News HNB Film 128/129.

35   Today Cheb in the Czech Republic.

36   Klemperer, *To the Bitter End*, 539–40.

Chapter 15: A Chance Find in Zossen

1   W. Warlimont, *Inside Hitler's Headquarters, 1939–1945*, trans. R. Barry (London: Presidio, 1964), 510.

2   General Buhle was present in the Rastenberg map room on July 20, 1944, standing a short distance from the table, when the bomb designed to kill Hitler exploded. He made a good recovery from his injuries. Hitler was photographed visiting him in the hospital, but his chance for promotion, imminent at the time of the explosion that July, had now passed. At the time of the explosion, Buhle was close to Admiral von Puttkamer, whose recuperation took place in the same hospital ward, and who was also visited by Hitler that day. See Gilbert, *Second World War*, figure following p. 592.

3   G. Buchheit, *Der deutsche Geheimdienst: Spionageabwehr im Dritten Reich* (Beltheim-Schnellbach, Germany: Lindenbaum, 2010), 479, cited in Höhne, *Canaris*, 591.

4   It has not thus far proven possible to know more of Buhle's motivation: he survived the war, was flown to the USA for interrogation, and died without issue in 1959.

5   See chapter 27 for further discussion on timings.

Chapter 16: Departure from Buchenwald

1   Falconer, *Most Improbable Hostage*, 111–12.

2   Fey von Hassell (married name Fey Pirzio-Biroli; she wrote under her maiden name) was the twenty-five-year-old daughter of Ulrich von Hassell, German ambassador to Italy, executed in late 1944 for his involvement in the July 20 plot against Hitler. At the family villa in north-eastern Italy, Fey's two little boys, Corrado and Roberto Pirzio-Biroli, were torn weeping from her side when the SS seized her as "complicitous" kin of the bomb plotters. In the ensuing nine months, Fey was shuttled in cattle cars from Germany to Poland and back again, where she was detained in concentration camps at Stutthof, Matzkau, and Lauenburg, provided with inadequate rations, and almost died of typhoid.

3   Von Stauffenberg, *Aufzeichnungen aus unserer Sippenhaft*, 110 and 111. Countess Marie-Gabriele Schenk von Stauffenberg was a young cousin (aged thirty) on her father's side of Claus Graf Stauffenberg, the army officer who detonated the July 20

bomb intending to kill Hitler. After the failure, all generations of the family were arrested, and children separated and removed into institutions. Estates were requisitioned, and after a brief period of house arrest the countess was sent from prisons in Augsburg, Friedberg, and Nördling on to one concentration camp after another; the list included Stutthof, Matzkau, Lauenburg, and Buchenwald.

4   By this stage of the war, Allied air superiority was such that it was perilous for any German vehicle to use a public road during daylight. This was due to the imminent risk of strafing by low-flying enemy aircraft.

5   F. von Hassell, *Hostage of the Third Reich: The Story of My Imprisonment and Rescue from the SS* (New York: Macmillan, 1989), 180. (German edition: *Niemals sich beugen: Erinnerungen einer Sondergefangenen der SS* [Munich: Piper, 1993], 175f.)

6   The story of Isa Vermehren and her family, which has a distant link with the demise of Admiral Canaris, and hence Bonhoeffer, is recounted in appendix 9.

7   Vermehren took religious vows soon after the war, was accepted as a nun, and had a remarkable career as a broadcaster and Catholic head teacher.

8   Vermehren, *Reise durch den letzten Akt*, 198–200. The arrival time in Regensburg next day on April 4 is hence recorded here as being at just before midday.

9   Léon Blum was a French socialist politician, and leader of the Front Populaire. Although he was Jewish, he had refused to leave France when the Germans invaded. He had twice been prime minister before 1938, and following the French defeat in 1940 became a staunch opponent of Vichy France. Tried by Vichy on trumped-up charges, he had conducted his defence so brilliantly that the Germans had stopped the trial and had him deported to Buchenwald concentration camp. He was joined voluntarily by his long-standing companion Jeanne Reichenbach, and they were married there. At this point, a week or so short of his seventy-third birthday, he was stricken with sciatica and temporarily unable to move, and hence spent the journey lying on the back seat of the car. His account indicates that his powers of observation, together with his clarity of insight and expression, were not correspondingly reduced: indeed, it is more that the reverse proves to be the case.

10 Blum, *Dernier mois*, 41.

11 On this number Best, Pünder, Falkenhausen, Heberlein, Richardi, and Sayer concur.

12 Best, *Venlo Incident*, 190.

13 Best, *Venlo Incident*, 190.

14 Von Hassell, *Hostage of the Third Reich*, 184.

15 Commander-in-chief of the German army in 1938.

16 Oberstleutnant Ficht was the line head of the Abwehrstelle Munich.

17 Müller, *Bis zur letzten Konsequenz*, 243.

18 The three passengers rendered unconscious by the fumes were General Rabenau, Heidel Nowakowski, and Margot Heberlein.

19 Falconer, *Most Improbable Hostage*, 113ff.

20 Von Hassell, *Hostage of the Third Reich*, 180f.

Chapter 17: Unbeknown Companions

1   R. Cohen, *Soldiers and Slaves: American POWs Trapped by the Nazis' Final Gamble* (New York: Random House, 2005), 183.

Chapter 18: The Hostage Journey Continues

1   From early on during the war, the UK, in preparation for imminent invasion, had removed most if not all road signs, leading to immense inconvenience, accompanied by a very high loss of life in road traffic accidents. It remained a source of constant and thankful disbelief to all advancing Allied troops on German soil to discover that in Fortress Germany all road signs were conveniently still in place.

2   Von Stauffenberg, *Aufzeichnungen aus unserer Sippenhaft*, 111.

3   The closest the convoy actually came to Steinwiesen was a distance of around forty-six kilometres. The fact that Müller countenanced this thought is testimony, if any further were needed, to his determination to resist.

4   Müller, *Bis zur letzten Konsequenz*, 243.

5   Blum, *Le dernier mois*, 41.

6   P. Best, letter to Professor Liebholz, 1951, quoted in Schlingensiepen, *Dietrich Bonhoeffer*, 419.

Chapter 19: Herman Pünder and Vasily Kokorin

1   Marianne plays a key support role during the period of Pünder's incarceration.

2   Pünder, statement taken in Capri, May 30, 1945, TNA, WO 328/30.

3   Readers of Russian-language texts may already be well aware, or be pleased to discover, that Kokorin is the subject of a book (published in Russian) in 2000 by A. Ivakin, entitled Племянник Молотова и сын Сталина [Molotov's Nephew and Stalin's Son].

4   See also L. Reshin and A. Pochtarev, "Molotov's 'Nephew' under Investigation and on Trial," *Independent Military Review* 20 (2000); and V. Zvyagintsev and A. Beznasyuk, *Tribunal. Arbat, 37* (Moscow: Terra-Knizhnyj Klub, 2006), 159–61.

5   Sayer has Kokorin ranked as a sergeant in the 1st Soviet Airborne Brigade who had infiltrated behind German lines in 1942. The Germans spotted the infiltration and the Waffen-SS were awaiting them. One company of Russian paratroopers managed to engage the SS in hand-to-hand fighting, from which Kokorin was a (frostbitten) survivor. See Sayer and Dronfield, *Hitler's Last Plot*, 286.

6   Molotov and his sister Olga were born in Kukarka (now in Sovetsk). The village of Kukarka is only around a hundred kilometres from Moloki.

7   Best, *Venlo Incident*, 156.

Chapter 20: A Bankrupt Nation

1   I. Sayer and D. Botting, *Nazi Gold: The Story of the World's Greatest Robbery—and Its Aftermath* (London: Granada, 1984), 3–5. US dollar currency amounts are from this source.

2   Not only that, but the very files he was carrying were those of Bonhoeffer's fellow resister Fabian von Schlabrendorff, who—as a direct consequence—would survive the war.

3   Between six hundred and seven hundred soldiers from the 712th Tank Battalion and the 357th Infantry were assigned to guard the five entrances to the mine.

4   Goebbels, *Tagebücher 1945*, 516.

5   Gilbert, *Second World War*, 659.

6   A. Williams, *A Passing Fury: Searching for Justice at the End of World War II* (London: Penguin Random House, 2016), 20. Ten thousand inmates had been evacuated on a death march.

Chapter 21: Greatly Exaggerated Rumours

1   BBC News HNB Film 128/129.
2   BBC News HNB Film 128/129.
3   Joachimsthaler, *Last Days of Hitler*, 47.
4   Warlimont, *Inside Hitler's Headquarters*, 513. Warlimont cites Jodl's *Naval Affairs* diary and Schramm's *Kriegstagebuch des Oberkommando der Wehrmacht*.
5   Joachimsthaler, *Last Days of Hitler*, 89.
6   Speer, *Inside the Third Reich*, 613.
7   Witte and Tyas, *Himmler's Diary*, 116.
8   Hillgruber and Hümmelchen, *Chronik des zweiten Weltkrieges*, 276.
9   M. Middlebrook and C. Everitt, *The Bomber Command War Diaries: An Operational Reference Book, 1939–1945* (Harmondsworth, UK: Penguin Books, 1987), 691.
10   Witte and Tyas, *Himmler's Diary*, 115.
11   The People's Commissariat of Internal Affairs: the Soviet police and secret police from 1934 to 1943.
12   Beevor, *Berlin*, 187.
13   BBC News HNB Film 128/129.
14   Williams, *Passing Fury*, 5.
15   Blatman, *Death Marches*, 178.
16   *The War in Pictures*, 6 vols. (London: Odhams Press, 1946), 5:176–77.
17   Gilbert, *Second World War*, 659.
18   "Befreiung Städte," Das Jahr 1945: Die Befreiung von Faschismus, accessed February 23, 2024, https://dasjahr1945.de/category/befreiung-staedte.
19   Gilbert, *Second World War*, 659.

Chapter 22: The Hostages

1   H. Pünder, unposted and unpublished letters to family, Schönberg, April 14 and 23, 1945, Bundesarchiv Koblenz, Nachlass Hermann Pünder, nos. 663, 664 (handwritten source in the Bundesarchiv, transcribed by Dr Tilman Pünder).
2   Von Stauffenberg mentions Hof and Wunsiedel as points where the convoy waited and regrouped. See *Aufzeichnungen aus unserer Sippenhaft*, 111.
3   It is unclear which VIP prisoners were on this vehicle.
4   Blum, *Dernier mois*, 41–43.
5   Best records (presumably incorrectly) that they halted at Weiden. This mistake has been much repeated by other authors. Neustadt an der Waldnaab is actually en route to Flossenbürg, as opposed to Weiden, given the southerly direction of travel. It is named by Müller, Blum, Dünninger, and even Liedig. (In an interview in the 1950s with Dr H. Krausnick and Prof H. Deutsch, Liedig recalls it as Neumarkt in der Oberpfalz. See https://www.ifz-muenchen.de/archiv/zs/zs-2125.pdf, accessed May 2023.) Best's (partly mistaken) record continues: the guards went and called ahead to the camp, whereupon one of them, more friendly than the others, shared the news: "You will have to go farther, they can't take you here.

[There]. Too full." See Best, *Venlo Incident*, 192. See 1945 image of Neustadt, including the police station, demolished in 1956.

6   Sayer and Dronfield, *Hitler's Last Plot*, 42.

7   Blum, *Dernier mois*, 45.

8   Both of these two would (shockingly) survive the war, so the basis upon which they were so conspicuously removed from the transport at this point remains unknown. If the objective were to gather "the Canaris group" in Flossenbürg, which has been surmised but is illogical, given their survival, the omission of Bonhoeffer appears as an oversight. Be that as it may, Bonhoeffer's inclusion on the RSHA's actual death list would occur only the following day.

9   The tragedy of Gehre's story, outlined in chapter 6, is compounded at this point. Here he reveals how he had been duped by the cynical "glass of wine" ploy adopted by the brutal Stawitzki into considering him a friend. In "staying with Müller," he was still half-following Gestapo orders. Yet in volunteering to go with Stawitzki back to Flossenbürg, he travels to his death, a death he had previously sought at his own hand. It is possible that the stool pigeon / informer arrangement he had agreed with the Gestapo, also mentioned in chapter 6, also involved his own execution by the authorities, so here he helps them by correcting their mistake. It is even conceivable that this manner of collection was an agreed ruse. If so, this serves further to add to the mystery surrounding the reasons for Müller and Liedig's dramatic extraction and subsequent survival. In Flossenbürg Stawitzki's assaults on Müller were a demonstration of uninhibited violence. It seems beyond implausible that this was a ploy.

10 Müller, *Bis zur letzten Konsequenz*, 244.

11 Von Hassell, *Hostage of the Third Reich*, 181.

12 The town is likely to have been Nabburg, according to an article published in 2000 by Prof E. Dünninger (see fig. 22-1).

13 Blum, *Dernier mois*, 46.

14 Falconer, *Most Improbable Hostage*, 116.

15 NSV means National Socialist *Volkswohlfahrt* (welfare; Klemperer, *To the Bitter End*, 539). I have modified the published translation.

16 Goerdeler, *Verschleppt*, 203, in Zimmermann, *Begegnungen mit Dietrich Bonhoeffer*. Anneliese was the wife of Carl Goerdeler, the monarchist and conservative politician who would have served as chancellor in the new government had the July plot succeeded, and who was executed in Plötzensee prison on February 2, 1945. As Goerdeler's wife, Anneliese had been arrested under German *Sippenhaft* law in July 1944, along with his brother Gustav, sons Ulrich and Reinhard, daughters Benigna and Marianne, daughter-in-law Irma, and niece Jutta. Thinking to play a long game, Goerdeler had from the moment of his arrest talked openly and freely with his captors, naming dozens of individuals. It was a decision that proved costly for many. He may have been hoping thereby to create so many webs of follow-up questioning that the legal processes thus initiated would be overtaken by the defeat of Nazism. The Gestapo kept him alive for longer as a result, and whereas other key resisters executed had their families released in the early autumn of 1944, it proved otherwise with the Goerdeler clan. All of the Goerdeler family members were on the transport.

17 Von Hassell, *Hostage of the Third Reich*, 182.

18   Von Stauffenberg, *Aufzeichnungen aus unserer Sippenhaft*, 111.

19   Von Stauffenberg, *Aufzeichnungen aus unserer Sippenhaft*, 111.

20   Blum, *Dernier mois*, 48–49.

21   Blum, *Dernier mois*, 48–49. They were not the only married couple in Regensburg that night to be roughly informed, initially, that they were to be separated, only to be subsequently reunited. The same treatment was afforded to the Heberleins. In 2021 the diaries of both Margot and Erich Heberlein, long retained by the family, came to light, and are being prepared by this author for publication. These also mention an initial (but not enforced) separation.

22   Von Stauffenberg, *Aufzeichnungen aus unserer Sippenhaft*, 111 (German: "schlafen wie die Ratzen").

23   Von Hassell, *Hostage of the Third Reich*, 182.

24   Best, *Venlo Incident*, 193.

25   T. Pünder, *Windbriefe: Transkription nicht abgesandter Briefe meines Vaters Hermann Pünder an die Familie während seiner Zeit in den Fängen des NS-Staates und nach der Befreiung durch die Amerikaner 1945* (Münster: self-pub., 2020), 39.

26   Payne Best writes that he shared with Hugh Falconer, Colonel von Petersdorff, Vasily Kokorin, and (also) Alexander von Falkenhausen. Falconer's account also names Falkenhausen as being billeted with him. Pünder's account was written within a week, whereas the two others were compiled after a longer interval.

27   Erich Heberlein, Margot's husband, was in the end permitted to stay with her, according to Margot's diary, which adds the detail that no bedding was provided. He is overlooked in Best's account.

28   By this Pünder means Buchenwald.

29   Pünder, *Windbriefe*, 39. As indicated above, Best's account has Falkenhausen billeted elsewhere, and this likely mistake is repeated by Hassell.

30   In Regensburg, the local chemist, Mayer, whose pharmaceutical premises were in close proximity to the hostages' accommodation, at Landshuterstraße 44, kept a detailed diary account of all air strikes and air raid alarms for the period. During the month of April, the record indicates there were very frequent air raid warnings. From this source we learn that an air raid alarm or air raid happened on April 4 between 3:00 and 3:30 p.m. and on the next day, April 5, between 10:30 a.m. and 1:45 p.m. (information to the author from Peter Schmoll, author of *Die Messerschmitt-Werke im Zweiten Weltkrieg: Die Flugzeugproduktion der Messerschmitt GmbH Regensburg von 1938 bis 1945* (Regensburg, Germany: Mittelbayerischen, 1998). In addition, a website named Chronology of the Oil Campaign in World War II (which could not be verified) appeared to indicate that on April 4, 1945, eighty B-24s from the USAF's Mission 941 bombed Regensburg's oil depot and that 31 B-24s bombed the munitions depot.

31   Falconer, *Most Improbable Hostage*, 117.

32   Falconer, *Most Improbable Hostage*, 118.

33   Evelyn Smith, the daughter of Hugh Falconer, provided this information to the author in July 2019.

34   Falconer, *Most Improbable Hostage*, 107.

35   Falconer, *Most Improbable Hostage*, 107.

Chapter 23: Horst Hoepner, Payne Best, and Horst von Petersdorff

1   Before his arrest Hoepner was in contact with a young Frenchwoman named Arlette Jacquard, who had spent nine months imprisoned in Fresnes as a suspected Allied spy (TNA, WO 328/14).

2   International Tracing Service Digital Archive, Wiener Holocaust Library Collections, London, register of those arrested as relatives, dated December 15, 1944; 1.2.2.1; 11395926#1.

3   The cause of her death on June 17, 1918, at the age of thirty, is given as emphysema of both pleural cavities, which almost undoubtedly means that she died from the Spanish influenza epidemic. On her wedding certificate, she was registered as a woman of independent means. On her death certificate ten years on, Payne Best, Captain, Intelligence Corps, is noted as being of independent means (GRO, 11566554–20).

4   Best indeed showed greater caution than some of his superiors. See C. Andrew, *Secret Service: The Making of the British Intelligence Community* (London: Heinemann, 1985), 434.

5   In 1940 SS officer Walter Schellenberg was instructed by Gestapo director Reinhard Heyrich to compile an arrest list for the soon-to-be-conquered British Isles. Based on the interrogations of the abducted British MI6 agents Best and Stevens and on his own preconceptions, Schellenberg compiled a handbook on Britain for Gestapo use after a successful invasion. Schellenberg's *Informationsheft GB* offers a glimpse of his and Heydrich's perception of a country supposedly run by Freemasons, Jews, and a small public-school-trained elite. "Democratic freedom in Britain" was described as a sham, while the archbishop of Canterbury and Church of England Council on Foreign Relations were held responsible for anti-German propaganda. At the end of the list, the "Sonderfahndungsliste GB" (Special Search List GB) listed 2,800 individuals for special Gestapo attention, of whom 30 were to be arrested immediately after the invasion. Had the Nazis ever conquered Britain, the Gestapo would have arrested not only Winston Churchill and the leader of the Labour Party, Clement Attlee, but also pacifists like Norman Angell, writers such as H. G. Wells, and German emigrés such as the novelist Stefan Zweig. See W. Schellenberg, *Invasion 1940: The Nazi Invasion Plan for Britain* (London: St Ermin's Press, 2001). See, too, Heydrich's memorandum of May 5, 1939, in IfZ, MA 451; and R. Gerwarth, *Hitler's Hangman: The Life of Heydrich* (New Haven: Yale University Press, 2011), 177. From the German point of view, the Venlo Incident, though a brilliant tactical victory, was a strategic failure. The British SIS' slowness in realising that the conspirators were bogus, even after the capture of Best and Stevens, is evidence of how easily Schellenberg could have inaugurated a long-term system of deception. After a fortnight he tired of the charade and radioed a mocking message using the conspirators' call sign to tell SIS it had been duped. See Andrew, *Secret Service*, 439. For the Germans, an espionage "open goal" was missed.

6   Now Poznań, Poland.

7   Petersdorff mentions his friendship with Gruppenführer Ernst, who could be found dressed in women's clothing at the homosexual club Silhouette on Berlin's Hollendorfplatz (IfZ, 2094157/ZS-7473–2).

8   See chapter 6. The loud arguments between Alvensleben and Petersdorff contin-
     ued day and night.
9   This was a further experience he had in common with General von Falkenhau-
     sen, in the sense that Falkenhausen's brother did not survive, and Falkenhausen
     was out of the country, having just left for China. Petersdorff believed his close
     connections with Gregor Strasser were the reason for the danger.
10   Petersdorff informed Payne Best that he was only the third individual to receive
     this award. German records have not been accessed to verify this claim.
11   IfZ, 2094157/ZS-7473-2.

Chapter 24: Far from Over

1   Beevor, *Second World War*, 704.
2   BBC News HNB Film 128/129.
3   Dobbs, *Six Months in 1945*, 151.
4   Churchill, *Second World War*, 6:394.
5   "Amantium irae amoris integratio ist" (Lovers' quarrels always go with true love).
     See Dobbs, *Six Months in 1945*, 155.
6   H.-G. von Studnitz, *Als Berlin brannte: Tagebuch der Jahre 1943-1945* (Bergisch
     Gladbach, Germany: Gustav Lübbe, 1985), 308. Reference supplied by Dr E.
     Bucholtz, Stiftung Topographie des Terrors, Berlin.
7   W. Giebel, ed., "Haushaltsbuch von Ursula Kleinmichel," in *Bomben auf Berlin:
     Zeitzeugen berichten vom Luftkrieg* (Berlin: Berlin Story Verlag, 2012), 222–25.
8   Beevor, *Berlin*, 191.

Chapter 25: A New Low Point

1   E. Chowaniec, *Der „Fall Dohnanyi" 1943–45: Widerstand, Militärjustiz, SS-Willkür*
     (Munich: R. Oldenburg, 1991). There is another version of events derived from
     depositions submitted by SS-Standartenführer Huppenkothen after the war.
     Despite the obvious need for caution surrounding such a self-protective source
     of information, this account has been accepted by many. In this version Ratten-
     huber handed the diaries over to the RSHA, whose chief, Kaltenbrunner, in turn
     presented them triumphantly to Hitler at the daily midday briefing. On the basis
     of Hitler's irate directive to proceed with the immediate liquidation of the con-
     spirators, which in this account was issued at the end of that meeting, Kalten-
     brunner subsequently instructed Heinrich Müller to issue the relevant orders.
     But the speed with which we know events subsequently moved renders this ver-
     sion less likely.
2   See G. Ritter, *Carl Goerdeler und die deutsche Widerstandsbewegung* (Munich:
     Deutscher Taschenbuch Verlag, 1964), 535.
3   Von Schlabrendorff, *Revolt against Hitler*, 122.
4   Fritz Weidemann, one of Hitler's adjutants, said, "I have sometimes secured deci-
     sions from him, even ones about important matters, without his ever asking to
     see the relevant files" (Rees, *Nazis*, 52).
5   Canaris had long since taken precautions with the diaries to ensure that their
     contents were harmless to his protestations of loyalty. What is known is that the
     RSHA made microfilm copies of them, which Kaltenbrunner (or Müller acting
     in his name) ordered be destroyed along with all physical materials surrounding

Canaris. Nothing in writing from Canaris' hand was to survive him. Huppen-kothen duly burnt all the files at the end of April in Schloss Mittersill before link-ing up for active service with SS Division Nibelungen. See Buchheit, *Deutsche Geheimdienst*, 479. The link-up was an astute move, one he knew would both defend him from accusations of desertion and increase his chances of survival.

6 Deutsch, *Conspiracy against Hitler*, 228, citing the Groscurth diaries, entry of November 5.

7 Deutsch, *Conspiracy against Hitler*, 204. Deutsch cites Kordt, *Nicht aus den Akten*, 357, and conversations with Erich Kordt, December 1945.

8 Kurt Kerstenhahn (see Höhne, *Canaris*, 579, n. 55).

9 A measure that had the unintended consequence of introducing delays to the trial processes of many resisters.

10 J. C. Fest, *The Face of the Third Reich: Portraits of the Nazi Leadership*, trans. M. Bullock (New York: Pantheon Books, 1970).

11 W. Stevenson, *The Bormann Brotherhood* (New York: Harcourt Brace Jovanovich, 1973), 88.

12 If the scars had arrived as a result of the sabre rituals of his university years, he would have been following in the footsteps of his own duelling father, but they were in fact acquired for a far less glamourous reason. They were simply the result of an accident in which he was involved while driving under the influence of alcohol.

13 While Kaltenbrunner was still a virtual unknown in Austria, Heydrich had even planted spies in his office, one being Walter Schellenberg, who together with a cer-tain Untersturmführer Adolf Eichmann was sent to Vienna on March 12, 1938, with lists of political enemies and Jews scheduled for arrest. Heydrich also ensured Kaltenbrunner's subordinate postings were replete with men personally loyal to him (Heydrich), and in the end succeeded in entirely emasculating Kaltenbrunner. What had helped Heydrich in this respect was a glaring case of intelligence incom-petence: Kaltenbrunner was completely "duped." He was taken in by a Swiss man named Burri who claimed to have a large following. Himmler and Kaltenbrunner were taken in, but Heydrich decidedly not. Some aspects of Kaltenbrunner's expe-rience evidently helped establish him in Himmler's mind as a man who knew intel-ligence work, and the fact that the Austrian was a rank amateur did not seem to dis-turb Himmler, for after all, the Reichsführer himself was nothing more. Following the Vienna humiliation at Heydrich's hands, Kaltenbrunner took his defeat badly, but was ordered by Himmler to initiate a reconciliation, an order that he dutifully obeyed. But underneath this external show of line obedience simmered a lasting spirit of resentment. When Heydrich fell victim in 1942 to a British strike, and in due course Kaltenbrunner was somewhat surprisingly summoned to Berlin to fill his shoes, Kaltenbrunner exacted his revenge on Heydrich's widow by refusing to release to her a file of family papers that had remained in a safe at the RSHA. See Lina Heydrich to Kaltenbrunner, September 1, 1943, and October 1, 1944, cited in P. Black, *Ernst Kaltenbrunner: Ideological Soldier of the Third Reich* (Princeton, N.J.: Princeton University Press, 1984), 110.

14 Black, *Ernst Kaltenbrunner*, 192.

15 In fact, by April 1–9, the period covered by this book, the consequences of Kaltenbrunner having this direct access to Hitler, and his corresponding stand-

ing in Hitler's eyes, had long been producing acute problems for Himmler. Himmler actually became frightened of him. Kaltenbrunner, like others, began to use his increased sense of his own importance to open up a dialogue with the Allies—endeavours that were, however, not taken seriously at any point. Kaltenbrunner also had responsibility for destabilising the Allied currency, so had vast quantities of counterfeit notes printed, sequestering quantities for his own purposes. In a further example of how the latter's change of allegiance proved challenging, Himmler had secretly (or so he imagined) arranged with former Swiss federal president Jean-Marie Musy a release of Jews against a payment of 20 million Swiss francs from Jewish sources in the US. On February 6, 1945, the first trainload of Jews from Theresienstadt had actually reached Switzerland and 5 million Francs were deposited in Musy's account. Kaltenbrunner actively sabotaged this deal, not only informing Hitler of press reports on the release but also telling Hitler (wrongly) that Himmler had negotiated with Musy about asylum for 250 Nazi leaders in Switzerland. Enraged, Hitler promptly ordered that any German who helped a Jew escape would be executed on the spot. Himmler, although growing increasingly impervious to displeasing the Führer, immediately halted these transports: although soon he would try another route, via Sweden, and there is also (even) some thought that he perhaps used this outrage as a way to position himself as more serious towards the Allies.

16   In particular, the desertion of the Vermehren diplomatic couple (from the Abwehr).

17   Ashdown, *Nein!* 259.

18   Report from Kaltenbrunner to Bormann, September 19, 1944, quoted in H. Jacobsen, *Opposition: Gegen Hitler und der Staatsstreich*, 2 vols. (Stuttgart: Mundus, 1989), 1:425.

19   Black, *Ernst Kaltenbrunner*, 212.

20   F. Zipfel, *Kirchenkampf in Deutschland 1933–1945*, vol. 1 of *Publikationen der Forschungsgruppe Berliner Widerstand beim Senator für Inneres von Berlin* (Berlin: De Gruyter, 1965), 4.

21   Albert Speer records that this is how Hitler behaved between 1936 and 1940 towards the architect and Berlin mayor Julius Lippert in relation to architectural plans for the capital. Lippert could not work up any enthusiam for Hitler's ideas. At first Hitler was merely annoyed, remarking that Lippert was petty, incapable of governing a metropolis, and even more incapable of understanding the historical importance he (Hitler) planned to give it. As time wore on, these remarks mounted in intensity: "Lippert is an incompetent, an idiot, a failure, a zero." What was astonishing for Speer, however, was that Hitler never showed his dissatisfaction in the mayor's presence and never tried to win him over to his views.

22   Speer, *Inside the Third Reich*, 120.

23   Goebbels, *Tagebücher 1945*, 498.

24   In post-war testimony Sonderegger stated that Hitler had ordered the "merciless extermination" of those in Flossenbürg, but that the "soft Austrian" ("Gestapo" Müller's name for Kaltenbrunner) had decreed that no one should be condemned to death without a trial and verdict. See Bonhoeffer-Forschungsstelle, Heidelberg, Landgericht München, VIII, 7, 29, cited in Chowaniec, „Fall Dohnanyi", 133.

25   H. Eberle and M. Uhl, *Das Buch Hitler* (Mülheim, Germany: Gustav Lübbe, 2007), 351.

Chapter 26: Interpreting Hitler's Commands

1   By "black" Rattenhuber means "associated with things clerical and religious." Josef Müller had first been interrogated by none other than Heinrich "Gestapo" Müller, with Himmler in the adjacent room, on February 9, 1934. Heinrich Müller later apologised to Josef Müller for the unprofessional and inappropriate conduct of his superior, Heydrich. Josef Müller's friendship with Rattenhuber, whom he refers to as Hans, dated from the same day. From that day onwards, the SS top echelons, excluding Heydrich, formed a grudging respect for him, which was never withdrawn. In a further instance of this, Rattenhuber was the individual who made sure that Müller was warned that he was "on the list" for assassination in the Night of the Long Knives in June 1934 and that he should flee. See Müller, *Bis zur letzten Konsequenz*, 62, 67, 280.

2   See chapter 3, n. 1.

3   Black, *Ernst Kaltenbrunner*, 190.

4   Black, *Ernst Kaltenbrunner*, 450.

5   See chapter 25, n. 1 and n. 24.

6   The Berlin team understood Hitler well. "His originality lay in his realisation that effective revolutions, in modern conditions, are carried out with, and not against, the power of the state: the correct order of events was first to secure access to that power and then begin his revolution. Hitler never abandoned the cloak of legality: he recognised the enormous psychological value of having the law on his side" (Bullock, *Hitler*, 257).

7   In a remarkable sequence of events, the original was retrieved and published by Sayer and Dronfield in 2019: "Müller Order," April 5, 1945, in *Hitler's Last Plot*, 184.

8   Elser was someone in whose story Hitler had taken a particular interest, tinged with respect. He was also someone whom, according to his valet, Heinz Linge, he had allowed to remain alive only so that he might in the end know that he (Elser) was wrong and that Hitler was right. See Linge, *With Hitler to the End*, 15–18. Elser was murdered on April 9 in Dachau as part of the "tidying-up" work of the RSHA.

9   In Hitler's imagination, Elser was being preserved for a show trial alongside Payne Best, which would show the Allies had tried to eliminate him. Most likely Müller had decided it was time to "clear the decks."

10   IfZ, MB 3/1, Huppenkothen deposition, record of witness' testimony in Huppenkothen trial, February 4–14, 1951, day 1, p. 193.

11   It would not have suited or built Huppenkothen's post-war defence case to have brought any sensationalising revelations.

12   As mentioned above, how Liedig was exempted from being listed remains a mystery.

13   The phrase, quoted earlier, is used by Prof Ian Kershaw, quoted in Rees, *Nazis*, 53.

14   Chowaniec, *„Fall Dohnanyi"*, 131.

Chapter 27: The Wheel of History Turns

1   E. Wiesel, *Night*, trans. M. Wiesel (London: Penguin Books, 2006), 113. Buchenwald's prisoner uprising, almost uniquely in its context, experienced success on April 11.

2   Helm, *If This Is a Woman*, 568.

3   Sajer, *Forgotten Soldier*, 545. The name of the point between Danzig and Kiel is
     not specified, but Rødbyhavn is likely to have been the port in question.
4   P. Hoare, *Albert and the Whale* (London: 4th Estate, 2021), 275.
5   Vassiltchikov, *Berlin Diaries*, 274–75.
6   Hansen, *Disobeying Hitler*, 238.
7   Australian front-line war correspondent Alan Moorehead observed, "The Were-
     wolves and other last-minute ad hoc formations were never a serious menace.
     They were merely symptomatic of the general break-up. Here and there a Gau-
     leiter who himself was entirely compromised to the Party found he could stir a lit-
     tle temporary spirit by invoking the Führer and giving the local youth formation
     a romantic name and a few machine guns and grenades. But it never lasted. These
     children, some of them no more than fourteen or fifteen, fought hysterically for a
     day or a week, and then there was no more ammunition" (*Eclipse: A Classic Eye-
     witness Account of the Decline and Fall of Nazi Germany, 1943–1945* [1945; repr.,
     London: Sphere, 1967], 228).
8   BBC News HNB Film 128/129.
9   Beevor, *Berlin*, 190.
10   C. Bösendahl, *Rinteln Stadtgeschichte(n) neu erzählt* (Hamelin, Germany: Heimat-
     bund der Grafschaft Schaumburg, 2021), 169. Reference provided by Dr Stefan
     Meyer, Museum Director, Eulenburg. Universitäts- und Stadtmuseum Rinteln.
11   Hillgruber and Hümmelchen, *Chronik des zweiten Weltkrieges*, 64.
12   K. Schuschnigg, *Ein Requiem in Rot-Weiss-Rot: Aufzeichnungen des Häftlings
     Dr. Auster* (Zurich: Amstutz, Herdeg, 1946), 486.

Chapter 28: The Hostages

1   Pünder, *Windbriefe*, 39.
2   Best, *Venlo Incident*, 194.
3   Von Stauffenberg, *Aufzeichnungen aus unserer Sippenhaft*, 113.
4   Pünder, *Windbriefe*, 40.
5   Dagmar Ruscheinsky-Rogl, in *Die Woche*, April 6, 1995, Zeitgeschichtsarchiv
     Pragser Wildsee, 2aPW. T/C 19.01 T/C216. Keindl survived the war and died in
     1968.
6   For fuller details on the (remarkable) subject of the humanity of Bonhoeffer's
     Berlin guards, see Bethge, *Dietrich Bonhoeffer*, 827, 848.
7   Von Hassell, *Hostage of the Third Reich*, 184.
8   Best, *Venlo Incident*, 194.
9   Von Stauffenberg, *Aufzeichnungen aus unserer Sippenhaft*, 113.

Chapter 29: An SOE Sabotage Operation

1   Best, *Venlo Incident*, 194.
2   Falconer, *Most Improbable Hostage*, 115.
3   Blum, *Dernier mois*, 59.

Chapter 30: Hugh Falconer, Heidel Nowakowski, and Alexander Falkenhausen

1   In 2003 the author purchased a book in French in an antique bookstore in Bue-
     nos Aires, published in March 1940, soundly proclaiming the inviolability of

the Maginot line: P. Dehillotte, *Gestapo: L'Organisation. -Les chefs.- Les Agents. L'Action de la Gestapo en Europe. Aux Etats-Unis et en Amerique du Sud* (Paris: Payot, 1940). Other such maps are extant.

2   E. Smith, email to the author, January 14, 2021.

3   Fortunately—whether by luck or judgement is not known—the plain clothes outfit Falconer was wearing at the time of arrest included an RAF shirt with the collar attached and the labels taken out. Later, when flown to Italy, and still wearing a shirt that his captors would have recognised as originating with the RAF, he was able by stating his rank and number to pass more credibly for (only) the RAF squadron leader he in truth also was.

4   The Germans had been given copious quantities of information by Best and especially Stevens after capturing them in 1939.

5   The safety net was only as good as the "friends back home" and would often prove disastrous for the British, in occupied Holland particularly.

6   Out of all the British officers who could happen to have been placed at the right spot at the right time to be asked to identify SS-Standartenführer Kaindl at the moment of his capture in Paderborn after the war, none could have been more fitting, or more sure, than Falconer.

7   Sayer and Dronfield, *Hitler's Last Plot*, 292.

8   Copy of list of forced labourers, Bischofswerda, 2.1.4.2 / 71046248, in conformity with ITS Digital Archive, Arolsen Archives.

9   This record has a different initial. However, in Dortmund census records in 1950 and 1955, Heidel listed herself as a widow, which may possibly have been a flag of convenience. In a separate account, she was reported as married in 1953 to Harold Kaiser, divorced in 1955, and remarried to Hans Liell in 1956. See Sayer and Dronfield, *Hitler's Last Plot*, 293.

10 A location only twenty kilometres distant from the birthplace, thirty-six years later, of Nowakowski.

11 The author assumes that the hereditary title *baron* passed from father to eldest son. Falkenhausen's father (also Alexander) died in 1909.

12 Rev Dr Lepsius' work provided much material for the Jewish writer Franz Werfel, author of *Die vierzig Tage des Musa Dagh* (1933; repr., Frankfurt: Fischer, 2002), published as a warning to Jews on this subject in Germany in 1933. It became a bestseller in many countries and was banned, and burned, in Germany. The genocide took place in 1915/1916.

13 D. Orbach, *The Plots against Hitler* (London: Head of Zeus, 2017), 166.

14 Deutsch, *Conspiracy against Hitler*, 314. This information is from the post-war Falkenhausen trial testimony of Colonel Goethals.

15 The commanders included Leeb, Witzleben, Kluge, and List. See Deutsch, *Conspiracy against Hitler*, 313.

16 Issued in three languages: German, French, and Flemish. https://www.belgiumwwii.be/de/belgien-im-krieg/artikel/deutsche-militarverwaltung.html.

17 In one notable instance of this, which took place as early as May 1940, he was approached by a Chinese scientist known to him from his time in China and who was in Europe to work with the Marie Curie laboratory, called Qian Xiuling. She came to him with a plea on behalf of a young man who had buried a mine under a railway that destroyed a German military train and who been sentenced to death by hanging. Falkenhausen, although not yet in post, intervened. The life of a Belgian resister was spared.

18 Von Hassell, *Diaries*, August 2, 1941, 134.

19 Bethge, *Dietrich Bonhoeffer*, 726.

20 IMT, doc. 1594, Ps 6, p. 60, cited in E. Crankshaw, *Gestapo: Instrument of Tyranny* (London: Putnam, 1956), 211f.

21 Padfield, *Himmler*, 430.

22 The categories *Haftgeiseln* (arrest hostages), *Zuggeiseln* (hostages accompanying trains), and *Wahlgeiseln* (selected hostages) are explained in M. Courtoy, "La question des otages en Belgique pendant la seconde guerre mondiale," in *Occupation et répression militaire allemandes, 1939–1945: La politique de "maintien de l'ordre" en Europe occcupée*, ed. G. Eismann and S. Martens (Paris: Institut historique allemand, 2007), 106ff.

23 Courtoy, "Question des otages," 109.

24 D. Roden, "'In naam van het Duitse volk!' Het Duitse krijgsgerecht en de openbare orde in bezet België (1940–1944)" (PhD diss., University of Gent, 2015). The majority of 1944 deaths were attributable to Falkenhausen's successor.

25 Orbach, *Plots against Hitler*, 208. This would have meant, for example, carrying out the orders to arrest all SS troops in the same manner as took place in Paris in the failed plot of July 20, 1944. On July 11 the leading conspirator in the plot to kill Hitler, Claus von Stauffenberg, entered the Führer's staff meeting with a bomb. If he had detonated it and killed Hitler, the prepared orders would have gone out across Europe, and Falkenhausen would have been able to play a key supportive role. But Stauffenberg decided not to use the bomb because Himmler was not present.

26 By this time Qian was pregnant and about to give birth to her first daughter. Nevertheless—despite being warned that it was dangerous for a pregnant woman to drive at night—with so many lives on the line, she drove that very night to Brussels.

27 After the war, Qian Xiuling was modest about her role, ascribing credit simply to Falkenhausen's integrity. Her testimony at his subsequent trial was to prove decisive in the shortening of his sentence.

Chapter 31: Events Cascade

1   BBC News HNB Film 128/129.

2   Gilbert, *Second World War*, 659.

3   Dulles, *Secret Surrender*, 151.

4   Dobbs, *Six Months in 1945*, 155.

5   Beevor, *Berlin*, 199.

6   BBC News HNB Film 128/129.

7   Joachimsthaler, *Last Days of Hitler*, 91.

8   It was a conscious strategy to self-infect, with diptheria, and play for time until the regime collapsed.

9   Chowaniec, „*Fall Dohnanyi*", 134. For this author, Dohnanyi appeared convinced right to the end that he had an understanding of some kind with Himmler. While Chowaniec's work and exhaustive scholarship is generally exceptional, her silence on this feature of Dohnanyi's story is puzzling.

10 Assize Court (Landgericht München I), judgment against Walter Huppenkothen, February 16, 1951 (Munich Judgement), 30; *Material des amerikanischen CIC aus den Jahren 1945–1949 v. Dr Walter Huppenkothen*, 321, cited in Chowaniec, „*Fall Dohnanyi*", 125.

11   Bethge, *Dietrich Bonhoeffer*, 940.
12   Höhne, *Canaris*, 592.
13   Hastings, *All Hell Let Loose*, 620. A separate, specialist, source identifies the nationality of the POWs as American and British (Blatman, *Death Marches*, 263).
14   Blatman, *Death Marches*, 264.

Chapter 32: Deceptions and Killings Abound

1   W. Ribhegge, E. Schönbach, and M. Witt, *Geschichte der Stadt und Region Hamm im 19. und 20. Jahrhundert* (Düsseldorf: Schwann im Patmos, 1991), 371.
2   "Operation Annie—April 6, 1945," US Holocaust Memorial Museum, RG-91.0583, https://collections.ushmm.org/search/catalog/irn722630.
3   Kershaw, *Liberator*, 325.
4   Kershaw, *Liberator*, 234.
5   Wiesel, *Night*, 114.
6   Kershaw, *Liberator*, 332, citing Dr M. Gero, Hamburg. Murderer untraced.
7   Kershaw, *End*, 326. Kohlhass has fourteen victims, including those shot at but not actually hit. See A. Kenkmann and E. Kohlhaas, "Frühe Zeugnisse über den Holocaust: Die Befragungen von Kindern in Polen nach der Befreiung von der deutschen Herrschaft," *BIOS* 23, no. 1 (2010): 138–52. Dranz was executed in 1946.
8   S. Eminger, E. Langthaler, and K. Mulley, *Nationalsozialismus in Niederösterreich: Opfer. Täter. Gegner* (Innsbruck: Studienverlag, 2021), 298.
9   R. Streibel, *April in Stein* (Vienna: Residenz Verlag, 2015), 6.
10   Streibel, *April in Stein*, 6.
11   K. Ferihumer and W. R. Garscha, "Der 'Stein Komplex': Nationalsozialistische Endphaseverbrechen im Raum Krems und ihre gerichtliche Aufarbeitung," in *DÖW Jahrbuch 2016, Fanatiker, Pflichterfüller, Widerständiger*, ed. C. Schindler (Vienna: DÖW, 2017), 52.
12   Ferihumer and Garscha, "'Stein Komplex,'" 52.
13   A. Rose, *Werewolf 1944–1945: Eine Dokumentation* (Stuttgart: Motorbuch, 1980), 276.
14   Trigg, *To VE-Day*, 246.
15   Vassiltchikov, *Berlin Diaries*, 277.
16   Klemperer, *To the Bitter End*, 544–45.

Chapter 33: The Hostages

1   Pünder, *Windbriefe*, 40.
2   This bridge remained intact until April 27, 1945.
3   Best, *Venlo Incident*, 196.
4   Pünder, *Windbriefe*, 41.
5   Dachau, the next stop for the majority of the hostage convoy, was at this point deemed too full to accommodate this size of group under the required special conditions.
6   Pünder, *Kalenderblätter 1945*, 15.
7   Falconer, *Most Improbable Hostage*, 121.
8   Von Stauffenberg, *Aufzeichnungen aus unserer Sippenhaft*, 114.
9   Pünder, *Windbriefe*, 42 (German: "gaffen").
10   Von Hassell, *Hostage of the Third Reich*, 184.

11   J. Reinsburger, journal entry for April 7, 1945, Zeitgeschichtsarchiv Pragser Wild-
     see. Original text supplied by Erna Bachhuber (née Sterlich).

12   Falconer, *Most Improbable Hostage*, 121.

13   Best, *Venlo Incident*, 196.

14   Pünder, *Windbriefe*, 42, 43.

15   Best, Falconer, and Pünder all published some partial record of the arrangement.

16   Falconer, *Most Improbable Hostage*, 122.

17   Falconer, *Most Improbable Hostage*, 122. The ceramic wood-burning oven men-
     tioned (*Kachelofen*) was of green colour with the heat-retention properties of a
     storage heater, according to local resident Magdalena Ebner, born in 1932, who
     visited this school in the period 1938–1945 (information to the author from
     Bernd Bachhuber, October 12, 2021).

18   Falconer, *Most Improbable Hostage*, 123.

19   In 1942 the church's three main bells were removed, presumably for melting
     down for ammunition, such that in 1945 only the "call to worship/summoning"
     bell (*Sterbeglocke*) remained. With the frequency of Allied air strikes, most of the
     restrictions on bellringing were rescinded by Martin Bormann on February 15,
     1945. (W. Adolph, *Unveröffentlichte Bormann-Akten*, Anm. III/68, 150, cited in
     Zipfel, *Kirchenkampf in Deutschland*, 227, n. 31.) As of (most likely) this date,
     the bell was chimed at the following intervals: **Friday, April 6**: 6:00 a.m., dawn
     ring; 7:00 a.m., early service; 12:00 midday, the Angelus; 3:00 p.m., hour of Jesus'
     death; and 6:00 p.m., evening prayer ring. The hostages would have heard the
     reassuring sound either once or twice on that day. **Saturday, April 7**: 6:00 a.m.,
     7:00 a.m., 12:00 midday, and finally 6:00 p.m. **Sunday, April 8**: 6:00 a.m., dawn
     ring; 7:00 a.m., early service; 9:00 a.m., main service; 12:00 midday, the Angelus;
     2:00 p.m., rosary prayers; and finally 6:00 p.m., evening prayer ring (Very Rever-
     end Michael Bauer, incumbent, Parish Church of St. Margareta, Schönberg, email
     to the author, January 16, 2022).

20   Dr Hermann Pünder, *Bericht über die gemeinsame Haft mit Dietrich Bonhoeffer*
     [Report on shared imprisonment with Dietrich Bonhoeffer], compiled for Eber-
     hard Bethge, September 9, 1945, Münster, Zeitgeschichtsarchiv Pragser Wildsee.

21   Best, *Venlo Incident*, 198.

22   Best, *Venlo Incident*, 198.

Chapter 34: Erich and Margot Heberlein

1   Paris was liberated only six weeks later.

Chapter 35: World News

1   Hillgruber and Hümmelchen, *Chronik des zweiten Weltkrieges*, 276.

2   B. Ireland, *Jane's Naval History of World War II* (London: HarperCollins, 1998),
     230.

3   Gilbert, *Second World War*, 659.

4   J. Lelyveld, *His Final Battle: The Last Months of Franklin Roosevelt* (New York:
     Vintage Books, 2016), 316.

5   Dobbs, *Six Months in 1945*, 154.

6   Dulles, *Secret Surrender*, 151.

7   Jenkins, *Churchill*, 785.

8   BBC News HNB Film 128/129.
9   BBC News HNB Film 128/129.

Chapter 36: Ramming

1   Middlebrook and Everitt, *Bomber Command War Diaries*, 692.
2   Over Norway British bombers sank the freighter *Oldenburg* (4,595 GRT) that
     day in Vadheim fjord. At sea German submarine U 1195 was depth-charged and
     sunk south-east of the Isle of Wight by the British destroyer *Watchman*. Else-
     where, in the Irish Sea, the German U-boat U 1024 (captained by Lieutenant
     Gutteck) torpedoed and sank the US freighter *James W. Nesmith* (7,176 GRT)
     from the HX 346 convoy. See "Seekrieg 1945, April," last updated November 20,
     2021, https://www.wlb-stuttgart.de/seekrieg/45-04.html.
3   The ME Bf 109 aircraft they used were heavily stripped down for the purpose,
     with only one synchronized machine gun instead of up to four automatic weap-
     ons, and they were provided with only sixty rounds of ammunition, normally
     a totally insufficient amount for bomber-interception missions. Under the
     terms of engagement, they were instructed to make a diving firing attack on the
     selected victim. If this failed to send the bomber down, it was to be rammed.
     Striking the bomber's fuselage forward of the tail with the wing of the fighter
     was the advised method. It was believed that the bomber's fuselage would break
     in two and at the same time the ram pilot would have an opportunity to bail
     out safely. Of course, rehearsal was impossible, so theory rarely matched what
     would transpire in practice.
4   R. A. Freeman, *Mighty Eighth War Diary* (London: Jane's, 1981), 483. Other sources
     offer alternative statistics (for example, Gilbert, *Second World War*, 660, records
     133 German aircraft lost and 77 pilots killed, with only 23 US bombers being shot
     down). But not all B-17s were carrying explosives. Throughout the period April 1–9,
     the US 8th dropped propaganda leaflets on an almost nightly basis to encourage
     civilians towards the cessation of hostilities. While, for example, on April 7, 1945,
     a total of 3,451 tons of explosives were dropped by the US 8th Air Force across six-
     teen German towns and cities, from July 1944 onwards some aircraft were loaded
     only with leaflets, with an average of eight aircraft on every heavy bomber mission
     carrying leaflets only. The leaflets were packed in a special bomb designed to burst
     open at between 2,000 and 2,500 feet from the ground and cover a 200 x 50–yard
     area with its contents. See Freeman, *Mighty Eighth War Diary*, 483, 286. Examples
     of leaflets used for this purpose are provided in appendix 8.
5   Goebbels, *Tagebücher 1945*, 519.

Chapter 37: Berlin's Gestapo

1   After his meeting with Bernadotte on March 5, 1945, Kaltenbrunner spent most
     of his time at his headquarters in Austria, alternately toying with peace projects of
     his own and fantasies of continued resistance (Black, *Ernst Kaltenbrunner*, 232).
     His existing dependence on alcohol further intensified (Black, *Ernst Kaltenbrun-
     ner*, 239). His mistress had rented a small villa in Alt Aussee, and she had given
     birth to twins there on March 31.
2   S. Kratzer, review of *Der Tod Auf Steilem Berge: Die 'Standgerichtsprozesse' gegen
     Dietrich Bonhoeffer und Hans von Dohnanyi und die Freilassung ihrer Mörder*, by

C. Schmink-Gustavus, 5, https://ebw-oberpfalz.de/wp-content/uploads/2021/04/Rezension-Kratzer-Schminck-Gustavus.pdf. Kratzer in this instance does not footnote his source, and in the same review does cite with approval a separate disputed source. After the war Kaltenbrunner insisted forcefully that Müller had in repeated instances simply affixed Kaltenbrunner's signature to orders that were issued. But at least on this matter they appear to have worked together, in some measure.

3   Sayer and Dronfield, *Hitler's Last Plot*, 72–74, provides a full account.

4   H.-G. Richardi, *SS-Geiseln im Markt Schönberg: Dramatische Tage am Ende des Zweiten Weltkrieges im Bayerischen Wald* (Schönberg, Germany: Markt Schönberg, 2010), 140.

5   Höhne, *Canaris*, 593.

6   F. von Schlabrendorff, *Begegnungen in fünf Jahrzehnten, 1979*, 2nd ed. (Hamburg: Rainer Wunderlich, 1979), 287.

7   Müller, *Bis zur letzten Konsequenz*, 250.

8   Richardi, *SS-Geiseln im Markt Schönberg*, 126. The pilot was Countess Melitta Schenk Stauffenberg; see C. Mulley, *The Women Who Flew for Hitler: The True Story of Hitler's Valkyries* (London: Macmillan, 2017), 310. In a further Regensburg Gestapo link, in Huppenkothen's encoded message sent on April 9 from Flossenbürg, he refers Müller to the Regensburg Stapoleiter in relation to addressing the inadequacy of the Schönberg group's accomodation arrangements (Richardi, *SS-Geiseln im Markt Schönberg*, 123). As of April 1, 1945, the Stapoleiter Regensburg was SS-Colonel Friedrich Sowa (US NARA, RG 165, entry 179, box 751, USFET Interrogation Report no. 10, June 21, 1945, section 4, "The Gestapo in Regensburg," given by Fritz Popp). Both Popp and Sowa featured high up on the Allied (including Russian) "wanted" list of war criminals.

9   E. Endrass, *Bonhoeffer und seine Richter: Ein Prozess und sein Nachspiel* (Stuttgart: Kreuz, 2006), 8.

10   Flossenbürg camp records provide ample evidence of how meticulously well run the garage was. In one instance a memo dated August 25, 1944, shows that Grüne Minna vehicles of the type Bonhoeffer had been travelling in had been banned "with immediate effect" by Camp Commandant Koegel from starting their engines inside the garage, to avoid the spreading of the noxious fumes they emitted. Even their detoxing and cleaning had to take place outdoors. See NS4/FL-296/1_F30_1359.

11   Hansen, *Disobeying Hitler*, 201.

12   Speer, *Inside the Third Reich*, 587, 614, 615.

Chapter 38: Mounting Chaos

1   No. 3 Commando was part of the 1st Commando Brigade, commanded by Brigadier Mills-Roberts.

2   *Western Daily Press*, April 7, 1945, Findmypast, Collection: British Newspapers, 1710–1965, accessed February 12, 2022, https://www.findmypast.co.uk.

3   *News Chronicle*, April 7, 1945, Findmypast, Collection: British Newspapers, 1710–1965, accessed February 12, 2022, https://www.findmypast.co.uk. This sentiment was known to informed combatants. In connection with the mass surrender of the troops trapped in the Ruhr pocket, a front-line war correspondent

wrote, "There would be no general and instantaneous act of collapse: as soon as the flood raced around an island of German resistance then the island was going to abandon itself to the torrent: and in the end, the Third Reich was to be submerged not by the signing of a document or the issuing of an order, but by the impetus of force majeure" (Moorehead, *Eclipse*, 220).

4   Norwegian NRK-TV, broadcast of June 20, 2021. In 2020 a bracelet, inscribed on the facing with the name of its owner, "Lt. Richard A. Bosch 0–783238," was discovered by Jorn Loite, who found it while cleaning out the attic of his grandparents' home in Drangedal, Norway. An inscription on the underside, possibly from a girlfriend, said, "Ever with me, Jo." Loite was able to trace Bosch's family and return the bracelet to his niece. See R. Sisk, "Fallen US Bombardier's Bracelet Tells Story of Secret Missions to Norway in Last Days of WWII," Military.com, July 5, 2021, https://www.military.com/daily-news/2021/07/05/fallen-us-bombardiers-bracelet-tells-story-of-secret-missions-norway-last-days-of-wwii.html.

5   His actions made an exceptional contribution to the hard-won success of his battalion, and in 1997 he was posthumously awarded the Congressional Medal of Honour—the US military's highest award for valour, the equivalent of the United Kingdom's Victoria Cross—after a review under the Clinton administration had identified a number of such instances where the contributions of black people had been overlooked. See C. W. Hanna, *Black Recipients of the Medal of Honor: A Biographical Dictionary, Civil War through Vietnam War* (Jefferson, N.C.: McFarland, 2010), 130–31 (adapted).

6   "Were the Germans so very different?" asks Moorehead (*Eclipse*, 233).

7   Blatman, *Death Marches*, 158. Over the next few days in Lüneburg, a consensus emerged that the best thing to do with the remainder was to liquidate them. Under the "leadership" of SS-Oberschütze (Private First Class) Gustav Jepsen, a group of killers passed among the sick, injured, and dying prisoners at the railway station on the evening of April 11 and killed them one by one. They were buried in the Tiergarten Forest in Lüneburg. Jepsen was hanged on July 26, 1947. The military tribunal that tried Jepsen determined that all the local municipal bodies, ranging from the mayor to the police chief and the railway officials, made no attempt whatsoever to help the injured prisoners who lay out in the open, and did nothing to prevent the murders committed over the course of the several days during which the killings were "in the offing." See Blatman, *Death Marches*, 159.

8   Kershaw, *End*, 328.

9   Beevor, *Berlin*, 187.

10   Kershaw, *End*, 330. In a footnote to p. 491, Kershaw writes that the Western Allies went to considerable lengths after the war to establish the precise routes of these marches, the number killed in each place they passed through, and the exact burial place of those murdered. The extensive files are housed at the International Tracing Service, especially Bestand "Tote" (83 boxes) and "Evak" (9 boxes).

11   Blatman, *Death Marches*, 209–10 (adapted). The roads were crammed with refugees, the railway tracks were defective, and trains could not proceed smoothly. The evacuation train was bombed several times by the Americans. There was no additional food available for the prisoners, and the longer the journey went on, the clearer it became that they could be of no further use, either as slaves or as human material for barter. Consequently, the guards passed through the cars, converting

them into travelling extermination installations; those prisoners who did not die of starvation and exhaustion were shot in the head. On several occasions, when the train halted because of constant disruptions, the guards boarded the cars and murdered those prisoners who appeared unable to endure the conditions. The doors of the cars were opened as the train stood not far from the camp in Dachau on April 29 after it had covered in two weeks a distance that in normal times would have taken only one day. There were more than 2,300 corpses aboard.

12 The word used was "transport," which was another example of a euphemism current at the time for a walking group being harried onwards.

13 Blatman, *Death Marches*, 228–32 (adapted). Blatman also refers to W. Anzenberger, H. Halbrainer, and H.-J. Rabko, *Zwischen den Fronten: Die Region Eisenerz von 1938–1945* (Loeben: Institut für Strukturforschung und Erwachsenenbildung der AK-Steinermark, 2000), 60–67; and E. Lappin, "The Death Marches of Hungarian Jews through Austria in the Spring of 1945," *Yad Vashem Studies* 28 (2000): 203–42.

14 The English edition of Klemperer's diary states that it was twenty-five miles from Munich and sixty-nine miles from Nuremberg.

15 Klemperer, *To the Bitter End*, 546–48.

16 Vassiltchikov, *Berlin Diaries*, 277.

Chapter 39: Schönberg

1 Margot's unpublished diary entry records the initiative as being hers.

2 Richardi, *SS-Geiseln im Markt Schönberg*, 136.

3 Richardi, *SS-Geiseln im Markt Schönberg*, 136 (see diagram for *Metzgerei*).

4 Richardi, *SS-Geiseln im Markt Schönberg*, 133.

5 Falconer, *Most Improbable Hostage*, 124; and Vermehren, *Reise durch den letzten Akt*, 206–7.

6 Best, *Venlo Incident*, 199. In John Galsworthy's *The Man of Property*, James Forsyte is described as wearing a frock coat, on which was "the speckless gloss imparted by perfect superintendence. . . . Emily saw to that: that is, she did not, of course, see to it—people of good position not seeing to each other's buttons, and Emily was of good position—but she saw to it that the butler saw to it." See J. Galsworthy, *The Forsyte Saga* (London: Heinemann, 1976), 93.

7 Pünder, *Windbriefe*, 44.

8 Falconer's true sentiments (collaborator!) towards Best are equally disguised (although readily imaginable) in the sentence "Best was immaculate in the clothes the Gestapo had obligingly brought him after the invasion of the Netherlands from his flat in The Hague" (Falconer, *Most Improbable Hostage*, 106). Ian Sayer and Jeremy Dronfield provide a corresponding and revealing photograph of Best wearing an immaculate set of clothes in Sachsenhausen in 1943 (*Hitler's Last Plot*, 184).

9 Best, *Venlo Incident*, 200.

10 Best, *Venlo Incident*, 199. The deputy transport leader was SS-Untersturmführer Friedrich Bader.

11 Best, *Venlo Incident*, 200.

12 Falconer, *Most Improbable Hostage*, 124.

13 Pünder, *Windbriefe*, 43.

14 See Schönberg map (fig. 39-1), no. 2: courageous neighbour (information to the author from local historian Bernd Bachhuber). In Jehle's account, held in the Archiv of Markt Schönberg, Monika supplied the Grüne Minna party with "food, provisions and other necessities."

15 Best, *Venlo Incident*, 199.

16 Falconer, *Most Improbable Hostage*, 124.

Chapter 40: Bonhoeffer's Reading

1 A lectionary of daily Bible texts. See Pünder, *Von Preussen nach Europa*, 175.

2 It has not (yet) proven possible to identify which edition of Goethe's works Bonhoeffer retained. An obituary of Jürgen Moltmann published in the *Church Times*, June 7, 2024, stated that in his 1945 kitbag he also carried the writings of Goethe.

3 One source states that it was a gift from Karl-Friedrich for his 39th birthday, with the German title *Große Griechen und Römer: Ausgewählte Lebensbilder*.

4 Greeks Themistokles, Perikles, Alkibiades, and Alexander; and Romans Tiberius and Gaius Gracchus, Gaius Julius Caesar, and Marcus Antonius. Bonhoeffer was most likely reading a selective German edition, translated by J. Kaltwasser, published by Dietrich Meyer, of *Plutarchi Libellus* (Plutarch's lives). The Bonhoeffer family are currently unable to trace the original edition (returned to them in 1945) used by Dietrich Bonhoeffer (email to the author, April 14, 2022).

5 Plutarch, *Grosse Griechen und Römer* [*Lives of the Noble Greeks and Romans*], ed. D. Mikusch (Cologne: Anaconda, 2009; originally published Berlin: Propyläen, 1935), 375, my translation (throughout).

6 Plutarch, *Lives*, 227.

7 Plutarch, *Lives*, 312.

8 Plutarch, *Lives*, 156.

9 Plutarch, *Lives*, 346.

10 "Being well brought up" in German is *eine gute Erziehung erhalten*, which also has connotations of education and the acquisition of wisdom.

11 Plutarch, *Lives*, 252.

12 B. Russell, *A History of Western Philosophy* (London: George Allen and Unwin, 1946), 254.

13 P. Tillich, *The Courage to Be* (London: HarperCollins, 1986), 9. A contemporary of Bonhoeffer, Tillich was instrumental in obtaining the latter's teaching post in 1939 in the Union Theological Seminary of New York.

Chapter 41: Sunday in Schönberg (I)

1 Rabenau lived in Münster, Pünder's home town, between 1934 and 1936, and Rabenau lectured at the University there in May, July, and September 1935. Pünder also held the role of Münster's Examination Board (*Volkswirtschaftliches Prüfungsamt*) chair in economics (email to the author from P. Worm, *Leiter des Stadtarchivs*, March 10, 2023).

2 Pünder, *Von Preussen nach Europa*, 175.

3 W. Cavanaugh, *Torture and Eucharist* (Oxford: Blackwell, 1998), 34. For a fuller discussion of Christian subversion of the social order, see p. 63. In the schoolroom nearly all those present had experienced torture directly or adjacently, and at least one member of the group, Rascher, had actively perpetrated it.

4 Records for all members of the group have been traced on Ancestry.com, other than for Nowakowski and the (obvious) exceptions of Rascher and Kokorin.

5 In the year in which Reverend Falconer took his turn as head of the Presbyterian Church in England, he travelled round the world. If he got lost, he would look around for a Catholic priest and ask the way in Latin (email to the author from Evelyn Smith, Falconer's daughter, June 11, 2022). Bonhoeffer was a fluent user of Hebrew, Greek, Latin, and English.

6 After the early death of his first wife, Dorothy, in June 1918 from Spanish flu, Best had chosen to marry his second wife, Maria van Rees, in a civil ceremony, as opposed to a religious one, in Gravenhage, Holland, on September 13, 1921.

7 According to the family (telephone conversation between the author and Sofia Ceballos Garcia-Escudero, June 15, 2022), the marriage ceremony was followed by a celebration at the Ritz.

8 Pünder, *Kalenderblätter 1945*, 14. This pocket diary, size 7 cm x 10 cm, from the year 1945, is written in the Stolzte-Shrey annotation system, transcribed by Rosemarie Koller from Gossau. Dr Tilman Pünder commented on the discrepancies between the diary entries and the publication *Von Preussen nach Europa*: "For reliability the diary is the source I trust. It is more authentic than the book. For the composition of [my father's] memoirs the diary was not on hand. Working from memory—20 years after events—errors crept in, understandably. Similar inaccuracies also exist in the accounts of others concerning that time." See Pünder, *Kalenderblätter 1945*, 14; email to the author from Tilman Pünder, August 19, 2017.

9 The Moravian Daily Texts. The pattern of the *Losungen* is that there is always a "chosen word" text from the Old Testament, in conjunction with a suitably linked passage from the New Testament. Next there is, for each Bible passage, a phrase or verse from a song taken out of the society's hymn-book, as indicated by the numbers that follow, together with the composer's name. From this it may be seen that use of the *Losungen* was still a relatively "in-house" affair: for example, if the reader was (like Bonhoeffer) from the Lutheran or the United Church, it was not possible to look up the song, which may well have been unknown to him or her, so it was not able to be sung. This was also in part owing to the fact that the *Brüdergemeinde* pattern was to use a wide variety of local tunes that were not known at all in the more established churches across Germany. Along with the hymns of Paul Gerhardt and the Bible, especially the Psalms, the *Losungen* grew from being already significant to being a vital source of daily nourishment for Bonhoeffer during the war. For example, see DBWE 15:217–37; and the many references in DBWE 8. In one of these (DBWE 8:237), Bonhoeffer celebrates with Bethge the joy that still flows from their exchanging of *Losungen* as a Christmas gift. (On this, see further DBWE 5:58, n. 27.)

10 German: *Zusammengehörigkeitsgefühl.*

11 German: *gemeinschaftstiftende Kraft.*

12 In their use of the *Losungen*, Bonhoeffer and his illegal ordinands were in one sense ahead of their time. But they were not alone. Reverand Paul Schneider, before he was murdered in 1939 by lethal injection in Buchenwald, is reported to have shouted out the daily Bible readings of the *Losungen*, up to the day when he had to pay with his death for his unflinching steadfastness (J. Rieger, *The Silent*

Church: The Problem of the German Confessional Witness [London: SCM Press, 1944], 46). The Moravian texts have been published annually (and continuously, with an interruption in Germany in 1943) since 1722. Across Germany in 1942, around 400,000 copies were issued (Rieger, *Silent Church*, 88). Since the war, the circulation of these texts has experienced an extension in popularity: in 1998, 1,250,000 copies were printed in thirty-four languages and dialects, making the *Losungen* the most widely read daily worship guide in the world next to the Bible (DBWE 5:59, n. 27). There can be little doubt that their association with Bonhoeffer, other resisters (see his advocacy in DBW 5:43), and the Finkenwalde ordinands has played a contributory role in this respect. The *Losungen* passages for the period April 1–8, 1945, are listed in appendix 6.

13   On Monday, April 9, Bonhoeffer's belongings deposited in the Flossenbürg guard room included a Bible and a volume of Goethe, in both of which the name "Dietrich Bonhoeffer" was inscribed. See von Schlabrendorff, *Revolt against Hitler*, 173.

14   Pünder, *Von Preussen nach Europa*, 175. A *Schott Messbuch* is a small Catholic book of readings and prayers detailing set passages throughout the calendar of the Christian year. The Bible texts are laid out in Latin on the left-hand side with the German on the right. From a comparison of editions from 1907 to 1940, it appears likely that the version used for this service was the edition published in 1936. (The text of the 1907, 1936, and 1940 editions is provided in appendix 4.) In a further connection, the church in Flossenbürg is named after St Pancras, the saint named for that day in the *Schott* Bonhoeffer used at the time.

15   In the English-language matched version provided here (my translation), I have adapted and corrected the American 1945 edition held in the archives and translated the hymn stanza. Across Protestant Germany, surprisingly, the Sunday in question is known more widely by the Latin name Quasimodogeniti Sunday than by the Catholic *Weißer Sonntag* designation.

16   Quasimodogeniti Sunday 1944, in DBWE 8:342.

Chapter 42: Sunday's Total War

1   Lelyveld, *His Final Battle*, 286.
2   Lelyveld, *His Final Battle*, 36.
3   The strain of the war was showing through at multiple levels. Broadcasters themselves were pushing beyond their limits. That month Grisewood's cousin Harman collapsed in his office and had to be carried out unconscious. See Hendy, *BBC*, 286.
4   The Allied discussions on this thread are amply recounted elsewhere, for example: Churchill, *Second World War*, 6:198. By implication and omission, this guarantee did not apply for other countries experiencing the arrival of Soviet troops, whether they were Nazi collaborators or not.
5   BBC News HNB Film 128/129.
6   In one instance of reporting subsequently found to be inaccurate, the BBC reported on April 8 that French forces had taken Pforzheim. But in fact only its northern suburb had been captured. It would take a further ten days of the bitterest struggle, with ensuing loss of life and related destruction, before the city was in Allied hands.

7   BBC News HNB Film 128/129.

8   The Special Boat Services—a Special Forces unit specialising in lightning raids to harass the enemy.

9   The 1945 Pünder diary mentioned in fig. 41-1 shows April 9 as the anniversary of the occupation of both Denmark and Norway.

10   These 6,775 works of art included 40 Italian paintings of the famous Linz collection from Amsterdam, along with paintings by Brueghel, Titian, Rembrandt, Tintoretto, van Dyck, Rubens, Reynolds, Nattier, Lancery, Hals, and Veronese. The cache also included Vermeer's *Portrait of the Artist in His Studio*, van Dyck's *Adoration of the Mystic Lamb*, 50 kg of gold bars, 4.5 million Reichsmarks of army funds, $2 million, $2 million in Swiss francs, five cases of jewels, and a stamp collection worth 5 million gold marks. See B. O'Connor, *Operation Ebensburg: SOE's Austrian "Bonzos" and the Rescue of Looted European Art* (self-pub., Lulu.com, 2018), 79–80.

11   O'Connor, *Operation Ebensburg*, 56–57. For his services, Gaiswinkler was remunerated at the rate of 3 shillings per day up to April 7/8, 1945, and then 10 shillings thereafter. Over the course of the next month, Gaiswinckler proceeded to navigate (successfully) through a maze of complex plot twists in the saga of Nazi orders to blow up the mine at Altaussee, where the priceless collection of art treasures was stored. Gaiswinkler's personnel file (P/F), dated August 12, 1945, in which he is recommended by Lt Colonel C. H. Villiers for the award of a medal, states, "Dropped 8 April 1945 wrong place but made his own way to Bad Aussee and held place for 4 days before arrival of own troops, the 400 resistors his party had organised. The party thus immobilised approx. one regt. of SS troops. . . . This man played an important part in immediately serving the co-operation of civilians with occupying troops. He recovered large sums of German gold and currency for the Allies which had been concreted in by the Germans in the area. . . . In view success achieved rousing and organising Austrian resistors and qualities shown in leading his party and organising Austrian civil life after the surrender, recommend on discharge: £250. 1 suit clothes" (TNA, HS9/553/3). Post-1945 politics, however, meant that the medal was never awarded. "Held pending ban on Ex-enemy national" is written on the file. Perhaps unsurprisingly, in Austria, an alternative narrative, casting aspersions on Gaiswinkler and distributing credit among other Austrians, has gained traction.

12   B. Horn and A. Balasevicius, *Casting Light on the Shadows* (Toronto: Dundurn Press, 2007), 187.

13   C. P. Stacey, *The Victory Campaign: The Operations in North-West Europe, 1944–1945*, vol. 3 of *Official History of the Canadian Army in the Second World War* (Ottawa: Queen's Printer and Controller of Stationery, 1966), 552–56.

14   Stacey, *Victory Campaign*.

15   Horn and Balasevicius, *Casting Light on the Shadows*, 188.

16   Described in chapter 5.

17   Goebbels, *Tagebücher 1945*, 502–7.

18   Beevor, *Berlin*, 184.

19   "This was quite different from the German manner. They had seized not odd bottles of wine but a whole year's crop. They seized the products of entire factories. They seized rolling stock from the railways, gold from the banks, iron from the

mines, and in the end they stole the conquered people themselves" (Moorehead, *Eclipse*, 223).

20 Moorehead, *Eclipse*, 225.

21 The KL Ravensbrück commandant, Fritz Suhren. SOE's Odette Samson testified at his subsequent trial. He was hanged on June 12, 1950.

22 Despite the town coming under intense assault from April 2 onwards.

23 Helm, *If This Is a Woman*, 571–72 (adapted). The German text has not been sourced.

24 Beevor, *Berlin*, 187.

25 Celle was the safe destination to which Bonhoeffer's fiancée, Maria von Wedemeyer, led an extraordinary trek escaping westwards from the family estate in Pätzig, which began on January 31 and concluded safely on February 10, 1945.

26 Blatman, *Death Marches*, 266. This differs from Freeman's inventory, which was published at a much earlier date (*Mighty Eighth War Diary*, 483).

27 Kershaw, *End*, 332.

28 Blatman, *Death Marches*, 265–71 (adapted).

29 Klemperer, *To the Bitter End*, 548–50 (adapted).

30 Vassiltchikov, *Berlin Diaries*, 277.

Chapter 43: Sunday in Flossenbürg

1 B. A. James, *Moonless Night: The Second World War Escape Epic* (Barnsley, UK: Leo Cooper, 1983), 169.

2 T. Siegert, *30 000 Tote mahnen! Die Geschichte des Konzentrationslagers Flossenbürg und seiner 100 Aussenlager von 1938 bis 1945*, 3rd ed. (Weiden, Germany: Taubald, 1987), 61.

3 Exerpt from Thorbeck's statement in Staatsanwaltschaft München, 17452/10, fol. 1ff., cited in C. Schmink-Gustavus, *Der Tod auf steilem Berge: Die "Standgerichtsprozesse" gegen Dietrich Bonhoeffer und Hans von Dohnanyi und die Freisprechung ihrer Mörder* (Bremen: Donat, 2020), 264–65.

4 Theodor Strünck, a captain in the army reserve closely associated with General Oster at the Abwehr, had already been condemned to death in October 1944 at the People's Court. He was "included in the list" for the next morning.

5 Text adapted from indictments dated December 20, 1944, and April 9, 1945, in DBWE 16:460, 466.

6 DBWE 16:463.

7 This was an Oster decision implemented unbeknown to Abwehr chief Canaris, and represented a decision to which he would not have consented.

8 Zipfel states that this was not so and that there was insufficient evidence (*Kirchenkampf in Deutschland*, 240, n. 66). There are inaccuracies in this publication.

9 Chowaniec, „Fall Dohnanyi", 130. The footnote states: *Aussage Huppenkothen*, in Bfst (Bonhoeffer-Forschungsstelle, Heidelberg), Landgericht München, I, p. 149 (for Sack and Gehre, as well as for Oster), and II, p. 15 (for Canaris and Bonhoeffer). Bonhoeffer's transfer from Tegel to Prinz-Albrecht-Straße on October 8, 1944, is believed, however, to be connected with the Zossen find, as we know it took Huppenkothen three weeks to read and digest the contents, and become convinced of Bonhoeffer's connections with resistance activities (Chowaniec, „Fall Dohnanyi", 129).

10   During (one of) these interrogation sessions, Stawitzki's Gestapo colleague Valentin had come into the room waving a piece of paper, a telegraphic message in which from higher up the fate of the prominent prisoners was decreed. From the document, Valentin read out the words "For legal representation no opportunity for fee generation is to be allowed" (German: "Für Avokat keine Absatzmöglichkeit"). See Müller, *Bis zur letzten Konsequenz*, 248.

11   J. Müller, statement under oath, January 16, 1946, declassified, NA, Authority 745001, RG 498, box 66.

12   Müller, *Bis zur letzten Konsequenz*, 247–49 (adapted).

13   Staatsanwalt München, 17452/10, fol. 1ff., cited in Schmink-Gustavus, *Der Tod auf steilem Berge*, 264–66. Another account places this and the death sentences as being handed down around midnight.

Chapter 44: Sunday in Schönberg (II)

1   H. Pünder, *Bericht über die gemeinsame Haft mit Dietrich Bonhoeffer* [Report on shared imprisonment with Dietrich Bonhoeffer], compiled for Eberhard Bethge on September 9, 1945, in Münster, Zeitgeschichtsarchiv Pragser Wildsee, Prags, South Tyrol, Italy (my translation; German: "Schergen").

2   Falconer, *Most Improbable Hostage*, 125.

3   In Bonhoeffer's 1911 Luther Bible, Isaiah 53 is a very well-annotated chapter. In it the passage 1 John 5:4–10 is accompanied by a bracketed reminder that it is the set passage for Quasimodogeniti Sunday.

4   Falconer, *Most Improbable Hostage*, 125. In *The Prayerbook to the Bible: An Introduction to the Psalms*, which appeared in 1940, Bonhoeffer writes, "Perhaps it is precisely the case that we must pray against our own heart in order to pray rightly. It is not just that for which we ourselves want to pray that is important, but that for which God wants us to pray. If we were dependent on ourselves alone, we would probably often pray only the fourth petition of the Lord's Prayer. But God wants it otherwise" (DBWE 5:157). (The fourth petition of the Lord's Prayer is "Give us this day our daily bread.") A collection of Bonhoeffer's thoughts on the relevant passages, notably John 20:19–31, as well as Isaiah 53, is included in appendix 7.

5   DBWE 4:323.

6   Even, or especially, in circumstances where the presence of death might be impending or imminent.

7   Pünder, *Bericht*.

8   Best, *Venlo Incident*, 200.

9   These were Best and Falconer, as well as General von Falkenhausen, who later stated that the time at which Bonhoeffer was collected was 1:00. See Richardi, *SS-Geiseln im Markt Schönberg*, 299. Falkenhausen's account of May 16, 1952, from a military archive record supplied to the author by Tilman Pünder, places the service at 12:00, with Bonhoeffer collected soon thereafter. Pünder's *Taschenkalender* note from 1945 itself is more likely to be accurate.

10   C. Marsh, in *Strange Glory: A Life of Dietrich Bonhoeffer* (London: SPCK, 2014), 395, suggests this, but does not cite a source. In the composition of the group as currently understood, the number able to sing along a capella in German, without sight of the words, would have been low.

11   Pünder, *Bericht.* Anneliese Goerdeler wrote that Bonhoeffer was collected
     between 2:00 and 4:00 p.m. (A. Goerdeler, *Meine Erinnerung an Dietrich Bon-
     hoeffer*, cited in Richardi, *SS-Geiseln im Markt Schönberg*, 120).
12   Best, *Venlo Incident*, 200. In a report written in 1946, stored among Best's per-
     sonal papers in London's Imperial War Museum, a clearer memory comes back to
     Best as he recalls the formula of the German words used for the same situation by
     the Gestapo men when they collected three of them the following day: "Falken-
     hausen, Best and Kokorin, fertig machen zur Abreise." It is reasonable to assume
     that the rough command which summoned Bonhoeffer to his death on April 8
     was "Bonhoeffer, fertig machen zur Abreise." Certainly the impression left on the
     men by the words the next day was that death awaited them.
13   "With a blunt pencil he'd written his name and address in large letters in the front,
     back and middle of the book, which he had kept placed on a table in his cell [in
     Buchenwald] as a kind of buoy" (Marsh, *Strange Glory*, 388).
14   The likelihood of these words being accurate has rightly been questioned. That
     likelihood is further increased by a recent testimony from Fiametta Curcio about
     the farewell exchange between her father, Captain Dante Curcio, and Dietrich
     Bonhoeffer, which took place in Tegel at the point when Bonhoeffer was trans-
     ferred to Prinz-Albrecht-Straße. "When DB was taken away from Tegel, he
     wanted to say farewell to my father, who was surprised to see him, when the
     guards opened his cell. He said something like: 'I am going, they are taking me
     away, I can easily guess where and why. My friend, this is the end, but for me this
     is the beginning instead. Farewell.' . . . My father perceived he was very, deeply
     serene. My father, clumsy, said few words, thanking him for their friendship, the
     importance of it, hoping the future could evolve in a different away and meet
     again. But all was clear to both" (email to the author, June 17, 2021).
15   Bonhoeffer had most recently met Bishop Bell undercover in Sweden in 1942.
     Best wrote originally to Bishop Bell on October 17, 1946, conveying the message
     that Bonhoeffer assured the bishop of his warm regard, and of his unswerving
     adherence to the principles of universal brotherhood that he (Bonhoeffer) and
     Bell shared. In the same letter, Best apologises for the tardiness of his message.
     He explains that at the time the survival of any of them seemed doubtful, and
     that on his return to England he found such a hatred of all things German that
     he hesitated to deliver it. Following the sensed rebuff of only a formal acknowl-
     edgement, written by Bell's private secretary, it was only in 1953 that Best would
     pluck up the courage to write again. In a letter dated October 13, 1953, he apol-
     ogises, this time for failing to convey Bonhoeffer's actual words, explaining that
     his reluctance stemmed not only from the hatred of all things German to which
     he had alluded, but also from his awareness of Bell's close relations with Martin
     Niemöller, a man whose character (in Best's words) was the antithesis of every-
     thing for which Bonhoeffer stood. This time he writes, as nearly as he can now
     remember, with Dietrich's actual words, which are those included above, adding
     that in the brief period that they were together he learned to love Dietrich very
     dearly. London, Lambeth Palace Library, Bell Papers vol. 42; handwritten and
     typed; in original English, including errors; excerpts from letters dated October
     13, 1946, folio 154b., and folio 151, dated 23 September 1953.
16   Schlingensiepen, *Dietrich Bonhoeffer*, 418.

17   Pünder, *Bericht*. Subsequent to this momentary disappointment, Pünder would over time make an exceptional contribution to Bonhoeffer's legacy, much built on by his son Tilman.

18   Falconer, *Most Improbable Hostage*, 125.

19   Von Hassel, *Hostage of the Third Reich*, 185.

20   Goerdeler, *Meine Erinnerung an Dietrich Bonhoeffer*, cited in Richardi, *SS-Geiseln im Markt Schönberg*, 120.

21   Information provided to the author concerning Jehle, Häring, police protocol, and route details from Bernd Bachhuber, Schönberg historian, August 2022.

22   Goerdeler, *Verschleppt*, 206 (German: "in grosser Unruhe"), in Zimmermann, *Begegnungen mit Dietrich Bonhoeffer*.

23   *Passauer Neue Presse*, no. 122, October 12, 1951, 2.

Chapter 45: Transfer to Flossenbürg

1   One source names the room as the SS casino. Another stated that it was one of the rooms in the main camp headquarters block (16 in the 1945 plan). (There were ten rooms on the ground floor and ten on the first floor to choose from.) Another suggests the laundry annex (presumably adjacent to block marked 3 in the 1945 plan).

2   Testimony of Thorbeck in post-war hearing, Staatsanwalt München, 17452/10, fol. 1ff., cited in Schmink-Gustavus, *Der Tod auf steilem Berge*, 264–66. On December 19, 1944, Bonhoeffer had written to his fiancée, including the poem "Von Guten Mächten." The third stanza runs, "And should you offer us the cup of suffering / though heavy, brimming full and bitter brand / we'll thankfully accept it, never flinching / from your good heart and your beloved hand" (DBW 8:607). See also Bonhoeffer's meditation on Psalm 119 (1939–1940; DBW 15:506).

3   In Bonhoeffer's Luther Bible, there is a line in the margin beside Isaiah 53:7: "He did not open his mouth; like a lamb that is led to the slaughter."

4   Møgensen, cited in Mayer, *Todesstunde*, 283ff., cited in R. Mayer and P. Zimmerling, eds., *Dietrich Bonhoeffer: Beten und Tun des Gerechten: Glaube und Verantwortung im Widerstand* (Giessen, Germany: Brunnen, 1997), 107ff.

5   In Heinrich Himmler's initial decree of 1940 on the subject of harvesting dental gold from the deceased within the scope of Operation T4, the process was not conducted systematically. However, as of his second decree of 1942, it was. Amounts were tallied on a Hermann Hollerith device (the company making Hollerith machines would subsequently become IBM) and sent to the Berlin Reichsbank on a monthly basis, where they were remelted into conventional ingots for exchange with Switzerland (information from Xavier Riaud to the author, August 2022). Under a secret agreement between Himmler and the Nazi president of the Reichsbank Funk, the loot was deposited to the credit of the SS main account with the name of Max Heiliger (Max the Saint). See Bullock, *Hitler*, 701.

6   Müller, *Bis zur letzten Konsequenz*, 251.

7   "The letter kills, but the Spirit gives life" (2 Corinthians 3:6) and "Love is the fulfilling of the law" (Romans 13:10).

Chapter 46: The Administration of Death

1   April 23, 1945, was (also) the occasion of the twenty-first birthday of Bonhoeffer's fiancée, Maria von Wedemeyer.

2   W. Flynn, *A History of the 90th Division in World War II, 6 June 1944 to 9 May 1945* (Baton Rouge, La.: 90th Infantry Division, 1946), 79.

3   In post-war interrogations Huppenkothen, a man of astonishing and razor-sharp recollection in relation to facts and details that built his case for exoneration from culpability, stated repeatedly that he had no memory at all of the events of that morning and that insofar as his blank memory served him, he had already left and was only informed retrospectively that the executions had been carried out. In one of the 1950s' hearings, captured on video, Rapportführer Geissberger, in response to the question "Was Huppenkothen present?" is seen to turn towards Huppenkothen. He does so with a knowing glance of cynical amusement, and responds to the judge, "Maybe he was, maybe he wasn't." The truth was discernible only in the witnessing of this exchange. The fact of the presence in Flossenbürg on April 9 of the supervising senior SS officer, Huppenkothen, and the detail leader responsible for the carrying out of the death sentences, Geissberger, remains—as a result—unrecorded.

4   Von Schlabrendorff, *Revolt against Hitler*, 172.

5   Baumgartner held this role twice: from the spring of 1940 until March 1943, and then again from March 1944 onwards.

6   A. Papagos, Δύο χρόνια στά Χιτλερικά στρατόπαιδα συγκεντρώσεως [Two years in Hitler's concentration camps] (Athens: Ekdoseis "Epikaira," 1945), 66–67.

7   Geissberger joined the SS on May 1, 1933, with membership number 5.020.697.

8   J. Mogensen (1946), cited in R. Mayer and P. Zimmerling, *Dietrich Bonhoeffer Aktuell: Biographie, Theologie, Spiritualität* (Giessen, Germany: Brunnen, 2013), 92–93.

9   Information from Stephanie Lahousen to Michael Mueller, January 3, 2006, cited in Mueller, *Canaris*, 258.

10   After the war the camp doctor, the administrator of many a lethal injection, sought to distance himself from his own involvement. He spoke while under oath with disapprobation of the guards' (alcohol-fuelled) mocking of Bonhoeffer's male anatomy, a particular subject for derision, given his office as a priest, at the moment of execution. Ten years after the event, the same individual applied the natural gravitas he was endowed with to good effect. He invented a rose-tinted account of the moment of Bonhoeffer's death, of which also the evident and self-serving benefit was the casting of the doctor's role in a more humane light.

11   The characters in box 26 are underlined.

Epilogue

1   Petersdorff, statement to Dr H. Heiber, May 28, 1957, IfZ, 2094157/ZS-7473-2, https://www.ifz-muenchen.de/archiv/zs/zs-1473.pdf. Dr Heiber writes about his interview with Petersdorff that "this record is to be treated with the greatest circumspection, as Von Peterdorff knows a lot and is very talkative, so much so that it is hard to know where truth ends and fairy-tale begins. This is even harder because Von Petersdorff does not manipulate in order to deceive or to conceal but simply seems to love to 'tell a tale.'"

2   The paradox of von Hessen's own criminal record relating to Hitler advocacy and euthenasia, along with many other such puzzles from the era, remains.

3   Bonhoeffer's death, along with that of the others, was known to a number of associates on the day itself. Foremost among these was Josef Müller, to whom

the connected news of his own survival came as an even greater surprise. A source that could not be verified suggested that his secretary Anni Haaser was informed on April 9 that Müller was on his way to Dachau and could be brought food and clothing.

4 Author's collection.

5 Falconer's initial offer from the Sachsenhausen Fund was a paltry £750, which Airey Neave is believed to have helped increase.

6 Falconer, *Most Improbable Hostage*, 132.

7 The day's outgoing commandant of Dachau was SS-Obersturmbannführer Wilhelm Weiter. "Obese, apoplectic, he drunkenly bragged that he had ordered the execution of some two thousand prisoners before leaving Dachau for the last time" (S. Harding, *The Last Battle: When U.S. and German Soldiers Joined Forces in the Waning Hours of World War II in Europe* [Boston: Da Capo, 2013], 95). Weiter committed suicide six days later, on May 2.

8 Hans-Günter Richardi's German-language account, published in 2010, allocated much more credit to German participants. Only with the appearance in 2019 of *Hitler's Last Plot* by Ian Sayer and Jeremy Dronfield did a suitably balanced rendition finally appear.

9 Bethge obliged by handing over the voice of narrator to Best for the conclusion of his extensive biography on Bonhoeffer, lifting entire swathes of text from *The Venlo Incident*, in turn adding still further to the international success of Best's publication.

10 Klemperer, *To the Bitter End*, 628–29.

Appendix 4

1 Sofern sie das Gott feindliche Reich des Bösen ist; der Glaube vermittelt alle durch Christus gewordene Kraft und Hilfe.

2 Aus Nazareth kam Jesus durch Wasser, b.i. mit der Taufe im Jordan, zur Übernahme seines Sühnamtes; er kam durch Blut zur Vollendung seines Mittleramtes in das Allerheiligste des Himmels. Man kann "Wasser und Blut" auch auf die Eröffnung der heiligen Seite beziehen.

3 Durch die Propheten, bei der Taufe im Jordan, am Pfingstfest, durch die Wirksamkeit in der Kirche.

4 Der Vater bei der Taufe im Jordan, der Sohn durch seine Lehre und Wunder.

5 Im Wesen, untrüglichem Wissen und heiligstem Wollen.

6 Hier die Seele, welche der Heiland sterbend ausathmete.

7 Geben Zeugnis für seine wirkliche Natur: Jesus ist als Gottmensch bezeugt; oder: der Geist in der Firmung und in den Gnaden, das Wasser in der Taufe, das Blut im Meßopfer und Communion.

8 Durch den Glauben.

9 Am Freitag nach dem Weißen Sonntag wird an manchen Orten das Fest der Lanze und Nägel unseres Herrn Jesu Christi gefeiert. Die Messe ist dieselbe wie am Freitag nach dem ersten Fastenmontag (s. im Proprium der Heiligen) mit Hinzufügung von drei Alleluja im Eingang und von zwei zum Offertorium.

10 Der Glaube vermittelt alle Gnaden zur Befreiung der Welt.

11 Bei der Taufe im Jordan (Wasser) bezeugte der Vater die Gottheit seines Sohnes; am Kreuze im blutigen Tode (Blut) bezeugte der Sohn sich selbst.

Appendix 7

1   Isaiah 53:4–5: "Surely he has borne our infirmities and carried our diseases; yet we accounted him stricken, struck down by God, and afflicted. But he was wounded for our transgressions, crushed for our iniquities; upon him was the punishment that made us whole, and by his bruises we are healed." V. 4 is quoted in Matthew 8:17: "This was to fulfil what had been spoken through the prophet Isaiah: 'He took our infirmities and bore our diseases.'" (In Bonhoeffer's Luther Bible, Isaiah 53 is among texts marked with pencil, including underlining in v. 1a, "Who has believed what we have heard?" [in German the text literally reads, "But who believes our preaching?"] and a line in the margin beside v. 7 ["He did not open his mouth; like a lamb that is led to the slaughter"]).

2   The footnote in DBWE 8 states, "This *present* aspect, the 'now' in which Isa. 53 is fulfilled in the present moment, is noteworthy because until then Bonhoeffer had *always* seen the suffering of God's servant as accomplished on the cross of Golgotha" (emphasis in original); see letter of April 8, 1936, to Rüdiger Schleicher (above) and the outline for a lecture on October 20, 1936 (DBWE 8:481).

Appendix 9

1   Never published in English.

2   Vermehren, *Reise durch den letzten Akt*, 202.

3   M. Wegner, *Ein weites Herz: Die zwei Leben der Isa Vermehren* (Munich: Claassen, 2003), 25.

4   This he was delighted to be offered, second time around, only to have his passport confiscated by the Gestapo when his ship passage was already booked, as someone "unworthy of representing overseas the young people of the Third Reich." It was an insult—and frustration—he would not forget.

5   Elliot was being exploited by Kim Philby by this time in that he—like all in MI6—was unaware of Philby's Russian loyalties.

6   Grove Court, Drayton Gardens, Kensington (David Tremain, email to the author, April 13, 2023).

7   M. Hastings, *The Secret War: Spies, Codes and Guerillas, 1939–1945* (London: Collins, 2017), 365.

8   As late as 1986, far-right observer Gerhard Frey—albeit a discredited and marginal voice by then—dubbed it "a treasonable affair." In fact the "Vermehren affair" made German headlines as "treason" early in the new year of 1944. In Germany's Foreign Office at the time, it was the cause of considerable uproar. What the Vermehrens could not have anticipated was that their actions, those of just two people, could be used as a pretext to unleash a chain of events with such far-reaching consequences. Those closest to Hitler conspired to represent their decision to side with the Allied cause, together with who they were, as the "final straw" in an extended catalogue of events. Both Isa brothers were married to a countess: they thus represented and personified, even embodied, a strata of German society that Hitler overtly tolerated and inwardly despised. But much more than this. By early 1944 the ever-suspicious Hitler—apt to smell treason at the best of times—was now in possession of evidence that entirely confirmed and underlined his most neurotic of suspicions: his very chief of counter-intelligence, Admiral Wilhelm Canaris, head of the Abwehr, German military counter-intelligence, whose office

in Istanbul Erich Vermehren had been seconded to—and whom Oster, Dohnanyi, and Bonhoeffer worked for—was not only involved in such an affair as the desertion of the Vermehrens; he was in fact at the centre of an undermining web of intrigue against him personally. What the Vermehrens could not have known was the extent to which they lit the touchpaper that contributed with astonishing speed and directness to Canaris' undoing—and with it, a further reduction in Bonhoeffer's own chances of survival.

Erich Vermehren knew he could rely on Adam von Trott zu Solz to be supportive of his plans to bring his wife to Istanbul. What he may not have been aware of is that in his earlier visit to Istanbul in June 1943, Trott zu Solz had attempted, linked with Helmut Graf von Moltke's forthcoming visit, to win over Ambassador von Papen to active participation in the German resistance. By December 1943, feelers were being put out by von Moltke, with Canaris' knowledge, via US spy rings for the "Herman plan"—the coordination and cooperation of German democratic opposition in the assumption of German defeat and territorial losses. Moltke had planned a third excursion to Turkey for January 1943, but the Gestapo were on to them, and on January 19 he and fellow Solf Resistance circle member Otto Kiep were arrested, together with Kiep's wife, Hanna—the latter couple both on friendly terms with the Vermehrens. It may well have been that this news finally confirmed the Vermehrens' decision to jump ship. At just that time, a German spy ring was exposed in Argentina, causing the government in Buenos Aires to sever diplomatic ties with the Reich—a period when international friends of that stature towards Germany were few in number. Moreover, as partly alluded to in chapter 25, this scandal offered the German ambassador in Madrid—Dieckhoff, who was German foreign minister Ribbentrop's brother-in-law—the chance to strike against Canaris' Abwehr, whose sabotage activities in Spain had long vexed him. He demanded the cessation in Spain of Abwehr activity and the withdrawal of Abwehr people. For this he gained—naturally—Ribbentrop's support, and he in turn secured Hitler's, such that by February 8 the Führer had ordered the cessation in Spain of sabotage activity. To add spice to the explosive cocktail, in the Vermehren affair, together with the couple themselves, three further staff had also disappeared. Immediately—in response—twelve embassy staff and three other Abwehr workers were recalled from Istanbul. The shock waves in diplomatic circles would reverberate for months. Writing about the German ambassador, Goebbels noted in his diary on March 4, 1944—"Papen has evidently gathered in Ankara—as previously in Berlin—a motley crew of dubious characters around himself." In fact Papen himself was not party to any of Erich Vermehren's plans, but Erich Vermehren's flight provided grounds for Goebbels to voice suspicion about the German ambassador—while at the same time strongly discouraging Hitler from dismissing him.

Accordingly, these events helped bring to a climax the tempo of events adding pressure onto Canaris' position within the German high command: as recounted in chapter 26, Canaris was dismissed from military service on February 12, 1944, "with permission to wear his former uniform." But even Hitler would regain something of his equilibrium. In June of that year, as the Allies landed in France, Hitler countermanded his original order about Canaris. He rehabilitated him on July 1, 1944, to the role of leading "Special Staff for Shipping, Warfare and Economic War Measures" at OKW, based at HWK Potsdam-Eiche, possibly at Himmler's behest. Canaris' international standing, it seemed, might be useful after all. But the events of July 20, 1944, changed everything once again.

9   Isa's role in keeping up the spirits of the travelling hostages is well captured in the documentary *Wir, Geiseln der SS*, directed by Christian Frey and Carsten Gutschmidt, produced by Reinhardt Beetz (Berlin: Gebrüder Beetz Filmproduktion, 2015). The film is also available in French, but not in English.

BIBLIOGRAPHY

Archival Material

BBC News HNB Film 128/129, April 1–9, 1945. BBC Archive, Reading, Berkshire.

Pünder, H. *Bericht über die gemeinsame Haft mit Dietrich Bonhoeffer* [Report on shared imprisonment with Dietrich Bonhoeffer]. Compiled for Eberhard Bethge on September 9, 1945, in Münster. Zeitgeschichtsarchiv Pragser Wildsee, Prags, South Tyrol, Italy.

———. Unposted letters to family, Schönberg, April 14 and 23, 1945, Bundesarchiv Koblenz, Nachlass Hermann Pünder, nos. 663–64.

Interviews

Author with Evelyn Smith née Falconer, June 24, 2019.

Primary Sources in German

Dietrich Bonhoeffer Werke in 16 Bände. Munich: Chr. Kaiser, 1986–2002.

DBW 1 (2000). *Sanctorum Communio: Eine dogmatische Untersuchung zur Soziologie der Kirche*. Edited by J. von Soosten.

DBW 2 (2002). *Akt und Sein: Tranzendenzphilosophie und Ontologie in der systematischen Theologie*. Edited by H.-R. Reuter.

DBW 3 (2002). *Schöpfung und Fall*. Edited by M. Rüter and I. Tödt.

DBW 4 (2002). *Nachfolge*. Edited by M. Kuske and I. Tödt.

DBW 5 (2002). *Gemeinsames Leben: Das Gebetbuch der Bibel*. Edited by G. L. Müller and A. Schönherr.

DBW 6 (1998). *Ethik*. Edited by I. Tödt, H. E. Tödt, and C. Green.

DBW 7 (1994). *Fragmente aus Tegel*. Edited by R. Bethge and I. Tödt.

DBW 8 (1998). *Widerstand und Ergebung*. Edited by C. Gremmels, E. Bethge, and R. Bethge.

DBW 9 (1986). *Jugend und Studium, 1918–1927*. Edited by H. Pfeifer.

DBW 10 (2005). *Barcelona, Berlin, Amerika*. Edited by R. Staats and H. von Hase.

DBW 11 (1994). *Ökumene, Universität, Pfarramt, 1931–1932*. Edited by E. Amelung and C. Strohm.

DBW 12 (1997). *Berlin, 1932–1933*. Edited by C. Nicolaisen and E. Scharffenorth.

DBW 13 (1994). *London, 1933–1935.* Edited by H. Goedeking, M. Heimbucher, and H.-W. Schleicher.

DBW 14 (1996). *Illegale Theologenausbildung: Finkenwalde, 1935–1937.* Edited by O. Dudzus and J. Henkys.

DBW 15 (1998). *Illegale Theologenausbildung: Sammelvikariate, 1937–1940.* Edited by D. Schulz.

DBW 16 (1996). *Konspiration und Haft, 1940–1945.* Edited by J. Glenthøj, U. Kabitz, and W. Krötke.

DBW 17 (1999). *Register und Ergänzungen.* Edited by H. Anzinger and H. Pfeifer.

Other Primary Works in German

Bonhoeffer, D., and M. von Wedemeyer. *Brautbriefe Zelle 92.* Munich: C. H. Beck, 2001.

Primary Works in English

English Translations of the DBW. Minneapolis: Fortress, 1996–2013.

DBWE 1 (1998). *Sanctorum Communio: A Theological Study of the Sociology of the Church.* Edited by C. J. Green. Translated by R. Krauss and N. Lukens.

DBWE 2 (1996). *Act and Being: Transcendental Philosophy and Ontology in Systematic Theology.* Edited by W. W. Floyd. Translated by H. Rumscheidt.

DBWE 3 (1997). *Creation and Fall: A Theological Exposition of Genesis 1–3.* Edited by J. W. de Gruchy. Translated by D. Bax.

DBWE 4 (2001). *Discipleship.* Edited by J. Godsey and G. Kelly. Translated by B. Green and R. Kraus.

DBWE 5 (1996). *Life Together: Prayerbook of the Bible.* Edited by G. Kelly. Translated by D. Bloesch.

DBWE 6 (2005). *Ethics.* Edited by I. Tödt, H. E. Tödt, E. Feil, and C. Green. Translated by R. Krauss, C. West, and D. Stott.

DBWE 7 (2000). *Fiction from Tegel Prison.* Edited by C. Green. Translated by N. Lukens.

DBWE 8 (2010). *Letters and Papers from Prison.* Edited by J. W. de Gruchy. Translated by I. Best, L. Dahill, R. Krauss, and N. Lukens.

DBWE 9 (2003). *The Young Bonhoeffer, 1918–1927.* Edited by P. Duane Matheny, C. Green, and M. Johnson. Translated by M. Nebelsick.

DBWE 10 (2008). *Barcelona, Berlin, New York, 1928–1931.* Edited by C. Green. Translated by D. Stott.

DBWE 11 (2012). *Ecumenical, Academic, and Pastoral Work, 1931–1932.* Edited by V. Barnett, M. Brocker, and M. Lukens. Translated by I. Best, N. Humphrey, M. Pauck, A. Schmidt-Lange, and D. Stott.

DBWE 12 (2009). *Berlin, 1932–1933*. Edited by C. Nicolaisen and E. Scharffenorth. Translated by I. Best and D. Higgins.

DBWE 13 (2007). *London, 1933–1935*. Edited by K. Clements. Translated by I. Best.

DBWE 14 (2013). *Theological Education at Finkenwalde, 1935–1937*. Edited by H. Gaylon Barker and M. Brocker. Translated by D. Stott.

DBWE 15 (2012). *Theological Education Underground, 1937–1940*. Edited by V. Barnett. Translated by V. Barnett, C. Bergmann, P. Frick, and S. Moore.

DBWE 16 (2006). *Conspiracy and Imprisonment, 1940–1945*. Edited by M. Brocker. Translated by L. Dahill.

Other English Translations of Bonhoeffer's Works

Creation and Fall. Translated by J. Fletcher. London: SCM Press, 1959.

Ethics. Translated by N. Horton Smith. London: SCM Press, 1955.

Letters to London: Dietrich Bonhoeffer's Previously Unpublished Correspondence with Ernst Cromwell, 1935–36. Translated by I. Best. London: SPCK, 2013.

Letters and Papers from Prison. Edited by R. Fuller, F. Clarke, and J. Bowden. New York: Touchstone, 1997.

Love Letters from Cell 92. Edited by R.-A. von Bismarck and U. Kabitz. Translated by J. Brownjohn. London: HarperCollins, 1994.

No Rusty Swords. Edited by E. Robertson. London: Collins, 1965.

Temptation. Translated by K. Downham. London: SCM Press, 1955.

True Patriotism. Edited by E. Robertson. London: Collins, 1973.

The Way to Freedom. Edited by E. Robertson. London: Collins, 1966.

Secondary Sources

Allen, M. *The Hitler/Hess Deception: British Intelligence's Best-Kept Secret of the Second World War*. London: HarperCollins, 2003.

Andrew, C. *Secret Service: The Making of the British Intelligence Community*. London: Heinemann, 1985.

Anonymous. *A Woman in Berlin: Diary, 20 April 1945 to 22 June 1945*. Translated by P. Boehm. London: Virago, 2005.

Anzenberger, W., H. Halbrainer, and H.-J. Rabko. *Zwischen den Fronten: Die Region Eisenerz von 1938–1945*. Loeben: Institut für Strukturforschung und Erwachsenenbildung der AK-Steiermark, 2000.

Arndt, H. *The Economic Lessons of the 1930s*. Oxford: Oxford University Press, 1944.

Ashdown, P. *Nein! Standing Up to Hitler, 1935–1944*. London: Collins, 2018.

Baker, N. *Human Smoke: The Beginnings of World War II, the End of Civilisation*. London: Simon and Schuster, 2008.

Bär, S. *Der Untergang des Hauses Rascher.* Self-published, 2011. Later published as *The Fall of the House of Rascher: The Bizarre Life and Death of the SS-Doctor Sigmund Rascher.* Self-published, Kindle, 2014.

Barnes, J., and P. Barnes. *Nazis in Pre-war London, 1930–1934.* Brighton, UK: Sussex Academic Press, 2005.

Barnett, V. *For the Soul of the People: Protestant Protest against Hitler.* Oxford: Oxford University Press, 1992.

Bassett, R. *Hitler's Spy Chief: The Wilhelm Canaris Mystery.* London: Weidenfeld and Nicholson, 2005.

Beevor, A. *Berlin: The Downfall, 1945.* London: Penguin Books, 2003.

———. *D-Day: The Battle for Normandy.* London: Penguin Books, 2012.

———. *The Second World War.* London: Weidenfeld & Nicholson, 2012.

Benson, R. *The Way of Holiness: An Exposition of Psalm CXIX.* London: Methuen, 1901.

Best, P. *The Venlo Incident: A True Story of Double-Dealing, Captivity, and a Murderous Nazi Plot.* London: Frontline, 2009. First published 1950.

Bethge, E. *Dietrich Bonhoeffer: A Biography.* Minneapolis: Fortress, 2000. First published 1967.

Bidez, J. *Julian der Abtrünnige.* 4th ed. Munich: Verlag D Callway, 1940.

Binet, L. *HHhH.* Translated by S. Taylor. London: Vintage, 2013.

Black, P. *Ernst Kaltenbrunner: Ideological Soldier of the Third Reich.* Princeton, N.J.: Princeton University Press, 1984.

Blatman, D. *The Death Marches: The Final Phase of Nazi Genocide.* Translated by C. Galai. Cambridge, Mass.: Harvard University Press, 2011.

Blum, L. *Le dernier mois.* Paris: Arléa, 2004. First published 1946.

Bösendahl, C. *Rinteln Stadtgeschichte(n) neu erzählt.* Hamelin, Germany: Heimatbund der Grafschaft Schaumburg, 2021.

Boyd, J. *Travellers in the Third Reich: The Rise of Fascism through the Eyes of Everyday People.* London: Elliott and Thompson, 2017.

Boyle, A. *The Climate of Treason: Five Who Spied for Russia.* London: Hutchinson, 1979.

Breitman, R. *Official Secrets: What the Nazis Knew, What the British and the Americans Withheld.* London: Penguin Books, 1999.

Broszat, M., E. Fröhlich, and F. Wiesmann. *Bayern in der NS Zeit: Soziale Lage und politisches Verhalten der Bevölkerung im Spiegel vertraulicher Berichte.* Munich: Oldenburg, 1977.

Bücheler, H. *Hoepner: Ein deutsches Soldatenschicksal des XX Jahrhunderts.* Herford, Germany: Mittler, 1980.

Buchheit, G. *Der deutsche Geheimdienst: Spionageabwehr im Dritten Reich.* Beltheim-Schnellbach, Germany: Lindenbaum, 2010.

Bullock, A. *Hitler: A Study in Tyranny.* London: Penguin Books, 1962.

Burleigh, M. *The Third Reich: A New History.* London: Macmillan, 2000.

Cavanaugh, W. *Torture and Eucharist.* Oxford: Blackwell, 1998.

Cave Brown, A. *Bodyguard of Lies.* London: W. H. Allen, 1977.

Chowaniec, E. *Der „Fall Dohnanyi" 1943–45: Widerstand, Militärjustiz, SS-Willkür.* Munich: R. Oldenburg, 1991.

Churchill, W. *The Second World War.* 6 vols. London: Cassell, 1948–1954.

Clements, K. *Bonhoeffer and Britain.* London: CTBI, 2006.

Cohen, R. *Soldiers and Slaves: American POWs Trapped by the Nazis' Final Gamble.* New York: Random House, 2005.

Courtoy, M. "La question des otages en Belgique pendant la seconde guerre mondiale." In *Occupation et répression militaire allemandes, 1939–1945: La politique de "maintien de l'ordre" en Europe occupée,* edited by G. Eismann and S. Martens, 104–26. Paris: Institut historique allemand, 2007.

Crankshaw, E. *Gestapo: Instrument of Tyranny.* London: Putnam, 1956.

Crew, D. *Nazism and German Society.* London: Routledge, 1994.

Davies, N. *Europe: A History.* London: BCA, 1996.

Dear, I. *Sabotage and Subversion: The SOE and OSS at War.* London: Cassell, 1996.

de Gruchy, J. W. *Bonhoeffer and South Africa.* Grand Rapids: Eerdmans, 1984.

———. *Bonhoeffer for a New Day: Theology in a Time of Transition.* Grand Rapids: Eerdmans, 1997.

———. "Bonhoeffer's English Bible. UTS Archives, Bonhoeffer Secondary Papers, Series 2A Box 2. July 1976." *Dialog: A Journal of Theology* 17, no. 3 (1978): 211–15.

———, ed. *The Cambridge Companion to Dietrich Bonhoeffer.* Cambridge: Cambridge University Press, 1999.

———. *Daring, Trusting Spirit: Bonhoeffer's Friend Eberhard Bethge.* London: SCM Press, 2005.

Dehillotte, P. *Gestapo: L'Organisation. -Les Chefs.- Les Agents. L'Action de la Gestapo en Europe. Aux Etats-Unis et en Amerique du Sud.* Paris: Payot, 1940.

de Jonge, M. P. *Bonhoeffer's Reception of Luther.* Oxford: Oxford University Press, 2017.

Deutsch, H. *The Conspiracy against Hitler in the Twilight War.* Minneapolis: University of Minnesota Press, 1968.

Dobbs, M. *Six Months in 1945: From World War to Cold War.* London: Hutchinson, 2012.

Doerries, R. *Hitler's Last Chief of Foreign Intelligence: Allied Interrogations of Walter Schellenburg.* London: Frank Cass, 2003.

Doussinague, J. *España Tenía Razón: 1939–1945.* Madrid: Espasa-Calpe, 1949.

Dulles, A. *Germany's Underground: The Anti-Nazi Resistance*. Boston: Da Capo, 1947.

———. *The Secret Surrender*. London: Harper and Row, 1966.

Dumas, A. *Theologian of Reality*. Translated by R. McAfee Brown. London: SCM Press, 1971.

Dunkel, T. *White Knights in the Black Orchestra: The Extraordinary Story of the Germans Who Resisted Hitler*. New York: Hachette, 2022.

Eberle, H., and M. Uhl. *Das Buch Hitler*. Mülheim, Germany: Gustav Lübbe, 2007.

Eminger, S., E. Langthaler, and K. Mulley. *Nationalsozialismus in Niederösterreich: Opfer. Täter. Gegner.* Innsbruck: Studienverlag, 2021.

Endrass, E. *Bonhoeffer und seine Richter: Ein Prozess und sein Nachspiel*. Stuttgart: Kreuz, 2006.

Ericksen, R. P. *Theologians under Hitler: Gerhard Kittel, Paul Althaus and Emmanuel Hirsch*. London: Yale University Press, 1985.

Ericksen, R. P., and S. Heschel. *German Churches and the Holocaust: Betrayal*. Minneapolis: Fortress, 1999.

Evans, R. *The Coming of the Third Reich*. London: Penguin Books, 2003.

Falconer, H. *The Gestapo's Most Improbable Hostage*. Barnsley, UK: Pen and Sword, 2018. First published 1975.

Ferihumer, K., and W. R. Garscha. "Der 'Stein Komplex': Nationalsozialistische Endphaseverbrechen im Raum Krems und ihre gerichtliche Aufarbeitung." In *DÖW Jahrbuch 2016, Fanatiker, Pflichterfüller, Widerständiger*, edited by C. Schindler, 51–82. Vienna: DÖW, 2016.

Fest, J. C. *The Face of the Third Reich: Portraits of the Nazi Leadership*. Translated by M. Bullock. New York: Pantheon Books, 1970.

———. *Hitler*. Translated by R. Winston and C. Winston. London: Weidenfeld and Nicholson, 1974.

———. *Plotting Hitler's Death: The German Resistance to Hitler, 1933–1945*. Translated by B. Little. London: Weidenfeld and Nicholson, 1996.

Feuersenger, M. *Mein Kriegstagebuch: Führerhauptquartier und Berliner Wirklichkeit*. Freiburg, Germany: Herder, 1982.

Fitzgibbon, C. *To Kill Hitler: The Officers' Plot*. Stevenage, UK: SPA Books, 1994. First published 1956.

Flynn, W. *A History of the 90th Division in World War II, 6 June 1944 to 9 May 1945*. Baton Rouge, La.: 90th Infantry Division, 1946.

Frankopan, P. *The Silk Roads: A New History of the World*. London: Bloomsbury, 2015.

Freeman, R. A. *Mighty Eighth War Diary*. London: Jane's, 1981.

Frey, Christian, and Carsten Gutschmidt, directors. *Wir, Geiseln der SS*. Produced by Reinhardt Beetz. Berlin: Gebrüder Beetz Filmproduktion, 2015.

Freytag von Loringhoven, B. *In the Bunker with Hitler*. New York: Pegasus, 2005.

Fry, H. *The King's Most Loyal Enemy Aliens*. Cheltenham, UK: History Press, 2007.

Fulbrook, M. *A Concise History of Germany*. Cambridge: Cambridge University Press, 1990.

Gaevernitz, G. *The Plots to Kill Hitler: The Account of Fabian von Schlabrendorff*. Self-published, CreateSpace, 2017.

Galsworthy, J. *The Forsyte Saga*. London: Heinemann, 1976.

Gardiner, G. *The Thirties: An Intimate History*. London: HarperCollins, 2010.

Gellately, R. *Backing Hitler: Consent and Coercion in Nazi Germany*. Oxford: Oxford University Press, 2001.

George, S. *How the Other Half Dies*. Harmondsworth, UK: Penguin Books, 1986.

Gerwarth, R. *Hitler's Hangman: The Life of Heydrich*. New Haven: Yale University Press, 2011.

Giebel, W., ed. "Haushaltsbuch von Ursula Kleinmichel." In *Bomben auf Berlin: Zeitzeugen berichten vom Luftkrieg*. Berlin: Berlin Story Verlag, 2012.

Gilbert, M. *Second World War*. London: Phoenix Giant, 1989.

Goddard, D. *The Last Days of Dietrich Bonhoeffer*. New York: Harper and Row, 1976.

Goebbels, J. *Tagebücher 1945: Die letzten Aufzeichnungen*. Hamburg: Bastei Lübbe, 1977.

———. *Die Tagebücher von Joseph Goebbels, Teil II, Diktate 1941–1945*. Munich: E. Fröhlich, 1993.

Graber, G. *History of the SS*. London: Robert Hale, 1978.

Green, C. *Bonhoeffer: A Theology of Sociality*. Grand Rapids: Eerdmans, 1999.

Grundmann, S. *Der Geheimapparat der KPD im Visier der Gestapo*. Berlin: Dietz, 2008.

Halder, F. *Kriegstagebuch*. Stuttgart: H. A. Jacobsen, 1964.

Hale, C. *Himmler's Crusade: The True Story of the 1938 Nazi Expedition into Tibet*. London: Transworld, 2003.

Hanna, C. W. *Black Recipients of the Medal of Honor: A Biographical Dictionary, Civil War through Vietnam War*. Jefferson, N.C.: McFarland, 2010.

Hansen, R. *Disobeying Hitler: German Resistance in the Last Year of WWII*. London: Faber and Faber, 2014.

Harder, T. *Special Forces Hero: Anders Lassen VC MC**. Barnsley, UK: Pen and Sword, 2021.

Harding, S. *The Last Battle: When U.S. and German Soldiers Joined Forces in the Waning Hours of World War II in Europe*. Boston: Da Capo, 2013.

Hastings, M. *All Hell Let Loose: The World at War, 1939–1945*. London: Harper, 2011.

———. *Overlord: D-Day and the Battle for Normandy, 1944*. Oxford: Pan, 1999.

———. *The Secret War: Spies, Codes and Guerrillas, 1939–1945*. London: Collins, 2017.

Hauerwas, S. *Performing the Faith: Bonhoeffer and the Practice of Non-violence*. London: SPCK, 2004.

Haynes, S. *The Bonhoeffer Phenomenon: Portraits of a Protestant Saint*. Minneapolis: Fortress, 2005.

Helm, S. *If This Is a Woman: Inside Ravensbrück: Hitler's Concentration Camp for Women*. London: Little, Brown, 2015.

———. *A Life in Secrets: The Story of Vera Atkins and the Lost Agents of SOE*. London: Little, Brown, 2005.

Hendy, D. *The BBC: A People's History*. London: Profile Books, 2022.

Heppel, M. *George Bell and Nikolai Velimirovic*. Birmingham, UK: Lazarica Press, 2001.

Hermiston, R. *The Greatest Traitor: The Secret Lives of Agent George Blake*. London: Aurum Press, 2015.

Hibbert, C. *The English: A Social History, 1066–1945*. London: Paladin Press, 1987.

Hillgruber, A., and G. Hümmelchen. *Chronik des zweiten Weltkrieges*. Bindlach, Germany: Gondron, 1978.

Hitler, A. *Mein Kampf*. Munich: Franz Eher, 1943.

Hoare, P. *Albert and the Whale*. London: 4th Estate, 2021.

Hoffmann, P. *The History of the German Resistance, 1933–1945*. London: Macdonald and Jane's, 1977.

Höhne, H. *Canaris*. Translated by J. Maxwell Brownjohn. London: Secker and Warburg, 1979.

Holland, T. *Dominion: The Making of the Western Mind*. London: Little, Brown, 2019.

Horn, B., and A. Balasevicius. *Casting Light on the Shadows*. Toronto: Dundurn Press, 2007.

Huntemann, G. *Dietrich Bonhoeffer: An Evangelical Reassessment*. Translated by Todd Huizinga. Grand Rapids: Baker Books, 1996.

Hutton, W., and A. Giddens. *On the Edge: Living with Global Capitalism*. London: Jonathan Cape, 2000.

Ireland, B. *Jane's Naval History of World War II*. London: HarperCollins, 1998.

Jacobsen, H. *Opposition: Gegen Hitler und der Staatsstreich*. 2 vols. Stuttgart: Mundus, 1989.

James, B. A. *Moonless Night: The Second World War Escape Epic*. Barnsley, UK: Leo Cooper, 1983.

Janssen, G. *Das Ministerium Speer: Deutschlands Rüstung im Krieg*. Berlin: Ullstein, 1968.

Jardim, T. *The Mauthausen Trial: American Military Justice in Germany*. Cambridge, Mass.: Harvard University Press, 2012.

Jasper, R. *George Bell, Bishop of Chichester*. London: Oxford University Press, 1967.

Jeffreys, D. *Hell's Cartel: IG Farben and the Making of Hitler's War Machine*. London: Bloomsbury, 2008.

Jenkins, R. *Churchill: A Biography*. London: Pan, 2003.

Joachimsthaler, A. *The Last Days of Hitler: Legend, Evidence and Truth*. London: Cassell, 2000.

Jørgen, B., and L. F. Mogensen. "Ein Zeuge aus dem KZ Flossenbürg." In *Dietrich Bonhoeffer, Mensch hinter Mauern: Theologie und Spiritualität in den Gefängnisjahren*, edited by R. Mayer et al. Giessen, Germany: Brunnen, 1993.

Junge, T. *Until the Final Hour*. London: Phoenix, 2002.

Jünger, E. *Storm of Steel*. Translated by Michael Hofmann. London: Penguin Books, 2004. First published 1920 as *In Stahlgewittern*.

Kahn, D. *Hitler's Spies: German Military Intelligence in World War II*. London: Hodder and Stoughton, 1978.

Keegan, J. *The Penguin Book of War*. London: Viking, 1999.

Kele, M. H. *Nazis and Workers: National Socialist Appeals to German Labour, 1919–1933*. Chapel Hill: University of North Carolina Press, 1972.

Kenkmann, A., and E. Kohlhaas. "Frühe Zeugnisse über den Holocaust: Die Befragungen von Kindern in Polen nach der Befreiung von der deutschen Herrschaft." *BIOS* 23, no. 1 (2010): 138–52.

Kern, K.-H. *Die Geheimnisse des Dr. Josef Müller: Mutmassungen zu den Morden von Flossenbürg (1945) und Pöcking (1960)*. Berlin: Frieling, 2000.

Kershaw, A. *The Liberator: One World War II Soldier's 500-Day Odyssey*. London: Arrow, 2013.

Kershaw, I. *The End: The Defiance and Destruction of Hitler's Germany, 1944–1945*. London: Penguin Books, 2012.

———. *Hitler*. London: Penguin Books, 2009.

Kiltzer, L. *Hitler's Traitor: Martin Bormann and the Defeat of the Reich*. Novato, Calif.: Presidio, 2000.

Kirchliche Handlungen. Vol. 2 of *Agende für die Evangeliche Landeskirche*. Berlin: Mittler and Sohn, 1895.

Klemperer, V. *I Shall Bear Witness*. Vol. 1 of *The Diaries of Victor Klemperer*. London: Phoenix, 1999.

———. *To the Bitter End.* Vol. 2 of *The Diaries of Victor Klemperer.* London: Phoenix, 2000.

Knigge, V., R.-G. Lüttgenau, B. Ritscher, and H. Stein. *Konzentrationslager Buchenwald 1937–1945: Speziallager Nr. 2 1945–1950. Zwei Lager an einem Ort—Geschichte und Erinerrungskonstruktion.* Weimar: Gutenberg, 1998.

Lang, B., ed. *Writing and the Holocaust.* New York: Holmes and Meier, 1998.

Lappin, E. "The Death Marches of Hungarian Jews through Austria in the Spring of 1945." *Yad Vashem Studies* 28 (2000): 203–42.

Leese, K. *Der Protestantismus im Wandel der neueren Zeit.* Stuttgart: Alfred Kroner, 1940.

Lelyveld, J. *His Final Battle: The Last Months of Franklin Roosevelt.* New York: Vintage Books, 2016.

Levi, P. *Survival in Auschwitz: The Nazi Assault on Humanity.* New York: Collins, 1961.

Levy, A. *Nazi Hunter: The Wiesenthal File; How Simon Wiesenthal Hunted Down the Nazi War Criminals.* London: Robinson, 2002.

Lewis, D. *The Nazi Hunters: The Ultra-secret SAS Unit and the Quest for Hitler's War Criminals.* London: Quercus, 2015.

Lifton, R. *The Nazi Doctors: Medical Killing and the Psychology of Genocide.* New York: Basic Books, 2000.

Linge, H. *With Hitler to the End: The Memoirs of Adolf Hitler's Valet.* London: Simon and Schuster, 2009.

Lofgren, S. *Southern Philippines: The US Army Campaigns of World War II.* Self-published, CreateSpace, 2015.

Longerich, P. *Heinrich Himmler.* Oxford: Oxford University Press, 2012.

Lucas, J. *Last Days of the Reich: The Collapse of Nazi Germany, May 1945.* London: Cassell, 1986.

Macdonald, C. *The Killing of SS Obergruppenführer Reinhard Heydrich, 27 May 1942.* London: Macmillan, 1989.

Macintyre, B. *Agent Zigzag: The True Wartime Story of Eddie Chapman.* London: Crown, 2007.

Madsen, C. "Victims of Circumstance: The Execution of German Deserters by Surrendered German Troops under Canadian Control in Amsterdam, May 1945." *Canadian Military History* 2, no. 1 (1993): 93–113.

Marsh, C. *Reclaiming Dietrich Bonhoeffer: The Promise of His Theology.* Oxford: Oxford University Press, 1994.

———. *Strange Glory: A Life of Dietrich Bonhoeffer.* London: SPCK, 2014.

Marshall, P., ed. *The Cambridge Illustrated History of the British Empire.* Cambridge: Cambridge University Press, 1996.

Mayer, A. *Why Did the Heavens Not Darken? The Final Solution in History.* London: Verso, 1990.

Mayer, R., and P. Zimmerling, eds. *Dietrich Bonhoeffer: Beten und Tun des Gerechten: Glaube und Verantwortung im Widerstand.* Giessen, Germany: Brunnen, 1997.

———. *Dietrich Bonhoeffer Aktuell: Biographie, Theologie, Spiritualität.* Giessen, Germany: Brunnen, 2013.

Mazower, M. *Dark Continent: Europe's Twentieth Century.* London: Allen Lane, 1998.

Metaxas, E. *Bonhoeffer: Pastor, Martyr, Prophet, Spy.* Nashville: Thomas Nelson, 2010.

Meyer, W. *Unternehmen Sieben: Eine Rettungsaktion für vom Holocaust Bedrohte aus dem Amt Ausland/Abwehr im Oberkommando der Wehrmacht.* Meisenheim, Germany: Anton Hain, 1993.

———, ed. *Verschwörer im KZ: Hans von Dohnanyi und die Häftlinge des 20. Juli 1944 im KZ Sachsenhausen.* Berlin: Hentrich, 1998.

Meyer-Krahmer, M. *Carl Goerdeler: Mut zum Widerstand: Eine Tochter erinnert sich.* Leipzig: Leipziger Universitätsverlag, 1998.

Middlebrook, M., and C. Everitt. *The Bomber Command War Diaries: An Operational Reference Book, 1939–1945.* Harmondsworth, UK: Penguin Books, 1987.

Moorehead, A. *Eclipse: A Classic Eyewitness Account of the Decline and Fall of Nazi Germany, 1943–1945.* London: Sphere, 1967. First published 1945.

Morison, S. E. *Victory in the Pacific, 1945.* Oxford: Oxford University Press, 1960.

Mowat, C. *Britain between the Wars, 1918–1940.* London: Methuen, 1955.

Mueller, M. *Canaris: The Life and Death of Hitler's Spymaster.* Barnsley, UK: Frontline, 2007.

Müller, C. *Dietrich Bonhoeffers Kampf gegen die nationalsozialistische Verfolgung und Vernichtung der Juden.* Munich: Chr. Kaiser, 1990.

Müller, J. *Bis zur letzten Konsequenz.* Munich: Süddeutscher Verlag, 1975.

Mulley, C. *The Women Who Flew for Hitler: The True Story of Hitler's Valkyries.* London: Macmillan, 2017.

Neillands, R. *The Conquest of the Reich: D-Day to VE Day: A Soldier's History.* London: Weidenfeld and Nicholson, 1995.

Nowak, K. *Adolf von Harnack als Zeitgenosse: Reden und Schriften aus den Jahren des Kaiserreichs und der Weimarer Republik.* Berlin: De Gruyter, 1996.

O'Connor, B. *Operation Ebensburg: SOE's Austrian "Bonzos" and the Rescue of Looted European Art.* Self-published, Lulu.com, 2018.

Orbach, D. *The Plots against Hitler.* London: Head of Zeus, 2017.

Padfield, P. *Himmler: Reichsführer SS*. London: Papermac, 1990.

Papagos, A. Δύο χρόνια στά Χιτλερικά στρατόπαιδα συγκεντρώσεως [Two years in Hitler's concentration camps]. Athens: Ekdoseis "Epikaira," 1945.

Plant, S. *Bonhoeffer*. London: Continuum, 2004.

Plutarch. *Plutarch: Grosse Griechen und Römer [Lives]*. Edited by D. Mikusch. Cologne: Anaconda, 2009. Originally published Berlin: Propyläen, 1935.

Popov, D. *Super Spion: Der Doppelagent im Zweiten Weltkrieg*. Vienna: Molden, 1974.

Pünder, H. "Pervertierung des Polizeirechts in Nationalsozialismus (Teil 1)." *JURA—Juristische Ausbildung* 1 (2023): 10–18.

———. *Von Preussen nach Europa: Lebenserinnerungen*. Stuttgart: Deutsche Verlags-Anstalt, 1968.

Pünder, T. *In den Fängen des NS-Staats: Staatssekretär Dr. Hermann Pünder 1944/45*. Munich: Aschendorff, 2018.

———. *Kalenderblätter 1945: Hermann Pünders Taschenkalender-Eintragungen im ersten Halbjahr 1945*. Transcribed from Stolze-Schrey shorthand by Rosemarie Koller from Gossau. Münster: self-published, 2014.

———. *Windbriefe: Transkription nicht abgesandter Briefe meines Vaters Hermann Pünder an die Familie während seiner Zeit in den Fängen des NS-Staates und nach der Befreiung durch die Amerikaner 1945*. Münster: self-published, 2020.

Ramm, H.-J. *Mich trägt mein Glaube: Friedrich von Rabenau: General und Christ im Widerstand: Tagebuch einer Gestapohaft*. Beau-Bassin: Fromm, 2011.

Rees, L. *The Nazis: A Warning from History*. London: BBC Books, 2005.

Reshin, L., and A. Pochtarev. "Molotov's 'Nephew' under Investigation and on Trial." *Independent Military Review* 20 (2000).

Ribhegge, W., E. Schönbach, and M. Witt. *Geschichte der Stadt und Region Hamm im 19. und 20. Jahrhundert*. Düsseldorf: Schwann im Patmos, 1991.

Richardi, H.-G. *SS-Geiseln im Markt Schönberg: Dramatische Tage am Ende des Zweiten Weltkrieges im Bayerischen Wald*. Schönberg, Germany: Markt Schönberg, 2010.

———. *SS-Geiseln in der Alpenfestung: Die Verschleppung prominenter KZ-Häftlinge aus Deutschland nach Südtirol*. Bozen, Italy: Edition Raetia, 2009.

Riebling, M. *Church of Spies: The Pope's Secret War against Hitler*. New York: Basic Books, 2015.

Rieger, J. *The Silent Church: The Problem of the German Confessional Witness*. London: SCM Press, 1944.

Ritter, G. *Carl Goerdeler und die deutsche Widerstandsbewegung*. Munich: Deutscher Taschenbuch Verlag, 1964.

Robertson, E. *Unshakeable Friend: George Bell and the German Churches.* London: CCBI, 1995.

Roden, D. "'In naam van het Duitse volk!' Het Duitse krijgsgerecht en de openbare orde in bezet België (1940–1944)." PhD diss., University of Gent, 2015.

Rose, A. *Werewolf 1944–1945: Eine Dokumentation.* Stuttgart: Motorbuch, 1980.

Royce, H. *20. Juli 1944.* Bonn: Berto-Verlag, 1952.

Runcorn, D. *Spirituality Workbook: A Guide for Explorers, Pilgrims and Seekers.* London: SPCK, 2011.

Russell, B. *A History of Western Philosophy.* London: George Allen and Unwin, 1946.

Sajer, G. *The Forgotten Soldier: War on the Russian Front—A True Story.* London: Cassell, 1999.

Sands, P. *The Ratline: Love, Lies and Justice on the Trail of a Nazi Fugitive.* London: Weidenfeld and Nicholson, 2020.

Sayer, I., and D. Botting. *Nazi Gold: The Story of the World's Greatest Robbery—and Its Aftermath.* London: Granada, 1984.

Sayer, I., and J. Dronfield. *Hitler's Last Plot: The 139 VIP Hostages Selected for Death in the Final Days of World War II.* New York: Da Capo, 2019.

Schellenberg, W. *Invasion 1940: The Nazi Invasion Plan for Britain.* London: St Ermin's Press, 2001.

Schlingensiepen, F. *Dietrich Bonhoeffer: Martyr, Thinker, Man of Resistance.* Translated by I. Best. London: T&T Clark, 2010.

Schmink-Gustavus, C. *Der Tod auf steilem Berge: Die "Standgerichtsprozesse" gegen Dietrich Bonhoeffer und Hans von Dohnanyi und die Freisprechung ihrer Mörder.* Bremen: Donat, 2020.

Schmoll, Peter. *Die Messerschmitt-Werke im Zweiten Weltkrieg: Die Flugzeugproduktion der Messerschmitt GmbH Regensburg von 1938 bis 1945.* Regensburg, Germany: Mittelbayerischen, 1998.

Scholder, K. *Preliminary History and the Time of Illusions, 1918–34.* Vol. 1 of *The Churches and the Third Reich.* London: SCM Press, 1977.

———. *The Year of Disillusionment: 1934, Barmen and Rome.* Vol. 2 of *The Churches and the Third Reich.* London: SCM Press, 1988.

Schuschnigg, K. *Ein Requiem in Rot-Weiss-Rot: Aufzeichnungen des Häftlings Dr. Auster.* Zurich: Amstutz, Herdeg, 1946.

Sereny, G. *Albert Speer: His Battle with Truth.* London: Macmillan, 1995.

Shakespeare, C. *Kim Philby, Our Man in Moscow: The Life of a Cold War Masterspy.* 2nd ed. Self-published, CreateSpace, 2015.

Shirer, W. *The Rise and Fall of the Third Reich.* London: Pan, 1979. First published 1960.

Siegert, T. *30 000 Tote mahnen! Die Geschichte des Konzentrationslagers Flossenbürg und seiner 100 Aussenlager von 1938 bis 1945*. 3rd ed. Weiden, Germany: Taubald, 1987.

Sifton, E., and F. Stern. *No Ordinary Men: Dietrich Bonhoeffer and Hans von Dohnanyi, Resisters against Hitler in Church and State*. New York: New York Review of Books, 2013.

Sisk, R. "Fallen US Bombardier's Bracelet Tells Story of Secret Missions to Norway in Last Days of WWII." Military.com, July 5, 2021. https://www.military.com/daily-news/2021/07/05/fallen-us-bombardiers-bracelet-tells-story-of-secret-missions-norway-last-days-of-wwii.html.

Speer, A. *Inside the Third Reich: The Classic Account of Nazi Germany by Hitler's Armaments Minister*. London: Weidenfeld and Nicholson, 1970.

Stacey, C. P. *The Victory Campaign: The Operations in North-West Europe, 1944–1945*. Vol. 3 of *Official History of the Canadian Army in the Second World War*. Ottawa: Queen's Printer and Controller of Stationery, 1966.

Stafford, D. *Mission Accomplished: SOE and Italy, 1943–1945*. London: Vintage Books, 2011.

Stein, H., ed. *Konzentrationslager Buchenwald 1937–1945: Begleitband zur ständigen Ausstellung*. Gedenkstätte Buchenwald, Germany: Wallstein, 1999.

Stevenson, W. *The Bormann Brotherhood*. New York: Harcourt Brace Jovanovich, 1973.

Streibel, R. *April in Stein*. Vienna: Residenz Verlag, 2015.

Tillich, P. *The Courage to Be*. London: HarperCollins, 1986.

Toland, J. *Adolf Hitler*. London: Book Club Associates, 1977.

Trevor-Roper, H. *The Last Days of Hitler*. London: Macmillan, 1947.

Trigg, J. *To VE-Day through German Eyes: The Final Defeat of Nazi Germany*. Stroud, UK: Amberley, 2020.

Trotsky, L. *The Struggle against Fascism in Germany*. New York: Pathfinder, 1971.

Tyas, S. *SS-Major Horst Kopkow: From the Gestapo to British Intelligence*. London: Fonthill Media, 2017.

Vassiltchikov, M. *The Berlin Diaries, 1940–1945*. London: Pimlico, 1985.

Vermehren, I. *Reise durch den letzten Akt: Ravensbrück, Buchenwald, Dachau: Eine Frau berichtet*. Hamburg: Rowohlt, 2005. First published 1946.

Vinogradov, V. K., J. F. Pogonyi, and N. V. Teptzov. *Hitler's Death: Russia's Last Great Secret from the Files of the KGB*. London: Chaucer Press, 2005.

von Hassell, F. *Hostage of the Third Reich: The Story of My Imprisonment and Rescue from the SS*. New York: Macmillan, 1989.

von Hassell, U. *The Ulrich von Hassell Diaries: The Story of the Forces against Hitler inside Germany*. London: Frontline, 2011.

von Kellenbach, K. *The Mark of Cain: Guilt and Denial in the Post-war Lives of Nazi Perpetrators*. Oxford: Oxford University Press, 2013.

von Meding, D. *Courageous Hearts: Women and the Anti-Hitler Plot of 1944*. Translated by M. Balfour and V. Berghahn. Oxford: Berghahn Books, 1997.

von Rabenau, F. *Die alte Armee und die junge Generation: Kritische Betrachtungen*. Berlin: Mittler, 1925.

———. *Buch und Schwert: Rede des Generals der Artillerie Friedrich von Rabenau: Gehalten am 28. Okt. 1940 zu Leipzig*. Leipzig: Bibliographisches Institut, 1940.

———. *Vom Sinn des Soldatentums. Die innere Kraft von Führung und Truppe*. Bonn, Germany: Bernard and Graefe, 1939; repr., Cologne: DuMont/Schauberg, 1941.

———. *Vom Geist und Seele des Soldaten*. Vortrag vom 27. Mai 1940; Berlin: Schriftenreihe der NSDAP Gruppe I Deutsche Wehrkraft, 1940; repr., Munich: Eherverlag/Zentralverlag der NSDAP, 1941

———. *Ernste Laiengedanken*: Archiv Rabenau, circa 1940.

von Schlabrendorff, F. *Begegnungen in fünf Jahrzehnten, 1979*. 2nd ed. Hamburg: Rainer Wunderlich, 1979.

———. *Revolt against Hitler: The Personal Account of Fabian von Schlabrendorff*. Edited by G. Gaevernitz. London: Eyre and Spottiswood, 1948.

von Stauffenberg, M. *Aufzeichnungen aus unserer Sippenhaft 20. Juli 1944 bis 19. Juni 1945*. Stuttgart: Haus der Geschichte Baden-Württemberg, circa 2012.

von Studnitz, H.-G. *Als Berlin brannte: Tagebuch der Jahre 1943–1945*. Bergisch-Gladbach, Germany: Gustav Lübbe, 1985.

von Stülpnagel, J. *75 Jahre meines Lebens*. Oberaudorf, Germany: Obb, 1955.

Wachsmann, N. *KL: A History of the Nazi Concentration Camps*. New York: Farrar, Straus and Giroux, 2015.

Waite, C. *Survivor of the Long March: Five Years as a POW, 1940–1945*. Stroud, UK: History Press, 2012.

The War in Pictures. 6 vols. London: Odhams Press, 1946.

Warlimont, W. *Inside Hitler's Headquarters, 1939–1945*. Translated by R. Barry. London: Presidio, 1964.

Weale, A. *Army of Evil: A History of the SS*. New York: NAL Caliber, 2012.

Wegner, M. *Ein weites Herz: Die zwei Leben der Isa Vermehren*. Munich: Claassen, 2003.

Werfel, F. *Die vierzig Tage des Musa Dagh*. Frankfurt: Fischer, 2002. First published 1933.

Wiesel, E. *Night*. Translated by M. Wiesel. London: Penguin Books, 2006.

Williams, A. *A Passing Fury: Searching for Justice at the End of World War II*. London: Penguin Random House, 2016.

Williams, R. *Bonhoeffer's Black Jesus: Harlem Renaissance Theology and an Ethic of Resistance.* 2nd ed. Waco, Tex.: Baylor University Press, 2021.

Witte, P., and S. Tyas. *Himmler's Diary, 1945: A Calendar of Events Leading to Suicide.* London: Fonthill Media, 2014.

Zimmermann, W., ed. *Begegnungen mit Dietrich Bonhoeffer.* 4th ed. Munich: Christian Kaiser, 1964.

Zimmermann, W., and R. Gregor Smith. *I Knew Dietrich Bonhoeffer.* Translated by K. Gregor Smith. London: Collins, 1964.

Zipfel, F. *Kirchenkampf in Deutschland 1933–1945.* Vol. 1 of *Publikationen der Forschungsgruppe Berliner Widerstand beim Senator für Inneres von Berlin.* Berlin: De Gruyter, 1965.

Zvyagintsev, V., and A. Beznasyuk. *Tribunal. Arbat, 37.* Moscow: Terra-Knizhnyj Klub, 2006.

INDEX